G
Conceptual
History

Global Conceptual History

A Reader

Edited by Margrit Pernau and Dominic Sachsenmaier

Bloomsbury Academic
An imprint of Bloomsbury Publishing Plc

B L O O M S B U R Y
LONDON · OXFORD · NEW YORK · NEW DELHI · SYDNEY

Bloomsbury Academic

An imprint of Bloomsbury Publishing Plc

50 Bedford Square	1385 Broadway
London	New York
WC1B 3DP	NY 10018
UK	USA

www.bloomsbury.com

BLOOMSBURY and the Diana logo are trademarks of Bloomsbury Publishing Plc

First published 2016

British Library Cataloguing-in-Publication Data
A catalogue record for this book is available from the British Library.

ISBN: HB: 978-1-4742-4254-7
PB: 978-1-4742-4255-4
ePDF: 978-1-4742-4257-8
ePub: 978-1-4742-4256-1

Library of Congress Cataloging-in-Publication Data
A catalog record for this book is available from the Library of Congress.

Typeset by Integra Software Services Pvt. Ltd.
Printed and bound in Great Britain

Contents

Part IV   Outlook 337

13 Forty Years of Conceptual History – The State of the Art *Willibald Steinmetz* 339

List of Figures

Acknowledgements

Coffee breaks matter, all the more during international conferences. It was in Bangkok, at a workshop on the concept of 'The Social in Europe and Asia' that Bo Stråth toyed with the idea that someone should put together a reader bringing together conceptual history and global history. Already before we had finished our coffee, we agreed that this was an excellent idea, and this volume is the result of that conversation.

We thank Bo Stråth for this initial inspiration, and all the scholars who encouraged us to further pursue this project during the past few years. In addition, we are grateful to all the contributors who graciously agreed to the republication of their articles. We also thank Joy Titheridge for her dedicated work on the translation of the texts by Rolf Reichardt, Dietrich Busse und Willibald Steinmetz.

We are glad about the fact that research funds provided by Duke University and the Alexander von Humboldt Foundation could be used to finance parts of the work on our reader. We also appreciate the reliable collaboration with Claire Lipscomb and Emma Goode of Bloomsbury Publishers.

Finally, this work would never have been possible without the untiring work of Anja Berkes and her team of student assistants at the Max Planck Institute for Human Development: Juliane Boehm, who explored the possibilities for reprinting the articles with the publishers; Rachel Johnson and Frederik Schröer, who first were among the students serving as guinea pigs to test how the collection worked in class, and then took over the entire copyediting process and more.

Permissions Information

The following material is reproduced with kind permission of the copyright holders:

Chapter 1: Introduction (*Einleitung*) to the *Geschichtliche Grundbegriffe*

Reinhart Koselleck, 'Introduction (*Einleitung*) to the *Geschichtliche Grundbegriffe*', *Contributions to the History of Concepts*, 6/1 (2011), 7–25. Reproduced by permission of Klett Cotta.

Chapter 2: Social History and Conceptual History

Reinhart Koselleck, 'Social History and Conceptual History', *International Journal of Politics, Culture and Society*, 2/3 (1989), 308–25. Reproduced by permission of Suhrkamp.

Chapter 3: For a Socio-historical Semantics as a Middle Course between 'Lexicometry' and 'Conceptual History'

Rolf Reichardt, 'Einleitung', in Idem (ed.), *Handbuch Politisch-Sozialer Grundbegriffe in Frankreich 1680–1820*, München: De Gruyter, 1985, 60–85. Translated and reproduced by permission of De Gruyter.

Chapter 4: Conceptual History or a History of Discourse? On the Theoretical Basis and Questions of Methodology of a Historical-Semantic Epistemology

Dietrich Busse, 'Begriffsgeschichte oder Diskursgeschichte? Zu theoretischen Grundlagen und Methodenfragen einer Historisch-Semantischen Epistemologie', in Carsten Dutt (ed.), *Herausforderungen der Begriffsgeschichte* (Heidelberg: Univeritätsverlag Winter, 2003), 17–38. Translated from the original by permission of the Universitätsverlag Winter GmbH.

Chapter 5: Rhetoric and Conceptual Change

Quentin Skinner, 'Rhetoric and Conceptual Change', *Finnish Yearbook of Political Thought*, 3 (1999), 60–73. Reproduced by permission of SoPhi Publishing.

Chapter 6: Translation as Cultural Transfer and Semantic Interaction: European Variations of *Liberal* between 1800 and 1830

Jörn Leonhard, 'Translation as Cultural Transfer and Semantic Interaction: European Variations of Liberal between 1800 and 1830', in Martin Burke and Melvin Richter (eds), *Why Concepts Matter: Translating Social and Political Thought* (Leiden: Brill, 2012), 93–108. Reproduced by permission of Klartext Verlag GmbH

Chapter 7: Translation, Politics and Conceptual Change

Kari Palonen, 'Translation, Politics and Conceptual Change', *Finnish Yearbook of Political Thought*, 7 (2003), 15–35. Reproduced by permission of SoPhi Publishing.

Chapter 8: The Question of Meaning-Value in the Political Economy of the Sign

Lydia Liu, 'The Question of Meaning-Value in the Political Economy of the Sign', in Lydia H. Liu (ed.), *Tokens of Exchange* (Durham: Duke University Press, 1999), 13–45. Republished by permission of the copyright holder. www.dukeupress.edu

Chapter 9: The Resonance of *Culture*: Framing a Problem in Global Concept-History

Andrew Sartori, 'The Resonance of "Culture": Framing a Problem in Global Concept-History', *Comparative Studies in Society and History*, 47/4 (2005), 676–99. © Society for the Comparative Study of Society and History, published by Cambridge University Press, reproduced with permission.

Chapter 10: The Conceptualization of the Social in Late Nineteenth- and Early Twentieth-Century Arabic Thought and Language

Ilham Khuri-Makdisi, 'The Conceptualization of the Social in Late Nineteenth- and Early Twentieth-Century Arabic Thought and Language', in Hagen Schulze-Forberg (ed.), *A Global Conceptual History of Asia, 1860–1940* (London: Pickering & Chatto, 2014), 91–110. Reproduced by permission of Taylor and Francis.

Chapter 11: *Ustaarabu*: A Conceptual Change in Tanganyikan Newspaper Discourse in the 1920s

Katrin Bromber, '*Ustaarabu*: A Conceptual Change in Tanganyikan Newspaper Discourse in the 1920s' in Roman Loineier and Rüdiger Seesemann (eds) *The Global Worlds of the Swahili: Interfaces of Islam, Identity and Space in 19th and 20th-Century East Africa* (Münster: LIT Verlag, 2006), 67–81. Reproduced by permission of LIT Verlag.

Chapter 12: Pictures, Emotions, Conceptual Change. Anger in Popular Hindi Cinema

Imke Rajamani, 'Pictures, Emotions, Conceptual Change: Anger in Popular Hindi Cinema', *Contributions to the History of Concepts*, 7/2 (2012): 52–77. Reproduced by permission of Berghahn.

Chapter 13: Forty Years of Conceptual History – The State of the Art

Willibald Steinmetz, '40 Jahre Begriffsgeschichte – *The State of the Art*', in Heidrun Kämper and Ludwig M. Eichinger (eds), *Sprache – Kognition – Kultur* (Berlin: De Gruyter, 2008), 174–97. Translated and published with permission of De Gruyter.

Editors' Biographies

Margrit Pernau coordinates the India group at the Max Planck Institute for Human Development, Center for the History of Emotions, in Berlin. She teaches at the Freie Universität Berlin, where she also holds an extraordinary professorship. She studied history and public law at the University of Saarland and University of Heidelberg; she took her PhD at the latter in 1991. During the period 1997 to 2003 Margrit Pernau conducted research in Delhi on 'Plural Identities of Muslims in Old Delhi in the 19th Century', and has been a research fellow at the Social Science Research Centre Berlin and at the Modern Orient Centre in Berlin. Beside the history of emotions, her areas of interest include modern Indian history, the history of modern Islam, historical semantics, comparative studies, and translation studies. Her publications include *Ashraf into Middle Classes: Muslims in Nineteenth-Century Delhi* (2013), *Information and the Public Sphere: Persian Newsletters from Mughal Delhi* (edited with Yunus Jaffery, 2009), *The Delhi College: Traditional Elites, the Colonial State, and Education before 1857* (edited, 2006), and *Family and Gender: Changing Values in Germany and India* (edited with Imtiaz Ahmad and Helmut Reifeld, 2003).

Dominic Sachsenmaier is a professor of 'Modern China with a special Emphasis on Global Historical Perspectives' at Georg-August-University Göttingen. In the past, he held faculty positions at Jacobs University Bremen, Duke University as well as the University of California, Santa Barbara. He received his education at Freiburg University, St. Andrews University, Nanjing University and Harvard University. Sachsenmaier's main current research interests are Chinese and Western approaches to global history as well as transnational connections of political and intellectual cultures in China. Furthermore he has published in fields such as seventeenth-century Sino-Western cultural relations, overseas Chinese communities in Southeast Asia, and multiple modernities. His most recent single-authored monograph is *Global Perspectives on Global History. Theories and Approaches in a Connected World* (2011). Sachsenmaier serves on several editorial and advisory boards in Asia, Europe and the United States.

List of First Publication

Chapter 1

German: Reinhart Koselleck, 'Einleitung', in Otto Brunner, Werner Conze and Reinhart Koselleck (eds), *Geschichtliche Grundbegriffe: Historisches Lexikon zur Politisch-Sozialen Sprache in Deutschland*, vol. 1 (Stuttgart: Klett-Cotta, 1972), viii–xxvii.

English: Reinhart Koselleck, 'Introduction (*Einleitung*) to the *Geschichtliche Grundbegriffe*', *Contributions to the History of Concepts*, 6/1 (2011), 7–25.

Chapter 2

German: Reinhart Koselleck, 'Sozialgeschichte und Begriffsgeschichte', in Wolfgang Schieder and Volker Sellin (eds), *Sozialgeschichte in Deutschland: Entwicklungen und Perspektiven im internationalen Zusammenhang*, vol. 1 (Göttingen: Vandenhoeck & Ruprecht, 1986), 89–109.

English: 'Social History and Conceptual History', *International Journal of Politics, Culture and Society*, 2/3 (1989), 308–25.

Chapter 3

German: Rolf Reichardt, 'Einleitung: III. Für eine sozialhistorische Semantik als Mittelweg zwischen "Lexikometrie" und "Begriffsgeschichte"', in idem (ed.), *Handbuch Politisch-Sozialer Grundbegriffe in Frankreich 1680–1820* (Munich: Oldenbourg, 1985), 60–85.

English: First translation into English.

Chapter 4

German: Dietrich Busse, 'Begriffsgeschichte oder Diskursgeschichte? Zu theoretischen Grundlagen und Methodenfragen einer Historisch-Semantischen Epistemologie', in Carsten Dutt (ed.), *Herausforderungen der Begriffsgeschichte* (Heidelberg: Winter, 2003), 17–38.

English: First translation into English.

Chapter 5

Quentin Skinner, 'Rhetoric and Conceptual Change', *Finnish Yearbook of Political Thought*, 3 (1999), 60–73.

Chapter 6

German: Jörn Leonhard, 'Von der Wortimitation zur semantischen Integration: Übersetzung als Kulturtransfer', *Werkstatt Geschichte*, 48 (2008), 45–63.

English: Jörn Leonhard, 'Translation as Cultural Transfer and Semantic Interaction: European Variations of *Liberal* between 1800 and 1830', in Martin Burke and Melvin Richter (eds), *Why Concepts Matter: Translating Social and Political Thought* (Leiden: Brill, 2012), 93–108.

Chapter 7

Kari Palonen, 'Translation, Politics and Conceptual Change', *Finnish Yearbook of Political Thought*, 7 (2003), 15–35.

Chapter 8

Lydia H. Liu, 'The Question of Meaning-Value in the Political Economy of the Sign', in, *Tokens of Exchange: The Problem of Translation in Global Circulations* (Durham: Duke University Press, 1999), 13–41.

Chapter 9

Andrew Sartori, 'The Resonance of "Culture": Framing a Problem in Global Concept-History', *Comparative Studies in Society and History*, 47/4 (2005), 676–99.

Chapter 10

Ilham Khuri-Makdisi, 'The Conceptualization of the Social in Late Nineteenth- and Early Twentieth-Century Arabic Thought and Language', in Hagen Schulze-Forberg (ed.), *A Global Conceptual History of Asia, 1860–1940* (London: Pickering & Chatto, 2014), 91–110.

Chapter 11

Katrin Bromber, '*Ustaarabu*: A Coneptual Change in Tanganyikan Newspaper Discourse in the 1920s', in Roman Loimeier and Rüdiger Seesemann (eds), *The Global Worlds of the Swahili: Interfaces of Islam, Identity and Space in the 19th and 20th-Century East Africa* (Münster: Lit Verlag, 2006), 67–81.

Chapter 12
Imke Rajamani, 'Pictures, Emotions, Conceptual Change: Anger in Popular Hindi Cinema', *Contributions to the History of Concepts*, 7/2 (2012), 52–77.

Chapter 13
German: Willibald Steinmetz, '40 Jahre Begriffsgeschichte – *The State of the Art*', in Heidrun Kämper and Ludwig M. Eichinger (eds), *Sprache – Kognition – Kultur* (Berlin: de Gruyter, 2008), 174–97.

English: First translation into English.

History of Concepts and Global History

Margrit Pernau and

Dominic Sachsenmaier

Let us dwell for a moment on three scenes from different centuries. The first takes us to Europe, where a group of scholars led by the Belgian Jesuit Philippe Couplet published the first annotated translation of major Confucian texts in 1687. The resulting book, entitled *Confucius Sinarum Philosophus*, sparked rather intensive discussions in many parts of Europe, which were partly related to the question of how to develop a new vision of man, society and politics. In the second scene, we see Shah Wali Ullah, an eighteenth-century religious scholar from northern India, travel from his native Delhi to the Arab Peninsula. He performs the pilgrimage to Mecca and Medina, where he establishes close interaction with the religious reformers of the Jemani tradition. Back in Delhi, he becomes one of the most influential leaders of the Islamic reform movement. The third scene is set in Japan during the late 1800s where the influential author, translator and educator Fukuzawa Yukichi sought to contribute to the Meiji Reform. In his widely influential writings he used a wealth of concepts and topoi that, in his eyes, were drawn from works coming out of 'advanced societies'.

These scenes could be multiplied at will. What holds them together are two elements: already prior to the twentieth century, historical development can no longer be explained by looking at only one country or society. Men (as well as women, to a somewhat lesser extent) and ideas had always moved across boundaries, even though in many regards such movements became even more important and multifaceted from the nineteenth century onwards. Today, historians have become increasingly interested in the historical flows, transfers and interconnections which have shaped the world's nations, regions and languages more profoundly than scholars had often assumed before.

This reader seeks to contribute to the understanding of a specific aspect of border-crossing movements and connections. All three scenes discussed earlier depict particular types of encounters across various types of borders: encounters leading to the transformation of the concepts through which the respective protagonists perceive and interpret the world. Sometimes we forget the extent to which all of them, and indeed almost every transnational encounter, hinge on translation processes. In the cases mentioned earlier, there are the rethinking of concepts of republican virtue in English and the translation of Confucian texts to European audiences; the ability of Shah Wali Ullah to communicate in Arabic and the importance he accorded to the translation of the Islamic sacred texts first to Persian and then to Urdu; as well as the presentation of Western concepts to Japanese reformers and the general public during the Meiji Period.

As we can see, global encounters can take place in many different periods and regions and involve a large variety of practices, from migration to the writing of history. This is not a new insight for historians – after all, global encounters of this kind have long been investigated as part of the history of cross-cultural encounters and even of cultural translation processes. What has received less attention is that almost all of these encounters occur not only across geographical but also linguistic boundaries and hence involve the necessity for a translation of words and concepts, which bring together the actors' interpretation of the world they are living in and constitute the basis for all meaningful action. Certainly, not all communication is based on language, but a large part, especially of what is accessible to the historian, usually is. Cultural translation in almost every case is mediated through linguistic translation.

If we focus on the linguistic dimensions of border-crossing exchanges, we are moving outside of the mainstream of historiography. We hence need to pay more attention to research fields that have played only a rather marginal role in global historical scholarship. This has certainly been the case with conceptual history, a field which long had chiefly focused on the study of European languages. Yet as this reader shows, there have been important developments in this field, and the range of languages and regions it covers has grown significantly wider. Today, conceptual history can even be regarded as more than a sub-field of global history, namely as an approach cutting across many of them. It is through concepts – based on language and other semiotic sign systems like pictures[1] – that actors make sense of their experiences and create the knowledge about the world they are living in, which in turn permits them to act meaningfully. Making sense and creating knowledge are not individual but social activities, premised on communication. Conceptual history thus focuses on communication in the broad sense of the term, that is, not only on harmonious forms of mutual understanding but equally on misunderstanding and on communication as the basis of power relations.

For a long time, the history of concepts focused on projects within individual nations and languages. While conceptual transformations within particular languages and countries have never been viewed in isolation from one another, researchers paid relatively little attention to processes of transfer, translation and other entanglements. Certainly, the field has witnessed some important multinational projects, particularly since the beginning of the twenty-first century. Yet these mainly focused on comparisons between the developments in two or more countries. In that manner they drew together conceptual historians from different regions and brought forth many fascinating new insights.[2] However, it was only in a successive step that the 'methodological nationalism'[3] inherent in the project of conceptual history was being challenged directly. Global history has not only shown the extent of encounters and connections across different regions but also the measure to which these very encounters brought forth nations, societies and cultures. It almost goes without saying that such entanglements also had a formative influence on concepts and languages. Moreover, global historians are increasingly becoming aware of the mutuality of influence between colonial powers and their colonies. If we proceed further on this route we discover that this bidirectional pattern impacted the development and transformation of the concepts as well. A number of projects have pursued research directions of this kind and raised concomitant questions.[4] Hopefully the increasing dialogue of conceptual historians with global history will yield many more projects heading in these directions. This book intends to address some of the methodological challenges facing this approach and to contribute to finding new paths for coping with them.

If the history of concepts can profit from a closer collaboration with global history, what about the reverse? How can the input of the history of concepts enrich global history? As the brief scenes at the beginning of this introduction show, global encounters at the micro and the macro level always involved encounters between languages. The transfer and transformation of knowledge, as well as the establishment of relations of power and hegemony, were based on the necessity of communication across linguistic boundaries. Among other fields, the Orientalism School and postcolonial studies have devoted increasing levels of attention to questions of language in recent years. However, investigations in this field have often focused exclusively on the 'creation of colonial knowledge'. This means that the field was usually far less interested in changes within the local languages of colonized societies, as well as the conflicts surrounding these changes.

Yet we not only ought to inquire into the ways in which hegemonic powers and languages interpreted and created their world. We need to pay attention to those at the receiving end of this hegemony, at a global no less than at a societal scale. Such an approach runs counter to a tendency in many otherwise excellent studies in global history to focus primarily on materials written in either English or French. In combination with translation studies, conceptual history offers a tool box for investigating encounters between many languages and ensuing transformations with methodological precision. Within this framework, tracing concepts to their moorings in specific languages and focusing on their contested character help deconstruct the still powerful notion of a 'Europeanization' of concepts and ideas elsewhere. Instead, globally oriented conceptual history can point to a world of linguistic entanglements – a world in which the 'West' was not an unmoved mover but rather subject to outside influence and change, just as other parts of the world were. Moreover, the field can show which interpretation of a concept gained influence at which particular time – across national, semi-colonial and colonial boundaries.[5]

A growing field of conceptual history will thus add many facets to our understanding of how languages were entangled in – and contributed to – the wider contexts of power systems, global flows and shared transformations. An evolving landscape of case studies will certainly further complicate our picture of conceptual transformations in terms of their global interconnections and local dynamics. For instance, already at the present stage we should not crudely assume that languages spoken in the so-called 'Global South' can be treated as a quasi-homogenous category. Also here, there were significant varieties, for instance between different cultures, regions or specific types of colonial regimes. Moreover, there were dissimilarities between widely spoken languages like, for instance, Arabic or Mandarin and much more regional tongues spoken by a limited number of people. Then there were languages like Swahili (which had developed through the encounters between speakers of different African languages and Arabic traders) evolving into a lingua franca in parts of East Africa under the conditions of European colonialism. These and plentiful other languages experienced very specific conceptual transformations; yet at the same time, the latter were entwined with larger regional, if not global, patterns and constellations. At first sight, the newly digitized bodies of texts in a growing number of languages will continue to ease the possibilities for the practitioners of conceptual history to move their field onto a transnational and global level[6] – more and more texts become accessible online. However, digitalization does not resolve the problem of power relations between languages; even in digital format, sources in French or English will make it more easily into historiography than those in Telugu, Malay or Yoruba – or for that matter Czech or Finnish. The fact that digital projects are spread out very unevenly might even, at least in a mid-term perspective, exacerbate these inequalities.[7]

Global History and the Cultures of Historiography

If taken to global and trans-continental scales, conceptual historical research will be able to engage in fruitful dialogues with other branches of historiography. After all, the growing interest in the history of transfers, comparisons, flows and other dynamics was not a development unique to conceptual history. Instead, a surge of new types of border-crossing research has become visible across almost the entire spectrum of historiography as well as other disciplines belonging to the social sciences and the humanities. This has particularly been the case during the past two to three decades.

The growing presence of global and transnational historical research has changed the landscapes of important historiographical sub-disciplines such as cultural history, political history or economic history. For instance, in the latter field some highly influential works challenged the idea of European economic exceptionalities prior to the 1800s, and they did so from new comparative and global historical perspectives.[8] Likewise, within the field of labour history a growing number of scholars were drawn to the study of trans-continental entanglements. As part of this development, the concept of *labour* itself was problematized since Western concepts did not necessarily match experiences in Sub-Saharan Africa and other parts of the world.[9] Drawing on fields of this kind, there have now been significant efforts to rethink the history of single regions or nations by viewing them through global and transnational lenses.[10] Facets of nationalism have also been studied from global perspectives, for example by focusing on the transfers underlying the global spread of national identities. In fact, even the history of historiography itself experienced its own turn to global history in recent years – for example, some researchers have come to deal with the transformations leading to the global spread of university-based history departments.[11]

At the same time, the growing emphasis on border-crossing connections gave new impulses to hitherto marginalized research fields ranging from maritime history to the history of diseases. For instance, the study of non-governmental organizations and other global civil society initiatives has received a strong boost of energy during the past one or two decades.[12] The same is true for the field of environmental history, which received much more attention when its scholarly efforts were purportedly transgressing political and geographical boundaries.[13] Moreover, the history of migration has developed fascinating global perspectives which no longer focus on single diasporic communities but instead seek to gain comprehensive pictures of human movements across and between continents.[14]

Additionally, fields regarded as adjacent to conceptual history have in some measure started to depart from their original Eurocentric grounds. This is the case with the history of ideas and intellectual history, fields which at least in Western academia had for a long time focused almost exclusively on European and North American cases.[15] Yet recent publication patterns of flagship journals such as *Modern Intellectual History* and (to a slightly lesser extent) the *Journal for the History of Ideas* give evidence that the study of cases from other parts of the world has come to be recognized as highly relevant for the field.[16] As part of this development, there has been a growing body of literature comparing intellectual developments between societies in different world regions. Perhaps more importantly, there are now a growing number of studies exploring ideas, thoughts and discourses which in and of themselves can be considered to be transnational or even 'global' in terms of their spread, impact and scope.[17]

The history of ideas and intellectual history have started to shift away from their original focus on the history of prominent thinkers – certainly in their programmatic writings and, more slowly, also followed by empirical studies. Already since a generation ago, the field has witnessed a growing interest among researchers in the history of wider opinion climates, public discourses and broader intellectual transformations.[18] This implied that historians became increasingly aware of the need to study a wide range of authors, journals and newspapers, many of which had long been forgotten. Also primary sources like pamphlets and even objects of material culture became parts of the body of primary sources with which intellectual historians worked. There are certainly significant overlaps between the research agendas of intellectual historians and conceptual historians. Both share a critical attitude towards older approaches to the history of ideas, which investigated ideas independently of both their context and their foundation in language; both increasingly focus on local case studies in a global context. The global turn of conceptual history, as presented in this reader, hence also speaks to a wider historiographical field which also encompasses the history of ideas, intellectual history as well as the history of discourses.

Within the context of rapidly evolving fields, conceptual history will continue having a rather focused research agenda, and it will still draw on a clearly defined methodological toolbox. This might be seen as a rather exceptional character trait within the current landscapes of border-crossing historiography. Within many subfields of history, the surging interest in global and transnational perspectives has certainly taken researchers into fascinating and promising directions. Yet for better or for worse, the global turn in historiography is not characterized by a core set of methodologies or research questions. In fact, the recent wave of scholarship heading into global and transnational directions has still not come to be connoted by a single, all-encompassing and commonly accepted term. Rather, there have been a good number of terminological possibilities and – adding to the confusion – quite some debates on how to distinguish different field designations from one another. Among several expressions, 'global history' has emerged as a rather prominent term. Contrary to what the concept 'global' suggests, the expression is not only being used for studies that are covering the world in its entirety. Many publications published under the rubric of 'global history' actually focus on sample cases from different world regions and only implicitly situate their research within a global framework of analysis.

In that sense, much of 'global history' is hard to differentiate from 'transnational history', another neologism that is now being used rather frequently in academic circles and general education systems. As the term 'transnational' suggests, this field designation tries to provide an alternative to the older 'international history', a field that had long been centred on the study of international relations and diplomatic interactions, hence taking the nation state as a primary unit of analysis. By contrast, transnational historical scholarship is purportedly moving towards the study of flows and interactions across borders, which in many cases are neither framed nor conditioned by the nation state as a key agent.[19] Actually, scholarship is becoming increasingly sensitive to the dynamics and exchanges which led to the emergence of nations, respectively national or cultural identities in the first place. This means that units such as nations, regions or languages are no longer seen as the frameworks but, much rather, as the products of historical interactions.[20]

In addition to now rather well-established expressions like 'transnational history', an array of additional newly coined terms has been emerging. Many of the latter are seeking to demarcate single aspects of border-crossing scholarship or express certain methodological predilections. Among them are, for instance '*histoire croisée*'[21] as well as 'entangled histories'[22] and 'connected histories'.[23] Without a doubt, each of these terms conveys a specific idea. However, none of these terms has become established enough to be able to constitute an established research community of its own. The boundaries between these terms remain indistinct, and they are also not categorically separate from other recently coined field designations like 'global history' or 'transnational history'.

The picture of programmatic terms is becoming even more complex since some older concepts remain influential and have come to be filled with new contents. For example, the aforementioned field of international history has also witnessed some movements which are actively pursuing alternatives to its earlier focus on encounters between states and statesmen.[24] In other words, parts of the international historical community have started departing from the close methodological connections of their own field with the study of international relations, a branch of the political sciences which is particularly dominated by realist outlooks. In this context, themes like cultural flows, joint transformations and shared ideologies have moved closer to the foreground of research agendas. Developments of this kind, marked by the influence of cultural and social historical questions and concepts, are making it hard to distinguish international history sharply from transnational history and other terms.

World history is another field which has been the arena of great conceptual and methodological changes. The term 'world history' has a much longer history than any of the aforementioned expressions and was already commonly used among historians during the Enlightenment period. Yet particularly from the nineteenth century onwards, 'world history' started developing into a field dominated by often unabashedly Eurocentric assumptions. Both in Western but also in many non-Western societies, many of the most influential world historical works were centred on a narrative string depicting European history as the autochthonous rise of a civilization to unique global influence. As a consequence, many world histories published during that time period either implicitly or explicitly treated the past of entire world regions, including East Asia, South Asia and Africa, as of little global significance. Hegel's famous dictum that societies like China or India lacked genuine history in the sense of progress had its equivalents in much of world historical literature, and it did so for a significant amount of time.

Within the landscapes of Western historiography, world history long also had a rather marginal standing.[25] In contrast to the dominant national historiographies, it was also not commonly regarded as a research field but rather as an arena for general education. For all these reasons, during the 1990s and early 2000s a group of prominent scholars suggested a clear separation of global history from world history.[26] However, at the same time, world history experienced some strong institutional and epistemological transformations, which can even be understood as a process of renovation. For instance, it developed its own journals and graduate programmes, which were indicative of the transformation of the field into a genuine research community.[27] Moreover, many scholars with an area studies background became involved with the new institutions and forums of world history. These changes in personnel further intensified critical currents flowing against Eurocentric outlooks.

As a consequence of these developments, it is also no longer possible to distinguish world history so clearly from global history. A closer look at different authors and institutions suggests that today many influential scholars use these terms as largely synonymous with one another, and that the same is the case with other field designations like 'transnational' history.[28] In the future, these rather blurred semantic fields emanating from new directions in historiographical activity might eventually be well worth being studied from the perspectives of conceptual history. A project of this kind would become even more challenging since many of these terms, including 'global history', have become frequently used in a large variety of languages and academic systems around the globe. For example, the English term 'transnational history' has its matches in words ranging from the German '*transnationale Geschichte*' to the Chinese '*kuaguo lishi*'.

However, for the purpose of situating recent developments in conceptual history within wider currents in the field of historiography, it is not of primary importance to clearly map out the aforementioned field designations in the sense of coming up with sharply defined categories. Rather, it suffices to observe that the growing presence of these terms together indicates an important trend in historiography – a trend which also affected the study of conceptual history. Yet what characterizes this academic trend? The mere fact that global and transnational research attracts an increasing number of scholars, journals and institutions points to an important mood swing within the guildhalls of academic historiography. It can be roughly described as a growing discomfort with the mental maps which have dominated the professional field since the nineteenth century. Within the canon of modern scholarship, arguably no other field was as closely tied to the institution and the ambitions of the emerging nation-state as historiography.[29] In many parts of the world, academic historiography was primarily institutionalized as national history, which meant that a large number of scholars were trained as experts of one particularly nation, be it their own or an outside country.

Certainly, even in the nineteenth and early twentieth centuries academic historiography did not completely ignore the study of outside connections and entanglements. Yet nation-centred perspectives clearly dominated the ways in which exchanges and interactions were being studied, which often led to rather distorted images of the past. Moreover, for a long time most historians doing research on border-crossing flows and transnational dynamics did so within the confinements of single world regions. Up until the present day the vast number of historians of Europe, for example, do not seek to relate their own area of expertise to the study of other world regions. Similar statements could be made about many East Asianists, Latin Americanists and other representatives of area studies. As a consequence, many transnational, transregional and transcontinental connections of the past had been sidelined by modern historical scholarship. For example, since East Asia was the domain of East Asian specialists and South Asia of

South Asian specialists, comparatively little historical scholarship has come to investigate the quite dense patterns of historical interaction between China and India.[30]

The field of conceptual history can contribute as much to these academic developments as it can benefit from them. For instance, as the following sections will show, overcoming Eurocentric and nation-centred historiographical traditions remains a major challenge for the study of concepts and entire languages. Perhaps most importantly, like other branches of historiography, the field of conceptual history, too, is beginning to evolve into a meeting ground for hitherto separate research traditions. For example, also here scholars with an expertise in different world regions have started interacting with each other, and such modes of collaboration are even intensifying. Such encounters can often trigger important debates that touch upon foundational issues and conceptual questions. The exhilaration of a pioneering era has come back to the field.

Conceptual History Goes Global[31]

This book proceeds in three steps. In the first part, we present three of the foundational texts[32] of conceptual history (*Begriffsgeschichte*), which all stem from its origins within the German academic environment. As pieces from the early stages of conceptual history, they are not representative of the global and transnational turn within the field but they grant important insights into the field's contours and research agendas. The first two texts were authored by Reinhart Koselleck, one of the leading spirits of conceptual history. He was among the editors of *Geschichtliche Grundbegriffe*, a dictionary in eight thick volumes covering the key concepts of the political and social language.[33] Though the emphasis is on German concepts such as *Gesellschaft* (society) or *Nation* from the mid-eighteenth to the mid-nineteenth century, almost each article takes into account the longer history of each concept, very often starting in classical antiquity and ending with an outlook into the twentieth century. This enables the dictionary to transcend the exclusive focus on German texts when presenting the formative period of key concepts. The dictionary draws on a source base which mainly consists of canonical works in political philosophy as well as a wide range of theoretical writings. It is from these texts that the transformation of key concepts – those concepts which were so foundational at a certain point in time that a debate was not possible without them – is being traced. Furthermore, in Koselleck's work social history and the history of concepts are closely linked with each other, but they never merge. Yet although he accorded a central role to language, Koselleck always kept his distance from the linguistic turn and insisted that there was a social reality beyond language. Concepts could, therefore, be viewed as both indicators of change and as forces behind them.[34]

At an early stage, Rolf Reichardt, another important figure who was already active in the formational period of conceptual history, aimed at overcoming the exclusive focus of the *Geschichtliche Grundbegriffe* on canonical texts. He adopted suggestions from the French *lexicometrie* and proceeded to develop his own dictionary, the *Handbuch politisch-sozialer Grundbegriffe in Frankreich, 1680–1820* (Handbook of political and social key concepts in France).[35] Focusing on the everyday use of language, the articles are based on a digitalized common corpus consisting mainly of tracts and pamphlets. This allowed the authors involved in this work to go beyond individual concepts and look at the shifting positions a concept can hold in a semantic net. The latter they did through the interpretation of co-occurrences, that is, the tracing of words which are used together in the same sentence or the same paragraph. Reichardt's dictionary shows the traces of an important development in conceptual history. There was a growing presence of approaches leaning towards corpus linguistics and frequency analysis on the one hand and towards pragmatics, that is the focus on the work concepts are being made to perform through their use, on the other hand.[36]

The second part of our reader focuses on three important challenges to conceptual history which have been articulated in the past but remain relevant to the present day. The first comes from representatives of the linguistic turn who, on epistemological grounds, defied the possibility of a social reality outside of language.[37] While the distinction between social and conceptual history had permitted Koselleck and the *Geschichtliche Grundbegriffe* to look for social factors to explain conceptual change and vice versa, this approach placed the burden of explanation on language alone. In turn, this implied that the focus was no longer on concepts but on systems of meaning which transcended single concepts, even those bound together through co-occurrence. This in turn implied abandoning the notion of a history of concepts and replacing it with historical semantics. However, even within conceptual history, the linguistic turn has been a dominant influence on theoretical and methodological developments during the last thirty years. The boundaries towards historical semantics thus remain fluid.[38]

Another challenge came from the Cambridge school of intellectual history, represented mainly by Quentin Skinner and John Pocock. Both the history of concepts and intellectual history had developed from a wider turn against the traditional history of ideas, but it was not until 1995 that Skinner and Koselleck became aware of each other's work. While for Koselleck conceptual change – in the *longue durée*, in the development of a philosophy of historical time – was close to the centre of his enquiry, Skinner's interest focused on synchronicity, on short-term changes in the use of words within argumentative structures. He conceded – perhaps slightly tongue-in-cheek – that the investigation of diachronic conceptual transformations might constitute the final goal. Yet he voiced doubts as to whether enough detailed investigations had already been conducted to base the study of conceptual transformations across time on a solid empirical basis. At the same time, he reserved for himself the topic of rhetorical changes and redescriptions, which he regarded not only as more feasible but also less given to speculation.[39]

The third part of our reader presents more recent examples of scholarship that are taking the field of conceptual history into global and transnational directions. The selection of texts aims at giving an idea of the plurality of theoretical and methodological approaches and topics and of the geographical spread of global conceptual history today.[40] In this part, a recurrent theme is translations, which had not been a central issue in the first decades of conceptual history. At the same time, translations had also not been completely neglected – the index of the *Geschichtliche Grundbegriffe* contains entries in no less than six languages, ranging from Greek and Latin to French, English and Italian, plus four pages of *varia*, including Spanish, Gothic, Hebrew and Russian. The interest of the first generation was initially less directed at translation issues between than within languages. For instance, in the eyes of Otto Brunner, one of the co-editors of the *Geschichtliche Grundbegriffe*, the starting point for conceptual history was the need to avoid the anachronism involved in not being aware of conceptual transformations. The concepts from the mediaeval texts he was working with and the present-day analytical language did not have the same meaning, even if they seemed to use the same words; rather, they stood in need of a translation. For Koselleck, this need for translation was one of the criteria marking the watershed period of intense conceptual transformation around the French Revolution, which he termed '*Sattelzeit*' (literally 'saddle period'). While older concepts required the kind of translation for which Brunner had been arguing, after 1840 concepts became self-evident in their meaning to present-day readers.[41] This is also of great relevance for the necessary conceptual self-reflectivity of historians – after all, concepts such as *nation* or *society* (just to name two) change in their meanings, so scholars working with historical documents need to negotiate between the conceptual worlds of their own times and the ones of their primary sources. Since its inception, conceptual history has hence contributed to destabilizing what felt like an intuitive knowledge.

Koselleck explored the possibilities of taking conceptual history into comparative studies in a co-authored article on the middle classes in Germany, France and Britain.[42] Comparisons of concepts, he put forth, can run into an *aporia*, as they need a translation of the actors' experiences from the language by which these experiences have been formed and which they have in turn shaped into a different language, to which they lack this intimate connection – translation is thus simultaneously indispensable and impossible. He further argued that a meta-language would be needed to reflect and mediate the differences between the languages – a meta-language that for him did not exist.[43]

This is certainly an important objection, and we will come back to the problem of the meta-language in the last section of this introduction. However, the way Koselleck poses the question puts a heavy emphasis on both the isolated character of the experiences which went into the formation of the concepts of *Bürgertum*, *middle classes* and *bourgeoisie* and also of the languages used to describe them: as long as experiences are distinct, and as long as language reflects these specific experiences, using concepts embedded in one language to describe the experiences framed by another language is hardly possible. Global history, however, has pointed out how fragile and brittle this isolation was: present-day historians are by no means the first ones to bring developments within different nations and languages into a common framework and hence can draw on a long history of mutual interpretation, which marked the experience of the historical actors no less than their language. Even if translations were theoretically impossible, in practice they have always happened and produced if not perfect, then at least good-enough results for communication to continue.

Jörn Leonhard was the first to investigate systematically in a book-length study the change of one semantic field, *liberalism*, through transfer in several European countries.[44] The fact that the different concepts use the same word with only minimal local modification (*libéralisme*, *Liberalismus*, *liberalism*) does not mean that no translation took place. Opening up the field for investigation, Leonhard brings out that the same concept of translation contains (at least) three different operations, deployed in three different stages of encounter. Firstly, the imitative translation transposes the word but not the experience, which means that it uses the translated word to refer to an experience in its original context. Secondly, the adapting translation applies the new word to real or anticipated experiences in the target language. Thirdly, the discursive translation proceeds to integrate the new concept into the political language, no longer marking out its foreign origin but treating it on a par with the other concepts in a larger semantic field.[45]

The history of transfers, between nations as well as between languages, was an important step in shifting the attention from intrinsic explanations to encounters as one of the important moving forces behind transformation. Nevertheless, it usually does little to challenge the ontological priority of the objects between which the transfers are taking place. Here it might be valuable to link up with the parallel movements which have transformed global history, anthropology and translation studies since the late 1990s through the reconfiguration of their foundational categories of nation, locality and language. In a parallel development, the history of entanglements, with a focus on British imperial history, and the *histoire croisée*, initially devoted to Franco-German relations in the eighteenth and nineteenth centuries, claimed that nations do not precede transfer but, on the contrary, are the result of encounters.[46] For anthropology, locality came to no longer constitute the protected counterpart to globalization, untouched by modern transformation, but the place where globalization took shape.[47] In translation studies, the cultural turn destabilized the notion of pre-given languages.

Translation has traditionally been viewed as taking place between two languages considered to be entities complete in themselves and endowed with stable boundaries. The translator aimed to identify the meanings of words in one language and to transport them as faithfully as possible into the other language. Of course it has long been known that meaning could only rarely be transported one-to-one, as not all words had equivalents in every language. The traditional bon mot of '*traduttore, traditore*' (traitor-translator) conveys this problem very well. But whether this translation-treason was to be deplored or celebrated as adding new meaning to the original,[48] the translator was still commonly seen as working with given languages which he or she did not change. According to this logic, equivalences either existed or not. If they did, they were quasi natural; if not, there was little the translator could do.

The cultural turn in translation studies brought the translator into perspective as an active and creative agent. Translators, it was proposed, did not 'find' equivalents between languages but created them and thus transformed both of the languages with which they were working.[49] For instance, research on multilingual dictionaries, most notably in the colonial context, has shown that the equivalences that were considered as 'given' were actually the results of negotiations and contestations.[50]

At the same time, researchers ceased to perceive translations as activities that were marginal within the languages that were involved. Introducing a concept from another language and embedding it in a new context changed the meaning of the word itself. This holds true for both types of translations that Schleiermacher distinguished: the domesticating translation, which brings the text to the reader and the foreignizing translation, which confronts him with unfamiliar language and concepts.[51] Simultaneously, the translation of each concept restructures the semantic field into which it has been imported. Translations not only transfer content from one language to the other but in the process also transform the languages. However, this only rarely leads to a complete break with previous language use. Even if a word continues to be used without a translation, it has to be at least explained to the readers through words and concepts with which they are already familiar, thus embedding the new concept into a linguistically shaped previous experience.[52] Like nations, languages are both constituted and concurrently develop their separate identity through encounters. For example, dictionaries and their systematic creation of equivalents not only bridge the gap between languages but also constitute them as distinct and more and more internally homogenized entities.

The cultural turn in translation studies also facilitated the link-up to the debate on cultural translation which had been going on in anthropology since the 1950s and came to the forefront again in the 1990s discussions on the representation of the 'other'.[53] Neither representation nor translation is a 'neutral' activity, taking place in a power-free zone. Both the creation of colonial knowledge with the aim to secure hegemony and the appropriation of the colonizers' knowledge with the aim to resist colonial rule and induce transformation relied heavily upon translation. For example, some leaders of nationalist movements from Egypt to Japan believed that translation not only brought forth a reform of the language, making it more apt to express new ideas, but also opened the pathways to new experiences. To put it more concretely, translating modernity was perceived as the means to modernization.[54] While much of the research has concentrated on the interaction between European and Asian concepts, a similar movement between European languages and concepts in the different African languages can also be shown.[55] Some studies have shown that power patterns and hierarchies played a strong role in framing the encounters between languages and the flow of concepts, particularly under colonial conditions. When studying colonial encounters, it would certainly be misleading to assume that semantic exchanges took place in reciprocal ways. Certainly there have been conceptual transfers from places such as China and Africa to European languages, but it can hardly be argued that these flows matched the influences in the opposite direction, both in terms of breadth and impact. However, not all the conceptual transfers, even since the late eighteenth century, did involve Europe – this still remains a much under-researched field.[56]

When analysing the transfer and translation of concepts, we thus have to consider the relations between languages and also between their respective speakers and translators. After all, translations usually neither occur symmetrically nor do they carry the same meaning in both directions.[57] This means that we also have to take into account the mutual perceptions speakers have of their own and other languages. Such perceptions contribute not only to the hierarchization of languages but also to what forms of translation are deemed possible and significant.[58] The translation of the Qur'an, for instance, was opposed for a long time, as the meaning of the verses was held to be inextricably linked to their sound in Arabic and hence not reproducible in any other language. If we want to understand the meaning translators attached to their activities, the very idea that it is possible to say the same thing in different languages, that languages are interchangeable as they have an equivalent function, needs to be historicized, as Lisa Mitchell has pointed out for South India. For instance, *monoglossia* – using the same language for the private sphere, the administration of the state, commerce and religion – is but one possible way of organizing communication, one that regards languages as parallel and not as complementary.[59]

The notion of the mother tongue, the language which members of a certain community learn at a very early age and through which they negotiate their entire experiences and endow their world with meaning, is a quite recent phenomenon. Its emergence is linked to the eighteenth-century perception of the nation as a cultural and linguistic community. Most translation studies, and especially those which focus on the transfer of concepts through translation, take this model as their starting point – thus viewing translations as something which would primarily happen through texts and involve only a small group of professionals. Though it involves meticulous research, these texts and the path a concept or a semantic field followed across the linguistic border can be traced and, in a best-case scenario, the translators can be identified. However, this mode of conceptual transfer may well be the exception rather than the general rule. This becomes particularly clear if we regard the wide prevalence of multilingualism up until the present day.

Translators are rarely the sole guardians of language transfers. Much more commonly, we encounter situations in which a substantial percentage of speakers and readers are multilingual, accessing texts and concepts directly in the other language. This is as true for the Chinese students in Japan at the turn of the nineteenth century as for the French-speaking Ottoman and Arab intellectuals and for the largely bilingual, if not trilingual, Indian national movement.[60] All of them read the relevant texts in the original (or in Japanese, French or English translations). In that manner, the first mediation between the two languages and the integration of the concepts into new semantic nets often took place without leaving written traces. In turn, these intellectuals may have worked as translators in a very wide sense of the term, writing reviews, summaries and explanations in their mother tongue, which might then look like the first 'translation' of a concept. Such translations may be even more hidden if the reference to the original text is missing altogether and the authors simply start using the translated concepts in their writings. Word-to-word translations of canonical texts, once they occur, may then draw on a history of linguistic encounters rather than being their starting point.

Two of the three vignettes at the beginning of this introduction pointed to professional translators, or at least scholars with a high level of competence in both the source language and the target language. However, the third example, the Meiji reformer Fukuzawa Yukichi, suggests that this may be just the tip of the iceberg of translations actually taking place on a day-by-day basis (and anyone who has tried to make sense of translated instruction manuals for new electronic devices will tend to confirm this). Yet once we have given up the notion of pre-existing equivalences, which a translator can get right or wrong, it is not without problems to include mistranslations in our investigation. Can we still distinguish between successful and failed translations? Translation, first of all, should be regarded not as an individual undertaking, in which a translator working in solitude creates equivalents out of nothingness and imposes them on a passive audience. Rather, negotiating meaning at the interstice of languages needs to be seen as a social process in which translations and equivalents will be created but nevertheless also remain contested. The latter is particularly evident in the process demarcating the boundaries of the semantic field within which the translation will be understood and accepted. These boundaries are not immovable but neither are they inexistent. The second approach starts from the pragmatics of translation: every translation is a communicative act in a chain of consecutive actions. Thus viewed, a translation is successful if and in so far as it permits the communicative action to go on – whether it is the arrival of the explorer who proclaims that he has come with peaceful intentions, the traveller who asks for food or the overseer of a prison who orders a group of convicts to build a road. To an even greater degree than conceptual history in a monolingual environment, the investigation of the transfer of concepts through translation has to take into account the practices into which the use of concepts is being embedded. This is the case for both the source as well as the target language. These practices sometimes can be deduced from the translated texts themselves; often this will require enlarging the corpus of sources we draw upon as scholars in the field.[61]

Concepts in Global History Writing

As we hope to have shown, conceptual history can greatly benefit from the wider trend of global history, for instance by absorbing the growing literature on the history of trans-lingual and global transfers. But at the same time, conceptual history also has important elements to offer to the rapidly evolving landscapes of global historical research. For instance, it would certainly enrich many global historical studies to pay more attention to the history of concepts and their usage by historical agents in languages other than French or English. In addition, a greater emphasis on the role of concepts in history and historiography leads to challenging – but at the same time rewarding – theoretical questions. After all, historians are not only researching concepts, they are also using them. We are all part of the ongoing evolution of concepts. Which, then, are the concepts we want to use in the writing of global history? In which language shall our writing be, if the history we are investigating is multilingual and so increasingly are the colleagues with whom we are interacting?

As Reinhart Koselleck has pointed out, the translation of source concepts into analytical concepts used as tools in the historian's workshop lies at the basis of all conceptual history, even if it limits itself to a single language. Things become even more complex once the languages of the sources and of the analytical concepts fall apart. Historians often write their text while implicitly assuming that they have access to a quasi-neutral analytical language which is equally distant from all other languages. According to some historians, concepts like *economy, middle class* or *religion* can even be used as common universal categories if they are carefully defined.[62] Though languages can and do evolve – and historians are certainly agents of this change – the idea of converting concepts into universals by means of definition seems overly hopeful. Concepts, as their historical analyses have shown over and again, do not depend on definitions alone but carry with them the heritage of their past use. They cannot easily be separated from the semantic nets thus created – semantic nets that consist not only of other concepts but also of the metaphors, images and stories which embed their meaning.[63] The seemingly universal concepts thus transport their particular history. Moreover, if we take the basic assumption of conceptual history seriously, the concepts also convey the experiences and world interpretations embedded in their particular language. Through the strong role of English as a language of communication, global history may therefore inadvertently run into the danger of undermining its own project of bringing together the history of the different world regions on an equal footing. The global role of Eurocentric ideas, concepts and languages has already been problematized by schools such as subaltern studies and post-colonialism.[64]

But are we left only with the choice of epistemic violence or the confusion of the tower of Babel? Is refusing to translate key concepts from their original languages, hence leaving the readers bewildered in front of an abundance of words in italics they can neither pronounce nor remember, the only alternative to using a hegemonic language? It is here that the systematic integration of the history of concepts to global history may show, if not the solution of the problem, then at least a way to a higher degree of self-reflexivity. Tracing the history of the key concepts used in the sources will show the readers the concepts' places in their respective semantic networks, that is, the ways in which they have been delimited and distinguished from other concepts, how they have been used and applied, as well as their transformations. In a next step, such information could then be correlated to the semantic load carried by analytical concepts. Instead of a translation of nineteenth-century Chinese or Ottoman concepts into present-day English, in which the process of establishing equivalents would remain hidden, the analysis could instead bring the two concepts into an open dialogue. This will not bring about a more 'faithful' translation, but it will show the chasms facing the translation, as well as the connecting bridges already built.

This might not change the languages in which global historians communicate across the globe – in very many cases English has already become the common language, at least for the time being. It certainly makes sense to use the current possibilities already existing to talk to each other at a conference and to read each other's books and articles. What conceptual history, particularly after having opened up to global history, can do in this situation is to enhance the awareness of the conceptual reconfigurations and translation processes involved in our everyday communication. It can also greatly enrich the ways in which we as historians approach the past, as well as the ways in which we debate the contours of our field. The pieces collected in this reader provide examples of scholarship heading into this direction.

Notes

1   For a discussion of the possibility of using multiple (not only language based) media for conceptual history see Imke Rajamani, 'Pictures, Emotions, Conceptual Change: Anger in Popular Hindi Cinema', *Contributions to the History of Concepts*, 7/2 (2012), 52–77 (also Chapter 12 in this volume).

2   For an overview of this development see Margrit Pernau, 'Whither Conceptual History. From National to Entangled Histories', *Contributions to the History of Concepts*, 7/1 (2012), 1–11.

3   Jani Marjanen, 'Undermining Methodological Nationalism: Histoire Croisée of Concepts as Transnational History', in Matthias Albert et al. (eds), *Transnational Political Spaces: Agents – Structures – Encounters* (Frankfurt a.M.: Campus, 2009), 239–63.

4   For an early work on linguistic encounters see Anuradha Dingwaneyand and Carol Maier (eds), *Between Languages and Cultures. Translations and Cross-Cultural Texts* (Pittsburgh: University of Pittsburgh Press, 1995); with a special focus on moving concepts Carol Gluck and Anna Lowenhaupt Tsing (eds), *Words in Motion: Towards a Global Lexicon* (Durham: Duke University Press, 2009); Michael Lackner, Iwo Amelung and Joachim Kurtz, *New Terms for New Ideas: Western Knowledge and Lexical Change in Late Imperial China*, (Leiden: Brill, 2001); on the adaptation of the concepts of society and economics in different Asian countries see Hagen Schulz-Forberg (ed.), *A Global Conceptual History of Asia, 1860–1940* (London: Pickering & Chatto, 2014). See also the large collaborative projects on conceptual change in Spain, Portugal and Latin America, *Iberconceptos*, coordinated by Javier Fernandez Sebastian

(<www.iberconceptos.net> (accessed 31 May 2015)), and the equally large project on concepts in Korea, China and Japan at the Hallym Academy in Korea (<http://has.hallym.ac.kr/science_E/?c=5/29> (accessed 31 May 2015)).

5   See the path breaking studies of Lydia Liu, *Translingual Practice: Literature, National Culture and Translated Modernity-China, 1900–1937* (Stanford: Stanford University Press, 1995); Douglas Howland, *Translating the West: Language and Political Reason in Nineteenth Century Japan* (Honolulu: University of Hawaii Press, 2002); Andrew Sartori, *Bengal in Global Concept History: Culturalism in the Age of Capital* (Chicago and London: University of Chicago Press, 2008).

6   A challenge that cannot be overlooked is that the current wave of digitizing historical materials prioritizes larger languages or languages that continue being relevant today. Global interpretations of conceptual history need to take this distorted pattern of historiographical accessibility into account.

7   Global history has emphasized the colonial legacy framing these power relations. For a global conceptual history it might be important to also look at the importance the size of a language community plays: transfers and translations play out differently for Korean than for Chinese, or for Dutch than for English.

8   For example, Kenneth Pomeranz, *The Great Divergence: China, Europe and the Making of the Modern World Economy* (Princeton: Princeton University Press, 2001).

9   For example, Marcel van der Linden, *Workers of the World: Essays Towards a Global Labor History* (Leiden: Brill, 2008).

10   For example, Thomas Bender, *Rethinking American History in a Global Age* (Berkeley: University of California Press, 2002); and Prasenjit Duara, *The Global and Regional in China's Nation Formation* (New York/London: Routledge, 2009).

11   For instance, Georg Iggers, Edward Wang and Supriyah Mukherjee, *A Global History of Modern Historiography* (Harlow, England: Pearson Longman, 2008), 117–56; and Eric Woolf, *A Global History of History* (Cambridge: Cambridge UP, 2011).

12   For example, Akira Iriye, *Global Community: The Role of International Organizations in the Making of the Contemporary World* (Berkeley: University of California Press, 2002).

13   John R. McNeill, *Something New Under the Sun: An Environmental History of the Twentieth-Century World* (New York: W.W. Norton, 2000).

14   See Dirk Hoerder, *Cultures in Contact: World Migrations in the Second Millennium* (Durham, NC: Duke University Press, 2002).

15 See Dominic Sachsenmaier, 'Global Challenges to Intellectual History', *Fudan Journal of the Humanities and Social Sciences*, 6/1 (2013), 128–47.

16 Shruti Kapila and Faisal Devji (eds), *Political Thought in Action: The Bhagavad Gita and Modern India* (Cambridge: Cambridge University Press, 2013); Shruti Kapila (ed.), *An Intellectual History for India* (New York: Cambridge University Press, 2010).

17 For instance, Samuel Moyn and Andrew Sartori (eds), *Global Intellectual History* (New York: Columbia University Press, 2013).

18 For a general overview of developments within intellectual history see Anthony Grafton, 'The History of Ideas: Precepts and Practice, 1950–2000 and Beyond', *Journal of the History of Ideas*, 67/1 (2006), 1–32; and David Armitage, ' "The Fifty Years" Rift: Intellectual History and International Relations', *Modern Intellectual History*, 1/1 (2004), 97–109.

19 See for examples Pierre-Yves Saunier, 'Learning by Doing: Notes about the Making of the Palgrave Dictionary of Transnational History', *Journal of Modern European History*, 6/2 (2008), 159–80. See also Patricia Clavin, 'Defining Transnationalism', *Contemporary European History*, 14/4 (2005), 421–39.

20 See for example Ulrike Freitag and Achim von Oppen, 'Translokalität als ein Zugang zur Geschichte globaler Verflechtungen', *H-Soz-u-Kult* (10 June 2005), <http://hsozkult.geschichte.hu-berlin.de/index.asp?pn=forum&uid=2005-06-001&view=pdf> (accessed 31 May 2015); see also Ulrike Freitag and Achim von Oppen (eds), *Translocality. The Study of Globalizing Processes from a Southern Perspective* (Leiden: Brill, 2010).

21 Michael Werner and Bénédicte Zimmermann, 'Beyond Comparison: Histoire Croisée and the Challenge of Reflexivity', *History and Theory*, 45/1 (2006), 30–50.

22 For example: Jorge Cañizares-Esguerra, 'Entangled Histories: Borderland Historiographies in New Clothes?' *American Historical Review*, 112/3 (2007), 787–99.

23 For example, Sanjay Subrahmanyam, 'Connected Histories: Notes towards a Reconfiguration of Early Modern Eurasia', *Modern Asian Studies*, 31/3 (1997), 735–62.

24 About reform movements and new trends in international history see Akira Iriye, *Global and Transnational History: The Past, Present and Future* (New York, Palgrave: 2013). See also Ursula Lehmkuhl, 'Diplomatiegeschichte als internationale Kulturgeschichte: Theoretische Ansätze und empirische Forschung zwischen Historischer Kulturwissenschaft und Soziologischem Institutionalismus', *Geschichte und Gesellschaft*, 27/3 (2001), 394–423.

25 Outside of the West, modern academic and education systems put more emphasis on world history. See Dominic Sachsenmaier, *Global Perspectives on Global History: Theories and Approaches in a Connected World* (Cambridge: Cambridge University Press, 2011), esp. chapter one.

26 See for example Bruce Mazlish, 'Comparing Global History to World History', *Journal of Interdisciplinary History*, 28/3 (1998), 385–95.

27 See for example Patrick Manning, *Navigating World History: Historians Create a Global Past* (New York: Palgrave Macmillan, 2003); and David Christian and Marnie Hughes-Warrington (eds), *Cambridge Companion to World History* (Cambridge: Cambridge University Press, 2015).

28 On this topic see for example Dominic Sachsenmaier, *Global Perspectives on Global History. Theories and Approaches in a Connected World* (Cambridge: Cambridge University Press, 2011), esp. chapter two; and Akira Iriye, *Global and Transnational History: The Past, Present and Future* (New York: Palgrave, 2013).

29 Compare Stefan Berger, 'Introduction: Towards a Global History of National Historiographies' in idem (ed.), *Writing the Nation: A Global Perspective* (Basingstoke: Palgrave Macmillan, 2007), 1–29; and Immanuel Wallerstein et al. (eds), *Open the Social Sciences: Report of the Gulbenkian Commission on the Restructuring of the Social Sciences* (Stanford: Stanford University Press, 1996).

30 Important examples of literature heading into this direction are the publications on the history of the Indian Ocean or parts thereof. For example: Sugata Bose, *A Hundred Horizons: The Indian Ocean in the Age of Global Empire* (Cambridge, MA: Harvard University Press, 2006); or Sunil Amrith, *Crossing the Bay of Bengal: The Furies of Nature and the Fortunes of Migrants* (Cambridge, MA: Harvard University Press, 2013).

31 This interpretation draws partly on an earlier article, (Pernau 2012).

32 Editorial footnotes in the texts are marked with squared brackets and provide updated references or give further references or translations.

33 Otto Brunner, Werner Conze and Reinhart Koselleck (eds), *Geschichtliche Grundbegriffe: Historisches Lexikon zur Politisch-sozialen Sprache in Deutschland*, 8 vols (Stuttgart: Klett, 1972–90).

34 See Reinhart Koselleck, 'Introduction to the *Geschichtliche Grundbegriffe*' (Chapter 1 in this volume); Reinhart Koselleck, 'Social History and Conceptual History' (Chapter 2 in this volume).

35 Rolf Reichardt and Eberhard Schmitt (eds), *Handbuch politisch-sozialer Grundbegriffe in Frankreich, 1680–1820* (München: Oldenbourg, 1985).

36 See Rolf Reichardt, 'For a Social-historical Semantics as a Middle Course between "Lexicometrie" and "Conceptual History"' (Chapter 3 in this volume).

37 Dietrich Busse, *Historische Semantik: Analyse eines Programms* (Stuttgart: Klett-Cotta, 1987).

38 See Dietrich Busse, 'Conceptual History or a History of Discourse? On the Theoretical Basis and Questions of Methodology of a Historical-semantic Epistemology' (Chapter 4 in this volume).

39 See Quentin Skinner, 'Rhetoric and Conceptual Change' (Chapter 5 in this volume). For a more in-depth introduction into the programme of Cambridge Intellectual History see Quentin Skinner, 'Meaning and Understanding in the History of Ideas', *History and Theory*, 8/1 (1969), 3–53.

40 For further reading refer to the continuously expanding bibliographic database on <www.historyofconcepts.org> (accessed 31 May 2015) and the bibliography on <http://www.concepta-net.org/links> (accessed 31 May 2015) listing works until ca. 2010.

41 Kari Palonen, 'Reinhart Koselleck on Translation, Anachronism and Conceptual Change', in Melvin Richter and Martin Burke (eds), *Why Concepts Matter: Translating Social and Political Thought* (Leiden: Brill, 2012), 73–92.

42 Reinhart Koselleck, Ulrike Spree and Willibald Steinmetz, 'Drei bürgerliche Welten? Zur vergleichenden Semantik der bürgerlichen Gesellschaft in Deutschland, England und Frankreich', in Hans-Jürgen Puhle (ed.), *Bürger in der Gesellschaft der Neuzeit. Wirtschaft–Politik–Kultur* (Göttingen: Vandenhoeck & Ruprecht, 1991), reprinted in Reinhart Koselleck, *Begriffsgeschichten* (Frankfurt am Main: Suhrkamp, 2006), 402–61.

43 Koselleck, Spree and Steinmetz (2006), 413.

44 Jörn Leonhard, *Liberalismus – Zur historischen Semantik eines europäischen Deutungsmusters*, Veröffentlichungen des Deutschen Historischen Instituts London, vol. 50 (Munich: Oldenbourg, 2001).

45 See Jörn Leonhard, 'Translation as Cultural Transfer and Semantic Interaction: European Variations of Liberalism between 1800 and 1830' (Chapter 6 in this volume); Kari Palonen, 'Translation, Politics and Conceptual Change' (Chapter 7 in this volume).

46 Ann Laura Stoler and Frederic Cooper (eds), *Tensions of Empire: Colonial Cultures in a Bourgeois World* (Berkeley: University of California Press, 1997); Kathleen Wilson, *A New Imperial History: Culture, Identity and Modernity in Britain and the Empire, 1660–1840* (Cambridge: Cambridge University Press, 2004); Werner and Zimmermann (2006).

47 James Clifford, *Routes: Travel and Translation in the Late 20th Century* (Cambridge, MA: Harvard University Press, 1997); Arjun Appadurai, *Modernity at Large: Cultural Dimensions of Globalization* (Minneapolis: University of Minnesota Press, 1996); Ulf Hannerz, *Transnational Connections: Culture, People, Places* (London: Routledge, 1996).

48   Walter Benjamin, 'The Task of the Translator', trans. Harry Zohn, in
      Lawrence Venuti (ed.), *The Translation Studies Reader* (New York:
      Routledge, 2000), 9–15.

49   Susan Bassnett and André Lefevere (eds), *Constructing Cultures: Essays
      on Literary Translation* (Clevedon: Multilingual Matters, 1998); Susan
      Bassnett and Harish Trivedi (eds), *Post-colonial Translation: Theory and
      Practice, Translation Studies* (London: Routledge, 1999). For a good
      summary of the issues debated see Mary Snell-Hornby, *The Turns of
      Translation Studies: New Paradigms or Shifting Viewpoints?* (Amsterdam:
      J. Benjamins, 2006). See also Yves Gambier and Luc van Doorslaer,
      Handbook of Translation Studies, 3 vols (Amsterdam: J. Benjamins,
      2010–12).

50   Walter Nils Hakala, 'Diction and Dictionaries: Language, Literature
      and Learning in Persianate South Asia', PhD dissertation, University
      of Pennsylvania, 2010; Javed Majeed, 'Modernity's Script and a Tom
      Thumb Performance: English Linguistic Modernity and Persian/Urdu
      Lexicography in Nineteenth Century India', in Michael S. Dodson and
      Brian A. Hatcher (eds), *Trans-Colonial Modernities in South Asia* (London:
      Routledge 2012), 95–115.

51   Friedrich Schleiermacher, 'Über die verschiedenen Methoden des
      Übersetzens', Berlin, Königliche Akademie der Wissenschaften, 24
      June 1813, reprinted in *Friedrich Schleiermacher's sämmtliche Werke,
      Dritte Abtheilung: Zur Philosophie*, vol. 2 (Berlin: Reimer, 1938),
      207–45; idem, 'On the Different Methods of Translation', trans. English
      Waltraud Bartscht, in Rainer Schulte and John Biguenet (eds), *Theories
      of Translation: An Anthology of Essays from Dryden to Derrida* (Chicago:
      University of Chicago Press, 1992), 36–54; Lawrence Venuti, 'Translation
      as Cultural Politics: Régimes of Domestication in English', in Mona Baker
      (ed.), *Critical Readings in Translation Studies* (London: Routledge, 2010),
      65–79.

52   Kurt Mueller-Vollmer, 'Übersetzen–Wohin? Zum Problem der
      Diskursformierung bei Frau von Staël und im amerikanischen
      Transzendentalismus', in Beate Hammerschmid and Hermann Krapoth
      (eds), *Übersetzung als kultureller Prozess: Rezeption, Projektion und
      Konstruktion des Fremden* (Berlin: Erich Schmidt Verlag, 1998), 11–31.

53   Talal Asad, 'The Concept of Cultural Translation in British Social
      Anthropology', in Baker (2010), 7–27; Doris Bachmann-Medick,
      'Meanings of Translation in Cultural Anthropology', in Theo Hermans
      (ed.), *Translating Others* (Manchester: St. Jerome Publishing, 2006), 33–43;
      Martin Fuchs, 'Reaching Out; Or, Nobody Exists in One Context Only:
      Society as Translation', *Translation Studies*, 2/1 (2009), 2–40.

54   Howland (2002); Samah Selim, 'Nation and Translation in the Middle East: Histories, Canon, Hegemonies', *The Translator*, 15/1 (2009), 1–13; Tejaswini Niranjana, *Siting Translation: History, Poststructuralism and the Colonial Context* (Berkeley: University of California Press, 1992). See Lydia Liu, 'The Question of Meaning-Value in the Political Economy of the Sign' (Chapter 8 in this volume); and Andrew Sartori, 'The Resonance of "Culture": Framing a Problem in Global Concept-History' (Chapter 9 in this volume).

55   See Katrin Bromber, '*Ustaarabu*: A Conceptual Change in Tanganyikan Newspaper Discourse in the 1920s' (Chapter 11 in this volume).

56   Sajjad Alam Rizvi, 'Loving the Master? The Debate on Appropriate Emotions in North India (ca. 1750–1830)', PhD dissertation, Freie Universität Berlin, 2012, mainly chapter three.

57   For an overview of the unequal translation flows between languages see UNESCO, *Index Translationum*, <http://portal.unesco.org/culture/en/ev.php-URL_ID=7810&URL_DO=DO_TOPIC&URL_SECTION=201.html> (accessed 31 May 2015).

58   Debendra K. Dash and Dipti R. Pattanaik, 'Translation and Social Praxis in Ancient and Medieval India', in Paul St. Pierre and Prafulla C. Kar (eds), *Translation Reflections, Refractions, Transformations* (Amsterdam: John Benjamins, 2007), 153–73; Maria Tymoczko, 'Reconceptualizing Translation Theory: Integrating Non-Western Thought about Translation', in Hermans (2006), 13–32.

59   Lisa Mitchell, *Language, Emotion and Politics in South India: The Making of a Mother Tongue* (Bloomington: India University Press, 2009).

60   Özlem Berk, *Translation and Westernization in Turkey from the 1840s to the 1980s* (Istanbul: Yaninlari, 2004); Chandrani Chatterjee, *Translation Reconsidered: Culture, Genre and the 'Colonial Encounter' in Nineteenth Century Bengal* (Newcastle: Cambridge Scholars Publishing, 2010).

61   See Rajamani (2012) (also Chapter 12 in this volume).

62   About the complexity of defining *labour* in various global and local historical contexts see Marcel van der Linden, 'The "Globalization" of Labour and Working Class History and Its Consequences', in Jan Lucassen (ed.), *Global Labour History: A State of the Art* (Bern, Switzerland/New York: Peter Lang, 2006), 13–36.

63   See Rieke Schäfer, 'Historicizing Strong Metaphors: A Challenge for Conceptual History', *Contributions to the History of Concepts*, 7/2 (2012), 28–51, and Rajamani (2012).

64   See for example Robert J.C. Young, *Postcolonialism: A Historical Introduction* (Oxford/Malden, MA: Blackwell, 2001); Rochona Majumdar, *Writing Postcolonial History* (London: Bloomsbury Academic, 2010).

Part I

Classical Texts in Conceptual History

Reinhart Koselleck, widely considered the founding father of German conceptual history (*Begriffsgeschichte*), can be seen one of the most influential German historians of the twentieth century. Koselleck lived through the catastrophic events of World War II, as a soldier and subsequently as a prisoner of war, until 1946. His subsequent studies in Germany and England included history, sociology, law and philosophy. He received his PhD from Heidelberg University in 1954 and later taught at a number of different universities. His intellectual biography bears the traces of his engagement with the philosophy of Heidegger and Gadamer, the philosophy of history of Karl Löwith and the political theory of Carl Schmitt. He played an instrumental role in rebuilding and reforming the post-war German academic landscape, notably through his involvement in the foundation of Bielefeld University.[1] It is from here that the renowned Bielefeld School of historians emerged.

Koselleck's research interests spanned from history, sociology and law to linguistics, epistemology and political iconography. His numerous publications, several of which are available in translation into English and other languages, include his PhD thesis *Kritik und Krise: Eine Studie zur Pathogenese der bürgerlichen Welt* (1954, published as a book in 1959; English edition: *Critique and Crisis: Enlightenment and the Pathogenesis of Modern Society*, 1988), his postdoctoral habilitation thesis *Preußen zwischen Reform und Revolution: Allgemeines Landrecht, Verwaltung und soziale Bewegung von 1791 bis 1848* (1965, published as a book in 1967; 'Prussia between Reform and Revolution: General Common Law, Administration and Social Movement from 1791 to 1848'), *Vergangene Zukunft: Zur Semantik geschichtlicher Zeiten* (1979; English edition: *Futures Past: On the Semantics of Historical Time*, 1985), *Zeitschichten: Studien zur Historik* (2000) and *The Practice of Conceptual History* (2002).

Reinhart Koselleck's work as editor (together with Otto Brunner and Werner Conze) on the monumental eight-volume *Geschichtliche Grundbegriffe: Historisches Lexikon zur politisch-sozialen Sprache in Deutschland* (1972–1997; 'Basic Concepts: A Historical Dictionary of the Socio-political Language in Germany') remains one of his most influential publications. The volumes cover a total of 115 diverse concepts, with contributions written by a variety of specialists. Koselleck decisively shaped the discipline of conceptual history in Germany and abroad. The text published here is the introduction to the first volume of *Geschichtliche Grundbegriffe*, published in 1972. It elucidates Koselleck's initial intentions regarding the project as well as his vision of conceptual history.

---

[1] Niklas Olsen, *History in the Plural: An Introduction to the Work of Reinhart Koselleck* (Berghahn: New York, 2012).

1

Introduction (*Einleitung*) to the *Geschichtliche Grundbegriffe*

Reinhart Koselleck

Ernst: *When I have a concept of something, I can also express it in words.*

Falk: *Not always, and at any rate not in a way that others, even if they use the same words, will form exactly the same concept as I do.*[1]

Social and political language is rich in concepts that define or categorize (*Leitbegriffe*), as well as in keywords (*Schlüsselwörter*) and in slogans (*Schlagwörter*). Some suddenly appear and then just as soon vanish. On the other hand, many basic concepts (*Grundbegriffe*) have remained in use ever since they were first coined in classical antiquity, and even today help constitute our political and social vocabulary (albeit with altered meanings). New concepts have come into use; old ones have changed, or died out. At all times, the diversity of historical experience – past and present – has been captured by concepts in different languages and in their translations. Thus the editors of this lexicon have had to choose which concepts to include.

(1) The Purpose of the Lexicon

The lexicon centres on the investigation and exposition of some 130 basic historical concepts (*geschichtliche Grundbegriffe*).[2]

(1.1) The term 'basic historical concepts', when used in this lexicon, means not those technical terms registered in the handbooks and methodological works of historical scholarship and the disciplines related to it, but those defining concepts (*Leitbegriffe*) which must be studied historically. Professional historians must, of course, take account of the distinctive linguistic usages prevalent at the times and places they investigate. Research centred on the past must sooner or later confront the language and self-interpretations both of that time and of the present. For the language used in the primary sources (*Quellensprache*) for a given period can be treated as a metaphor for the history that is to be comprehended.

For this reason, the lexicon is limited to those expressions which, because of their range of meanings and applications, make it possible to analyse historical structures and major complexes of events. To this end, the lexicon gathers together:

1   Concepts central to classifying constitutions.
2   Key terms used by political, social and economic organizations.
3   Self-characterizations used in the disciplines dealing with these organizations.
4   Concepts and slogans (*Schlagwörter*) crucial to political movements.
5   Designations of dominant professional groups and social strata.
6   Core concepts with a claim to the status of theory (including those of ideology), which articulate and interpret the domains of social and political action and of labour.

All these concepts may be treated as building blocks for a type of research that considers social and political language, particularly the specialized terminology of these domains, both as causal factors and as indicators of historical change. Given the nature of language, with its endless potential for multi-layered and ambiguous expression, the selection of concepts must be, to some extent, arbitrary. Yet such choices have also been determined by the theoretical issues addressed by the lexicon.

(1.2) The central problematic (*die leitende Fragestellung*) of this lexicon is the dissolution of the old society of orders or estates and the development of the modern world. These twin processes are studied by tracking the history of how they were conceptually registered. This theme imposed certain limitations which nonetheless, we hope, promote methodological clarity while doing justice to the richness of the primary materials.

This lexicon's primary focus is the period from about 1,700 to the threshold of our own time. Its research is meant to reveal what is distinctively *modern* about the way we conceptualize political and social life. Rather than treating *modern* simply as *contemporary*, this work explores how modern and old words began to overlap and shift their meanings. This investigation necessitated reaching back to classical antiquity, the Middle Ages, the Renaissance, the Reformation and humanism, insofar as the history of the concepts included in this lexicon can be traced to these periods. Furthermore, only the concepts of German-speaking Europe were investigated, although always within the context of the traditions found in Europe as a whole. Finally, detailed analysis has been reserved for those political and social concepts which registered the transformations resulting from the political and industrial revolutions (of the eighteenth and nineteenth centuries). Such concepts were demonstrably affected, altered, displaced or provoked by these two revolutionary processes.

Thus, to a considerable extent, the lexicon is oriented to the present. Its theme is how the modern world has been registered through language; how, in other words, it was comprehended and articulated through concepts which we still use. Nonetheless, the lexicon was never intended to treat the entire social and political vocabulary of our own time. Nor did it seek to provide a political semantics derived from present-day linguistics, although it does make some preliminary contributions in this still-uncharted area. Rather the aim of this work was to track the categorizing concepts (*Leitbegriffe*) from the period before the French Revolution, through the events and changes during the Revolution, down to the language of the present. Examples of such concepts are *civil society, the state* or (adaptations of)[3] Aristotelian constitutional concepts. Also charted are those neologisms related to this process of change (for example *Caesarism, communism* or *anti-Semitism*). Analysed as well is the history of successive meanings

(*Bedeutungsgeschichten*) of those words that acquired the status of concepts only in modern times (such as *class, need, progress* or *history*).

(1.3) The heuristic presupposition (*heuristischer Vorgriff*) guiding the research presented in this work is that since the middle of the eighteenth century a profound change has occurred in the meaning of the classical topics (topoi) of political discourse. Old words have taken on new meanings, which for us do not require translation. What is posited is the emergence of a threshold period (*Sattelzeit*) in which the past was gradually transformed into the present. Concepts registering this change became 'Janus-faced': facing backwards, they pointed to social and political realities no longer intelligible to us without critical commentary; facing forward to our own time, concepts have taken on meanings that may not need further explication to be directly intelligible to us. From this point on, we understand and conceptualize simultaneously.

With certain exceptions, this initial presupposition has been confirmed. The history of those political and social concepts included in this lexicon revealed a long-term, profound and at times convulsive transformation of every-day experience. The significance of old concepts was altered to fit the changing conditions of the modern world. Although the words themselves may not have changed, such concepts as *democracy, revolution, republic* or *history* underwent a process of modification that can be clearly traced. Alternatively, virtually new coinages appeared, such as *class* or *socialism* – old expressions that could be elevated into central concepts only as the result of economic planning and changed economic conditions. While some of these expressions became easily accepted neologisms, other traditional words, such as *estate* (order) and *aristocracy*, gradually lost their former social and political significance.

The same heuristic presupposition determined the thrust of the distinctive history presented in this lexicon, which traces the persisting and surviving meanings of concepts from their origins to the changes and shifts occurring over the course of (modern) revolutionary processes. Taken together, these histories of concepts testify to the novelty of what was being conceptualized, to the changing relationship of humans to nature, history and time – in short, to the beginning of the *modern world*.

As yet no unambiguous answer can be given to the question of whether the rate of change in social and political terminology has accelerated since 1750. While analogous developments can be discerned at the threshold of every epoch, a significant number of indicators do point to such an accelerated process of change in the political and social language of the period studied here. If so, then it is likely that the *modern world (Neuzeit)* was simultaneously experienced as a *new age (neue Zeit)*. Sudden changes permanently altered the once-familiar world, thus transforming the horizon of experience and with it the terminology (especially the central concepts) that had once been – reactively or proactively – tied to it. What is immediately striking (and here the lexicon confirms earlier research such as that of Stammler) is that since 1770, a flood of previously unknown words and meanings has appeared, thus testifying to a new understanding of the world, which soon infused the entire language.[4] Old expressions were enriched with novel content. This not only fed German classicism and idealism, but also reframed all the terms used to discuss state and society, including these very concepts.

For this reason, the distinguishing characteristics of this long-term process need to be identified. Needless to say, not every article in this lexicon will emphasize all of these characteristics to the same degree. Indeed, whether they are equally applicable to every social and political concept can only be ascertained after the completion of our project, when all our concepts will have been fully charted.

(1.3.1) As the old world of estates or orders disintegrated, its many social and political concepts came to be applied to a number of domains beyond those to which they had been restricted in the past. In this sense, we can speak – to use a contemporary term – of the *democratization* of political and social language. To be sure, something analogous had already occurred after the invention of the printing press. Especially from the Reformation onwards, religious, social and political conflicts were waged in pamphlets available to members of all social orders. But it was not until the Enlightenment, especially after it spread beyond France, that political language came into more general use. Fields of expression once specific to given social orders now were opened to everyone. Until the middle of the eighteenth century, the language of politics had been used exclusively by the upper ranks of the aristocracy, by jurists and by the learned. After this time, the circle of users rapidly expanded to encompass all educated persons. Indicative of this enlargement was not only the rising number of journals, but also the change in what was being read. Intensive, repetitive study of a few familiar texts gave way to more extensive and varied reading habits, fed by the craving for everything new and novel.[5] Finally, beginning roughly with the period between 1815 and the 1848 Revolution (*Vormärz*), there was a leap in the size of the public addressed. After unprecedented numbers of the lower strata consciously entered the speech community of those using political language, the significance of its terms expanded correspondingly. The number of readers increased, as did that of the writers and orators addressing them. Nevertheless, there remained considerable social differences between the audiences reached and those seeking to communicate with them. Numerous concepts – often in the form of slogans – penetrated social circles previously excluded from political discourse by the rigidities of social stratification. This process facilitated alterations of meaning. Thus to German Conservatives, 'freedom of the press' (*Preßfreiheit*) meant 'freedom of the press to be impudent' (*Preßfrechheit*), while to illiterate peasants it meant, even as late as 1848, freedom from oppression and its burdens. But such differences in meaning were perhaps less significant than the fact that the same concepts could now be used by different social strata.

On the other hand, as the hierarchical order of estates began to dissolve, so too did the concepts once tied to specific estates; such concepts no longer fitted the new reality. *Honour* or *dignity* could no longer be unambiguously reserved for members of a particular estate. Once exclusively aristocratic concepts, they were now either used to describe purely private virtues or else expanded to encompass *the nation* or *the people*. The very term for *estate* (*Stand*) decomposed into distinctive economic, social and occupational meanings. Previously these had been conjoined in a single concept, which corresponded to the political designation of a given estate. Such socially specific concepts were now replaced by new, more general concepts, even though these were often clothed in the guise of old words. Thus, the old concept of *Bürger* once described someone considered honourable within a given order or estate. Subsequently, the word remained the same, but it became transformed into the generic concept of *citizen*, which could exclude or cover all the terms that previously indicated an individual's social and political status.

(1.3.2) A second characteristic of those concepts that incorporated new experiences came with the introduction of a temporal dimension (*Verzeitlichung*) into categories of meaning. Outmoded themes (topoi) now became emotively charged, infused with a sense of expectation they had not had before. Thus the three Aristotelian forms of government, once regarded as a permanent and exhaustive repertoire of constitutions that could recur at any time, were undermined and superseded. *Republic* was originally a collective term applied to all constitutions. Once it became a party-political concept, however, it was declared to be the only legitimate constitution. Eventually, *republic* ceased to be a generic concept in a static system of classification, and instead came to mean the one constitution towards which human history was (said to be) moving. Expectations about the future also became an integral part of *republicanism*, which now functioned as a political concept that integrated and made meaningful the movements of history. Soon *democracy* took the place of *republic*. In German-speaking Europe, democracy was by no means universally accepted. Yet now those who did champion democracy declared it to be the only legitimate constitution. That claim, in turn, had the result that *aristocracy* and *monarchy* were no longer regarded as those forms of rule most directly opposed or contrary to *democracy*. This meant that democracy could no longer derive legitimacy by contrasting itself with these older, bipolar opposites or counter-concepts (*Gegenbegriffe*). It had to be legitimated, instead, by reasons that varied depending on whether it was associated with liberalism, Caesarism or socialism.

Numerous terms began to surface in the form of *isms*. They promoted and indicated a process of change which advanced at different speeds, depending upon the social strata affected. Yet none of these *isms* could give a complete account of this process. The entire (social and political) vocabulary was reoriented in terms of baselines set within a philosophy of history. A telling example is the concept of *emancipation* (*Emanzipation*). In its former setting, it had been understood in terms of a natural rhythm of generational change. Thus, in its original sense, it was a legal term applied to an individual's coming of age. Then *emancipation* was extended to mean the elimination of those privileges formerly granted to members of a given estate. Finally, it became a general concept oriented to the future and applicable to any context. In this form, the concept indicated the end not only of the type of personal domination by one person over another characteristic of the system of estates or orders (*ständische Herrschaft*), but of domination in general (*Herrschaft überhaupt*). To the extent that administrative organizations took the place of older forms of personal domination, the concept of *Herrschaft* became a metaphor with many shades of meaning (*dominion, domination, rule, authority, power*), while still invoking the original antithesis between lord (*Herr*) and servant (*Knecht*).

In contrast (to concepts that registered changes which had already occurred) were those defined in a manner that incorporated coefficients of future change into themselves. Vattel was the first to do this with the concept of *constitution*. For Friedrich Schlegel, *democracy* – precisely because it cannot be fully attained in practice – became the proper standard for determining the legitimacy of all future constitutions. To take another example: Until about 1780, human needs had been thought of as unchanging and static. Thereafter such needs were seen as rapidly escalating. This new dynamic component was incorporated into the concept of *escalation of needs*.

Finally, expressions appeared which articulated historical time itself: *development* understood in the reflexive sense (of cumulative additions); *progress* as an unending process (of future change); *history as such* (*Geschichte schlechthin*), which is simultaneously its own subject and object; or *revolution*, which, once detached from its previous setting, lost its original meaning of 'recurring cycle' and became instead a general concept projecting movement towards future goals and indeterminate outcomes. All these new concepts became situated within a temporal process that at every stage both registered historical change and gave meaning to it.

(1.3.3) Yet another characteristic that defines the domain of the incipient modern world is the increasing extent to which many expressions could be incorporated into ideologies (*Ideologiesierbarkeit*). A defining experience of the modern world is the loss of those specific and particularistic terms which once designated social conditions. For this reason many older concepts, increasingly overtaken by events or changes in social structures that they could no longer either articulate or explain, became more and more abstract. From that time on, the use of collective singular nouns proliferated. Concrete usages such as *stories* or *histories* (*Geschichten*) were replaced by the more abstract term *history* (*Geschichte an sich*). Separate advances in one or another field now were lumped together as *progress*. The plural *liberties*, or privileges derived from a position in the old social order of estates, was replaced by the singular – *liberty* – common to all. This new usage of *liberty* in the collective singular, in turn, necessitated the addition of adjectives meant to designate particular applications, such as *social liberty, economic liberty* (in both the older and present senses of *economic*), *Christian liberty, political liberty* and so forth.

Such terms formulated in the collective singular have the advantage of being general and ambiguous. These qualities facilitate open-ended, unspecified expressions that can be understood in different, contradictory senses depending on the class or interest of the person using them. Concepts in this form were thus easily incorporated into ideologies. Depending on the background and ideological perspective of those involved, these ideologies could assume a variety of forms: economic, theological, political or that of a philosophy of history. Such processes as the turning of concepts to ideological purposes can be detected by the methods of conceptual history. In this way, a structural transformation becomes evident: a growing trend away from life in settings of manageable size and relative stability, and towards new horizons of possible experiences. These prospects, however, were purchased at a price. For they required the use of concepts at an ever-rising level of abstraction, a characteristic that allowed them to be integrated into ideologies. (During this period of change), the best regime came to be discussed by reference to constitutions that had been adopted at one or another phase of the French Revolution. The politics of the future could still be depicted solely by reference to past models. But restricting concepts to purely historical references simplified the process of incorporating them into an ideology. History and ideology now complemented one another. It was in this way that many concepts were transformed into abstract formulas, defended only by evidence derived from party allegiances.

(1.3.4) Historians have long recognized that every use of a word is related to its user's social and political position. But establishing such a relationship became more difficult once the number of possible positions increased and society became more pluralistic. At this point, the pressure to politicize concepts increased, along with the number of opportunities for doing so. More and more individuals were addressed, drawn in, mobilized. Whether there was a quantitative increase in the number of abusive and derogatory terms available to propagandists is debatable. But there can be no doubt that such terms of abuse were applied ever more indiscriminately and to ever greater effect. There was a significant increase in the use of concepts derived from those bipolar oppositions (*Gegenbegriffe*) that are indispensable to polemicists. Such late-eighteenth-century paired contrasts as that between *aristocracy* and *democracy* could still be located within the system of estates and be limited to it. This was not the case with *revolutionary* and *reactionary*, paired concepts of a later age. These served as easily available designations for one's own side and for one's enemies, both of which could be defined arbitrarily. As such they could always be recycled; indeed they demanded to be recycled. At the level of politics, long-term processes of industrial and social change gave rise to neologisms and other means for manipulating language such as the production of slogans. In addition to slogans, more theoretical concepts were minted to deal with specific situations. Politically and economically, addressing the recipient of a bureaucratic correspondence as a member of a noble *estate* or as a *proprietor* or as a member of the possessing class may have been of equal significance. In the eyes of the Prussian reformers, however, these distinctions were crucial.

Diplomatic, bureaucratic and propagandistic usages were mutually coloured by their respective terms and forms of expression. All that, *mutatis mutandis*, may well be valid for every age. What was new, however, was the feedback between historical and philosophical plans for the future, with their own distinctive concepts and political planning, which required steering language in new directions. In other words, the relationship between a concept and what was conceived was reversed; concepts now depended upon linguistic anticipations meant to shape the future. Thus concepts arose which could point beyond what was empirically verifiable and yet not lose their political and social significance. Indeed, the contrary was true. To what extent this tendency amounted to a *secularization* of theological strands of meaning will be investigated in the pertinent articles.

(1.3.5) Democratization, temporalization, the transformability of concepts into ideologies and politicization not only share common characteristics, but also are mutually dependent. They may not completely cover every aspect of modern social and political language. Yet they can serve as a way to distinguish modern terms from those in use before the (French) Revolution. Although they are central to our heuristic presupposition, these four characteristics may not necessarily be present to the same degree in all of the concepts charted in this lexicon. On the contrary, the meaning of many concepts remained unchanged even after our threshold period. To identify the otherness – or sameness – of expressions in the period before circa 1770, we must investigate usage before that time, which once again has its own history. This history may differ from word to word, and therefore will be pursued to various degrees of depth in different time periods. Understanding how the origins of distinctively modern times were conceptually registered is possible only if we pay especially close attention both to earlier meanings of the words investigated and to those changes that required the new formulations. To track and register this process in its totality is the purpose of the historical analysis of basic concepts presented in this lexicon. Although the lexicon is meant to provide neither a historical–positivist stocktaking nor a catalogue of current usage, both enter into the investigation of the concepts included.

(1.4) The lexicon's overall contribution, therefore, can be measured in three ways:

(1.4.1) First, the lexicon contributes *information*. As we know, philological dictionaries like those of Grimm or Trübner often leave us in the lurch when it comes to social and political concepts.[6] In the word fields of the central concepts treated in our lexicon, one will find a wealth of new evidence as to when terms were first used, or when and how they came to be translated into German from Latin, French or English. Numerous citations and bibliographical references make the lexicon an invaluable source of information. Thus the history of concepts as applied in this lexicon serves as an aid to the social and language sciences.

(1.4.2) Second, beyond offering such a survey of findings, the lexicon traces – in accordance with its heuristic presupposition – the *process of transformation into modernity*. This is the lexicon's specific contribution to history as a discipline, and here it differs from analogous philosophical or philological projects. The history of concepts as developed in this lexicon thus goes beyond merely systematizing or accumulating evidence from historical sources. Rather it seeks to comprehend the process by which experiences came to be registered in concepts and – as far as possible – to identify the theories included in such concepts. Above all, it is through the ways that social and political concepts were articulated, used and applied that our lexicon seeks to describe and explain the epochal transformation (of language) in the modern age.

(1.4.3) Third, in this way we may also establish a degree of *semantic control* over the use of (social and political) language today. The extent to which undesirable or arbitrary contemporary meanings have been imposed upon earlier meanings of words may now be determined. Retrieving the historical background and meanings of words will illuminate today's expressions and slogans. Definitions need no longer remain ahistorical or excessively abstract because of ignorance of what they may have meant in the past. They can now take into account the traditional plenitude or poverty of meanings of concepts. Exposure to experiences that once seemed distant and unfamiliar may sharpen consciousness of the present; such historical clarification may lead to a more enlightened political discourse.

(2) Method

In the last few decades, research into the history of concepts and semantics, both within and outside Germany, has generated a series of new questions and methods. The present lexicon has incorporated suggestions from linguistics and the history of philosophical terminology. But it relies on a historical method that has been further developed so as to make the history of concepts more fruitful for the study of history and the social sciences. In this sense, the history of concepts does not claim to be a completely independent discipline within the historical sciences. Its method follows from the project's overall goal: to treat concepts historically. This method does not aim at a history of words, past events, ideas or problems, though it uses knowledge gained from such histories. In the first instance:

(2.1) It is historical-critical. Prior knowledge of historical conditions or events raises questions that, to begin with, lead us to those words whose conceptualization is to be investigated. The history of words serves as a point of entry, insofar as every investigation proceeds by way of a word that designates a specific social and political condition, or that harbours within it corresponding experiences, thoughts or theorems. Textual analyses circumscribe the possible range of meanings that words may contain. To be sure, a meaning may attach itself to a word, but that meaning is also fed by the spoken context; it originates in the situation to which it simultaneously refers. It is the actual use of words that is being investigated. To analyse such concrete situations and to make intelligible the social and political meanings historically derived from them has always been part of the historical-critical method.

A further issue addressed is for whose benefit or for which purposes (*cui bono*) a concept is used. Does the speaker include or exclude himself when applying a given concept? Who is the addressee? Such questions provide a concrete reference point for identifying polar opposites, or counter-concepts. It is almost never, or only rarely possible to derive polemical content from a word itself. Take for example the German concept of *citizen* (*Bürger*). In 1700, it referred generically to those living in a city; in 1800 it meant the citizen of a state, and in 1900 it meant a non-worker (*bourgeois*). Thus, by itself, the word *Bürger* conveys nothing of its origins in a society of estates, or its subsequent political or social (*bourgeois*) points of reference. Conversely, there are concepts that preserve their neutral connotation independent of any political context. Many are to be found especially in the conceptual world of the old society of estates, whose dissolution we are investigating.

For this reason, the lexicon also enquires into the social reach of a concept: what terminology is specific to a given stratum? Which concepts were restricted to members of an estate or social class, to given societies, churches, sects and so forth? The term *peasant*, for example, was a designation used almost exclusively by socially superior strata. That was no longer the case for the terms *agriculturalist* (*Landwirt*) or *economist* (*Ökonom*). Lacking a specific social connotation, these were self-designations chosen by those with aspirations to a new social position. In this way, the lexicon investigates the power of words and concepts to bind, stamp or destroy (social) connections. With its analysis of such phenomena, conceptual history comes closest to social history.

To be sure, older historical-philological[7] methods can also help to discover the meaning of words, their social and political content and their underlying intent, but only by addressing problems in certain specific contexts. In this method, words are read in their past social and political contexts; the relationship of the word to what it designates is analysed; the conceptual result defined.

(2.2) This procedure always implies a retranslation (*Rückübersetzung*) of the vanished content of words into our current language. Every analysis of a word or concept leads from ascertaining its past meanings to specifying what they mean for us today. This process is central to the method of conceptual history. But the history of concepts is more than the sum of concrete analyses of concepts. Rather than offering mere historical inventories of political and social concepts, conceptual history requires a further *diachronic* analysis of each term or concept. In this second stage of analysis, therefore, concepts are removed from their original context, their meanings during successive periods of historical time are examined and relationships among these meanings are then assigned. It is by adhering to this procedure alone that the historical-philological method can ascend to the level of conceptual history. Only in this way, for example, can we become aware of the social persistence of a meaning and the structures to which it corresponded. In and of itself, words' persistence over time is an insufficient index of their unchanging content. Only through a diachronic investigation of the layers of meaning contained in a concept can we uncover long-term structural transformations. Witness the slow and creeping change from *societas civilis* to *civil society* (*Bürgerliche Gesellschaft*), a designation which ultimately came to be consciously conceptualized as being separate from the state. Insight into this change, so highly relevant to social history, could not have been attained without that level of reflection achieved by the history of concepts.

To be sure, diachronic analysis alone cannot answer questions about how time acquires its successive layers and how social structures change. Every history of a concept must examine simultaneously both historical change and historical persistence. Only in this way can we perceive the disparity between merely chronological accounts of meanings and the more systematic findings made possible by the history of concepts. Then the fault lines separating older meanings of a concept that depended upon a now-vanished context from what is now meant by the same word can be identified. This procedure makes it possible to take account of overlapping meanings that no longer correspond to reality or of realities whose meaning remains unknown. Only diachronic analysis can detect how a word has moved from being a religious to a social concept, which layer of meaning applies to a concept such as *league* (*Bund*), or how juristic titles have been transformed into political concepts which then show up in scholarly language as well as in propaganda (as for example in the case of *legitimacy*). But identifying the many-layered quality of meanings leads beyond strict diachrony.

Only conceptual history can throw light on the contemporaneity of the non-contemporaneous (*Gleichzeitigkeit des Ungleichzeitigen*) contained in a concept. It alone can give systematic or structural character to this dimension of historical depth, which is not the same as its chronology. The method of conceptual history thus intertwines diachrony and synchrony.

(2.3) The lexicon's emphasis on the historical character of the basic concepts it charts distinguishes its method from that of modern linguistics, especially structural linguistics. Although linguistics and conceptual history may eventually converge, this lexicon focuses above all on the history of social structures. Attention is concentrated on the relationship of *word* to *thing*; concepts are discussed according to their socio-political rather than their linguistic function. To the extent that insights from linguistics proved helpful for this purpose, they were utilized as well. The use of semasiology, which takes into account all meanings of a term, is limited here to the domains covering social and political vocabularies and their alteration. At no point is the attempt made to survey the entire field of a term's meaning. Peripheral or secondary meanings irrelevant to our questions are omitted.

Conversely, the other extreme is also avoided, that of enumerating all meanings of every word found in existing or potentially available vocabularies for a given situation or problematic. Thus, onomasiology, which collects all designations for a given term, is taken into account only insofar as related designations or synonyms record the diverse effects of historical developments, or as new characterizations come into use that indicate social and political changes. The work of this lexicon alternates between these two approaches. For our purposes, there is some technical advantage in favour of semasiology, insofar as concepts are initially approached through the words used to express them. Alternatively, onomasiology moves to the foreground when we investigate how extra-linguistic developments, such as changes in historical structures, are articulated through the medium of language.

Given inherent limitations of finances and personnel, this lexicon could not aspire to provide a complete statistical account of lexical uses. Occasionally, however, such documentary evidence has been compiled to support our historical interpretations. In order to analyse concepts focused on social and political contexts and their transformations, the lexicon registered both the layers of meaning of a word as well as the different words used to arrive at a given meaning.

(2.4) This lexicon treats the distinction between *word* and *concept* pragmatically. Thus, for the purpose of our own investigations, we avoided using the linguistic triangle of word (designation)– signification (concept) – and object (thing) in all its variations. At the same time, empirical evidence from history indicates that most socio-political terms can be distinguished from those words here designated as basic historical concepts. The transition from word to concept may be fluid. In their historical quality both may be ambiguous, but they are ambiguous in different ways. The meaning of a word always points to what is meant, be it a thought or a thing. Yet meaning, though attached to a word, is also created by the conscious intentions of the speaker, by the written or spoken context, by a given social situation. A word can become unambiguous because it is ambiguous. To achieve the status of a concept, on the other hand, it must always remain ambiguous. A concept may be attached to a word, but it is simultaneously more than that word. In terms of our method, a word becomes a concept when a single word is needed that contain – and is indispensable for articulating – the full range of meanings derived from a given socio-political context.

Think of all the elements, for example, that enter into the word *state* so as to turn it into a concept: domination, territorial sovereignty, administration, citizenship, legislation, adjudication, administration, taxation and military force, to name just the most common ones. All of them, with their own complex subject matter and terminology, are incorporated into the word *state*, which then becomes elevated to the status of a concept. Concepts are thus concentrations of many semantic contents. It is possible to think separately of the meaning (*Bedeutung*) of a word and what is meant (*das Bedeutete*). In a concept, however, these two senses are always combined, insofar as the multifarious quality of historical reality enters into the ambiguity of a word in such a manner that this reality can be understood and conceptualized only in that word. A word may have several possible meanings, but a concept combines in itself an abundance of meanings. Thus a concept may be clear, but it must be ambiguous. It bundles together the richness of historical experience and the sum of theoretical and practical lessons drawn from it in such a way that their relationship can be established and properly understood only through a concept. To put it most succinctly: the meaning of words can be defined exactly, but concepts can only be interpreted.

The example of the word *state* also helps to clarify our use of the expression 'terminology'. Thus, *law* is a concept, whereas *the administration of law* is a technical term. To put it more precisely, the lexicon is not built on words but on social and political terminology. A term combines in it the characteristics of a given set of facts and the meaning of that term as defined either by those facts, or by the discipline of which it is a part, although such definitions may vary. But a concept emerges only at the point when the meanings of those individual terms which describe a common set of facts perform not merely a descriptive function, but also point to and reflect upon relationships among them. What changes in the history of a concept is not merely one meaning of a word to another meaning. Rather the change occurs in the entire complex of meanings that have entered into the word, in both their makeup and their interaction. The history of a concept always contains within it a multilayered and multilevel process. To quote Nietzsche: 'Concepts, insofar as they involve the entire process of semiotics, cannot be defined; only that which has no history can be defined.'[8]

(2.5) The theoretical premise underlying the method of conceptual history used here is not only that history finds expression in certain concepts, but that events only attain the status of history through the process of being conceptualized. This premise implies that the lexicon's project does not simply stand halfway between the history of words, to which it could not be restricted, and a conventional history of facts, which it was not intended to provide. Rather, the lexicon sets out to interpret history through its basic concepts, and it understands such concepts historically. Its principal theme, in other words, is the convergence of concepts and history.

This convergence, however, is not to be understood as the identity of concept and history, nor can their relationship be reduced to that. It rejects as naïve the circular conclusion that words explain what actually happened, or vice versa. Rather, it sees an inherent tension between word and concept that sometimes eases, sometimes resurfaces and sometimes seems insoluble. Changes in the meaning of a word (*Wortbedeutungswandel*) or of a thing (*Sachwandel*), changing situations and pressures to coin new terms relate to one another in different ways. When such larger historical processes intersect, a concept is created to designate that situation. An example is the history of institutions and their *secularization* and the history of that same term. Though *secularization* initially referred to the history of the Church as an institution, this term is no longer limited to that.

For this reason, our method moves among the theoretical questions posed by semasiology, onomasiology, conventional history and the history of ideas: all are required to determine the historical content of a concept. At times, there may be no appropriate concept to designate a new situation, or else one has to grope in the dark to discover it; an older concept may be used for this purpose, even if it has lost its traditional meaning; new words may be coined; hyphenated concepts proliferate as new experiences or expectations demand appropriate formulations (for example *social democracy*). The very inadequacy of certain concepts to designate certain events or situations may become linguistically noticeable. This can be seen in the heavy-handed debates over the constitution of the old German Reich during the early modern period. The lack of precision, the fading of old terms or the charging of such terms with new meanings creates the need for expressions based on a new horizon of expectations. Such a new horizon ultimately finds linguistic expression when it leads to coining a new concept, as when *federation* (*Bundesstaat*) appeared around 1800 to designate the Reich in the period of its dissolution.

Our method, therefore, does not draw conclusions about historical facts from linguistic sources. Nor is it limited to the intellectual expressions of past thinkers. It avoids intellectual history (*Geistesgeschichte*), whether understood as a history of ideas or as history that simply reflects material processes (*Reflexhistorie*). Instead the method employed here investigates concepts used in the past to order experience; it seeks to discover the theory such concepts contain. In other words, this method uncovers those concepts which can serve as the basis for theories, and then examines thematically how such concepts change over time.

In practice, there are many developments or modes of conduct that come to light before they can be properly named – such as those which became historical phenomena only after they were linguistically recorded. The linguistic record focuses in both cases on extra-linguistic processes that can be fully understood and conceptualized only after the changes in the concepts themselves are examined. This, of course, is the very purpose of conceptual history. Insofar as it points to structural change in history, it contributes to social history. But inasmuch as it does so only through the medium of concepts, it rests upon its own theories. The different articles in this lexicon will develop or highlight both of these aspects in a variety of ways.

(3) Sources

Not every entry will make use of all the methodological approaches sketched above, nor will they all rely on exactly the same source materials. Naturally, the choice of sources depends in large part on the concept itself. As for the sources, they can be found in every possible sphere of life and every area of scholarship, provided only that they have become important for social and political terminology. Especially for basic historical concepts, however, texts drawn from theology, law, economics and the natural sciences may be more important that those from historiography. Our sources fall into three groups:

1   All articles make use of the writings of representative authors. This is the level of 'classical' thinkers, whether philosophers, economists, legal theorists, theologians, poets or political philosophers. Citations from them have generally been taken from their collected works.
2   The semantic fields to be explored for a given concept required a wide range of source materials taken from everyday life. These primary sources include newspapers, journals, pamphlets and records of estates and parliaments, administration and government, as well as diaries and letters and, finally, chance discoveries in the secondary literature.
3   Thirdly, every entry is based at a minimum on consultation of the major dictionaries, encyclopaedias and lexica of a period being studied, even

if they ultimately proved unhelpful. It is at this level that the knowledge and self-understanding of particular generations is recorded, first for scholars, then for the educated and finally for the reading public at large. To understand the formation of concepts and their impact, it is always informative to compare and contrast the differences among these three categories of materials.

4 Extensive citations are often provided to support interpretations that help turn a collection of sources into our conceptual history. Citations from German sources – until 1700 – are given in their original written style. Thereafter, they have been modernized, especially since not all source materials were still available in the original. In this case the written style found in original sources was retained only when the distinctive mode of writing a word suggests its conceptual history, such as *Social-Democracy* (*Sozial-Demokratie*), which became *social democracy* (*Sozialdemokratie*), or the word *race* (*Race*), which became *Rasse*.

(4) Organization and Division

(4.1) The lexicon is organized alphabetically. A systematic ordering by subject (such as politics, economics, etc.) or by any temporal dimension (such as traditional concepts, concepts that changed in their entirety and neologisms) would have been impractical. It would have meant imposing an interpretation that could not have been maintained consistently.

For example, grouping together such concepts as *tyranny, despotism, dictatorship, Caesarism* and *fascism* might have been justified on objective, historical grounds, but it would have meant systematizing history in a way that cannot be derived from the concepts themselves. Similarly, concepts that today would have to be placed into different subject categories, such as *state* and *civil society*, or *state* and *estate* or *order*, for the most part could not have carried the same meaning in an earlier age. Even the traditional content of a concept rarely, if ever, coincides precisely with that of other concepts. Hence it is all but impossible to arrive at a single common denominator for all the temporal layers of persistent meanings. Only pure neologisms could be classified in this way. To have adopted any such (temporal) principle, therefore, would have distorted the history of at least some concepts. Thus only the neutrality of the alphabet provided a scheme that was both sufficiently elastic and appropriate to historical change.

(4.2) Within each article, of course, it was often necessary to bring together several concepts under one heading (*Stichwortgruppe*). Without including parallel or counter-concepts, without categorizing common and special concepts in relation to one another, without registering the overlapping of two or more expressions, it would be altogether impossible to determine a given concept's status within a social order, or the parameters of a political confrontation. The intersections, continuities or eliminations of meaning can be fully investigated only when changing groups of words appear together within the same article, such as *unification* (*Einung*), as well as *league* and *union* (*Liga* and *Union*), in the article on *federation, alliance* (*Bund, Bündnis*).

Some concepts whose meanings have almost completely converged – such as *histories* (*Historie*) and *history* (*Geschichte*) in the nineteenth century – must be examined together. This applies no less to words that once belonged to different conceptual fields before they gradually came together and became alternative, parallel concepts. Examples of such words are *revolution* and *civil war*. Used at times as synonyms, they may also become counter-concepts. Consequently, they must be considered together. Alternatively, a word can also signify several diverse concepts. Thus, the incorporation of the word *state* (*status, état*) into German was made possible only by excluding meanings derived from the (earlier) society of social orders or estates. Only after this distinction was made, towards the end of the eighteenth century, could the word *state* become a basic concept. Indeed, since that time the words *state* and *estate* – originally combined in the word *status* – could turn into contrasting concepts. For this reason, *estate* (*Stand*) is treated in the articles on both *state* (*Staat*) and *estate and class* (*Stand und Klasse*). That is all the more warranted because the developments in both concepts took place during the threshold period (*Sattelzeit*) assumed in our heuristic presupposition.

At what point can a concept be defined as a 'basic' concept? This ultimately depends on the resources of its language as a whole. Of course, it is no more possible to command all the socio-political terms of a period than to reconstruct the entire past. To ascertain whether a concept is or is not a basic concept, we must first ask what the prerequisites for such a determination are. This, of course, must be done whenever interpretation is attempted. The desirable but unattainable knowledge of the totality of linguistic relationships is at least given heuristic consideration, by treating a concept as more than a singular key word. Otherwise, both its quality as a concept and its function as a basic concept would be lost. For this reason, the lexicon contains a series of core articles that bring together concepts that are historically interdependent.

(4.3) Accordingly, the length of the articles varies. Depending on what the data yielded, they range – with some exceptions – between twenty and sixty pages. Many authors were thus forced to adhere to limits disproportionate to both their preliminary research and the wealth of the materials they had gathered. Since here too completeness was impossible, we opted to give the most space to articles related to our method. At least this has the advantage of encouraging future monographs that go beyond what was covered in the articles.

(4.4) Basically, every article is divided into three parts. The preview or opening section follows the history both of the concept and the words designating it up to the early modern period. In the main section, the central theme is the unfolding of the processes by which the concept acquired its distinctive modern qualities. The final section points to present-day uses of the concept.

The opening section highlights the contributions of antiquity – such as Aristotelian or classical Roman concepts – followed by those made by the Christian tradition, the Renaissance and the history of the French and German languages. To this end, relevant historical developments for each period had to be added. Every effort was made, however, to avoid artificially condensing the past. Frequently it can be demonstrated that the meanings of a concept's pre-history persevere deep into the nineteenth and twentieth centuries. Tracking these meanings, in turn, provides the foundation for raising those structural questions on the basis of which the range of modern meanings examined in the main section can be developed all the more clearly.

In this main section, synchronic cross-section analyses and diachronic depth analyses complement each other, as stipulated by our method. It is precisely the alternation between these two methods that reveals the history of a concept that can never be reduced to a single original meaning. The actual representation of that history rests on temporal sequencing, since permanence, change and novelty can be registered and historically interpreted only chronologically. Thus, strictly speaking, the history of concepts is the temporal history of concepts.

In this way, we may bring the historical claims of our history of concepts to bear on the central concerns of the final section, which touches on usage in our own time. To have undertaken a separate examination of contemporary usage, with its rapid changes and its universal neologisms, would have violated the precepts of our method, by ignoring all its criteria for delimiting the scope of this inquiry. At best, this lexicon furnishes the preliminary basis for a political semantics of the present time.

(4.5) As for our contributors, it was possible to attract scholars who were eminently qualified to record the history of a concept from the perspective of their own disciplines. Because this necessarily gave rise to certain disciplinary preferences, we occasionally added supplementary sections by other authors, whose names are indicated separately. Whenever the opportunity presented itself, joint execution of an article proved advantageous. For several articles, it was most appropriate to divide the work chronologically among several authors. Altogether, the contributors to this lexicon included, in addition to historians, representatives from several other disciplines: jurists, economists, philosophers, philologists, theologians and social scientists. Differences among the articles presented here that go beyond general methodological points of view and organizational issues resulting from them ultimately reflect the varied views of the authors and their own distinctive questions concerning the history of concepts. It is just as impossible to stipulate the meaning of a historical concept as it is to write its final history.

(Translation: Michaela Richter)

Notes

1 Gotthold Ephraim Lessing, *Ernst und Falk* (1776–78). [English translation: Gotthold Ephraim Lessing, 'Ernst und Falk: Conversations for the Freemasons', trans. William L. Zwiebel, in Peter Demetz (ed.), *Nathan the Wise, Minna von Barnhelm, and other Plays and Writings* (New York: Continuum, 1991), 277–308.]
2 Of the originally projected 130 concepts, 115 were ultimately included.
3 [Note: information added by the translator.]
4 Wolfgang Stammler, *Kleine Schriften zur Sprachgeschichte* (Berlin: Erich Schmidt, 1954), 48ff.
5 Rolf Engelsing, *Der Bürger als Leser: Lesegeschichte in Deutschland, 1500–1800* (Stuttgart: Metzler, 1974).

6 Jakob and Wilhelm Grimm, *Deutsches Wörterbuch* (16 vols, Leipzig: S. Hirzel, 1854–1965); Alfred Götze (ed.), *Trübners Deutsches Wörterbuch* (8 vols, Berlin/Leipzig: De Gruyter, 1939–57).

7 [Note: German original: '*historisch-philologischen*'.]

8 Friedrich Nietzsche, *The Birth of Tragedy and The Genealogy of Morals*, trans. Francis Golffing (New York: Doubleday, 1956), 212.

Reinhart Koselleck's understanding of conceptual history continued to evolve over the course of his work on the multi-volume project of the *Geschichtliche Grundbegriffe* (*Basic Concepts*). 'Social History and Conceptual History', a later text that engages with the relationship between conceptual history and social history, explains and exemplifies some of these changes.

Koselleck's work on conceptual history was fundamentally influenced by the Heidelberg philosopher Hans-Georg Gadamer and his theory of hermeneutics. For Gadamer the human subject is, in its understanding, itself dependent upon the objects it aims at understanding. The historically conditioned consciousness of an individual locates him or her within a specific socio-cultural context. This context in turn shapes the ways in which individual human beings interpret their world, for instance through the languages they speak and their dominant concepts. It is easy to see how this philosophy, which emphasizes the primacy of language, resonates in conceptual history.

As the following text selection illustrates, Koselleck argued that conceptual history needed to engage in an intimate dialogue with social history. Language and social formations are related, and they also influence each other. Yet they can never completely be mapped onto each other. Conceptual history therefore needs to be informed by, and contextualized through, social history, just as social history needs to pay attention to the constitutive influence of language. Here, Koselleck elaborates not only on the two disciplines' interdependence but also shows how conceptual history can develop beyond a primarily lexical undertaking like *Geschichtliche Grundbegriffe*.

2

Social History and Conceptual History

Reinhart Koselleck

Whoever is occupied with history – whatever that is – and defines it as social history obviously limits his or her theme. And the individual who narrows history to conceptual history obviously does the same thing. Nevertheless, with both determinations it is not the usual limitation of special histories which general history embraces within it. England's economic history, perhaps, or the history of diplomacy of early modernity or Western ecclesiastical history are special themes of this type which were materially, temporally and regionally present and worthy of investigation. Then it is a question of particular aspects of general history.

It is otherwise for social and conceptual histories. From their theoretical self-foundation, there arises a general claim which can be extended and applied to all special histories. Because what history has not in any case something to do with interpersonal relationships with social configurations of some type or with social strata, so that the characterization of history as social history involves an irrefutable – anthropological, so to speak – lasting claim that it is implicated in any form of history. And what history could there be which would not be conceived as such before it gels as history? The investigation of concepts and their linguistic transformation is so very much a minimal condition for cognizing a history as its definition of having to do with human society.

(1) Historical Retrospective

Both social history and conceptual history have been explicit hypotheses since the Enlightenment and the discovery of the historical world at that time: when the former social structures were breaking up and when linguistic reflection felt the pressure of change of a history which itself was newly experienced and articulated. If one follows the history of historical reflection and historical representation since then one finds both grasps again and again whether it is through mutual elucidation as with Vico, Rousseau or Herder, or by separate paths.

The claim that all historical manifestations of life and their transformations are to be based on and derived from social conditions has been advanced since the historical philosophies of the Enlightenment up to Comte and the young Marx. Following them are the histories of society and civilization, the cultural and folk histories of the nineteenth century which were already proceeding positivistically methodically, up to the regional histories including all areas of life, the synthetic achievement of which by Moeser through Gregorovius up to Lamprecht can rightly be named social-historical.

On the other hand, since the eighteenth century there have been consciously thematised conceptual histories[1] – obviously the expression comes from Hegel – which have retained their permanent place in histories of language and historical lexicography. Of course they were thematised by all disciplines working historico-philologically which must secure their sources by posing hermeneutic questions. Any translation into one's own present implies a conceptual history, the methodological inevitability of which Rudolf Eucken has shown in his *History of Philosophical Terminology* to be exemplary (paradigmatic) for all intellectual and social sciences.[2]

In the practice of research, then, reciprocal references also occur which bring special social and constitution-historical analyses together with conceptual historical questions. Their mutual connection was more or less reflected, always present, in ancient sciences and the scholarship of the Middle Ages, because what circumstances could be known, especially with sparsely available sources, without knowing the manner of its former and present conceptual shaping? Indeed it turns out that the reciprocal entwinement of social and conceptual history was first systematically treated in the 1930s; one thinks of Walter Schlesinger or above all of Otto Brunner. From closely related regions there were Rothacker for philosophical conceptual history, Carl Schmitt for legal sciences and Jost Trier for linguistic sciences who sponsored the sharpening of historical methods.

With respect to the politics of research, the combined social and conceptual history was oriented towards two different directions which dominated both in the 1920s: once it circumvented the differentiation of ideo- and spiritual-historical concepts, which were followed without their concrete political-social context, as it were, for the sake of their own value. On the other hand, it circumvented operating with history primarily as a political history of events to then inquire after the presuppositions maintained for so long.

Otto Brunner intended, as he maintained in the preface to the second edition of *Land and Domination*[3] 'to inquire about the concrete presuppositions of the politics of the Middle Ages, but not to represent them'. It then occurred to him to draw into view long-term structures of social composition and their – never instantaneous – transformation, and in so doing the respective linguistic self-articulation of the social groups, associations or strata as well as their concepts and interpretive history were expressly thematised. And it is no accident that the 'Annals', which came from an analogous research interest, provided the rubric 'Words and Events' in 1930. For Lucien Febvre and Marc Bloch, linguistic analysis was an integral component of their social historical investigations. In Germany, Gunther Ipsen acted as a trail blazer for modern history in supplementing his social-historical, special demographic researches through linguistic knowledge. Werner Conze took up all these suggestions when he founded the study group for modern social history in 1956–57.[4] Thanks to Conze's initiative, the bringing together of social-historical and conceptual-historical questions, as well as their differentiation, belong among those enduring challenges which are at issue in the following.

(2) The Impossibility of a 'Total History'

Without searching for social formations together with their concepts, by virtue of which – reflectively or self-reflectively – they determine and resolve their challenges, there is no history, it cannot be experienced, interpreted, represented or explained. Society and language insofar belong among the meta-historical givens without which no narrative and no history are thinkable. For this reason, social historical and conceptual historical theories, hypotheses and methods are related to all merely possible regions of the science of history. So at times, however, the wish to be able to conceive a total history creeps in. If for pragmatic reasons, empirical investigations or social or conceptual historians deal with limited themes, then this self-limitation still doesn't diminish the claim to universality that follows from a theory of possible history which must presuppose society and language in any case.

Under the pressure or methodologically required specializations, the social- and conceptual-historical grasp must necessarily proceed in an interdisciplinary way. Nevertheless, it doesn't follow from that, that its theoretical claim to universality can be posed absolutely or totally. Indeed, they are compelled to presuppose the entirety of social relations as well as their linguistic articulations and systems of interpretation. But the formally irrefutable premise that all history has to do with language and society does not admit the wider-ranging consequence that by virtue of its content it is possible to write or even merely to conceive a 'Total History'.

As numerous and plausible as the empirical objections to a total history are, there is one objection against its possibility which follows from its attempt at autonomous thinkability. Because the totality of a history of society could never be represented by the totality of its language. Even if the empirically unverifiable case is posed, that both regions would be thematised a finitely limited totality, an irreconcilable difference between any social history and the history of its concepts remains.

The linguistic conception neither takes in what happens or what was actually the case, nor does something occur that is not already altered through its linguistic shaping. Social history or history of society and conceptual history stand in a historically conditioned tension, both refer to one another without being able to supersede each other. What you do is first said to you the other day. And what you say becomes an event as it escapes from you. What occurs socially, among individuals and what is said at the time or about it, causes an always changing difference which prevents any 'Total History'. In anticipation, history takes place imperfectly/incompletely, so any interpretation appropriate to it must do without totality.

It is a characteristic of historical time that the tension between society and its transformation and its linguistic preparation and shaping is reproduced again and again. Every history draws on this tension. Social relations, conflicts and their resolutions and their changing presuppositions are never congruent with the linguistic articulations by virtue of which societies act, conceive themselves, interpret, change and form anew. This thesis should be tested in two respects, once in view of history occurring in actu or currently, and secondly from the point of view of past history which has happened.

(3) Occurring History, Speech and Writing

If social history and conceptual history are related to each other, then that qualifies their respective claim to universality. History does not become apparent in the way that its conception does, yet it is not thinkable without this.

In everyday events their connection is present without distinction. As a being endowed with language, the human individual originated with social existence. How can the relationship be determined? It is comparatively clear that individual events, in order to be realized, must admit to being expressed linguistically. No social activity, no political action and no economic action is possible without speech and reply, without discussion of plans, without public debate or secret utterance, without command – and obedience – or consensus of the participants or articulated disagreement of the contesting parties. Any everyday story in daily performance is oriented by language in execution, by talking and speaking, just as no love story is thinkable without at least three words – you, I, we. Any social event in its manifold connections is based on preparatory communicative acts and achievements of linguistic mediation. Institutions and organizations, from the smallest club to the United Nations are oriented by whether in spoken or written form.

As obvious as this is, it is just as obvious that this observation must be limited. What actually occurs is evidently more than the linguistic articulation which has led to it or interprets it. The command or the collegial resolution or the elementary cry to kill are not identical with the act of killing itself. The expressions of lovers are not merged in the love which the two individuals experience. The written rules of an organization or its spoken executive instructions are not identical with the action of the organization itself.

There is always a difference between a spontaneously occurring sequence of events or its story and its linguistic potentialization. The speech act which helps to prepare, cause and execute the act is not the act itself. Indeed it must be granted that often a word causes irrevocable consequences; one recalls Hitler's command to invade Poland to name a striking example. But precisely here the relationship is clear. A story does not evolve without speech, but it is never identical with it, it cannot be reduced to it.

Thus, beyond spoken language, there must be other preparatory performances and manners of execution which make events possible. Here perhaps the region of semiotics, which goes beyond speech, can be named. One thinks of the body's gestures in which a merely encoded language is imparted, of magic rituals including the theology of the sacrifice that has its historical place not in words but on the cross, of the power of its symbol ground into the behaviour patterns of groups or of modern traffic signs: they all concern a symbol for speech which is understandable without words. All the symbols named can be verbalized. They are also reducible to language but their achievement lies precisely in that spoken language must be abandoned so that the symbols can evoke or control the corresponding actions, attitudes or patterns of behaviour.

Other explicit preconditions for possible stories need only be recalled; spatially near or far, distances which are either pregnant with conflict or retardant of conflict, temporal differences between the ages within a living generation or the bipolarity of the species. All of these differences harbour events, strife and reconciliation which are made possible pre-linguistically, even if they can, but must not, be performed by virtue of linguistic articulation.

Thus there are pre-linguistic and post-linguistic elements in all actions which lead to a unit of events or to a story. They are rooted in the elemental, geographical, biological and zoological conditions which affect the human constitution all together in social events. Birth, love and death, eating, hunger, misery and disease, perhaps even happiness, at times plunder, triumph, destruction and defeat, all these are also elements and ways of performing human history which extend from the everyday to the identification of sovereign political entities, and the explicit givens of which are difficult to deny.

Within the concrete context of actions giving rise to events, the analytical schisms encountered here can hardly be reconstructed. All pre-linguistic givens are taken up by individuals in speech and mediated with their deeds and afflictions in concrete discussions. Language which is spoken and writing which is read, the effective or overhead discussions in the actual performance of the happening are knit into the event which is always composed from extra-linguistic and linguistic elements of action. Even when speaking ceases, remaining in the linguistic foreknowledge that [is] inherent in human individuals is the capability to communicate whether with people, things, products, plants or animals.

And the more highly aggregated human units of action are, as in modern work processes together with their economic interconnections or in more and more complex spheres of political action, the more important linguistic conditions for communication become in order to retain the ability to act. This is shown in the expansion of linguistic mediation: of the audible range of a voice through technological conveyers of news, writing, printing, the telephone, the radio, up to the screen of a television or a computer – together with the institutions involved with the technical aspects of their traffic, from messengers through the mail and press to news satellites – as well as the ramifications for any linguistic codification. It has always involved either extending the range of spoken language for coming ages in order to capture events or to extend and accelerate it in order to anticipate events so they can be resolved or controlled. This example may be sufficient to show the interpenetration of 'social history' and 'linguistic history' in any performance of speaking and doing.

Discussions which have been uttered or writing which has been read and the events taking place in actu cannot be separated; they can only be divided from one another analytically. When one is overwhelmed by a speech, one experiences it not only linguistically but throughout the entire body; and when one is silenced by a deed, her or his dependency on language is experienced all the more in order to be able to move again. This personal relationship of exchange between talking and doing can be carried over to all levels of social units of action which are becoming increasingly complex. The interpenetration of so-called speech-acts with 'factual' events extends from individual discussions and deeds to their multifarious social networks by virtue of which events are placed in their contexts. This finding, in spite of all historical variations, is essential to any story which occurs and has a considerable effect on the portrayal of past histories, on their types, especially on the difference between social and conceptual history.

(4) The Representation of Past History and Its Linguistic Sources

The empirical connection between doing and talking, acting and speaking outlined so far is ruptured as soon as the view reverts back from history taking place *in eventu* to the history with which the professional historian is occupied, that which has already occurred, *ex eventu*. The analytic separation between an extra-linguistic and a linguistic level of action takes on the status of an anthropological given without which no historical experience at all could be transformed into everyday or scientific expression. It is only through talking or writing that I can learn what has happened beyond my own experience. Even if in the performance of action and emotion language may be – at times – merely a secondary factor, as soon as an event has transpired in the past, language returns to being a primary factor without which no recollection and no scientific transposition of this recollection is possible. The anthropological priority of language for the representation of history taking place thereby takes on an epistemological status. This is so because whether what happened in the past was linguistically conditioned or not must be decided linguistically.

Anthropologically any 'history' is constituted through oral and written communication of the generations living together, who mediate their own experiences amongst themselves. And only if through the dying out of old generations, the range of orally transmitted recollection dwindles, writing reverts to the first-ranking conveyer of historical mediation.

Certainly there are numerous extra-linguistic remains which give evidence of past events and situations: ruins from catastrophes; coins from economic organization; buildings which indicate community, rule and servitude; streets which show activity or war; cultural landscapes; work carried out over generations; monuments which testify to triumph or death; weapons which show struggle; implements which show invention and application; in sum, relics, respectively, 'findings' – or pictures – which can attest to everything at the same time. Everything is prepared by special, historical disciplines. To be sure, what may have occurred 'factually' can be verified only through oral and written tradition, through linguistic testimony. The linguistic sources allow one to decide what in the past is to be recorded as 'linguistic' or as 'factual' in occurrence. From this perspective types and their differentiation can be reclassified.

What belonged together *in eventu* can still only be communicated *post eventum* through linguistic evidence; and with each association with this linguistic conveyance, oral or written tradition, the most different types come together and separate from each other.

Characteristic of mythology, fairy tales, drama, epics and novels is that they all presuppose and thematise the original connection between speaking and doing, of emotion, speaking and silence. The representation of such a history as it occurs generates the meaning which remains worthy of recollection. And it is precisely this that all (hi)stories achieve which use true or fictitious speeches in order to become truly convincing, or which call upon those words which give evidence of the amalgamation of talking and doing in written sources.

There are the non-reversible situations which drive out their own transformation and behind which then something like 'fate' can appear, which remains a challenge to be explored and handed down for any self- and world-interpretation. All memoires and biographies more or less accomplished belong in this category, in English emphasizing the interplay between life and language – 'Life and Letters' – further, all stories which trace causes and events in their imminent dynamic. 'He said this and did that, she said that did such and so, which caused something surprising, something new that changed everything' – numerous works have been built up according to this formalized schema, especially those which, like histories of political or diplomatic events and, thanks to the situation of sources, are able to construct proceedings in actu. Regarded from their linguistic achievement, these stories fall into a series which extends from mythology to the novel.[5] Only as objects of knowledge do they live from the authenticity – to be verified – of linguistic sources, which stand up for the totum of the formerly presupposed entwinement of speech-acts and deeds.

What is analytically separable, the pre-linguistic and the linguistic, is brought together again thanks to the linguistic achievement 'analogous to experience': It is the fiction of the factual. Since what has actually taken place – looking backward – is real merely in the medium of linguistic fiction.

In contrast to the speech of action in which history is taking place, language thus acquires an epistemological primacy, which always urges one to judge how language and acting have been related.

Then there are types which, placed under this alternative, are articulated extremely one-sidedly. There are annals which merely record events which have taken place, not how they came about. There are reference books and the so-called narrative works of history which deal with deeds, success or failure, but not with the words or discussion which led to them. Whether it is that great individuals are acting or that highly stylized subjects of action become active as it were without speech: States or dynasties, churches or sects, classes or parties or what is otherwise reified as units of action. Seldom, however, are the linguistic patterns of identification examined, without which such entities could not act at all. Even where spoken discussion or its written equivalent is brought into the portrayal, the linguistic testimony falls all too quickly under ideological suspicion or is read merely instrumentally as alleged prior interests and evil intentions.

Investigations undertaken from the historico-linguistic side which primarily thematise linguistic testimony itself – on the other side of our scale – also easily fall into the danger zone – that of sketching a real history which itself must first be constituted linguistically. But the methodological difficulties, to which especially socio-linguistics sees itself exposed, in relating speech and language to social conditions and changes, remain trapped in the aporia which is common to all historians of having to first produce the subject domain linguistically about which they prepare to speak.

For this reason one also finds the other extreme in the guild: the editing of linguistic sources as such, the written portion previously spoken or written discussion. Then, where the difference between extra-linguistic and linguistic action has been expressly thematised, transmission is left to chance. Everywhere it is the task of the good commentator to track down here the sense of the written fragments which could not be found at all without the differentiation of speech and facts.

In this way we have stylized three types, which under the alternatives speech-action and deed-action either relate both to each other or, in the extreme case, thematise them separately. Epistemologically, a two-fold task always falls to language: it refers to the extra-linguistic connections of occurrences as well as – while it does that – to itself. Historically understood, it is always self-reflective.

(5) Event and Structure: Speech and Language

Whereas up to now we have only spoken about and investigated history that has occurred or is taking place, how talking and doing have related to one another in actu, as it were, in a synchronous pattern, the issues broaden as soon as diachrony is thematised, too. Here too, as with the relationship of speaking and acting in the performance of an event, synchrony and diachrony cannot be empirically separated. The conditions and determinants, which being temporally various and deeply graduated extend from the so-called past into the present, include the occurrence at the time in the same way that acting parties act 'simultaneously' from their projections of the future at that time. Any synchrony is eo ipso diachronic at the same time. In actu, all temporal dimensions are always meshed and it contradicts any experience to define the so-called present as perhaps one of those moments which are added together from the past into the future – or which conversely slip from the future into the past as fleeting points of transition. Purely theoretically, all histories can be defined as permanent present in which the past and the future are contained – or, however, as the lasting meshing of past and future which constantly makes any present disappear. In one case, which is intensified on synchrony, history becomes depreciated as a sphere of pure consciousness in which all temporal dimensions are contained at once, whereas in the other case, which is intensified on diachrony, the active presence of human individuals would have no sphere for acting socially and politically. This thought experiment should merely indicate that the differentiation introduced by de Saussure between synchrony and diachrony can be analytically helpful everywhere, without being able to do justice to the complexity of temporal overlapping in spontaneously occurring history.

With this reservation, the analytic categories of synchrony, which tends toward the actual presentness of the occurrence at the time, and diachrony, which tends toward the temporal dimension of depths and is likewise contained in each actual occurrence, may be used. Many presuppositions influence spontaneously occurring history in the long-run or middle-run – and naturally also in the short-run. They limit the alternatives for action while they make possible or release only determinate alternatives.

Now it is characteristic of social and conceptual history that both – even if in different ways – theoretically presuppose just this connection. It is the connection between synchronic events and diachronic structures which is investigated social-historically. And it is the analogous connection between speech uttered at the time, synchronically, and the given language which always acts diachronically, which is thematised conceptual-historically. What occurs at some point in time may be unique and new, but it is never so new that longer-term, pre-given social conditions had not made the one-time event in question possible. A new concept may be coined which had never before expressed experiences or expectations which had been present in words. But it can never be so new that it was not virtually laid out in the pre-given language at the time and even drawing its sense from its conventional linguistic context. The interplay of speaking and doing in which events occur is thus extended by the two directions of research around its – variously defined – diachronic dimensions. Without this, history is neither possible nor comprehensible.

This can be elucidated with one series of examples. Marriage is an institution which besides its pre-linguistic biological implications represents a cultural phenomenon that exhibits numerous variations in the entire history of humanity. Since it concerns a social form of two or more individuals of different sex, marriage is one of the genuinely social-historical topics of research. At the same time it is obvious that something can only be discussed socially-historically if written sources inform us about how any given type of marriage has been brought to its concept.

Then two methodological versions, in abbreviated model form, can be constructed. One is primarily oriented towards events, actions in speech, writing and deed – the other is primarily directed to diachronic presuppositions and their long-term transformation. Thus it looks for social structures and their linguistic equivalents.

1 So an individual event can be thematised, perhaps a royal marriage about which dynastic sources offer us abundant information; what political motives came into play, what contractual conditions, what dowry was negotiated, how the ceremonies were staged and more of such matters. Also, the course of this marriage can be reconstructed and recounted again and again with the sequence of events, up to the terrible consequences if, say, with the death of a spouse the succession allowed for contractually was followed by a war to decide it. An analogous, concrete history of marriage can also be reconstructed today from the personal circle of the lower classes – an exciting theme of everyday history which employs numerous, previously unused

sources. Both times at issue are unique, individual histories which are likely to contain their unsurmountable tension between happiness and misery and which in both cases remain embedded in the religious, social and political context.

2 Social and conceptual history could not do without such individual cases, but exploring them is not its primary interest. To characterize the second methodological version, both are oriented – again in abbreviated model form – towards long-term conditions acting diachronically which have made the individual case possible, and they investigate the long-term events which can be derived from the sum of individual cases. Applied in another way, they investigate structures and their transformation. They inquire about the linguistic givens under which such structures have entered into social consciousness, been conceived and also changed.

Next we will follow specific social-historical, then specific conceptual-historical manners of procedure.

The synchrony of individual marriages and of the discussion or letters which were exchanged about them is not socially-historically faded. Rather it will develop diachronically. So, for example, under social-historical inquiries, the number of marriages will be prepared statistically in order to establish the increase of population by class. When did the number of marriages begin to exceed the number of houses and homesteads already present in the realm which had their limited area for subsistence? How did the number of marriages relate to the corresponding salary and price curves, to good or bad harvests to be able to balance the economic and natural factors for reproduction of the population against one another? How can the number of legitimate and illegitimate births be related to each other to measure the extent of social conflict? How do the figures for births and deaths of children, mothers and fathers behave towards one another in order to explain the long-term transformation of a typical married life? How does the curve of divorces run, which also permits conclusions on the type of a marriage? All such questions, almost randomly chosen here, have in common that they help to construct 'factual' events of a long-term nature which as such cannot be directly contained in sources.

Arduous preparatory work is required to make evidence from sources comparable, to compile series of figures from it, and finally – and foremost – systematic deliberation is necessary to be able to interpret the aggregated series of data. In no case is linguistic evidence from sources sufficient to be able to immediately derive from it evidence of longer-term structures. The sum of concrete and established individual cases occurring synchronically is itself mute and cannot 'prove' long- or middle-term, in any case diachronic structures. In order to extract lasting evidence of past history, preparatory theoretical work is thus necessary. Technical terminology must be used which alone can ferret out connections and interactions about which the individuals concerned at the time could have had no awareness.

What has happened 'factually' – and not perhaps linguistically – over the long-run in history remains social-historically a scientific construction, evidence of which depends on the credibility of its theory. To be sure, any theoretically grounded evidence must be submitted to the methodological control of sources to be able to maintain past factuality, but the character of reality of long-lasting factors cannot be adequately grounded from individual sources as such. For this reason, as in the train of Max Weber, ideal types can be formed which compile different criteria for the description of actuality so that presupposed connections can be interpreted consistently.

So – drawing from our series of examples – the ideal types of a peasant and an underprivileged marriage and family can be developed, into which go the respective average figures of births and deaths, the correlation to salary and price indices or to a succession of crop failures, to the period of work and to the tax burden in order to find out how a peasant marriage and family can be distinguished from an underprivileged marriage and family and how they have both changed in the transition from the pre-industrial to the industrial age.

It is not the individual cases themselves, then, but the factors which can be structured so that the economic, political and natural presuppositions – each according to the importance of salary and price structures, the tax burden or the yield of the harvest – become insightful of a typical marriage specific to a class. The questions about which factors are similar for how long, when dominant, when recessive, then permit the determination of terms, periods or epochal thresholds according to which the history of peasant and underprivileged marriages can be classified diachronically.

Up until now, our series of examples was deliberately selected on the basis of such clusters of factors that primarily extra-linguistic series of events could be structured diachronically and related to one another. As stated, the presupposition is a social-historical theory which with a technical terminology (here demography, economy and financial disciplines) permitted the constitution of duration and transformation which are never to be found in the sources as such. The theoretical claim thus grows in proportion to the distance which must be observed for the 'self-expression' of the sources in order to constitute long terms or typical social formations.

But naturally there is yet another cluster of factors which goes into the history of marriages to be posed as 'typical' than those named so far. These concern those factors which could not be investigated at all without interpretation of their linguistic self-articulation. With this we come to the required conceptual-historical procedures which – analogously to the differentiation of event and structure – must distinguish between actual speech and its linguistic pre-given nature.

Theology and religion, law, civility and custom set conditions for the sphere of any concrete marriage which are diachronically present before the individual case and commonly outlast it. On the whole it concerns institutionalized rules and interpretative patterns which found and limit the living space of a marriage. Indeed, there are also established 'extra-linguistic' patterns of behaviour but in all of the cases named, language remains the primary vehicle of mediation.

Linguistically articulated givens extend from custom through legal proceeding to sermon, from magic, through sacrament to metaphysics without which (even if to a dwindling extent) a marriage would neither be agreed to nor conducted. Thus various socially stratified texts must be examined in which marriage has been brought to its respective conception. These tests could have originated spontaneously like diaries, letters or newspaper reports; or in the other extreme case, they could have been formulated with normative intention such as theological treatises or legal codes together with their interpretations. In all cases traditions linked to language act here to diachronically fix in writing the living sphere of a possible marriage. It is only, then, when marriage has been brought to a new conception that changes emerge.[6]

So dominating into the eighteenth century is the theological interpretation of marriage as an indissolvable institution established by God the main purpose of which is the preservation and reproduction of the human species. Matching this were the conditions pertaining to class prerogatives that a marriage was only permissible if the economic basis of the household was sufficient to nurture and raise children and to insure the mutual assistance of the married couple. In this way, many individuals were legally excluded from the opportunity to agree to a marriage. As the nucleus of a household, marriage was only permissible if the economic basis of the household was sufficient to nurture and raise children and to insure the mutual assistance of the married couple. In this way, many individuals were legally excluded from the opportunity to agree to a marriage. As the nucleus of a household, marriage remained tied to class prerogative. This changed in the wake of the Enlightenment which newly founded marriage by contract law within the Prussian common law (*Allgemeines Landrecht*). The economic ties with the past were loosened and the freedom of the spouses as individuals came to extend so far that divorce – theologically forbidden – became admissible.

Common law had in no way relinquished theological or class-prerogative conditions, but the concept of marriage shifted – which can only be recorded conceptual-historically – by distinct nuances in favour of a greater freedom and self-determination of each partner.

Finally we find at the beginning of the nineteenth century a completely new concept of marriage. The theological foundation was dissolved through an anthropological self-grounding and the institution of marriage was stripped of its legal framework in order to provide room for ethical self-actualization of two persons who love each other. The *Brockhaus Encyclopedia* of 1820 extolls the postulated autonomy in emphatic words and raises up the innovative concept – marriage of love. With this, marriage loses its former primary purpose of producing children; the economic ties faded out and Bluntschli later goes so far as to declare a marriage without love as unethical. It becomes a duty to dissolve the marriage.

In this way three conceptual-historical periods would be outlined which at definite points innovatively re-structured the traditional normative household of argumentation at the time. The conceptual formation of Prussian common law and romantic liberalism has linguistic-historically, as it were, the character of the event. It then re-acts on the whole structure of language from which marriage could be conceived. It is not the diachronically given language as a whole which has changed but actually its semantics and the new pragmatics of language set free with it.

Now, it can in no way be derived from conceptual-historical procedures that the history of factual marriages had taken place along this linguistic self-interpretation. The economic forces portrayed in the social-historical perspective which limit, complicate and burden marriages continue to remain in effect. And even if legal barriers would be lowered, social pressures continue to be operative which keep the type of a marriage of love from being the only empirically normal case. To be sure, a lot can be said for the hypothesis that the conception of a marriage of love, once developed in temporal anticipation, as it were, has found increased chances for its actualization over the long-run.

Conversely, it cannot be denied that, before the formation of the romantic conception of marriage of love, love as an anthropological given had even found its way into marriages of class-prerogative that do not mention it.

For the determination of the relationship of social and conceptual histories it follows from this that they need and refer to one another without being able to coincide with each other. Since what was 'factually' operative over the long-run and has changed cannot be derived entirely from handed-down, written sources. Theoretical and terminological preparatory work is needed for this. And what, on the other hand, can be shown conceptual-historically – in written documents handed down – in fact refers us to the linguistically bounded sphere of experience and provides evidence of innovative breaches, intended to initiate or record new experiences. Inference to factual history, however, is still not thereby admissible. The difference between acting and speaking which we referred to for history taking place also keeps social 'actuality', in looking back, from ever converging with the history of its linguistic articulation. Even if in the synchronic cross-section, which is itself an abstraction, speech acts and deeds remain entwined, the diachronic transformation which remains a theoretical construction does not occur 'real-historically' or 'conceptual-historically' in the same temporal rhythm or temporal sequence. Actuality may have changed long before the transformation has been brought to its concept and similarly concepts may have been formed which have released new actualities.[7]

And yet there is an analogy between social and conceptual history which can be pointed out in closing. What occurs uniquely in history taking place is possible only because the conditions which must be supposed repeat themselves with a long-term regularity. The act of marriage may be subjectively unique; all the same, repeatable structures are articulated in it. The economic conditions of a marriage, dependent on the annually fluctuating harvest yield or on tax burdens which monthly or annually upset the planned budget – entirely apart from the regular services of the rural population – all these presuppositions are operative only by virtue of the regular repetition of greater or lesser constancy.

The same holds true for the social implications of a marriage that can only be specifically grasped linguistically. The pre-givens of custom, of legal strictures and possibly even theological interpretation, all these institutional bonds are only operative *in actu* in that they are repeated from case to case. And if they do change, they do so only slowly without rupturing their repetitive structures. What is called 'long duration' is historically actual in that each unique period of the event harbours repeatable structures, which range at a different velocity than the event itself. The thematic of all social history lies determined in this variant relationship, only inadequately defined through 'synchrony' and 'diachrony'.

The transformative linkage of any actual talking and pre-given language is to be determined analogously but not uniformly. If a concept, say of marriage, is employed, in it there are linguistically accumulated long-term actual experiences of marriage which have supported the conception. And the pre-given linguistic context likewise regulates the scope of its interpretive strength. With any actual application of the word 'marriage', linguistically conditioned pre-givens are repeated which structure its sense and understanding. There are also linguistic structures of repetition here which release as much as limit the sphere of discussion. And any conceptual change which becomes speech-event takes place in the act of semantic and pragmatic innovation which enables the old to be conceived differently and the new to be conceived at all.

Social and conceptual histories have various velocities of change and are grounded in different repetitive structures. For this reason, the scientific terminology of social history remains directed to the history of concepts in order to ascertain experience stored linguistically. And conceptual history must continue to consult the results of social history in order to keep the difference in view between vanishing actuality and its linguistic testimony which is never to be bridged.[8]

Notes

1   Hans G. Meier, 'Begriffsgeschichte', in Joachim Ritter, Karlfried Gründer and Gottfried Gabriel (eds), *Historisches Wörterbuch der Philosophie*, vol. 1 (Basel: Schwabe, 1971), 788–808.

2   Rudolf Eucken, *Geschichte der Philosophischen Terminologie* (Leipzig: Veit, 1879; reprint Hildesheim: G. Olms, 1964).

3   Otto Brunner, *Land und Herrschaft* (Brno: Rohrer, 1942), xi.

4   About this compare Werner Conze, 'Zur Gründung des Arbeitskreises für moderne Sozialgeschichte', *Hamburger Jahrbuch für Wirtschafts- und Gesellschaftspolitik. Festgabe für Karl Jantke*, 24 (1979), 23–32. Conze himself preferred the term 'structural history' in order to avoid use of the word 'social', being close to the delimitation of 'social questions'. Otto Brunner was happy to adopt the term 'structural history' in order to

avoid the temporally conditioned determination of a 'folk history' which from his theoretical start as early as 1939 tended towards structures. For this, compare the 2nd edition of Otto Brunner, *Land und Herrschaft* (Brno: Rohrer, 1942), 194, with the fourth, revised edition, Otto Brunner, *Land und Herrschaft* (Vienna: Rohrer, 1959), 164: A good example for showing that politically conditioned interests of knowledge could lead to theoretically and methodologically new insights which outlast their initial situation.

5 For this Hayden White, *Tropics of Discourse. Essays in Cultural Criticism* (Baltimore: Johns Hopkins University Press, 1978). [Note: German translation: idem, *Auch Klio dichtet, oder, Die Fiktion des Faktischen: Studien zur Tropologie des historischen Diskurses* (Stuttgart: Klett-Cota, 1986).]

6 For this compare Dieter Schwab, 'Familie', in Otto Brunner, Werner Conze and Reinhart Koselleck (eds), *Geschichtliche Grundbegriffe*, vol. 2 (Stuttgart: Klett-Cota, 1975), 271–301 and Edeltraud Kapl-Blume, 'Liebe im Lexikon', MA thesis, Universität Bielefeld, Bielefeld, 1986.

7 One may refer to the following books for the state of research in conceptual history: Eugenio Coseriu, *Synchronie, Diachronie und Geschichte* (Munich: Fink, 1974); Hans-Georg Gadamer, *Die Begriffsgeschichte und die Sprache der Philosophie* (Opladen: Westdeutscher Verlag, 1971); Reinhart Koselleck (ed.), *Historische Semantik und Begriffgeschichte* (Stuttgart: Klett-Cotta, 1978); John G. A. Pocock, *Virtue, Commerce and History* (Cambridge: Cambridge University Press, 1985), especially the introduction: 'The State of the Art'; Rolf Reichardt, 'Einleitung', in Rolf Reichardt and Eberhard Schmitt (eds), *Handbuch politisch-sozialer Grundbegriffe in Frankreich 1680–1820*, vol. 1 (Munich: Oldenbourg, 1985), 39–148 [Note: extract of it included as chapter three in this volume: Rolf Reichardt, 'For a Socio-historical Semantics as a Middle Course between "Lexicometry" and "Conceptual History" ']; Regine Robin, *Histoire et Linguistique* (Paris: Colin, 1973).

8 [Note: translator not mentioned in the 1989 first edition of the text in the *International Journal of Politics, Culture and Society*, 2/3 (1989), 308–25.]

Rolf Reichardt is a German historian, holding a professorship at the University of Gießen since 2008. He has directed a research project entitled 'Lexikon der Revolutions-Ikonographie' ('Lexicon of Revolutionary Iconography'). After writing his PhD thesis (1969) on the concepts of *revolution* and *reform* in the Enlightenment discourse of eighteenth-century France, Reichardt continued to focus on the French revolution, French political discourse, symbolism, the press and Franco-German cultural relations.

Reichardt's publications include *Französische Presse und Pressekarikaturen 1789–1992* ('The French Press and Press Caricature 1789–1992'), *Das Blut der Freiheit: Französische Revolution und politische Kultur* (2002; 'The Blood of Freedom: The French Revolution and Political Culture') and *Visualizing the Revolution: Politics and Pictorial Arts in Late Eighteenth-Century France* (2008).

Of particular importance to conceptual history is his contribution to the multi-volume publication *Handbuch politisch-sozialer Grundbegriffe in Frankreich 1680–1820* (1985–2000; 'Handbook of Basic Politico-Social Concepts in France 1680–1820'). Though in many ways inspired by Koselleck, he extends the scope of conceptual history in a number of ways: firstly, at the level of source materials, by going beyond canonical texts and including pamphlets and popular literature as well as exploring the possibilities opened up by the inclusion of visual material; and, secondly, at the level of methodology, by drawing on early corpus linguistic approaches (notably French lexicography) and focusing on semantic networks rather than single concepts.

3

For a Socio-historical Semantics as a Middle Course between 'Lexicometry' and 'Conceptual History'[1]

Rolf Reichardt

Chapter Outline

(1) Available Methodological Approaches

a) The first method that comes to mind, as the most modern and undoubtedly most exact, is the computer-aided frequency analysis of lexicometry as developed chiefly in St.-Cloud.[2] By first saving all of the words that occur in the selected political texts it automatically creates not only complete alphabetical indexes and concordances for the immediate contexts but also lists of words ranked according to frequency. These are used to establish the most common and, by this measure, central words, as well as tables of words often occurring in a single context ('co-occurrences'), whether associated as equivalents or appearing in oppositional relationships.[3] This kind of quantification does indeed represent the most objective way of, for example, establishing the obsession of leading revolutionaries with the word *peuple*, discovering temporal changes in frequency in an author's use of a word, determining the high rate, which has long been overlooked, of the personal pronouns *tu* and *vous* in the writing of the radical revolutionary journalist Leclerc or the close relation of the words *peuple*, *vertu* and *bonheur* in the speeches of Robespierre.[4] However, quite apart from the fact that there is little sense in competing with the valuable work undertaken in St.-Cloud, their findings one decade on are still patchy.[5] This points to the procedural and methodical/methodological reasons why lexicometry is unsuitable for long-term semantological research.

It obtains its precision by applying restrictions that largely exclude from analysis aspects we consider crucial, namely temporal changes and meaning. On the one hand it concentrates on comparatively small text corpora. This means that its findings rarely go beyond the personspecific, synchronic, or at most micro-diachronic – partly because of the labour involved, but also increasingly from a desire to work only with the structural qualities of the individual author and a great reluctance to compare different authors at all.[6] On the other hand, and this is the chief concern, the reduction of textual analysis to the frequency of individual word units becomes dogmatically systematic, to the extent that leading lexicometricians reject any transition from the description of word frequency to the interpretation and discussion of meaning (and despite statistical lists, this requires reference to the individual text passage) as a violation of linguistic exactitude, and rarely admit of inferences from the specific text and usage to language as a superindividual system.[7] Moreover, lexicometrical methods and findings can evidently only be described and presented in a form that is largely incomprehensible to non-specialist readers and has, to date, been almost completely neglected even in historical scholarship.[8]

b) Due to similar, if less fundamental, reservations, discourse analysis is likewise able to support but not to carry and sustain a project such as ours. It is itself not a single consistent method but a whole bundle of different procedures, some quantifying and some more qualitative, with the common objective of uncovering concealed rhetorical strategies and ideological elements, the unconscious, in specific texts.[9] It does take semantics into consideration and is useful, for instance, in revealing the key role of the concept of freedom in the reform discussions between Turgot and the supreme courts, exploring the underlying Jacobin tendency of the *Père Duchesne*, established as the organ of the *sansculotterie*, and observing how Raynal was forced into the role of militant *philosophe* by the social reception of his writings or how revolutionary slogans emerged and took hold.[10] But discourse analysis ascribes greater importance to the functioning and inner structure of texts than to the meaning of the terms adapted to new contexts therein and requires such intensive work on individual passages that larger masses of source material can only be analysed with a disproportionately great effort.

c) The methods of etymological and analytical linguistics that are most highly developed from a theoretical and technical point of view thus being of only limited use in answering the questions posed above, the obvious alternative would be to turn to 'conceptual history'. Following humble lexicographic beginnings[11] and intermittent abandoned attempts,[12] this discipline was largely developed by Reinhart Koselleck and, with his collaborative work *Geschichtliche Grundbegriffe*, has produced recognized results for the German-speaking world.

Indeed, our project would be almost inconceivable without this precedent. Koselleck's historical observations are thought-provoking working hypotheses that can also be effectively applied to France. They include the notions that nouns initially used in the plural such as *histories* are singularized into general terms like *history* ('collective singular'), that vocabularies once only employed by intellectuals enter into usage in other social strata (*Demokratisierung*, democratization), that basic expressions are increasingly used as polemical weapons and become more ambiguous (*Ideologisierbarkeit*, the potential ideologization of modern concepts), and that they are increasingly invested with expectations and objectives (at the expense of the accumulated experience they contain), thus becoming future-oriented concepts of movement (*Bewegungsbegriffe*) (*Verzeitlichung*, temporalization; *Politisierung*, politicization). Equally useful and relevant to France is his conceptual framework according to which this whole transformation in semantic structure from bygone, old-European concepts to 'modern' ones that are fairly generally understood today took place primarily and most rapidly during what he termed the *Sattelzeit* (literally 'saddle period') from around 1750 to 1850.[13]

We can of course also draw lessons from the criticism that the *Geschichtliche Grundbegriffe*, amidst considerable approbation, also incurred. It demonstrates that, for various reasons, the editors have not been completely successful in resolving their brilliantly formulated concept, in particular its claim to socio-historical relevance, in the collaborative work. This is because the undertaking's very broadly conceived chronological framework spanning antiquity and the present day, coupled with a neglect at times of the source texts recommended by all contributors as their key common source, have resulted in a certain amount of bias and in places to the favouring of an elite group of 'great', canonized theorists from Aristotle to Karl Marx while failing to demonstrate their social representativeness or address political vernacular. To these reservations is added the fundamental objection that the socio-historical relevance of conceptual history cannot be convincingly defended theoretically by citing the referential nature of concepts to historical events and circumstances, because changes in the socio-economic position of social strata, for instance, can be reconstructed more immediately and exactly from collective sources such as notarial acts than from verbal descriptions such as *bourgeois* or *capitalist*.[14]

(2) Outline of our Socio-historical Approach

For these reasons, and because while other historical semantological approaches do show an interest in problems of conceptual history, they fail to provide any practical methods for their solution,[15] our undertaking follows a different approach both theoretically and historically as well as with regard to method and sources.

a) Theoretical Background

The social significance of a socio-historical semantics as we understand it stems not from the material circumstances and things to which it more or less indirectly refers but directly from the social nature of language itself. It must of course go beyond isolated speech events and citations from literary classics and investigate the verbal conventions, the 'norm', that 'really does exert pressure on the individual and restricts his freedom of expression and the possibilities offered by the system to the limitations of traditional realisations'.[16] This social filtering and pre-sorting function of language can be explained not only linguistically but also with regard to the sociology of knowledge, drawing on the work of Alfred Schütz, Peter Berger and Thomas

Luckmann. In their now-classic formulation of a new theoretical foundation for the sociology of knowledge, the two last-mentioned make a number of statements about the social role of language which may appear self-evident in themselves but which assume systematic, fundamental validity in the context of their theory.

Put briefly, in order to get their bearings in the overabundance of unfamiliar ambient sense impressions, in order to act purposefully and to be able to coordinate this with their fellow human beings, the individual members of a society typify common and stored experiences ('sediments') in the same way, creating patterns specific to their era or society, expectations and behavioural dispositions and formations of meaning that acquire the validity of conventions irrespective of the facticity of the individual case ('objectivations') and that create certainty about reality in the form of 'social knowledge'. This process takes place primarily in the medium and through the sign system of language, especially everyday language.

It is itself a part of the social stock of knowledge and is accepted as such as a certainty. As a common 'store of accumulated experiences and significances' it depersonalises individual phenomena and specific occurrences, subsumes them under more universal significances, stabilizes these objectivations through the act of their verbalization and through daily conversation and is thus the chief instrument of social legitimation:

> Language makes common experience tangible and allows the experience to be accessible to all who belong to the language community. Language is simultaneously the foundation and the instrument of a collective body of knowledge. Furthermore, language provides the tool for the objectification of new experiences and enables introducing them into the already-existent body of knowledge. Moreover, language is the most important medium, through which the objectified sediments have become objects can be passed down as tradition in the respective society.[17]

This theory, as elaborated by Hans Ulrich Gumbrecht,[18] is particularly important for a socio-historical semantics because it encompasses a concept from the sociology of knowledge of 'type' that stems from the linguistic concept of 'meaning'. As 'uniform *Bestimmungsrelationen* sedimented in past experiences',[19] as contexts taken for granted and recognized by a speech community ('institutionalized'), types also belong to the social stock of knowledge. However, they are more highly developed, more complex and more closely related to history than the simpler and relatively constant habitual knowledge. They emerge and change in crisis situations where construction of meaning is more difficult, is problematic, when the available knowledge has lost credibility and proves too imprecise for dealing with such a situation. Types develop further the elements they contain within them in seminal form, cast off elements that are outmoded or no longer relevant and assume new ones. Hence they are always problem-oriented and have a history. Above all, it is types that give clear contours to a subject selected from the abundance of perceptions of one's surroundings, interpret it according to previous experiences, derive from it and make accessible unconscious attitudes and more conscious motives, and thus are one of the principal factors governing this 'process of constructing meaning' in all of its phases. In addition to the interpretation of and response to perceptions, they also serve as a basis for the articulation of expectations and predictions. They do not function in isolation but rather in the context of a semantic structure of relationships specific to the particular time or society:

> Through linguistic objectification, every type finds a 'special significance' in the semantic structuring of language. That means, that these types are embedded in a context of types, which is even stronger than when an individual type is detached from the subjective immediate experience. At the same time, this embedding means that the constitution of the type and the variation within the systems are cumulative, which means, that the shift/ change of the 'special significance' that happens to a type, has consequences for the 'special significance' of other types within the semantic structure.[20]

What this means for a socio-historical semantics is that terms – social products themselves – in turn have an effect on their 'producers' and acquire a dynamic that is not necessarily bound to material facts. It is no longer necessary to describe this dynamic intuitively as a somehow innate 'inherent force of words'[21]; it can be understood as the assertiveness and persistence of socially institutionalized knowledge. Thus in the 1780s, demands for the razing of the Bastille spread throughout broader sections of society and became more radical, and were ultimately satisfied, because this state prison was increasingly seen as a symbol of 'despotism' even though objectively and in reality this was less and less the case; and despite the changes introduced in 1789 the revolutionaries were incapable of understanding institutionalized power and politics other than as *despotisme*, because they remained ideologically tethered to the dualistic notion of 'freedom/ despotism' of the Enlightenment criticism of absolutism and their rejection of the formation of political parties in any form. Just as things only become socially and psychologically existent through their verbalization, conversely, terms are more real for social knowledge than material reality and can be a motivation and driving force behind actions that go against demonstrable facts. As common 'types' and guidelines, the meanings of terms are therefore not so much indicators as key factors of social life that concentrate collective experiences, form a key component of the psychological and cultural infrastructure of a time period ('outillage mental', Lucien Febvre), inform attitudes and mentalities, make possible and govern communication and collective action, and indeed even crystallize fundamental social values. The latter is particularly true of the elaborate, problem-oriented types, that is, the meanings of mostly abstract, basic terms that store complex, non-situation specific basic elements of social knowledge. As they are generally more subject to historical problematizations and changes than are the names of actual objects, they afford the greatest prospect of charting shifts in social attitudes and key conceptions via type and semantic changes. In other words, for our purposes basic terms are, on the one hand, 'the linguistically objectified social types…, through whose changes it is possible to trace a transformation of basic elements of the social knowledge which is neither initiated nor controlled by the historical agents'.[22] On the other hand, and particularly when they are closely connected with other types, these basic terms also reveal ideological-mental structures of resistance that outlast both economical and political changes and which can be important factors behind historical stasis and inertia. Unlike some, such as representatives of lexicometry (see note 7 above), we believe it is quite possible that semantics may at least approach this level of collective significance. The strict division taught from Saussure through to structural linguistics between 'language' as the autonomous, logical system of signs of a speech community on the one hand and its actualization in individual 'speech' (and in text) on the other is increasingly proving to be exaggerated, artificial and divorced from social realities. The social function of language – uncoupled from the shifting, historical conditions of its production, reproduction and application – can neither be correctly understood merely from its autonomy and through the construct of the ideal 'speaker' and 'receiver' (Noam Chomsky) nor should the examination of specific texts be necessarily restricted to understanding usage in isolated cases. While a 'language' as a system is really a product of state education policy and of academia, 'speech' draws on similar but less universal conventions, which, in its turn, it also influences.[23] Thus, in a broad transitional area underneath the abstract language system, the abundance of the particular usage aligns itself with basic patterns that are neither fixed nor entirely binding, though generally practised by broad sections of the particular society. It is precisely this intermediate zone of the social that we are interested in. It would be futile to want to apprehend it in its whole scope and to constantly explain which terms were common, in which sense, in which social groups and strata, at which time and to what extent. But with the help of the variety and accumulation of words used in an often situation-specific context in typical, collective sources that contribute to the institutionalization of knowledge (see below), we hope to gather sufficient evidence for the contours of a socio-historically constituted language.

To do this, we must round out this theoretical justification of our project with a socio-historical concept and illustrate it with reference to French history, defining it both chronologically and, in particular, with regard to the emergence, communication and dissemination of new social knowledge.

b) Social and Chronological Scope

First of all, it is important to be aware that the theory pertaining to the sociology of knowledge outlined in simplified terms above is not directly transferable to *the* society of the old France as a whole from a conceptual history point of view. As this society consisted in reality of the stark juxtaposition of various cultures with a wide education gap, and because the social knowledge of its lower classes was neither concentrated in prominent basic terms nor articulated over a prolonged period of time with a broad thematic scope in more or less homogeneous sources, our project must work with the language of the educated urban upper and middle classes. While it attempts also to explore the broader social resonance of this language, it can only take account of the social knowledge and culture of, in particular, the peasantry in certain favourable cases. If, in keeping with the above requirement for cross-epochal, chronological and yet clearly structured historical-semantic analyses, we concentrate on the period from around 1680 to 1820, this follows from the working hypothesis that the Enlightenment and Revolution have permanently changed the fundamental values and key concepts of the old France but that this structural change can only be proven by comparing the dominant usage during these putative periods of upheaval with the preceding and following periods. The first date was chosen because it marks the beginning of the series of general source texts on which our research is based (see below), and because more recent historio-cultural studies have confirmed statistically that in order to identify long-term changes in the eighteenth century, the period from 1680 to 1715/30 must be taken into account. On the one hand, it is during this period that the

Counter-Reformation, 'classicism', court life and aristocratic habits enjoyed their greatest social acceptance and exerted greatest influence as role models, while at the same time, Enlightenment developments, though not yet clearly revealed, were already beginning to make themselves felt.[24] If, following a different suggestion (see note 7 above), our study only began with the more specific, particularly relevant source of the socio-political (in the narrower sense) dictionaries of the 1760s, a significant part of the semantic tradition would be entirely overlooked, and it is in context of this very tradition that the redefinitions of the eighteenth century become clear. Correspondingly, the choice of our second date also draws on case studies from the sociology of culture and on the findings of socio-economic historical research, namely that it was not until 1820/30 that it became clear which of the reforms announced by the revolutionaries openly or covertly outlasted the attempts to restore the monarchy that gained strength after 1795.[25] It may be seen as a sign of the particularly accelerating effect in France of the Enlightenment and Revolution that the period we are looking at is a whole generation or more earlier than the *Sattelzeit* postulated for the conceptual shift in the German-speaking area (see note 13 above).

c) Outline of the Social Institutions and Multipliers of Conceptual Development between 1680 and 1820

If we want to understand the social institutionalization, dissemination and semantic transformation of basic terms in eighteenth-century France from a socio-historical point of view – beyond language acquisition in the family and at work – we must, first and foremost, consider the structure and development of the supraregional discursive fabric of society which is so crucial to the collective understanding of language and its influence. By this we mean a sociability network of intellectuals' associations and collective sources of information that were at least partially independent of church and state, and whose communication took place essentially through the medium of the spoken or printed word. These groups and sources picked up on and discussed new and established terms and their meanings and played a large role in their either being discredited or becoming more firmly ingrained, according to the interests and convictions of the majority of their members. In the course of the dwindling influence of religious/church and state authority and the liberation of the individual, the unified religious-political faith community was replaced by an increasingly pluralistic communication community, and language went from being an auxiliary tool that retroactively updated norms entrenched in ritual and symbolism, to the constitutive medium of understanding, coordination of action, and sociation among individuals.[26]

This discursive fabric initially consisted mainly of a few aristocratic salons, the academies in Paris and a dozen provincial capitals, the private correspondence of a small circle of theologians and polymaths (including French Protestant emigrants in Holland) and, finally, a few hand-written news-sheets and early review journals. From 1680 until 1715/30 it was only a very loosely-woven network, poorly organized, very academic and limited to a small, highly educated elite, and it exerted little public influence.

This underwent a sea change between 1720/30 and 1760, a period which also saw increasing literacy among the urban population (from 40 per cent to over 50 per cent in some places), an increasing production of books tacitly tolerated by the censors and increasing book ownership through to the petty bourgeoisie. Free-thinking salons became fashionable, the academy movement reached its peak with the founding of twenty one new academies in the provinces, the first hundred (albeit often short-lived) freemasons' lodges were established in regions with few academies, letters became a vehicle for the collaborative development of Enlightenment theory, for rallying together and for partisan tactics and newspapers not only almost tripled their circulation, they also shifted their emphasis from the sober reporting of news to political and literary commentary.[27] Sustained by a growing, ever-broader social desire for education, information and integration in view of the challenging of traditional values and the weakening of corporatist bonds, both the press and intellectuals' associations assumed the character of voluntary, relatively open and regular meetings around an organizational core or guiding spirit that sought to foster collective debate and to formulate policies on issues of both fundamental and topical interest. Not only the journals, but also the academies,[28] through their public meetings and competitions, now exerted an influence on the outside world and increasingly constituted a new civil public sphere distinct from government and state.

This process of consolidation and increasing organization, of pluralization and incipient democratization, of autonomization and emancipation, of actualization and politicization of the communication network, gained speed from 1760 to 1788. While the academy movement remained at a constant high level, the number of freemasons' lodges in the provinces increased from year to year to around 700 by the end of the ancien régime,[29] journal subscribers' circles, publicly-minded educational circles (*musées, lycées*), middle-class reading and literary societies and reading rooms run by book dealers were established in many places, the first daily newspapers were founded in addition to new journals, and by around 1788 there were around 400 press organs, seventy five of which were in the provinces.[30] The discursive fabric of society became increasingly diversified and indeed polarized both politically and socially as alternatives to the well-organized intellectuals' societies and moderately well-established newspapers emerged in the form of informal groups and café circles of little-known writers and their increasingly radical and inflammatory pamphlets.

This last point indicates that the sociability framework and discursive fabric of the eighteenth century was by no means uniformly limited to the upper echelon of intellectuals outlined above, but rather interacted with levels of communication of the middle and lower classes. To be sure, the fairly unorganized level of popular communication consisting of popular songs, fair theatres, pulp fiction, conversations in wine taverns and lemonade stands, can hardly reach the level of abstraction of basic theoretical concepts. However, the social distribution and reception of underground literature affiliated to the *bibliothèque bleue* about criminals such as Cartouche, Mandrin and Desrues or the diary of a Parisian glazier[31] are evidence that certain notions and catchwords prevalent among the cultural elites did indeed gain currency among the petty bourgeoisie, particularly from the 1750s onwards, and were used alongside pre-existing ones or merged with them. Between this basic level of knowledge communication and the sociability network of the educated classes was a broad intermediary zone of more or less informal cultural communication. Among other things, this was sustained by increasing literacy, social mediators such as priests (and their libraries), lawyers, newspaper vendors and servants, as well as by public communication situations regarding religious policy, conflicts between the crown and parliaments, sensational legal scandals and so on.[32] Indeed, this whole gradated discursive fabric presented an alternative to the information and propaganda tools of the absolute monarchy – from fairly unofficial gazettes to the issuance of royal proclamations from pulpits across the country, *repraesentatio maiestatis* at national festivals, and, in connection with the church, at Te Deums sung by order throughout the country to mark military victories, peace agreements or significant events in the royal family. And yet the state information system developed in the seventeenth century lagged further and further behind the growing level of organization and regularity of the civic communication media, as suggested by the rationalist infiltration of the *Mercure de France*, the less frequent portrayal of the royal image at festivals, and the end of Te Deums in the 1760s,[33] so that one may speak of the end of the ancient régime being marked by a withdrawal of the state from public life.[34]

With the French Revolution, particularly during the period 1789 to 1794, the discursive fabric fairly exploded and assumed new dimensions – a process that arguably constitutes a substantial part of the Revolution itself.[35] The flood of pamphlets multiplied after 1787/88 (approximately 1,500 titles) by a factor of more than thirty (approximately 50,000 titles, 18,000 of which were anonymous) and, together with the 2,000 or so newspapers and periodicals of the Revolutionary period, absorbed almost the entire available printing capacity[36]; the Jacobin clubs increased from nineteen in the autumn of 1789 to 921 in July 1791 and at least 5,000 in the spring of 1794, comprising on average every fifth to eighth community in the provinces, or one sixth of the adult male population.[37] This leap in quantity was closely connected to a qualitative structural upheaval in four respects:

1 Firstly, the Revolutionary pamphlets were not only more immediately and exclusively political than most of their Enlightenment-era precursors; they also appealed more strongly to the ordinary man. In some cases spokesmen of the lower classes were heard for the first time, people who had previously had little part in the written tradition, such as the 'patriote' Palloy, a former journeyman bricklayer turned building contractor.[38]

2 The press, secondly, experienced a similar transformation: Daily newspapers increasingly took the place of the more expensive weekly and monthly papers, and more neutral coverage of events gave way to political commentary.[39]

3 This accelerated democratization, politicization and actualization of the mass communication media had in turn a close functional connection to a new kind of sociability that had emerged in a smooth transition from the bourgeois late-Enlightenment and pre-Revolutionary intellectuals' societies. Because thirdly, subscriptions, reading together (reading aloud), and the discussion of newspapers were increasingly essential components not only of the predominantly bourgeois Jacobin clubs, but also of the sectional meetings of the *sansculottes* in the cities and the popular societies dominated by tradesmen, shopkeepers and

pettybourgeois intellectuals that sprang up throughout the country from the autumn of 1790 onwards, while the elite academies were completely discredited and ultimately dissolved.[40] Social strata previously confined to the lower level of communication thus became involved in the political public sphere at an organizational level also.

4   Fourthly, a parliamentary communications system emerged in France for the first time as a common reference point for both mass communication media and club culture. The ground was prepared for this system throughout the country in the provincial assemblies with their subdivisions (1787/88) and the awareness-raising election campaign for the Estates-General. It prevailed against the royal government on 17 June 1789,[41] spread to departments, districts and communes, and was repeatedly confirmed and consolidated in new elections. This new communications system was based on the social impact of public speeches and debate at assemblies, on a permanent context of discourse and on the exchange of information and opinions between the central parliamentary decision-making body in Paris and voters, Jacobin clubs, popular societies and elected provincial officials and governments – an exchange established and sustained with unprecedented intensity through public tribunes in the parliament, the press, reports from members of parliament, petitions, demonstrations, administrative correspondence, parliamentary commissioners, national festivals, etc.[42]

What was new here was not only each of these individual discursive elements, but above all the political public sphere they jointly created. This replaced the monarchical public sphere and generally involved all sections of society.[43] With the increased political significance, circulation speed, concentration/condensation of subject matter, and geographical and social distribution of information and opinions in this new public sphere, language as the key vehicle of this sociability assumed greater strategic value and exerted influence on political decision-making much more directly than before, and official parlance and party disputes about the definition of key concepts attracted greater interest and acquired greater social relevance.

This discursive fabric was initially favoured by almost complete freedom of the press and of assembly and the openness of parliamentary debate, then restricted by censorship and the prohibition of dissent under the Jacobin dictatorship. However, from 1795 to 1815/20, it sacrificed much of its freedom, diversity, density and scope as popular societies and Jacobin clubs were closed, *sansculottes* and Jacobins withdrew to their places of work and circles of friends, the parliament's legitimizing power diminished, and state information policy, police and censorship restricted the press. Total newspaper circulation dropped (by 90,000 copies) as did the number of readers of daily newspapers (approx. 300,000), ultimately reverting to the pre-Revolutionary level by 1803. For a short time in 1811, there were only four daily newspapers in Paris.[44] Nevertheless, development could not be turned back to the level of the ancien régime. The Revolution had so thoroughly established the puralistic, collective opinion forming process, which took place through language, in the public sphere that even conservatives began to found party-like clubs and electoral organizations. Certain groups, including some among the petty bourgeois, did continue to read newspapers in the reading rooms of the early nineteenth century. The newly founded academies never regained their 'enlightening' function, but the improved 'democratic' sociability of the Revolution was not completely lost. For all the attempts at Restoration, an autonomous, potentially revolutionary social discursive fabric continued to exist vis-à-vis the state.[45]

It remains to be noted that this brief and inevitably simplistic discursive history can perhaps provide a general outline of the social development of language in France between absolutism and Restoration but cannot explain it in detail. For within this changing discursive fabric, language did not develop automatically, as it were, in neutral spaces but rather functioned as the vehicle of the collective communication, discussion and interpretation of events, conflicts and possible responses specific to a particular time and society. This means that the individual utterance can only be properly understood if we take the particular communication situation into account; indeed, a socio-historical semantics could usefully concentrate on a limited sequence of particularly catalysing communication situations.

Enumerating all of the communication situations that could be considered for the period we are looking at would amount to a social history of the eighteenth century and is therefore not feasible here. But it would appear that in this domain also, from the largely philosophical/religious disputes of the early eighteenth century, the beginnings of reform and crises in the state system of the later Enlightenment through to the quick succession of decision-making situations during the Revolution, a similar process of politicization and democratization was taking place to that involved in the structural transformation of the discursive fabric itself.

(3) Selection of Terms and Scope of the Articles

How can the theoretical substantiation of our project and its model definition in the light of discursive history be translated into the practical study of conceptual history?

To reach the level of the social – not for each individual concept anew and in a different manner but uniformly and jointly for a base stock of concepts – our project draws on a common corpus of sources that are, as far as possible, representative, collective and that had a mass reception. This body of sources shall be described in greater detail below. The fact that the sources used are almost exclusively printed can be justified not only with respect to the labour involved but also and above all by the aim of apprehending as social knowledge the meanings of terms actually circulating in the public sphere. This is why we also draw on historical information regarding circulation figures and the dissemination and mass reach of publications as a key way of monitoring the social range of the meanings of words.

Consequently, evidence from representative sources, as banal as they may appear, is given priority over subsequently canonized and generally theoretical 'classic' literature. The latter can and should be drawn on for deeper analysis but is not conclusive in and of itself. What we are looking for here is not so much the first instance and philosophical insight as the actual social usage.

The selection and compilation of the basic terms examined in our study is the product of a whole range of considerations and procedures.[46]

a) As far as the *question of completeness* is concerned, we have for a number of reasons decided against the most obvious, certainly most empirical and objective method of considering, for instance, all of the nouns without exception used in the corpus of sources on which our research is based. On the one hand, historical lexicometry has already been following this principle for one and a half centuries, so a division of labour, instead of a doubling, is advisable. On the other hand, the lexicometrical studies published thus far are to such a large extent limited to individual cases or statistical charts that level the contours of problem oriented basic terms in the mass of uncontested habitual words, which other studies concentrating on a core stock of terms can be a meaningful addition to these. Nor would it appear advisable to base such studies on empirical-quantifying statistics, that is, on a reduced principle of completeness, because, as mentioned above, the corpus of sources would have to be severely limited at the expense of its social representativeness, and many of our questions would not be able to be answered. Finally, the limited working capacity of a team of four, the funding of the project being only possible for a limited period of time, publishing requirements and, not least, the principle that it is better to examine a smaller number of terms thoroughly and with a view to new findings, than to compile only summary information on all terms – all of these factors played a part in our project's lack of aspiration to any extensive completeness with regard to vocabulary.

b) As we are thus concentrating on a *selection* of terms, it remains to explain how and according to what criteria this selection was made. In order to keep potentially subjective and anachronistic influences to a minimum, the socio-political dictionaries that appeared from the 1760s onwards provide an ideal starting point. These works explore certain terms in articles and thus undertake a selection from the total vocabulary themselves.[47] In addition, we have taken into account all journal passages where terms are emphasized by expressions such as '*mot de…*', typographically or within the context of the presented argumentation. This produced a base stock of almost 500 terms – not counting proper names and technical terms – with dozens to hundreds of textual examples amassed for each. On the one hand this allowed us to rediscover terms such as *abus* or *petits maîtres* and names like *Bastille* and *Saint-Barthélemy* that had assumed almost mythical proportions and whose former function as catchwords had largely been forgotten. On the other hand, preparing our handbook purely on this basis would have resulted in a largely unbalanced, very disparate book in the style of a formal register. Alongside words that were generally discussed, with rich supporting documentation proving them key terms, such as *philosophe*, this word list also contained little-discussed, descriptive, general designations such as *armée* whose content was invariably identical to the thing designated; moreover, it contained catchwords such as *encyclopédistes* and *brissotins* that are only documented for a portion of the period from 1680 to 1820 and are not suitable for general articles, as well as words related to each other through association, derivation or opposition, whose arbitrarily alphabetical treatment would have separated subjects which belonged together. It was therefore advisable to subject the list of terms provided by the sources to yet another selection process and to divide the individual entries in our handbook in such a way that they did not appear too isolated.

c) By now it was time of course to consider the insight of the sociology of knowledge (see above) and of structural linguistics, namely that the meanings of words in a speech community form a tightly-woven network of interrelations that continually intersect and intertwine and that change not individually but as a group, in other words, that a semantic history must essentially be *structuralist*. But quite apart from the fact that this would be possible only with a narrower source base than ours and in a systematic monograph, not an encyclopaedic handbook, such theoretical views are still very difficult to apply, because as yet linguistics offers almost no methods that are practical and productive for historians. While lexicometrical analyses of 'co-occurrences' (see note 3 above) prefer to withhold comment on semantic history, structural semantics is so exclusively committed to linguistic oppositions of words that belong to the same part of speech, to comparatively small groups of words, and to purely synchronic studies,[48] that it seemed poorly suited to our purposes. And a more historical approach, of which Ulrich Ricken is the key exponent, has provided important insights[49] but is not yet far enough developed to be adopted completely.[50]

d) The focus of our project is therefore still squarely on individual concepts, but when it came to defining the *scope of the articles*, wherever possible we took into account both explicit and functional links between different concepts:

1   Most of the following articles are indeed devoted to individual concepts and words derived from them, where the collective analysis of the source material produced sufficient supporting documentation and an examination of the relevant semantic history requires more than just a few pages, as for example in the case of *fanatisme* and *terreur*. In some cases, terms such as *cosmopolitisme* and *individu(alisme)*, which were supported by not more than thirty textual examples each, were given (shorter) articles of their own if these provided an opportunity to reconsider traditional paradigms.

2   In addition, however, pairs of antonyms that often appeared together in the sources are also examined together – from *droite/gauche* and *lumières/ténèbres* to *riches/pauvres*.

3   We have likewise combined in a single article the semantic development of mutually highly complementary concepts that often appear as a group in contemporary definitions (e.g. *autorité-pouvoir-puissance*), that are related synonymously and are at times interchangeable (e.g. *banquier-capitaliste-financier*), or that only articulate a basic

social attitude such as status oriented thinking when used together (*condition-état-naissance-qualité-rang*).

4   The same applies to concepts expressing shifting collective attitudes towards a single phenomenon (e.g. *administration-bureaucratie; charité-bienfaisance*) or rapidly outmoded social stylizations that belong together functionally (e.g. *petits maîtres; jeuneusse dorée; muscadins merveilleuses*), whose semantic history can be traced on the basis not of the individual words but of the particular sequence.

5   Finally, certain terms that are only documented for brief periods within our time span are incorporated into more extensive articles if they may be considered new forms of general concepts, such as the terms *brissotins* (see art. 'Faction/Parti') or *sansculottes* (see art. 'Peuple') but are omitted if they have no such connection and their occurrence is too sporadic for our purposes.

The selection thus obtained of around 150 articles is still not ideal; not only does it largely omit fairly uncontentious, habitual designations such as *bonnes villes*, expressions limited to a particular place and time such as *frérêche*, and seigneurial terminology (but see art. 'Féodalité'), it also bypasses universal concepts such as *guerre* and *paix* that rarely feature in our sources (which deal mainly with domestic issues). It is also clear that important collective attitudes, particularly of the lower classes, towards farm work, marriage, birth, death, etc. do not get the attention they deserve because they are rarely reflected in specific terminology; our project is thus largely limited to the sphere of social consciousness and of ideology. All the same, we hope to have addressed the key themes of society, economics, politics and culture at this level at least – if not comprehensively, then at least with representative examples. The terms selected are therefore not 'socio-political' primarily because they describe things, circumstances and processes in this manner but chiefly because of their function and impact.

The fact that we also include seemingly purely abstract, unpolitical general terms from areas such as etiquette, philosophy and religion can be explained both by the key function they assume in the corpus of sources on which our study is based and, especially, by the high circulation for example, of etiquette books in the old France (see art. 'Civilité'[51]), by the legitimizing role for instance of *raison* during the Enlightenment and the Revolution and by the politicization of what initially were purely theological terms such as *fanatisme*.

(4) Working Methods

Even though our project cannot claim to apply a strict method in the scientific sense, the preparation of the articles was subject to a number of checks and rules and not left to mere 'impressionism'.

The basic prerequisite is a shift in perspective from the history of ideas as reflected in human thought to our concept of socio-historical semantics, from the history of events to that of mentalities. Concepts should be understood not as the markers of material circumstances but as autonomous social factors, which of course interact with other socio-economic forces. Each article is based on the textual examples derived from the collective analysis of the source material. As the fruit of a complete and thorough reading of a corpus analysed from beginning to end (see below), they are not scattered, chance findings but a guiding basis that is representative of the corpus and relatively homogeneous. However, special sources have generally been drawn on for additional information on each basic term. These are often numerous and can amount to whole 'genres' of their own.

The references thus collected should neither be lumped together on one and the same level nor should they immediately become narrowly defined, 'autonomous' conceptual histories. Rather they are first to be differentiated, assessed and ordered in three respects:

1 Firstly, the degree to which the documents are socially representative is to be determined as far as possible, along with the historical situations and processes surrounding their emergence and usage. The concept of the *honnête homme*, for example, can mean two very different things depending on whether it was adopted by a nobleman at court or a petty bourgeois in the provinces. This socio-historical 'situating' of the material is not so much with a view to finding responsible parties and tracing the meanings of terms as 'ideological superstructure' back to their 'socio-economic basis' (which would be at variance with our approach founded on the sociology of knowledge). Rather it serves, first and foremost, to assess the social scope of the concepts and to understand their specific, socio-political functions.

2 Closely related to this is, secondly, a differentiation of the material according to 'areas of practice'. In other words, it is to be established whether the documents are of a general nature, that is, tend to pertain to

society as a whole, or whether they pertain to more technical domains specific to a particular group such as philosophy, theology, law or business. This not only allows the individual semantic elements and their respective areas of applicability to be established more precisely than by a global treatment; a circumstance such as the dwindling usage of a term in one such area and its emergence in new areas of practice also reveals interesting shifts in priorities and expansions or contractions of meaning. According to Michel Foucault's theory of the 'order of discourse', such areas of practice can be understood as socially and thematically defined contexts of discourse, lines of argument and ways of thinking in a particular era about particular fields of knowledge.[52]

3   Thirdly, the material is to be differentiated according to the textual features of the type of source from which it is derived. While the defining entries in dictionaries that order stocks of knowledge according to the principles of nuance (synonym dictionaries) or classification (dictionaries of homophones/polysemous words) can be utilized fairly directly, material from journals or pamphlets, where the stocks of knowledge merge with information and instructions, can only be tapped in the greater textual and historical context.

Admittedly, any attempt to apply these distinctions to each individual piece of material and to mention them explicitly each time would result in a virtually unreadable study and is only feasible to a certain extent in a collaborative project such as ours. It is therefore necessary as far as possible to describe, assess and typify the sources on which our study is based in order to unburden the individual articles of the handbook of this task, as far as this can be achieved with general comments on each source as a whole.

Moreover, the favouring of 'classics' of the history of ideas is to be avoided as far as possible or at least approached with caution. Jumping between different eras or even from one country to another, for example from English or Italian to French authors, requires supporting documentation linking their reception – not simply indicating theoretical affinities but an equivalent social resonance and communication.

Wherever additional empirical information can be brought in to support the interpretation and presentation of the semantic history of a term, this should be used. The same applies of course to the findings of lexicometrical and discourse-analytical research, which, however, generally only pertain to details. But it also applies to a newer historical semantological approach, one which is tied to a chronological series of more or less homogeneous source texts mainly featuring the same term and consists in structuring, formalizing, and establishing a hierarchy of frequency in each text for the vocabulary grouped with the given term, thus eliciting for each text a semantic field and, by comparing these different semantic fields, an objectifying interpretative framework. In other words, if we note in a text for example, (1) all words and expressions that define a central term (paradigmatic field), (2) all words associated with it that imbue it with meaning, explain and elaborate it (syntagmatic field), (3) all of its systematic counter-concepts (functional antonyms) and (4) its actual historical occurrences, we arrive at the semantic field illustrated here (see Figure 3.1).[53]

Such semantic fields are established more empirically than the 'lexical fields' constructed on Jost Trier's model.[55] In addition to their control function, they can reveal structures and developments that thematic interpretation perceives less clearly or not at all, for example, the circle of complementary concepts and counter-concepts surrounding a given basic term and thus areas of overlap between different semantic fields.

(Translation: Joy Titheridge)

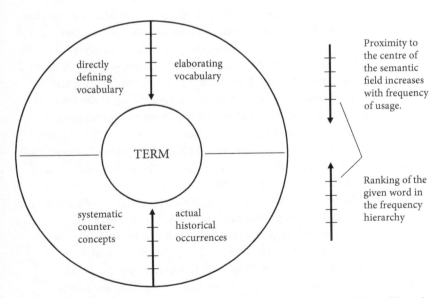

Figure 3.1 Recreated from Rolf Reichardt, 'Einleitung, III – Für eine sozialhistorische Semantik als Mittelweg zwischen "Lexikometrie" und "Begriffsgeschichte"', in Reichardt and Schmitt (1985), 85.[54]

Notes

1   [Note: this text is part III of the 'Introduction' to Rolf Reichardt and
     Eberhard Schmitt (eds), *Handbuch politisch-sozialer Grundbegriffe
     in Frankreich, 1680–1820* (Munich: Oldenbourg, 1985). Part I of the
     introduction concerns the general premise and necessity of conceptual
     history in the context of the dictionary. Part II gives an overview of the
     state of historico-lexicological scholarship on France.]

2   [Note: this refers to the Research Centre for Political Lexicology (centre de
     lexicologie politique) in Saint-Cloud, Hauts-de-Seine, France, founded in
     1965.]

3   [Note: this is footnote number 75 of the original chapter. For better
     readability, the numbering of the footnotes has been reformatted.] Cf.
     Maurice Tournier et al., 'Le vocabulaire de la Révolution. Pour un inventaire
     systématique des textes', *Annales historiques de la Révolution française*, 41
     (1969), 104–24; also Maurice Tournier, 'Travaux en cours. Vocabulaire
     politique et inventaires sur machine', *Cahiers de lexicologie*, 10 (1967), 67–81;
     idem, 'Méthode d'inventaire exhaustif du vocabulaire des textes politiques
     français', *Cahiers de lexicologie*, 10 (1967), 83–101; Annie Geffroy et al.,
     Traitement automatique des textes. 1: Perforation (Paris: 1970 (typescript
     copy)); Annie Geffroy, Pierre Lafon and Maurice Tournier, *Leximetrical
     Analysis of Co-occurences* (Paris: 1972 (typescript copy)); Maurice Tournier,
     'Approche d'une définition statistique des co-occurences de vocabulaire',
     Wissenschaftliche Zeitschrift der M. Luther-Univ. Halle-Wittenberg, 19 (1970),
     G3/4, 49–54; Annie Geffroy et al., 'Lexicometric Analysis of Co-occurences',
     in Adam Jack Aitken, Richard Bailey and Neil Hamilton-Smith (eds), *The
     Computer and Literary Studies* (Edinburg: Edinburgh University Press,
     1973), 113–33; Annie Geffroy, Jacques Guilhaumou and André Salem,
     'L'histoire sur mesures ou Pour une statistique du Discours', *Bulletin du
     Centre d'Analyse du discours*, 2 (1975), 15–60; Michel Launay, 'La lexicologie
     politique. Le traitement informatique du discours historique', *Bulletin de la
     Société d'histoire moderne*, 16/3 (1979), 2–12.

4   Cf. Annie Geffroy, *Vocabulaire politique. Etude statistique et sémantique.
     Saint-Just, discours et rapports à la Convention, 1792–1794*, 1966
     (Ms); excerpt thereof: 'Le people selon Saint-Just', *Annales historiques
     de la Révolution française*, 40 (1968), 138–44; eadem, 'L'étendue du
     vocabulaire chez Hébert et Robespierre', *Cahiers de Lexicologie*, 22
     (1973), 96–107; eadem, Formes de base et forms spécifiques dans le
     discours robespierriste, *Cahiers de Lexicologie*, 25 (1974), 96–134; eadem,
     ' "Terreur" et sa famille morphologique de 1773 à 1796', in Rosine Adda et
     al., *Néologie et lexicologie. Hommage à L. Gilbert* (Paris: Larousse, 1979),

124–34; eadem, 'Trois successeurs de Marat pendant l'été 1793. Analyse lexicométrique des spécificités', *Mots... Ordinateurs... Textes... Sociétés*, 1 (1980), 167–86; eadem, 'Personnes du discours et figures du pouvoir dans l' "Ami du Peuple" de Leclerc (juillet-septembre 1793)', *Bulletin du Centre d'Analyse du discours*, 9 (1981), 105–48.

5 According to the historian Pierre Vilar in the discussion on Launay (1979), 12.

6 Geffroy (1981), fn. 1 and 44, 139 and 145; eadem (1975), 52–1.

7 Maurice Tournier, 'D'où viennent les fréquences de vocabulaire? La lexicométrie et ses modèles', *Mots... Ordinateurs... Textes... Sociétés*, 1 (1980), 189–208.

8 According to Michel Vovelle at a round table discussion on 8 June 1982 at the Göttingen Max-Planck-Institut für Geschichte. A criticism from a linguistic perspective can be found for example in Peter von Polenz, 'Möglichkeiten satzsemantischer Textanalyse', *Zeitschrift für germanistische Linguistik*, 8 (1980), 133–53.

9 Michel Pêcheux, *Analyse automatique du discours* (Paris: Dunod, 1969); Régine Robin, 'Histoire et linguistique', *Langue française*, 9 (1971), 47–57; idem, 'Les historiens devant le champ linguistique', *Dix-huitième Siècle*, 5 (1973), 111–18; Denise Maldidier, Claudine Normand and Régine Robin, 'Discours et idéologie', *Langue française*, 15 (1972), 116–42; Michel Pêcheux, *Les vérités de La Palice. Linguistique, sémantique, philosophie* (Paris: Maspéro, 1975); Dominique Maingueneau, *Initiation aux méthodes de l'analyse du discours* (Paris: Hachette, 1976); Patrick Charaudeau, *Les conditions linguistiques d'une analyse du discours* (Lille/Paris: Service de reproduction des thèses, 1978); Jacques Guilhaumou and Denise Maldidier, 'Courte critique pour une longue histoire: l'analyse du discours ou les (mal) leurres de l'analogie', *Dialectiques*, 26 (1979), 7–23; Algirdas Julien Greimas et al., *Introduction à l'analyse du discours en sciences sociales* (Paris: Hachette, 1979); Heinz Georg Kuttner, *Zur Relevanz text- und inhaltsanalytischer Verfahrensweisen für die empirische Forschung* (Frankfurt am Main/Bern: Lang, 1981); Bernard Conein et al., *Matérialités discursives* (Lille: Presses Universitaires de Lille, 1981); Dominique Maingueneau, *Genèse du discours* (Brussels: Pierre Mardaga, 1984); see also the criticism, deserving of greater attention, by Jean-Claude Gardin, *Les analyses de discours* (Neuchâtel: Delachaux et Niestle, 1974).

10 Cf. the studies by Jacques Guilhaumou; also Denise Maldidier and Régine Robin, 'Polémique idéologique et affrontement discursif en 1776. Les grand édits de Turgot et les remontrances du Parlement de Paris', *Mouvement Social*, 85 (1973), 81–116; Hans-Jürgen Lüsebrink, 'Stratégies d'intervention, identité sociale et présentation de soi d'un "defenseur de l'humanité"'. La carrière de l'Abbé Raynal, 1713–1796', *Bulletin du Centre d'Analyse du discours*, 5 (1981), 28–64.

11   Otto Ladendorf, *Historisches Schlagwörterbuch. Ein Versuch* (Straßburg/
     Berlin: Karl J. Trübner, 1906); much further developed: Elisabeth Kredel,
     Hundert französische Schlagworte und Modewörter (Giessen: Romanisches
     Seminar, 1926).
12   *Beiträge zu einem Lexikon historischer Grundbegriffe*, ed. Pädagogische
     Hochschule Braunschweig. Internationales Schulbuchinstitut
     (Braunschweig: Limbach, 1960), 100 pages (also published in the
     Internationales Jahrbuch für Geschichtsunterricht, 7 (1959/60), 241–340);
     *Europäische Schlüsselwörter. Wortvergleichende und wortgeschichtliche
     Studien*, ed. Sprachwissenschaftliches Colloquium (Bonn), vol. I–III
     (Munich: Hueber, 1963–67); esp. Wolfgang Schmidt-Hidding, 'Zur
     Methode wortvergleichender und wortgeschichtlicher Studien', in ibid.,
     vol. I, 18–33.
13   Reinhart Koselleck, 'Richtlinien für das Lexikon politisch-sozialer
     Begriffe der Neuzeit', *Archiv für Begriffsgeschichte*, 11 (1967), 81–99; idem,
     'Introduction', in Otto Brunner, Werner Conze and Reinhart Koselleck
     (eds), *Geschichtliche Grundbegriffe*, vol. I (Stuttgart: Klett-Cotta, 1972),
     XIII–XXIII; Reinhart Koselleck, *Vergangene Zukunft. Zur Semantik
     geschichtlicher Zeiten* (Frankfurt am Main: Suhrkamp, 1979), esp. 107–29.
14   Helmut Berding, 'Begriffsgeschichte und Sozialgeschichte', *Historische
     Zeitschrift*, 223 (1976), 98–110; James J. Sheehan, 'Begriffsgeschichte:
     Theory and Practice', *The Journal of Modern History*, 50 (1978), 312–19;
     Irmline Veit-Brause, 'A Note on "Begriffsgeschichte"', *History and
     Theory*, 20 (1981), 61–7; Niklas Luhmann, *Gesellschaftsstruktur und
     Semantik. Studien zur Wissenssoziologie der modernen Gesellschaft*, vol.
     1 (Frankfurt: Suhrkamp, 1980), 13–21 (The fact that the application
     of systems theory to conceptual history attempted in this volume is
     difficult to adopt as a method is demonstrated in the double review by
     Thomas Luckmann and Bernhard Giesen, 'Symposium über: Niklas
     Luhmann, Gesellschaftsstruktur und Semantik, vol. 1', *Soziologische
     Revue*, 5 (1982), 1–10.); an initial systematic assessment of the various
     criticisms presented can be found in Heiner Schultz, 'Begriffsgeschichte
     und Argumentationsgeschichte', in Reinhart Koselleck (ed.), *Historische
     Semantik und Begriffsgeschichte* (Stuttgart: Klett-Cotta, 1979), 43–74.
15   Alphonse Dupront, 'Sémantique historique et histoire', *Cahiers de
     lexicologie*, 14 (1969), 15–25; idem, 'Langage et Histoire', *13e Congrès
     international des sciences historiques, t. 1: Communications* (Moscow,
     1973), 186–254; Louis Trenard, 'Histoire et sémantique', *Revue des
     études sud-est européennes*, 10 (1972), 423–48; Josef Macek, 'Pour une
     sémantique historique', in Abel W. E. Ashtor and M. Aymard (eds),
     Mélanges en l'honneur de Fernand Braudel (Toulouse: Edouard Privat,
     1973), 343–52; Nancy S. Sruever, 'The Study of Language and the Study

of History', *Journal of Interdisciplinary History*, 4/3 (1974), 401–15; Ruth Schmidt-Wiegand, 'Neue Ansätze im Bereich "Wörter und Sachen"', in Günter Wiegelmann (ed.), *Geschichte der Alltagskultur* (Münster: Coppenrath, 1980), 87–102; Maurizio Gribaudi, 'A proposito di linguistica e storia', *Quaderni Storici*, 46 (1981), 236–66.

16   Eugenio Coseriu, 'System, Norm, Rede', in idem, *Sprachtheorie und allgemeine Sprachwissenschaft* (München: Fink, 1975), 11–101, here 88.

17   [Note: the information contained in this quote can be found in the chapter 'Language and Knowledge in Everyday Life', in Peter L. Berger and Thomas Luckmann, *The Social Construction of Reality: A Treatise in the Sociology of Knowledge* (Garden City, NY: Anchor, 1966), 33–43. The English translation is a paraphrase of the German quote: '*Sprache vergegenwärtigt gemeinsame Erfahrung und macht sie allen zugänglich, die einer Sprachgemeinschaft angehören. Sie wird so zugleich Fundament und Instrument eines kollektiven Wissensbestandes. Darüber hinaus stellt sie Mittel zur Vergegenständlichung neuer Erfahrungen zur Verfügung und ermöglicht deren Eingliederung in den bereits vorhandenen Wissensbestand. Außerdem ist sie das wichtigste Medium, durch das die vergegenständlichten und zu Objekten gewordenen Sedimente als Tradition der jeweiligen Gesellschaft überliefert werden*', in Peter L. Berger and Thomas Luckmann, *Die gesellschaftliche Konstruktion der Wirklichkeit*, trans. Monika Plessner (Frankfurt: Fischer Taschenbuch, 1980), 39 and 72–1.] Such statements are not of course 'new' per se, but only in their application to/in the context of the sociology of knowledge; cf. for example Frédéric Paulhan, 'La double fonction du langage', *Revue philosophique de la France et de l'étranger*, 104 (1924), 21–73.

18   Hans Ulrich Gumbrecht, 'Für eine phänomenologische Fundierung der sozialhistorischen Begriffsgeschichte', in Koselleck (1979), 75–101 (forms the basis of the following).

19   Alfred Schütz and Thomas Luckmann, *Strukturen der Lebenswelt*, vol. 1 (Frankfurt am Main: Suhrkamp, 1979), 278; on the following see also ibid., 224–76 on 'relevance structures'. On changing definitions of reality, see also Berger and Luckmann (1966), 167–83.

20   '*Jeder Typ findet durch sprachliche Objektivierung einen "Stellenwert" in der semantischen Gliederung der Sprache. Das bedeutet, daß die Typen in einen Typenzusammenhang eingebettet sind, der noch viel stärker als der einzelne Typ von der subjektiven unmittelbaren Erfahrung abgelöst ist. Zugleich bedeutet diese Einbettung, daß Typenkonstitution und Abwandlungen innerhalb des Systems kumulativ sind, das heißt, die Veränderung des "Stellenwerts", die einem Typ widerfährt, hat Folgen für den "Stellenwert" der anderen Typen innerhalb des Systems.*' Schütz and Luckmann (1979), 282.

21 'Eigenkraft der Worte', Koselleck (1979b), 107; see also ibid., 301.

22 'jene sprachlich objektivierten sozialen Typen…, in deren Wandel eine von
    den historischen Akteuren nicht initiierte oder gesteuerte Transformation
    von Grundelementen des sozialen Wissens nachvollziehbar wird',
    Gumbrecht (1979), 86.

23 Thomas M. Scherer, Ferdinand de Saussure. Rezeption und Kritik
    (Darmstadt: Wissenschaftliche Buchgesellschaft, 1980), 77–120;
    Françoise Gadet and Michel Pêcheux, La langue introuvable (Paris:
    Maspéro, 1981); Pierre Bourdieu, Ce que parler veut dire (Paris: Fayard,
    1982).

24 Cf. for example Michel Vovelle, Piété baroque et déchristianisation en
    Provence au XVIIIe siècle (Paris: Pion, 1973); Daniel Roche, Le Siècle des
    Lumières en Province. Académies et académiciens provinciaux, 1680–1789,
    vol. I–II (Paris: Mouton, 1978); Jean Quéniart, Culture et société urbaines
    dans la France de l'Ouest au XVIIIe siècle (Paris: Klincksiek, 1978).

25 Cf. for example Michel Vovelle, Les métamorphoses de la fête en
    Provence de 1750 à 1820 (Paris: Flammarion, 1976). Further remarks
    in Rolf Reichardt and Eberhard Schmitt, 'Die Französische Revolution
    – Umbruch oder Kontinuität?', Zeitschrift für Historische Forschung, 7
    (1980), 257–321.

26 On the theoretical background, Jürgen Habermas, Theorie des
    kommunikativen Handelns, vol. I–II (Frankfurt am Main: Suhrkamp,
    1981), here especially vol. II, 118–69. Where not otherwise specified,
    the following sketch of the eighteenth century is based on the book
    Sozialgeschichte der Aufklärung in Frankreich, ed. Hans Ulrich Gumbrecht,
    Rolf Reichardt and Thomas Schleich, parts I–II (Munich: Oldenbourg,
    1981), particularly on the introductory section by the editor which
    includes detailed references (I, 4–25). Also comprehensive on aspects
    pertaining to the history of books, the Histoire de l'édition française,
    eds Henri-Jean Martin and Roger Chartier, tome II (Paris: Promodis,
    1984). – For further points I am indebted to conversations with Hans-
    Jürgen Lüsebrink and the unpublished presentations at the conference
    Vereinsleben und bürgerliche Gesellschaft in Frankreich, in Deutschland und
    in der Schweiz, 1750–1850, Bad Homburg, 7–9 April 1983.

27 See also the innovative analysis of content and reception using the
    example of causes célèbres undertaken by Hans-Jürgen Lüsebrink,
    Kriminalität und Literatur im Frankreich des 18. Jahrhunderts (Munich:
    Oldenbourg, 1983), 104–72.

28 Ibid., 173–240.

29 See the recent work by Ran Halévi, Les loges maçonniques dans la France
    d'Ancien Régime. Aux origines de la sociabilité démocratique (Paris:
    Armand Colin, 1984).

30   Basic data from a continuing community project on the French press in
     1788/89, carried out by the research centres for press history in Grenoble
     and Lyon.

31   Lüsebrink (1983), 14–103; Jacques-Louis Ménétra, *Journal de ma vie.*
     Jacques-Louis Ménétra, compagnon vitrier au 18e siècle. Présenté par Daniel
     Roche (Paris: Montalba, 1982); see also the collection of early essays on the
     proliferation of underground literature in the 1780s in Robert Darnton,
     Bohème littéraire et Révolution (Paris: Gallimard, 1983).

32   Hans-Jürgen Lüsebrink, 'Formen und Prozesse kultureller Vermittlung im
     Frankreich der Aufklärung', in idem, Ulrich Gumbrecht, Rolf Reichardt
     and Thomas Schleich (eds), *Sozialgeschichte der Aufklärung in Frankreich,*
     vol. I (München, Oldenbourg, 1981), 55–75.

33   Françoise Bardon, *Le portrait mythologique à la cour de France sous Henri*
     IV et Richelieu (Paris: Picard, 1974); Alain-Charles Gruber, *Les grandes*
     fêtes et leurs discours à l'époque de Louis XVI (Geneva: Droz, 1972); Pierre
     Retat (ed.), *L'Attentat de Damiens. Discours sur l'événement au XVIIIe siècle*
     (Paris: CNRS, 1979), 119–66; Michèle Fogel, 'Une politique de la parole.
     Publication et célébration des victoires pendant la guerre de Succession
     d'Autriche, 1744–1749', *Bulletin du Centre d'Analyse du discours*, 5 (1981),
     28–64; idem, 'Le système d'information ritualisé de l'absolutisme français',
     in idem, *Journalisme d'Ancien Régime. Questions et propositions*, Lyon
     1982, 141–49 (presentation) and 185 (discussion). See also Gilles Feyel, *La*
     'Gazette' en province à travers ses réimpressions, 1631–1752 (Amsterdam:
     Holland University Press, 1982).

34   François Furet, *Penser la Révolution française* (Paris: Gallimard, 1978), 42
     and 66–8.

35   In the absence of any methodical, synoptic accounts of our situation with
     regard to the French Revolution, the following survey shall be necessarily
     limited to hypotheses and examples of a less than universal nature.

36   In addition to the catalogue by André-Marie-Jacques Martin and Gérard
     Walter, *Bibliothèque nationale, Département des imprimés. Catalogue*
     de l'histoire de la Révolution française, t. I–V (Paris: Éditions des
     Bibliothèques nationales, 1936–55); cf. Eberhard Schmitt, *Repräsentation*
     und Revolution (München: Beck, 1969), 147–62; James Harvey
     Ojala, 'Education for Revolution. Pamphlets and the Politicization of
     French Society 1787–1789', PhD thesis, State University of New York,
     Binghampton, 1974; on the press in general, Jacques Godechot, *Histoire*
     générale de la presse française, ed. Claude Bellanger et al., vol. I (Paris:
     Presses Universitaires de France, 1969), 408–517.

37   Louis de Cardenal, *La province pendant la Révolution. Histoire des clubs*
     jacobins, 1789–1795 (Paris: Payot, 1929); Crane Brinton, *The Jacobins*
     (New York: Macmillan, 1930); Michael L. Kennedy, *The Jacobin Clubs in*

the French Revolution. The First Years (Princeton: Princeton University Press, 1981).

38   Victor Fournel, *La Patriote Palloy et l'exploitation de la Bastille* (Paris: Firmin Didot frères, fils et cie, 1872); Henri Lemoine, *Le démolisseur de la Bastille* (Paris: Perrin, 1930); Hans-Jürgen Lüsebrink is preparing a study on these issues. [Note: published as Hans-Jürgen Lüsebrink, Rolf Reichardt and Norbert Schürer, *The Bastille: A History of a Symbol of Despotism and Freedom* (Durham: Duke University Press, 1997).]

39   Further information in Jeremy D. Popkin, 'The French Revolutionary Press. New Findings and New Perspectives', *Eighteenth-Century Life*, 5 (1979), 90–104; Jacques Godechot, 'Les travaux des historiens anglo-saxons sur la presse révolutionnaire', in idem (ed.), *Regards sur l'histoire de la presse et de l'information. Mélanges offerts à J. Prinet* (Saint-Julien-du-Sault: Lobies, 1980), 61–83.

40   See note 37 above. Also Isabelle Bourdin, *Les Sociétés populaires à Paris pendant la Révolution française jusqu'à la chute de la royauté* (Paris: Librairie du Recueil Sirey, 1937); Albert Soboul, *Les Sans-culottes parisiens en l'an II* (Paris: Librairie Clavreuil, 1958); Michael L. Kennedy, 'Les clubs des Jacobins et la presse sous l'Assemblée nationale, 1789–1791', *Revue historique*, 264 (1980), 49–63; Robert B. Rose, *The Making of the Sans-Culottes: Democratic Ideas and Institutions in Paris, 1789–1792* (Manchester: Manchester University Press, 1982).

41   Schmitt (1969), 223–80; Rolf Reichardt, 'Die revolutionäre Wirkung der Provinzialversammlungen in Frankreich 1797–1791', in Ernst Hinrichs et al. (eds), *Vom Ancien Régime zur Französischen Revolution. Forschungen und Perspektiven* (Göttingen: Vandenhoek & Ruprecht, 1978), 66–124.

42   François A. Aulard, *L'éloquence parlementaire pendant la Révolution française*, vol. I–III (Paris: Hachette, 1882–86); Gaston Dodu, *Le parlementarisme et les parlementaires sous la Révolution* (Paris: Plon-Nourrit, 1911); Hans Ulrich Gumbrecht, *Funktionen parlamentarischer Rhetorik in der Französischen Revolution* (Munich: W. Fink, 1978), *passim*; Alison Patrick, 'Paper, Posters and People. Official Communication in France, 1789–1794', *Historical Studies*, 18 (1978), 1–23.

43   See also Furet (1978), 13–109.

44   On sociability, see Kåre D. Tønnesson, *La défaite des sans-culottes. Mouvement populaire et réaction bourgeoise en l'an III* (Oslo: Presse universitaires d'Oslo, 1959); Isser Woloch, *The Jacobin Legacy. The Democratic Movement under the Directory* (Princeton: Princeton University Press, 1970). On the press, cf. Godechot in Bellanger et al. (1969), 519–67; André Cabanis, *La presse sous le Consulat et l'Empire, 1799–1814* (Paris: Société des études robespierristes, 1975); Nathalie Lambrichs, *La liberté de la presse en l'an IV* (Paris: Presses universitaires

de France, 1976); Jeremy D. Popkin, *The Right-Wing-Press in France, 1792–1800* (Chapel Hill: University of North Carolina Press, 1980); idem, 'Les journaux républicains, 1795–1799', *Revue d'histoire moderne et contemporaine*, 31 (1984), 143–57. The figures are contemporary estimates by P. Roederer (*Annales de Normandie* 29/*Archives parlementaires*... 91, fol. I I8ff.), quoted in Popkin (1979), 100.

45   Cf. e.g. Françoise Parent-Lardeur, *Lire à Paris au temps de Balzac. Les cabinets de lecture à Paris, 1815–1830* (Paris: École des hautes études en sciences sociales, 1982); Daniel L. Rader, *The Journalists and the July Revolution in France* (The Hague: Nijhoff, 1973).

46   We are indebted to Gumbrecht (1979), 87ff. for key suggestions.

47   Here we follow the approach of R. Laplace and Maurice Tournier, 'Deux siècles de vocabulaire politique. Elaboration d'une nomenclature, 1770–1969', *Cahiers de lexicologie*, 17 (1970), 74–80.

48   Horst Geckeler, *Zur Wortfelddiskussion. Untersuchungen zur Gliederung des Wortfeldes 'alt -jung- neu' im heutigen Französisch* (Munich: Fink, 1971); idem, *Strukturelle Semantik des Französischen* (Tübingen: Niemeyer, 1973); idem (ed.), *Strukturelle Bedeutungslehre* (Darmstadt: Wissenschaftliche Buchgesellschaft, 1978), which includes the approach, unfortunately not yet further developed, by Eugenio Coseriu, 'Für eine strukturelle diachrone Semantik', in Geckeler (1978), 91–163; Horst Geckeler, 'Progrès et stagnation en sémantique structurale', in idem et al. (eds), *Logos semantikos* (Berlin: de Gruyter, 1981), 53–69.

49   As a selection, the following preparatory works of Ulrich Ricken shall be mentioned: 'Bemerkungen zu Struktur und Funktion des sozialen Wortschatzes in der französischen Literatur', *Wissenschaftliche Zeitschrift der M. Luther-Universität Halle-Wittenberg*, G 19 (1970), 9–35; Regarding 'nouveau' as a social term in L.-S. Mercier, ibid., 119–25; Semantic opposition as expression of societal contradictions, in ibid., G 24 (1975), 43–63; 'Le vocabulaire de la classification sociale dans la littérature française', *Langue française*, 9 (1971), 100–9; 'Oppositions et polarités d'un champ notionnel. Les philosophes et le despotism éclairé', *Annales historiques de la Révolution française*, 51 (1979), 547–57. As Ulrich Ricken prepares a systematic study about the vocabulary of descriptions of societies in the eighteenth century, a division of labour within our project presented itself here as well. [Note: Ulrich Ricken's study has since been published as *Linguistics, Anthropology and Philosophy in the French Enlightenment. Language Theory and Ideology* (London: Routledge, 1994).]

50   See note 52 below and the related methodological suggestions.

51   [Note: Roger Chartier, 'Civilité', in Rolf Reichardt and Eberhard Schmitt (eds), *Handbuch politisch-sozialer Grundbegriffe in Frankreich: 1680–1820*, vol. 4 (Munich: Oldenbourg, 1986), 7–50.]

52   Karlheinz Stierle, 'Historische Semantik und die Geschichtlichkeit der
     Bedeutung', in Koselleck (1979a), 154–89, esp. 163ff.

53   Substantiated and tested more thoroughly in Hans-Jürgen Lüsebrink and
     Rolf Reichardt, 'La "Bastille" dans l'imaginaire social de la France à la fin
     du XVIIIe siècle, 1774–1799', *Revue d'histoire modern et contemporaine*,
     30 (1983), 196–234; Rolf Reichardt, 'Zur Geschichte politisch-sozialer
     Begriffe in Frankreich zwischen Absolutismus und Restauration',
     Zeitschrift für Literaturwissenschaft und Linguistik, 47 (1983), 49–74.

54   Recreated from Rolf Reichardt, 'Einleitung, III – Für eine
     sozialhistorische Semantik als Mittelweg zwischen "Lexikometrie" und
     "Begriffsgeschichte"', in Reichardt and Schmitt (1985), 85.

55   Lothar Schmidt (ed.), *Wortfeldforschung* (Darmstadt: Wissenschaftliche
     Buchgesellschaft, 1973).

Part II

Challenges

Dietrich Busse is a German linguist and political scientist. He received his PhD in linguistics in 1984 after studying philosophy, linguistics, German, sociology and political science. Busse has held a professorship in German linguistics at the University of Düsseldorf, Germany since 2001. His main fields of research include historical semantics, language theory, textual linguistics, speech comprehension, linguistic use, discourse analysis and epistemology as well as legal linguistics.

Busse's publications include *Historische Semantik: Analyse eines Programms* (1987; 'Historical Semantics: Analysis of a Programme'), *Juristische Semantik: Grundfragen der juristischen Interpretationstheorie in sprachwissenschaftlicher Sicht* (1993; 'Legal Semantics: Fundamental Questions of Theory of Legal Interpretation from a Linguistic Perspective') and *Frame-Semantik: Ein Kompendium* (2012; 'Frame-semantics: A Compendium').

In the text presented here, Dietrich Busse analyses the relationship between conceptual history and the history of discourse. Originally published soon after the completion of Reinhart Koselleck's *Geschichtliche Grundbegriffe*, it reflects upon developments in conceptual history and linguistics in post-war Germany. He criticizes the balance between language and social history that had been so important to Koselleck and argues for its reconceptualization in light of the linguistic turn, thus emphasizing the constructive character of language.

4

Conceptual History or a History of Discourse? On the Theoretical Basis and Questions of Methodology of a Historical-Semantic Epistemology

Dietrich Busse

Chapter Outline

(1) Introductory Remarks

'Conceptual history or a history of discourse' – this formulation expresses an opposition that is often evoked but is essentially not entirely justifiable, and one which is ultimately only apparent. If, after twenty years of discussing the necessity, basis and methodological problems of discourse-historical research, such clarification is still required, may I draw attention to the more specific subtitle of this article. I would like to address in the following the theoretical basis and certain methodological issues around what I would describe today (perhaps more clearly than before) as a historical-semantic epistemology. The intentions of the concept[1] of historical semantics I propose[2] would be misconstrued if the 'or' in the title of my paper were to be understood as an exclusive 'or'. But it is not actually a matter of opposition. Rather (as I have repeatedly emphasized in the past also, although this has not always been heeded), it suggests a development and broadening of the methodological spectrum – not of the objectives! – of historical semantics.

I would like to develop my reflections on the basis and methodological problems of a historical-semantic epistemology in four steps. Following a brief explanation of the motives and objectives I associate with historical semantics, I would like to discuss, in the second step, the opportunities and limitations of conceptual history as a starting point for all subsequent approaches to historical semantics. In the third step I shall explain in detail the objectives and methods of an epistemologically oriented discourse analysis. Finally, I would like to consider how basic discourse-semantic paradigms function. I will illustrate this with the paradigm of 'the self and the other'.

(2) Motives and Objectives of Historical Semantics

The 'archaeology' (freely adapted from Foucault) of my own exploration of key questions of historical semantics revealed something that was surprising even to me when I discovered it – the first draft of my project later published under the title 'Historical Semantics' had borne the title 'Systems of Meaning'. This heading clearly sought to describe a semantics that was to be liberated from the constraints of the kind of narrowly defined lexical semantics that dominated the linguistic mainstream in the seventies. It was to be a 'rich' semantics that would overcome the methodological barriers of an isolated study of the meanings of individual words and of a reductionist componential semantics. It therefore had to be programmatically and theoretically formulated, and prevail, *against* the major linguistic-semantic trends. (A certain argumentative acerbity towards conceptual history in my earlier studies on historical semantics may occasionally have been the cause of some confusion. It doubtless stemmed from my concern that conceptual history might, despite its epistemological interests, revert to the constraints of an isolated concept of the meaning of words and thus obstruct important opportunities for the acquisition of epistemological knowledge.[3]) Although this polarity still applies to large areas of linguistic semantic research, the current state of the debate on semantic theory also suggests surprising points of contact between the goal I had over twenty years ago of analysing 'systems of meaning' and today's linguistic avant-garde. It appears that a direct link can be made to the analysis of 'semantic networks' and 'frames of knowledge' in contemporary cognitive semantics. The latter likewise (with different motives) advocates the concept of a 'rich' semantics that goes beyond componential analysis and the lexical semantic constraints of traditional linguistics.[4]

The analysis of 'semantic networks' and 'frames of knowledge' in contemporary cognitive semantics seeks to reconstruct the synchronic cognitive landscape of individuals or speech communities in order to implement or reproduce natural language processes on computing machines. By contrast, my reflections regarding the analysis of 'systems of meaning', with which my exploration of questions around historical semantics began, was from the outset *diachronic* in orientation, that is, socio-historically and historico-culturally motivated. In short, they were and are oriented towards an *historical* epistemology, a history of knowledge and consciousness that lays bare the representation of the social knowledge of an era in its genesis, its constituting conditions, its historico-cultural traditions and its epistemic undercurrents.

Theoretical connections appeared helpful in realizing this objective. They made it possible to interpret social semantics as the constitution of reality through language and to see in the epistemic conditions and networks the foundations of a contingent social consciousness of reality. An historical epistemology founded on (linguistic) semantics was to be framed by four areas of theoretical reflection. The first pertained to the general theoretical basis of an (historical) epistemology, whose frame of reference was provided by the uneasy triumvirate of Humboldt–Wittgenstein–Foucault. Wilhelm von Humboldt's theory of language seemed to me highly relevant with regard to the close interrelationship between linguistic and philosophical (epistemological and other) questions, and in particular with regard to the close connection between language and the constitution of reality. In my view, this made Humboldt one of the founding fathers of a semantically grounded epistemology. ('The word, which first makes an individual of the concept in the world of thought, will always add something more of its own significance, and while the idea gains shape through this, it is also at the same time kept restrained within certain bounds.'[5]) Wittgenstein II[6] provided the tools of philosophical theory that made it possible to explain the interplay of the constitution, transmission and changes of meaning with his concept of meaning, his language-game and rule model, and his concept of life-form. Finally, Foucault's discourse analysis created the link between the underlying theoretical philosophical questions and the specific historical and empirical localization of an historical epistemology, and called attention (as did the other two authors, albeit much more obliquely) to aspects of epistemic-semantic predispositions pertaining to the analytics of power.

The second area I touched upon at that time concerned the sociological foundations of an historical epistemology, the influence of the public sphere on the development of social semantics, and the public sphere as a space of signification and of the emergence and development of social knowledge.[7] The third theoretical area concerns the theory of language underlying historical semantics in the narrower sense. (By 'historical semantics' I meant and mean both the empirical description *and* the theoretical underpinnings of the explanation of semantic change.) This linguistic foundation of historical semantics was built on a concept of language deriving from action theory.[8] Its key aim was to clarify the following central problems of the theory of language:

1 The explanation of the conditions and functioning of the *constitution* of signification (i.e. meaning conveyed through language).
2 The explanation of the conditions and functioning of the *transmission* or handing down of signification (i.e. meaning conveyed through language).
3 The explanation of the conditions and functioning of *changes* (*shifts*) in signification (i.e. meaning conveyed through language), also and especially in the sense of *changing systems of meaning*.

Incidentally, the above-mentioned first draft of an analysis of systems of meaning did not include any reference to the objectives, programme or methodology of a conceptual history (for instance in the Koselleckian sense). However, (having been suggested[9]), it proved extraordinarily fruitful. In Koselleck's programme of 'Fundamental Concepts in History', I discovered an aspiration to a semantically grounded historical epistemology which bore a close affinity to my own reflections. The orientation expressed therein towards 'concepts' as theoretical and methodological touchstones of semantic analysis did, admittedly, pose a certain problem from my point of view. However, I wish to touch upon these problems only briefly at this point.[10]

(3) Conceptual History as a Starting Point for Historical-semantic Epistemology: Opportunities and Limitations

Even if it follows a programme as ambitious as the one developed for the 'Fundamental Concepts in History', conceptual history is only one of a number of ways in which historical semantics can be, and has been, conducted. Other common methods include

1 Traditional *lexical history* (rooted in etymology).
2 The standard *historical lexical semantics*, as conducted for instance in the context of historical lexicography.
3 The *history of ideas*, in philosophy and historiography, including the traditional *epistemology* from which Foucault so vehemently distanced his programme of discourse analysis. The history of ideas can be interpreted as an historical semantics *avant la lettre* in some of its aims and methods, if not in what it claims to represent.
4 Semantic tools can also be found in all *histories of consciousness*, for example as the history of everyday consciousness and of *mentalities* or as the *history of cultural memory*. These research approaches are often concerned precisely with the historically specific conditions of the constitution of social reality and awareness of reality.

5 Historical semantics then also includes *political speech analysis* and language criticism, which are concerned with uncovering the ideological tools of public language usage.

6 And, finally, there is the integrative approach of a *history of discourse*, involving, among other things, the analysis of discursive mechanisms and their thematic, textual and semantic expression – as a contribution to a semantically grounded historical epistemology in the post-Foucauldian sense.

Frequently, too little attention is paid to the specifics of what each of these disciplines hopes to achieve and the consequent need for theoretical groundwork *and* methodology *and* the practice of historical-semantic empiricism. These are all legitimate objectives in and of themselves, which may have a common underlying theory of language but *certainly cannot* share a single methodology and empirical practice. This means that there is not, and cannot be, a *single* historical semantics. Rather, there is at best a spectrum of partially overlapping, partially mutually exclusive aspects and perspectives.

Any semantic analysis that begins with a single sign or word and thinks it possible to have an isolated lexical semantics is, from an epistemological or depth semantic point of view, a kind of tip-of-the-iceberg semantics. This is because it leaves unexplained, ignores, or at best assumes to be obvious everyday knowledge – thus dismissing as uninteresting (for further study or semantic explication) – 80–90 per cent of the knowledge required to completely actualize the meaning of a word in the given context. When historical semantics are methodically justified as *conceptual* history, a linguistically motivated conception of depth semantics initially runs into problems for the chief reason that, in the context of the theoretical tradition of linguistics, the term 'concept' is intimately connected with an isolating, reductionist lexical semantics. This is not only true of the Fregean or Carnapian logical semantics, which are still influential today and clearly informed by the theory of concepts.[11] It is also true of the only analysis concept to have emerged to date out of linguistics itself, namely the structurally motivated feature semantics (or componential semantics). With its atomistic concept of features, which it shares with logical semantics, it draws on ideas at the root of the theory of concepts (with highly problematic ontological implications). This semantics based on the theory of concepts is sometimes dubbed the 'NSC concept' (i.e. 'concept of necessary and sufficient conditions') in the current discussion on semantic theory. Viewed from the perspective of an epistemologically motivated 'rich' semantics, it is tantamount to a reductionism of enormous proportions. Among other things, it ignores the very aspects that are of greatest interest with regard to the history of knowledge in the semantics of (elementary or more complex) verbal expressions.

There has, of course, never been any suggestion that the concept of conceptual history advocated by Reinhart Koselleck and others had anything to do with this reductionism based on the theory of concepts that is found in the linguistic-semantic mainstream. The epistemological perspective of their historiographical approach is enough to preclude this. But perhaps it explains a certain reluctance towards any positive adaption of the concept-concept and its application in the context of the historical-semantic analysis of 'systems of meaning' that I have in mind. Incidentally, and purely for the sake of completeness, I may mention that the concept-concept (concept semantics) is experiencing a renaissance in the context of cognitive semantics. In this incarnation, which deals with the analysis of semantic networks and systems of frames of knowledge, it is much more compatible with the objectives of an epistemologically motivated, 'rich' semantics than the reductionist semantic models of the intermediate linguistic-semantic phase in the 60s, 70s and 80s.[12]

I also believe I have a better understanding (than I did twenty years ago) of the motives behind Koselleck's formulation of his concept of conceptual history; and my impression, with all due respect, is that these motives have only partially been realized in the majority of the articles as they stand in the 'Fundamental Concepts in History'. Koselleck was and is concerned, I believe, with nothing more nor less than a cabinet of curiosities, a typology of concepts as *movens*, as agents of the historical process. His version of conceptual history is historical and historiographical in the complete, best sense because it seeks to analyse concepts as individuals, as it were, as driving forces in the historical process. Accordingly, concepts for Koselleck are epistemic entities that are not tied to individual words and their meanings, despite the fact that they can be named and identified with key words and often obtain their function as drivers of history precisely through this blatant, propagandistic identifiability.

In contrast to such a narrative – if I may call it this – of an animate, animated, and dynamic world of concepts, the sober perspective of an analytical linguistic approach comes across as the pure description of historical-epistemic conditions of possibility. It retains the scepticism expressed by Peter von Polenz in his concept of sentence semantic analysis towards any kind of 'agentification' of abstractive epistemic or linguistic entities, whether these be concepts, key words or discourses.[13]

Conceptual history and linguistically founded discourse analysis unquestionably share the same historical-epistemic objectives. Both, I believe, are equally concerned with the analysis of *systematic* connections in historical semantics. Strictly speaking, no historical discourse analysis can get by without Koselleckian conceptual history. But it is prepared to go further, shifting emphases, according in particular a greater role to networking, to the necessity of certain conditions, and to the discursive mechanisms that exert a profound and long-term influence. To use a central concept of Foucault's, there is a greater emphasis on the conditions of possibility, the historical a priori of epistemes in their particular historical form. Thus there is no absolute opposition between conceptual history and the history of discourse in either theory or methodology. Rather, they can perhaps be understood as different perspectives on a common theme in view of their comparable objectives.

A historical-semantic discourse analysis can make use of approaches and methods from conceptual history, just as it makes use of other traditional methods. These may be methods from lexical semantics and textual semantics (for instance by using the fruitful and hitherto under-exploited concept of isotopy from structuralist semantics). They may be methods used in sentence semantics, including aspects relating to speech act theory or methods from cognitive semantics such as the analysis of frames of knowledge and semantic networks. Finally, approaches taken from Toulminian argument analysis, from topology, presupposition analysis or political symbol analysis may also be fruitfully applied in the method system employed by discourse analysis.

(4) Objectives and Methods of an Epistemologically Oriented Discourse Semantics

In the following I would like to briefly outline a few objectives and procedures that characterize historical-semantic discourse analysis as a contribution to an historical epistemology. The programme I have formulated of an historical discourse semantics[14] borrows loosely from Foucault's discourse theory. Unlike a number of other advocates of discourse analysis, particular in Germany, I do not interpret this exclusively as ideology critique but as a descriptive project, similar to the way in which discourse analysis was applied to the methodology of linguistic analysis[15] by Michel Pêcheux and others.[16] The most important thing in our context is that Foucault regarded his discourse analysis as a *genealogy*, as the analysis of the genesis and conditions of social knowledge in discursive formations.

I consider the following elements of the Foucauldian concept of discourse[17] useful for the purposes of an historical-semantic epistemology.

Foucault's discourse model is based on the concept of the *énoncé*, the statement. He defines *discourse* as *a group of statements that belong to a single system of formation*. It is important to him that statements not be equated with utterances (*énonciations*). Statements (as *énoncés*) are abstract entities that can appear in different linguistic forms and are not necessarily tied to a particular form of verbal expression. (From this point of view, Foucault's *énoncé* could be compared to the concept of *proposition* in logical sentence semantics, which is also used in modern cognitive linguistics.) However, if we want to avoid too strong and too problematic a proximity between the level of statements in the Foucauldian sense and, for instance, Plato's 'heaven of ideas' or Frege's 'third realm of thoughts', we should speak not of 'statements' but of 'segments of knowledge' that can be articulated in different verbal forms.

Accordingly, discourses are systems of formation consisting of segments of knowledge, which, Foucault stresses, govern the conditions of possibility of the production of certain utterances. Thus, for Foucault, discourses are an epistemically effective 'historical a priori' that governs the production, occurrence, formation of series, formation and force of statements. Foucault's definition of discourse in the 'Order of Discourse' as the space between thought and speech is now famous. In this space, it is above all the discursive mechanisms that are at work. These may function as mechanisms of exclusion, as mechanisms of production constraints on discursive events, as structuring mechanisms of epistemes, or as systems of knowledge formation.

Foucault names the four concepts *event, series, regularity* and *condition of possibility* as the basic terms of discourse analysis. The concept of event refers to the spontaneous and often unforeseeable occurrence of an epistemic element in an utterance, a text, etc. This epistemic element (*énoncé* in Foucault's terminology) does not have to be absolutely new (and in fact rarely is); its unforeseen occurrence in a new discursive environment is enough to establish its character as an event. When such events occur more frequently, they form series and become the nuclei of discursive formations. New discursive structures are established when series of discursive events aggregate into regularities. Once established as systems of regularities, these discursive formations or structures act as conditions of possibility of the production of future, thematically related discursive events. They govern not only the actual occurrence but the very possibility of individual epistemic elements occurring in specific contexts. Foucault, then, also understands discourses as 'systems of dispersion' of statements. Thus discourse analysis examines discursive events in a field of knowledge, paying particular attention to the conditions of the occurrence of individual epistemic elements in given epistemic-discursive contexts. Discourses are shown to be regulated and discreet series of discursive events, the analysis of which is chiefly concerned with the identification of regularities. The analysis of these is, in Foucault's words, to ascertain 'how it is that a particular statement has appeared (at a given point) and no other in its place'.[18]

Following Foucault, discourse analysis was developed into a methodological apparatus by the prematurely deceased Michel Pêcheux and his colleagues, among others. (A fruitful approach, particularly for language-related discourse-analytical objectives, that has found little resonance in Germany thus far.) In Pêcheux's words, discourses become 'readable sequences of signs (indices), that form a corpus of socio-historical (one might add: epistemic) traces'.[19] The collective memory, the social episteme, is understood as a social body of traces that it is the job of discourse analysis to expose. Discourses are then able to be analysed as 'networks of signs, traces and trails'. A central characteristic of discourse analysis that Pêcheux particularly emphasizes is that it makes it possible to understand discursive relationships 'as the same thing that is repeated as such through all possible differences'. The inevitable conclusion, then, is that for the purposes of historical epistemology we should not be distracted by the superficial thematic and semantic level, that is, by the all too obvious textual structures of the underlying text corpora, from the differences in what appears to be the same and for what remains the same across all apparent distinctions. As Pêcheux's team demonstrated, the analysis of what appear to be counter-discourses (e.g. a 'right-wing' and a 'left-wing' discourse on a particular political subject) is particularly useful in identifying underlying discursive paradigms and similarities where a superficial, ideology-driven approach may not have suspected them.

My suggested exploitation of discourse analysis for the purposes of an historical-semantic epistemology was and is subject to some criticism. The most vehement is usually from the perspective of the guardians of a sacrosanct discourse analysis that is supposedly 'true' by virtue of its ideology critique. Its champions clearly take umbrage at the descriptive use of discourse analysis based on the Foucauldian model[20] and the association of 'exalted' post-structuralist approaches with 'vulgar' linguistic analytical ones. They may feel vindicated by Foucault himself, who has left us a long list of negative definitions telling us what he believes discourse analysis should *not* be: it is not lexical history, not conceptual history, not semantics, not the history of ideas, not the history of mentalities, not epistemology in the traditional sense. Discourse analysis should be none of these, but should rather inhabit a space *between* and *before* these by deciphering historical a prioris, the conditions of possibility and the genealogy of meanings, concepts, ideas, mentalities and epistemes. If, despite this, I lay claim to discourse analysis for an epistemologically oriented historical semantics, I appeal to Foucault himself, who once described his work in an interview as a box of tools to which anyone could help themselves.

In summary, I believe that the discourse analytical approach has the following advantages for an epistemologically oriented historical semantics: Any language-theoretic foundation of historical semantics which – as I have indicated – is to explain the processes of semantic change and of the constitution and the constancy or transmission of meaning, must also be able to explain how social knowledge influences the constitution and change of lexical and textual meanings. For the research objectives of historical semantics, it seems clear to me that the spectrum of semantically relevant knowledge must be widened, that a greater amount and broader scope of epistemic conditions of the textual constitution of meaning must be included in the analysis, than the narrow concept of meaning in traditional linguistic semantics would suggest. I am also speaking here of the field of *semantically relevant* or *comprehension-related knowledge* that has to be explained in a complete semantic analysis. This kind of 'rich' semantics or 'depth semantics' cannot limit itself to elucidating the 'obvious', as it were, epistemic elements of lexical and textual meanings. It must also explain the underlying, hidden knowledge that is normally overlooked because it is considered self-evident. This analysis also includes the elucidation of epistemic elements transported or insinuated in verbal utterances and of whose presence the speakers and recipients of the texts may not even be consciously aware. Any depth semantics, be it conceived as lexical semantics, conceptual history, sentence semantics, textual analysis or discourse analysis, requires this knowledge pertaining to the constitution of meaning to be made explicit. If such a depth semantics is now to make a contribution – and this applies to all varieties of historical semantics – to an analysis of epistemic conditions, tendencies, and the formation systems of semantically relevant knowledge, it must consider it its duty to make explicit and to describe such presupposed knowledge in its influence on the linguistic constitution of meaning.

The concept of discourse is *one* potential instrument that can be useful in drawing attention to the kind of epistemic elements that are often all but ignored in traditional semantic analyses. Clearly, then, the concept of discourse initially serves to shift the focus and attention of historical semantics in a new and specific way. I believe it can draw attention to things that other historical semantic approaches (whether conceptual history, the history of mentalities, etc.) fail to notice. This alternative historical-semantic focus can help, for instance, to explain epistemic conditions that would have been overlooked from other perspectives. Thus the overly rigorous focus on abstract nouns (or key words – even if they are only taken as headings for epistemic complexes) can sometimes blind us to the presence of textual elements pertaining to the constitution of concepts in which the antecedent is omitted entirely. (I have endeavoured to demonstrate this with examples for the conception of nation.[21])

Moreover, a discourse-analytical perspective can be better suited to drawing attention to the formation systems and conditions of semantically relevant knowledge. I often refer here to Wittgenstein's metaphor of the river-bed of thoughts. From a short-sighted, ahistorical point of view, the river-bed can easily be misconstrued as that which is absolutely immutable, fixed, given, whereas it can actually change, is historically constituted and hence contingent (Wittgenstein is thinking here of Western logic, for instance).[22] Foucault speaks in this context of the historical a priori that has a genealogy but often appears to discourse-dependent individuals as that which is simply given and to be accepted. It is my firm belief that analysis of the knowledge that is unreflected, unarticulated, taken for granted and consequently not addressed, despite its capacity to structure discourse, must be central to any historical semantics aspiring to make a serious contribution to an historical epistemology.

Finally – and Foucault stressed this time and again – a discourse-analytical perspective directs our attention to different source material from traditional conceptual history. Rolf Reichardt spoke out particular strongly in favour of this aspect in his methodological suggestions on historical semantics. Suffice it to recall the dictum concerning 'classic' literature as the source base of some conceptual history analysis. This is contrasted from a discourse-analytical perspective with an expanded source base featuring a strong emphasis on everyday texts.[23]

In the context of an epistemology proceeding along historical-semantic lines, discourse analysis need not entail a complete shift of focus to the micro-semantic level of corpus analysis. It requires rather a macro-semantic reorientation with regard to focus, selection of corpora and epistemic-semantic analysis. Its methodological value and its autonomy may consist chiefly in its formulation of a research strategy that is at once macro-semantic and depth-semantic. It does not stop where what is known anyway or tacitly considered self-evident is usually passed over and ignored as being irrelevant for semantic analysis. Rather, it begins precisely with the epistemic conditions of the linguistic constitution of meaning and focuses more heavily on the conditions that make the utterable and conceivable possible at all at a given point in time.

I once described historical semantics as a 'regulated transformation of meaning for others into meaning for us'.[24] A history of discourse is obviously equally entangled in the hermeneutic dilemma that it is only ever possible to explain those elements of the stocks of knowledge of past epochs and discourse formations that are thinkable and utterable against the backdrop of our own epistemes. The scepticism of historical semantics overall (and of semantics and textual analysis in general) with regard to methodology and the philosophy of science is therefore equally applicable to the discourse-historical approach. Even an inquiry made keener by the concept of discourse cannot prevent the fact that any selection of material, of cross-references, of key words, themes, figures of discourse and perspectives, will inevitably exclude other aspects. We cannot, therefore, expect of a discourse-analytical historical semantics and epistemology that it explain the *entire* network of epistemic references in which a text, a concept, an *énoncé* are embedded. Discourse analysis simply means tracing certain specific strands of knowledge in all manner of texts, text-types, fields of articulation and discourse, that is, undertaking to focus thematically on series of individual *énoncés*, individual epistemic elements. And so discourse analysis must also make a selection, guided by thematic guidelines but based on the fundamental methodological idea of a 'loosely-defined corpus that broadens during the research process'.[25] The purpose of discourse analysis can perhaps be aptly characterized by a citation from

Foucault: 'There is no knowledge without a particular discursive practice; and any discursive practice may be defined by the knowledge that it forms.'[26]

(5) 'The Self and the Other' – Aspects of a Discourse-semantic Paradigm

Finally, I would like to suggest the direction discourse-historical analysis can take, using the discourse-semantic paradigm of 'the self and the other' as an example.[27] I shall begin by outlining briefly what I mean by a *discourse-semantic paradigm* – something which can play a crucial role as the subject of a discourse-semantic analysis. One distinguishing feature of discourses is the recurrence of certain content elements in the texts attributable to them; another is that content elements aggregated into regularities are reflected in the texts that constitute (or contribute to) the corpus of individual discourses. This assumes that texts (and their components) are not original products formed ab ovo, as it were, by the intentionality of the producer – as an old preconception of language theory (and probably also everyday life) would have it. Rather, they use elements that are a part of the epistemic-cognitive make-up of the text producers or have been picked up ad hoc by them from previous texts. The rhetorical tradition provides a number of expressions such as 'rhetorical devices', 'topoi', etc. for some of these phenomena. Rather than proposing a topic in this traditional sense (as has been called for recently, for instance in the field of legal argumentation), I prefer to speak heuristically of *discourse-semantic paradigms*. Topoi tend to be static, are generally viewed as constituting a thesaurus, and are located at the level of 'surface semantics'. By contrast, discourse-semantic paradigms tend to concern the 'depths' of textual semantics (which are often hidden and only communicated via additional analysis operations). They can also become apparent (to the eye and ear of the knowing observer) where the 'producers' and 'recipients' of the text in question have no knowledge yet of their existence. While they are not completely removed from the speaker's volition, they often reveal themselves involuntarily. In doing so they also reveal specific traits of the text producer or rather his or her thought. Discursive paradigms do sometimes rise to the surface of the discourse and become the explicit subject or theme of texts, and we could perhaps go so far as to suggest that this temporary explicitness is a necessary condition of their (initial?) occurrence and their structural efficacy. But their normal efficacy is generally such that their existence does explain the appearance of certain discursive elements, but these elements do not make it particularly apparent that the discursive paradigms are a part of the explicit textual meaning at the superficial level.

Discursive paradigms order textual elements, govern their occurrence at certain points in the discourse, and give the discourse an inner structure. This structure may not be identical to the thematic structure of the texts in which they appear. They form a pattern that can function in turn as the basic structure of interdiscursive epistemic connections. In this sense, discursive paradigms are not necessarily bound to a particular discourse or limited to one individual discourse, but can emerge in multiple discourses at the same time. In this way they contribute to interdiscursive relationships that perhaps correspond at the discourse level to what have been studied as intertextual relationships at the textual level in text linguistics. And so, discursive paradigms have a history that is not necessarily limited to the time period and occurrence of the actual reference discourse (of the analysis). On the contrary, the appeal of the discourse-analytical perspective stems precisely from the fact that some discursive tendencies and paradigms have an historical-epistemic dimension that was initially (and from the surface semantic perspective) quite unsuspected.

The concrete form that discursive paradigms take in a discourse is not of immediate importance.

1 They may appear as semantic features and form historical isotopic chains.[28]
2 From an argument analysis perspective, they may be among the supporting elements of a text-based deduction rule.[29]
3 They may be linguistic pragmatic presuppositions or parts of what is implied and has to be deduced by inference.[30]
4 They may be hidden behind names or persons, things, circumstances or complexes of thoughts that are referred to.
5 And, finally, they may of course also be part of the superficial (lexical) meaning of words, concepts and texts in which they operate, whether noticed or unnoticed.

The standard methods of lexical semantics, concept analysis or textual analysis are often not sufficient to determine such discursive paradigms. For instance, they do not necessarily have to be expressed in 'abstract nouns' (as per the old distinction made in semantic theory between *autosemantica* and *synsemantica*), but can also be contained in the textual semantic function of what are known as 'function words' (*synsemantica*). This is illustrated in the discourse-semantic paradigm 'the self and the other' with the personal pronouns *we* and *they*. These can be seen as codes for an elementary discursive figure and are clearly used in this function in many texts.

What I am looking at with the following text example cannot be addressed with the methods of lexical semantics or concept analysis nor with the traditional methods of sentence semantics or textual semantics. I am interested here in epistemic elements of an emerging discourse. These could perhaps best be apprehended using the methods of the analysis of frames of knowledge from more recent cognitive semantics or indeed with the viewpoint and approach of an historical-epistemological discourse analysis. The function and situating of the text example are exemplary in this respect. In the nineteenth and early twentieth centuries, the politicization of the *collective self* achieved a scope and a dynamic that grew in proportion with the de-individualizing tendencies of modern mass societies. Much has been said about these socio-historical connections and it is not my intention to address them again here. What we are concerned with in our discourse-analytical context is how the paradigm of *self and other* comes into play here and is defined and canonized in the nineteenth century in a manner so explicit as to be almost inconceivable from today's historical point of view (following National Socialism and all it entailed).

My example illustrates the attempt to discursively establish a *collective ego* in such a way that this collective ego is to be founded on the discursive construct of a *collective self*, which is based in turn on an emotional, cultural-value-based dissociation from the other. What is key here is that this dissociation from the other, which is required for the formation of an identity as a *collective* ego, borrows conspicuously from the psycho-social make-up of the *individual* ego and the qualities it perceives in or attributes to itself. The discursive and psycho-social trajectory of this discourse paradigm could perhaps be described as follows: from the *individual self* to the *collective self* to the *collective ego* and on to the *individual ego*. (The *individual ego* is of course a *collectivized individual ego*, i.e. an ego that defines itself chiefly or exclusively via the qualities and attitudes of the *collective ego*.)

I would like to illustrate this with a text that is emblematic of the formation of a collective identity for nineteenth-century Germans, the novel 'Debit and Credit' by Gustav Freytag (published in 1855 and frequently reprinted in large numbers until the mid-twentieth century).[31] This novel brings together every aspect of the specifically German national discourse in a quite remarkable manner. It could perhaps be described as the quintessential novel of Germanness. Alongside the central theme of the social and economic emancipation of the middle classes (though they never cherish any democratic ambitions), the novel also contains a good deal of subtly administered anti-Semitism and cultural chauvinism, mainly directed towards the East. The novel is therefore a typical liminal text, that is, the author has situated the plot in the archetypal and paradigmatic situation of the dissociation of the self from the other. The collective self becomes more clearly defined as it distances itself further from the collective other. The self (i.e. the formation of a collective identity) and the other (here, in the form of the neighbouring Polish nation) determine each other. They define themselves by carefully drawing a precise line between their respective characteristics (which the author portrays as archetypal).

The novel's hero, Anton Wohlfahrt, explains to his cosmopolitan friend Fink why he, the merchant, intends to defend and preserve a nobleman's estate in the Polish countryside under Prussian occupation from the attacks of a Polish freedom fighter. He is proud of the German character, of the superiority of German culture, which he cites as justification: 'Culture, industry, and credit are on our side', in other words, 'German intelligence'. All of this gives him the right, he believes, 'as one of the conquerors . . . , in the behalf of free labor and civilization, [to usurp] the dominion of the country from a weaker race'. Everything Polish is portrayed negatively. The soil is 'neglected', the stable 'miserable' and the women 'dirty'. The men failed to 'inspire any confidence', the cattle are 'a poor set', the buildings 'cheerless' and the living quarters 'wretched'. By contrast, everything German is portrayed positively – and as typically German: the roof has been 'mended', a small garden dug, the child is blond and well-behaved, the woman neat and orderly, the man young and handsome, the room comfortable, coffee simmers on the stove, and of course there is a song-book and a rod, as symbols of German propriety and discipline. The passage ends with the exclamation: ' "This farm is the jewel of the estate," cried Karl . . . "There are actually signs of a dunghill here . . . And there is a myrtle in the window. Hurra! here is a *housewife*! here is the *fatherland*! here are *Germans*!" '[32]

The passage culminates in the revealing cry of the (fictitious!) protagonist, ' . . . now *we* have come into being, and a new German nation has arisen'.[33] We could replace the personal pronoun *we* with: '*now the (collective) We has come into being* . . . '! In this novel, then, the author invests the collective self with concrete features. An abstract rhetorical device becomes an idea with flesh and blood, which everyone who considers themselves a part of this collective We can then identify. The particular impact of the novel's discursive trajectory lies, on the one hand, in the fact that specific content that characterizes (or is intended to characterize) the collective self as opposed to the collective other is presented (fictionally) in the form of oppositions to concrete, existing others. It also lies in the fact that epistemic-ideological elements of the establishment of a collective identity are conveyed in this way, and made available for other discursive applications, to the novel's recipients. This includes recipients of the text and of the models for collective identification contained therein (supplied by the author) who have no genuine individual experience of the (fictionally) evoked, concrete 'other' and its (alleged) collective-other qualities.

What makes this nineteenth century text so unique is that it explicitly articulates what would generally be only implicitly conveyed (or presupposed) in modern texts. The paradigm of the self and the other is introduced into the narrative universe in a more or less definitional discursive act:

> He who has always trodden life's macadamized ways, hedged in by law, moulded by order, custom, form, handed down from generation to generation habits a thousand years old, and who finds himself suddenly thrown among *strangers*, where law can but imperfectly protect him, and where he must assert by daily struggles his right to exist – such a one realizes for the first time the full blessing of the *holy circle* woven round each *individual* by his *fellow-men*, his *family*, his *companions in labor*, his *race*, his *country*. Whether he lose or gain in *foreign parts*, he must needs [sic] change. If he is a weakling, he will sacrifice *his own manière d'être* to the *external influences* around him; if he has the making of a man in him, he will become one now. The possessions, perhaps the prejudices, that he has grown up with, will wax dearer to him than ever; and much that once he looked upon as things of course, like air and sunshine, will become his most prized treasures. It is in *foreign countries* that we first enjoy the *dialect of home*, and in *absence* that we learn how dear to us is our *fatherland*.[34]

The opposition between self and other is systematically established and extrapolated from the individual self to the collective self. Expressions such as *Heimat* in the original German (which conveys the idea of *home* or *homeland*), *holy circle*, and *fellow-men* function as links between the individual and the collective ego. This transition is systematically developed in the archetypal sequence *individual-family-companions in labor-race-country*. The individual's perception of him or herself is redefined collectively in expressions such as *his own manière d'être*. And, finally, the closing sentence expresses particularly well how the individually felt self has to become an abstract identification of the individual with his or her collective ego, presented here as *fatherland* but actually – and this is typically German – meaning *country*. The self is identified with the familiar and comforting *dialect of home* that envelops one in one's everyday life in a cocoon of self-related aspects of life and of one's own psycho-social situation. This allows it to function as a symbol for the collective self, which is presented here – ideologized and politicized as *fatherland* – as a greater, more all-embracing self, in which the individual can feel just as safe and secure as in his or her immediate experience of everyday life in the bosom of the *family*.

The quotations from the novel cited here reveal a way in which the discursive paradigm of the self and the other functions that is typical of the nineteenth century and indeed perhaps also illustrates a basic characteristic of how this paradigm operates. I am referring to the fact that the discursively founded collective identity (and hence the collective self as the actual content of a collective self-image) represents a negative image of the discursively postulated attributes of the collective other. This means that the collective self is the converse (negative) identity of the collective other. In this sense, the collective self is precisely what the discursively postulated collective other is not, or, to turn it around: it is (allegedly) not that which allegedly particularly distinguishes the collective other. Thus the self is only defined through the aid of the other, without which it would not only not be as it is but would arguably not be at all.

(6) Options, Opportunities and Limitations of Discourse-semantic Research

The historical discourse semantics I propose is situated (as is conceptual-history-related historical semantics) within the spectrum of historical epistemology. It is both descriptive and analytical in approach, without excluding outright the critical examination of discursive structures. Description and analysis are not, however, disparaged as the mere positivistic duplication of data (as some would evidently have it). Rather, semantic discourse analysis is founded on the belief that description and analysis are intrinsically linked in epistemological contexts, and that the convincing description of discursive structures and trajectories is in fact what makes it possible, in the network of epistemes, to explore their connections and how certain basic patterns operate. Only then can the latter be deciphered as patterns that may be related to and induced by power. From the descriptive and analytical standpoint of a discourse-semantic epistemology, any hasty criticism of discursive conditions is treading on precarious ground. It is a criticism of the very basis of our own thought and knowledge. This kind of criticism, which begins at the foundations, could initially be philosophical in nature rather than politically motivated. Even if post-Foucauldian discourse analysis cannot deny its origins in ideology critique,[35] an analytical description of the verbal knowledge and thought of a particular time or trend as materialized in texts cannot claim to be the final arbiter of epistemes. To do this, it would have to assume an Archimedean point outside the epistemes, the possibility of which has been rejected by every serious philosophical reflection since time began.[36] We must adhere strictly to the pre-eminence of meticulous description and analysis in the epistemological context. One reason for this is that no adequate description of depth-semantic epistemic conditioning can be satisfactorily realized from within the discourse, the epistemes of a particular time.[37] Moreover, any rash critique (of power) that disregards the limits of what it is possible to say and think at a particular time overlooks a key element of discourse analysis, namely the identification of the historical a priori. Any other form of examining epistemological-discursive conditions which presents itself as analysis, would, should it fail to observe these priorities, immediately be suspected of doing precisely what it criticizes: implementing a transparently interest-driven (and hence no longer descriptive) interpretation of the epistemic circumstances, an interpretation it would not hesitate to identify as a 'context of delusion' (in plain English: 'ideology') in its objects of study.

Despite its strictly descriptive and analytical approach, historical-epistemological discourse semantics must by no means ignore the fundamental dependence on interests and standpoint inherent in any study of cultural phenomena. If it professes a commitment to the 'happy positivism' exemplified by Foucault, it does so on the basis of a self-assessment of its own cognitive possibilities. This should by no means deny the validity of the epistemo-critical position of the hermeneutics of someone like Schleiermacher, for instance. Any historiography is concerned first and foremost with texts, and historical semantics all the more so. It would, therefore, be pious self-deception to deny its methodological and epistemological affinity with hermeneutics (in the advanced philosophical sense). While historical discourse semantics may not on any account be equated with hermeneutics (Foucault has convincingly expounded the problematic nature of the hermeneutic search for the 'true', 'hidden', 'latent' meaning), it does share its methodical problems and hence its self-reflection. This reflection upon its own possibilities also contains the seeds of its self-limitation. It would be denying its discourse-critical roots, were its primary objective the (re-)construction of a 'true' discourse 'behind' the manifest texts. Rather, it draws pictures, describes scenarios, creates maps of the epistemic landscape of a discursive network. In doing so it devotes as much attention to the dynamic aspect as it does to description of the structures, and it is perhaps this very process orientation that distinguishes it from earlier hermeneutics. Above all, however, it is not so presumptuous as to sideline the epistemes in their discursive structures and trajectories with the methods of the discipline, through description, analysis, and possibly also criticism. It examines, rather, the epistemic landscape (and hence the historical semantics) of a particular time or society as a social *conditio humana*, an historical a priori, that provides the foundation and raison d'être for its own activity in particular. To put it conservatively, it does no more than what Foucault himself describes with great foresight in the 'Order of Discourse' (we need only replace the word 'commentary' with 'discourse analysis'):

> *Mais, d'autre part, le commentaire n'a pour rôle, quelles que soient les techniques mises en œuvre, que de dire enfin ce qui était articulé silencieusement là-bas. Il doit, selon un paradoxe qu'il déplace toujours mais auquel il n'échappe jamais, dire pour la première fois ce qui cependant avait été déjà dit et répéter inlassablement ce qui pourtant n'avait jamais été dit. Le moutonnement indéfini des commentaires est travaillé de l'intérieur par la rêve d'une répétition masquée: à son horizon, il n'y a peut-être rien d'autre que ce qui était à son point de départ, la simple récitation.*[38]

(Translation: Joy Titheridge)

Notes

1   [Note: the word 'concept' is used in this article in both its abstract
     meaning, i.e. a conception or notion, and in the sense of conceptual
     history, i.e. relating to specific terms. In German, this is reflected by the

dichotomy of *Begriff*, as in *Begriffsgeschichte* (conceptual history), and *Konzept* (an abstract concept).]

2   Dietrich Busse, *Historische Semantik* (Stuttgart: Klett-Cotta, 1987); Dietrich Busse and Wolfgang Teubert, 'Ist Diskurs ein sprachwissenschaftliches Objekt? Zur Methodenfrage der historischen Semantik', in Dietrich Busse, Fritz Hermanns and Wolfgang Teubert (eds), *Begriffsgeschichte und Diskursgeschichte. Methodenfragen und Forschungsergebnisse der historischen Semantik* (Opladen: Westdeutscher Verlag, 1994), 10–28.

3   An apprehension that was not entirely groundless, judging by a methodological analysis of a number of articles of Otto Brunner, Werner Conze and Reinhart Koselleck (eds), *Geschichtliche Grundbegriffe: Historisches Lexikon zur politisch-sozialen Sprache in Deutschland*, 8 vols in 9 (Stuttgart: Klett, 1972–1997).

4   A 'richer' semantics was in fact proposed as early as 1934 in Karl Bühler, *Sprachtheorie* (Jena: G. Fischer, 1934; repr. Stuttgart: G. Fischer, 1999), and excellently formulated by the Germanist Peter von Polenz in his *Deutsche Satzsemantik: Grundbegriffe des Zwischen-den-Zeilen-Lesens* (Berlin: de Gruyter, 1985).

5   'On the Comparative Study of Language and Its Relation to the Different Periods of Language Development', in Theo Harden and Daniel J. Farrelly (eds), *Essays on Language* (Frankfurt: Lang, 1997), 15. (*Ueber das vergleichende Sprachstudium in Beziehung auf die verschiedenen Epochen der Sprachentwicklung*, 1820).

6   [Note: Wittgenstein II refers to the second major part of Ludwig Wittgenstein's works, the *Philosophical Investigations*, which formulates a complex philosophical theory with which language in use, or everyday language, can be analysed. The first and much earlier major work of Wittgenstein is the *Tractatus Logico-Philosophicus*, concerned primarily with logic and structural linguistics. Cf. Ludwig Wittgenstein, P.M.S. Hacker and Joachim Schulte (eds), *Philosophical Investigations* (Hoboken: Wiley-Blackwell, 2009).]

7   Individual reflections on this issue can be found in Busse (1987). However, I am well aware today that the realization of my original ideas would have required nothing more nor less than the formulation of my own sociology of knowledge, something which was simply not feasible for a linguist (let alone within a reasonable time frame).

8   I have been reproached by highly committed advocates of a discourse analysis of power relations for this very association of action theory concepts with concepts from Foucauldian discourse analysis. Quite apart from the fact that any reduction of Foucault's intentions to the criticism and destruction of power overlooks the enormous descriptive

potential and theoretical groundwork of his discourse theory (Michel Foucault, *L'archéologie du savoir* (Paris: Gallimard, 1969), 164: '*eh bien je suis un positiviste heureux*' in response to Sylvie LeBon, 'Un positiviste désespéré', *Les temps modernes*, 248 (1967), 1299–1319), which is as valid a source as his critique of power, this accusation fails to appreciate the theoretical groundwork laid by a pragmatic theory of language. This can by no means be reduced to a superficial linguistic intentionalism nor does it automatically exclude the consideration of the epistemic predispositions favoured by more recent post-structuralist approaches. (Cf. Dietrich Busse, 'Konventionalisierungsstufen des Zeichengebrauchs als Ausgangspunkt semantischen Wandels. Zum Entstehen lexikalischer Bedeutungen und zum Begriff der Konvention in der Bedeutungstheorie von H. P. Grice', in idem (ed.), *Diachrone Semantik und Pragmatik. Untersuchungen zur Erklärung und Beschreibung des Sprachwandels* (Tübingen: Niemeyer, 1991), 37–65.)

9   For which I am grateful to my university teacher Rainer Wimmer.

10   They are discussed in greater detail in Busse (1987).

11   On criticism of this, cf. Werner Wolski, *Schlechtbestimmtheit und Vagheit – Tendenzen und Perspektiven. Methodologische Untersuchungen zur Semantik* (Tübingen: Niemeyer, 1980), 44ff and 95ff; Busse (1991), 43ff and idem, *Juristische Semantik* (Berlin: Duncker & Humblot, 1993), 104ff.

12   I describe this as an 'intermediate phase' because prior to the rise of structuralism, the older, traditional linguistic semantics had no part in the subsequent semantic reductionism. There is ample evidence, particularly in studies from the period preceding the reception of Saussure's 'Cours' (i.e. before 1920) of an interest in semantics that was motivated by an interest in cultural phenomena. This can certainly be read as a prelude to a semantic epistemology or 'depth semantics'. In this regard and in the context of the history of research, more recent approaches in semantics (more recent, that is, at least for linguistics) which focus on cultural phenomena (whether as conceptual history, discourse analysis, the history of mentalities, etc.) are simply picking up on a thread that had been interrupted by the technologically motivated, formalistic concept of what is known as 'modern' linguistics. On earlier historical semantics, cf. the outline in Dietrich Busse, 'Semantischer Wandel in traditioneller Sicht. (Etymologie und Wortgeschichte III)', in David A. Cruse et al. (eds), *Lexikologie. Ein internationales Handbuch zur Natur und Struktur von Wörten und Wortschätzen* (Berlin: de Gruyter, 2002), 1306–24.

13   Cf. von Polenz (1985), 186ff.

14   Initially in Busse (1987).

15   Incidentally, many propositions on the theoretical foundations of historical semantics, which is what I am interested in, could have been formulated purely with reference to Wittgenstein. (I have been vigorously reproached for precisely this association of Foucault's discourse theory with Wittgenstein's philosophy of language and other approaches from linguistic analytical philosophy. The detractors were supporters of a discourse research with a clear emphasis on ideology critique – and also, mind you, scorners of analytical thought. This is actually a fairly platitudinous academic version of a structure of prejudice that enjoys great popularity among German intellectuals and is based on the implicit concept of a strictly antonymic relationship between Anglophilia and Francophilia.) However, I believe that Foucault's concept of discourse provided and continues to provide analytical possibilities and perspectives that would have first had to have been constructed on the basis of the fragmentary Wittgensteinian approach that has more to do with fundamental philosophical questions. Foucault's approach is much closer to the phenomena, the material, the social and historical analysis of an historical epistemology, and hence allows more direct connections to be made in this regard.

16   Cf. Michel Pêcheux, *Les vérités de la Palice* (Paris: Maspero, 1975); idem, 'Über die Rolle des Gedächtnisses als interdiskursives Material. Ein Forschungsprojekt im Rahmen der Diskursanalyse und Archivlektüre', in Manfred Geier and Harold Woetzel (eds), *Das Subjekt des Diskurses. Beiträge zur sprachlichen Bildung von Subjektivität und Intersubjektivität* (Berlin: Argument, 1983), 50–8.

17   I refer here largely to Foucault (1969) and idem, *L'ordre du discours* (Paris: Gallimard, 1971); cf. the in-depth discussion with individual examples in Busse (1987), 222ff.

18   [Note: quoted freely after Michel Foucault, *The Archaeology of Knowledge* (London/New York: Routledge, 2002), 30: 'how it is that one particular statement appeared rather than another'.]

19   Pêcheux (1983), 54.

20   These detractors are clearly unaware of the descriptive approach also taken by Pêcheux and others and ignorant of the descriptive content of Foucault's theory itself. Unlike their Cisrhenian disciples, the former certainly did combine description and critique in their analysis (quite in keeping with their secret role model Marx, who knew all along that penetrating and clear-sighted analysis and description of the prevailing conditions are the prerequisites for any germane critique of these conditions and thus for their subversion).

21   Busse and Teubert (1994), 19ff.

22   Ludwig Wittgenstein, *Über Gewißheit* (Frankfurt am Main: Suhrkamp, 1970), §95ff.

23 Cf. Rolf Reichardt, 'Zur Geschichte politisch-sozialer Begriffe in Frankreich zwischen Absolutismus und Restauration. Vorstellung eines Forschungsvorhabens', *Sprachgeschichte und Sozialgeschichte. Zeitschrift für Literaturwissenschaft und Linguistik*, 12/47 (1982), 49–74; idem, 'Einleitung', in Rolf Reichardt and Hans-Jürgen Lüsebrink (eds), *Handbuch politisch-sozialer Grundbegriffe in Frankreich 1680–1820* (München: Oldenbourg, 1985–2000), 39–148. [Note: extract included as chapter three in this volume.]

24 Busse (1987), 301.

25 Cf. Pêcheux (1983), 54.

26 Foucault (1969), 238.

27 Cf. Dietrich Busse, 'Das Eigene und das Fremde. Zu Funktion und Wirkung einer diskurssemantischen Grundfigur', in Matthias Jung, Martin Wengeler and Karin Böke (eds), *Die Sprache des Migrationsdiskurses. Das Reden über 'Ausländer' in Medien, Politik und Alltag* (Opladen: Westdeutscher Verlag, 1997), 17–35 for a more detailed account.

28 On the concept of isotopy, cf. Algirdas Julien Greimas, *Strukturale Semantik* (Braunschweig: Friedr. Vieweg + Sohn, 1971) [Note: English translation: idem, *Structural Semantics: An Attempt at a Method*, trans. Daniele McDowell, Ronald Schleifer and Alan Velie (Lincoln, Nebraska: University of Nebraska Press, 1983)]; on feature semantics, cf. Dietrich Busse, *Textinterpretation. Sprachtheoretische Grundlagen einer explikativen Semantik* (Opladen: Westdeutscher Verlag, 1991), 29ff.

29 On argument analysis, cf. Josef Kopperschmidt, *Argumentation* (Stuttgart: Kohlhammer, 1980) for an overview.

30 For a balanced analysis of implicit semantic content, cf. von Polenz (1985), 198ff.

31 I am extremely grateful to Fritz Hermann for pointing out (many years ago) the wealth of information this text conveys about the history of discourse and of mentalities. [Note: the English edition quoted in the following is Gustav Freytag, *Debit and Credit: a Novel*, trans. L. C. Cummings (New York: Harper, 1858).]

32 Freytag (1858), 317. [Note: '"Dies Vorwerk ist ein Juwel Gottes", rief Karl... '"Hier sind deutliche Spuren einer Düngestätte... Und hier steht ein Myrtenstock am Fenster. Hurra! hier ist eine Hausfrau, hier ist Vaterland, hier sind Deutsche."']

33 Ibid., 401.

34 Ibid., 313–14. [Note: 'Wer immer in den gebahnten Wegen des Lebens fortgegangen ist, begrenzt durch das Gesetz, bestimmt durch Ordnung, Sitte und Form, welche in seiner Heimat als tausendjährige Gewohnheit von Geschlecht zu Geschlecht vererbt sind, und wer plötzlich als einzelner unter Fremde geworfen wird, wo das Gesetz sein Rechte nur unvollkommen zu

schützen vermag, und wo er durch eigene Kraft die Berechtigung zu leben
sich alle Tage erkämpfen muß, der erst erkennt den Segen der heiligen
Kreise, welche um jeden einzelnen Menschen Tausende der mitlebenden
bilden, die Familie, seine Arbeitsgenossen, sein Volksstamm, sein Staat.
Ob er in der Fremde verliere oder gewinne, er wird ein anderer. Ist er ein
Schwächling, so wird er die eigene Art den fremden Gewalten opfern, in
deren Bannkreis er getreten ist. Hat er Stoff zu einem Manne, jetzt wird
er einer. Doppelt teuer werden seiner Seele die Güter, in deren Besitz er
aufgewachsen war, vielleicht auch die Vorurteile, die an seinem Leben
hingen; und manches, was er sonst gleichgültig angesehen hatte wie Luft und
Sonnenschein, das wird jetzt sein höchstes Gut. Erst im Auslande lernt man
den Reiz des Heimatdialektes genießen, erst in der Fremde erkennt man,
was das Vaterland ist'.]

35   Cf. Jacques Guilhaumou and Denise Maldidier, 'Courte critique pour une
       longue histoire. L'analyse du discours ou les (mal)leurres de l'analogie',
       Dialectiques, 26 (1979), 7–23.

36   Cf. in our context Michel Foucault, 'La pensée du dehors', *Critique*, 229
       (1966), 523–46.

37   However, this does not mean that we should automatically take as our sole
       benchmark Foucault's suggestion of one hundred years as the minimum
       distance between researcher and object.

38   'But on the other hand the commentary's only role, whatever the
       techniques used, is to say at last what was silently articulated "beyond",
       in the text. By a paradox which it always displaces but never escapes, the
       commentary must say for the first time what had, nonetheless, already
       been said, and must tirelessly repeat what had, however, never been
       said. The infinite rippling of commentaries is worked from the inside
       by the dream of a repetition in disguise: at its horizon there is perhaps
       nothing but what was at its point of departure – mere recitation'. Foucault
       (1971), 27. [Note: English translation: Michel Foucault, 'The Order of
       Discourse', trans. Ian McLeod in Robert Young (ed.), *Untying the Text: A
       Poststructuralist Reader* (Boston: Routledge and Kegan Paul, 1981) 57–8.]

Quentin Skinner is one of the most influential British intellectual historians, particularly of the early modern period. Since 2008, he holds the Barber Beaumont Chair of the Humanities at Queen Mary University of London. His research interests range from philosophical and political-theoretical topics to historical fields of study. Alongside J.G.A. Pocock, he is often associated with the so-called Cambridge School of Intellectual History. Though the disciplines of philosophy and history are not isolated from each other and share common ideas, intellectual history retains a primarily linguistic focus on synchronic change. Quentin Skinner investigates conceptual change mainly by analysing rhetoric and linguistic action (speech acts).

Among Quentin Skinner's publications are such titles as *The Foundation of Modern Political Thought*, volume I: *The Renaissance* and volume II: *The Age of Reformation* (1978); *The Return of Grand Theory in the Human Sciences* (as editor and contributor; 1985); *Political Discourse in Early-modern Britain* (as co-editor and contributor; 1993); *Liberty before Liberalism* (1998); *Visions of Politics*, volume I: *Regarding Method*, volume II: *Renaissance Virtues* and volume III: *Hobbes and Civil Science* (2002) and *Forensic Shakespeare* (2014).

The article presented here was first published in 1999 in response to Kari Palonen's discussion of the diverging approaches of Reinhart Koselleck and Quentin Skinner.[1] Palonen describes what he sees as the defining different features of both theories, namely Skinner's focus on linguistics and rhetoric and Koselleck's complex theory of time and temporalization. He concludes that the two approaches could indeed be made complementary 'either by including temporal elements of the Koselleckian inspiration to the Skinnerian programme…or by a consequent nominalization of the Koselleckian programme into one of temporal action'.[2]

---

[1]Kari Palonen, 'Rhetorical and Temporal Perspectives on Conceptual Change: Theses on Quentin Skinner and Reinhart Koselleck', *Finnish Yearbook of Political Thought* 3 (1999), 41–58.
[2]Ibid., 56.

5

Rhetoric and Conceptual Change

Quentin Skinner

> And therefore in reasoning, a man must take heed of words; which besides the signification of what we imagine of their nature, have a signification also of the nature, disposition, and interest of the speaker; such as are the names of Vertues, and Vices; For one man calleth *Wisdome*, what another calleth *feare*; and one *cruelty*, what another *justice*; one *prodigality*, what another *magnanimity*; and one *gravity*, what another *stupidity*, &c. And therefore such names can never be true grounds of any ratiocination.[1]

Kari Palonen begins his comments (in this volume[2]) by declaring that, when we address ourselves to the problem of conceptual change, we are (or ought to be) 'only concerned with the political aspects of concepts'.[3] He adds by way of explanation that 'for me the words "political" and "interesting" are more or less synonymous'.[4] I admire his epigram, but I faintly dissent from his narrowness of focus. For me the interest of studying the history of concepts arises from the moral and social as well as the political changes that we find reflected in – and to some extent engendered by – the groundswell of conceptual change itself.

This is a mere quibble, however, for I warmly endorse Palonen's contention that, if we are to treat the study of changing concepts as a distinct form of historical enquiry, we shall do well to concentrate on the concepts we employ to describe and appraise our moral and political world. This in turn means that we shall need to focus on the various terms – the entire normative vocabulary – in which such concepts are habitually expressed. These terms, the paradigms of which are perhaps the names of the virtues and vices, are those which perform evaluative as well as descriptive functions in natural languages. They are basically used to describe actions and the motives for which they are performed. But if the criteria for applying one or other of these terms can plausibly be claimed to be reflected in some given action or state of affairs, then the application of the term will not only serve to describe but at the same time to evaluate it. The special characteristic of the terms I am singling out is thus that (to invoke John L. Austin's jargon) they have a standard application to perform one of two contrasting ranges of speech-acts.[5] They are available, that is, to perform such acts as commending (and expressing and soliciting approval) or else of condemning (and expressing and soliciting disapproval) of any action or state of affairs they are used to describe.

As Palonen correctly notes, I began to make such terms a subject of my historical research in the early 1970s.[6] One reason for doing so was my wish to dispute the view – then prevalent in Anglophone philosophy – that it is appropriate to conceive of a distinctive grid of concepts marking off moral, political and other such domains. It was widely assumed that we can speak (as Thomas D. Weldon had done in the title of a classic text) of the vocabulary of politics[7] and that we can likewise speak (as Richard M. Hare had done in an even more influential book) of *the* language of morals.[8] This assumption seemed to me well worth disputing in the name of a more historically-minded acknowledgment that different societies may conceptualize these domains in different and possibly even incommensurable ways.

I had a second and yet more basic motivation for wishing to study the changing use of concepts. I wanted to question the assumption influentially propagated by Arthur Lovejoy and his school about the proper task of the historian of ideas. Lovejoy had argued that, beneath the surface of ideological debate, there will always be a range of perennial and unchanging 'unit ideas' which it becomes the task of the intellectual historian to uncover and trace.[9] Against this contention I tried once more to speak up for a more radical contingency in the history of thought. Drawing on a suggestion of Wittgenstein's,[10] I argued that there cannot be a history of unit ideas as such, but only a history of the various uses to which they have been put by different agents at different times. There is nothing, I ventured to suggest, lying beneath or behind such uses; their history is the only history of ideas to be written.

One way of expressing my underlying commitment would thus be to say that I wanted to treat the understanding of concepts as always, in part, a matter of understanding what can be done with them in argument. As Palonen points out, in announcing this belief I declared my allegiance to one particular tradition of twentieth-century social thought. The tradition may perhaps be said to stem from Nietzsche, although I originally encountered it in the social philosophy of Max Weber. It is characterised by the belief that our concepts not only alter over time, but are incapable of providing us with anything more than a series of changing perspectives on the world in which we live and have our being. Our concepts form part of what we bring to the world in our efforts to understand it. The shifting conceptualizations to which this process gives rise constitute the very stuff of ideological debate, so that it makes no more sense to regret than to deny that such conceptual changes continually take place. This commitment in turn gave rise in my own case – as in the case of Koselleck – to a particular view about what kind of history needs to be written if this general truth is to be illuminated. Koselleck and I both assume that we need to treat our normative concepts less as statements about the world than as tools and weapons of debate.

One reason why it is perhaps worth identifying my original targets in this way is that several commentators have supposed that what I was aiming to discredit was the very project of Koselleck's that Palonen seeks, very illuminatingly, to relate to my own research. It is no doubt deplorable, but it is nevertheless a fact, that when I wrote my polemical essays in the late 1960s and early 1970s I had no knowledge of Koselleck's research-programme. I did not come to appreciate the distinctiveness and magnitude of his achievement until Melvin Richter made his work available to Anglophone readers in his articles of the 1980s[11] and later in his important study, *The History of Social and Political Concepts*, published as recently as 1995.[12]

It is perhaps worth adding that I have not only been innocent of any desire to question Koselleck's methodological assumptions, but that I have even attempted to write some conceptual histories myself. I have written about the acquisition of the concept of *the State* as the name of a moral person distinct from both rulers and ruled.[13] And I have tried to sketch the rise and fall within Anglophone political theory of a particular view about *social freedom*, a view according to which our freedom needs to be seen not merely as a predicate of our actions but as an existential condition in contrast to that of the slave.[14] I do not consider these studies to be in tension with anything I have said about the need to understand what can be done with concepts as an element in the process of recovering their meaning and significance. On the contrary, part of my aim was to indicate why the concepts in question first came into prominence at particular historical periods by way of indicating what could be done with them that could not have been done in their absence.

As these remarks already make clear, I strongly endorse Palonen's insistence that we must be ready as historians of philosophy not merely to admit the fact of conceptual change but to make it central to our research. Not only is our moral and social world held in place by the manner in which we choose to apply our inherited normative vocabularies, but one of the ways in which we are capable of reappraising and changing our world is by changing the ways in which these vocabularies are applied. There is in consequence a genealogy of all our evaluative concepts to be traced, and in tracing their changing applications we shall find ourselves looking not merely at the reflections but at one of the engines of social change.

The only point at which I demur at Palonen's way of laying out these issues is that I am less happy than he is to talk about conceptual change *tout court*. It is true that he begins by asking 'what, then, does actually change when concepts change?' But his answer is simply that the transformations in question can be related both to language and to time. I have no quarrel with this formulation, but it seems worth trying to say something rather more detailed about it.

I have already gestured at what I take to be the most fundamental point we need to grasp if we are to study the phenomenon of conceptual change. My almost paradoxical contention is that the transformations we can hope to chart will not strictly speaking be changes in concepts at all. They will be changes in the use of the terms by which our concepts are expressed. These transformations will in turn be of various kinds. Palonen rightly notes that in my own work I have chiefly focused on what he describes as a rhetorical perspective. I have been interested, that is, in the kinds of debate that take place when we ask whether a given action or state of affairs does or does not license us to apply some particular evaluative term as an apt description of it. While this has been my principal interest, however, I should not want it to be thought that I take this to be the sole or even the most significant way in which the process of conceptual change may be initiated. Before turning to consider the rhetorical case in more detail, I should like to mention two other ways in which the phenomenon of conceptual change can be historically mapped.

We can hope in the first place to trace the changing extent or degree to which a particular normative vocabulary is employed over time. There are obviously two contrasting possibilities here. The rise within a given society of new forms of social behaviour will generally be reflected in the development of a corresponding vocabulary in which the behaviour in question will be described and appraised. As an example, consider the emergence in the English language for the first time in the early seventeenth century of a range of terms that came to be widely used to describe and at the same time to commend the behaviour of those who were *frugal, punctual* and *conscientious*. The alternative possibility is that a given society may gradually lose its sense that some particular style of behaviour needs to be singled out and evaluated. This will generally be registered in the atrophying of the corresponding normative vocabulary. An instructive example is offered by the disappearance in contemporary English of a complex vocabulary widely used in earlier generations to describe and commend an ideal of gentlemanly conduct, and at the same time to stigmatize any behaviour liable to undermine it. Such terms as 'cad' and 'bounder' – together with the contrasting concept of *gentlemanliness* – can still be found in historical dictionaries of the English language, but they are virtually obsolete as terms of appraisal now that the patterns of conduct they were used to evaluate have lost their social significance.

Such examples arguably provide the best evidence in favour of the claim that concepts have a history – or rather, that the terms we use to express our concepts have a history. I confess, however, that this kind of long-term shift in the fortunes of concepts is not one of my primary interests, as Palonen correctly points out. Here my approach differs from that of Koselleck, who as Palonen notes is chiefly preoccupied with the slower march of time and much less concerned with the pointillist study of sudden conceptual shifts. Palonen ends by asking why I am so much less interested in such broader chronologies. One reason is that, in the examples I have given, the shifting vocabularies are little more than indexes or reflections of deeper transformations in social life. This in turn means that, if a history of these conceptual changes were to have any explanatory value, the explanations would have to be given at the level of social life itself. But I have no general theory about the mechanisms of social transformation, and I am somewhat suspicious of those who have. Certainly I am deeply suspicious of all theories in which Time itself appears as an agent of change. As Palonen justly remarks, such metaphors have a nasty habit of reappearing as objectifications, thereby encouraging a discredited form of intellectual history in which Tradition is always doing battle with Progress, Superstition with Enlightenment, and so forth.[15]

I turn to consider a second form of conceptual change, or rather a second way in which the vocabularies we use to describe and appraise our social world continually wrinkle and slide. This process also occurs when the capacity of a normative vocabulary to perform and encourage particular acts of appraisal either alters in direction or else in intensity. Alterations of this kind will usually reflect an underlying attempt to modify existing social perceptions and beliefs, and these efforts will in turn be mirrored in the language of evaluation in one of two principal ways. A term generally used to commend an action or state of affairs may be used instead to express and solicit disapproval, or a condemnatory term may be used to suggest that, contrary to received assumptions, what is being described is also deserving of praise.

What is being suggested in these cases is that a society should reconsider and perhaps transvalue some of its moral values. Sometime we can even pinpoint such suggestions within individual texts. For example, we can arguably see this process at work in Machiavelli's *Il Principe*, in chapter XVI of which he appears to suggest that parsimony is not necessarily the name of a vice. Perhaps, he implies, a number of actions generally condemned by the courtly societies of Renaissance Europe as miserly and parsimonious actually deserve to be praised.[16] An even clearer example is provided by Sir Thomas Hoby's translation of Baldassare Castiglione's *Book of the Courtier*, first published in 1561. Faced with the term *sprezzatura*, which Castiglione had invented to commend an aristocratic style of nonchalance, Hoby chose to render it as *recklessness*, thereby confronting his puritan contemporaries with the astonishing thought that this might be the name of a virtue.[17]

When such suggestions are widely taken up, a whole society may eventually come to alter its attitude towards some fundamental value or practice and alter its normative vocabulary accordingly. Consider, for example, the fact that such terms as 'shrewd' and 'shrewdness' were widely employed in the Renaissance to condemn whatever actions they were used to describe, but were later employed in such a way that similar actions came to be commended. Or consider, by contrast, the fact that such terms as 'obsequious' were commonly used in the Renaissance to commend the behaviour they described, but were later applied in such a way as to make it clear that the obsequious are deserving of nothing but contempt.

These are examples of conceptual change in perhaps its purest sense. As Palonen correctly notes, however, I have again paid little attention to the long-term social transformations that cause such appraisive terms to lose or alter the direction of their evaluative force. Palonen is also right to note that this lack of interest again contrasts with Koselleck's approach. The reason for my neglect is the same as before. I lack any talent for writing the kind of social history that would be required. I also plead guilty to the further charge that, as Palonen expresses it, I neglect (by comparison with Koselleck) 'the possibility of including time into the very meaning of a concept'. I do indeed neglect this possibility, but only because I cannot make sense of it.

I turn finally to re-examine the form of conceptual change in which I have chiefly been interested, the form described by Palonen as rhetorical in character. Such changes originate when an action or state of affairs is described by means of an evaluative term that would not normally be used in the given circumstances. The aim is to persuade an audience that, in spite of appearances, the term can properly be applied – in virtue of its ordinary meaning – to the case in hand. The effect of successfully persuading someone to accept such a judgment will be to prompt them to view the behaviour in question in a new moral light. An action they had previously regarded as commendable may come to seem worthy of condemnation, while an action they had previously condemned may seem worthy of praise.

As Palonen notes, when in the early 1970s I first discussed this technique of rhetorical redescription, I operated with the assumption that for every evaluative term there will at any one time be a standard meaning and use. As a result, I portrayed the innovating ideologist as someone essentially engaged in the act of manipulating a normative vocabulary by a series of sleights of hand. Since then, however, I have immersed myself in the writings of the ancient theorists of eloquence who originally spoke of rhetorical redescription, and have come to share their more contingent understanding of normative concepts and the fluid vocabularies in which they are generally expressed. As a result, I have found myself adopting their assumption that it makes little sense to speak of evaluative terms as having accepted denotations that can either be followed or, with varying degrees of disingenuousness, effectively manipulated. Rather, as the ancient rhetoricians put it, there will always be a sufficient degree of 'neighbourliness' between the forms of behaviour described by contrasting evaluative terms for those terms themselves to be susceptible of being applied in a variety of conflicting ways. It now seems to me, in short, that all attempts to legislate about the 'correct' use of normative vocabularies must be regarded as equally ideological in character. Whenever such terms are used, their application will always reflect a wish to impose a particular moral vision upon the workings of the social world.

To illustrate the technique of rhetorical redescription, it will be best to turn to the analysis originally offered by the ancient rhetoricians themselves. The fullest account is supplied by Quintilian, although he owes an obvious debt to Cicero and even more to Aristotle's *Art of Rhetoric*. Quintilian's main discussion of the technique – to which he gave the name *paradiastole* – occurs in book IV of his *Institutio Oratorio*, where he discusses it in the course of considering how best to present a narrative of facts. Suppose you find yourself in a court of law facing an advocate who has managed to describe an act 'in such a way as to rouse up the judges and leave them full of anger against your side'.[18] Suppose too that you cannot hope to deny what happened. How are you to proceed? Quintilian's answer is that 'you should restate the facts, but not at all in the same way; you must assign different causes, a different state of mind and a different motive for what was done'.[19] Above all, 'you must try to elevate the action as much as possible by the words you use: for example, prodigality must be more leniently redescribed as liberality, avarice as carefulness, negligence as simplicity of mind'.[20]

Quintilian had already put forward this last and crucial suggestion in book II, in which he had quoted (although without acknowledgment) three examples of the same technique offered by Aristotle in *The Art of Rhetoric*: 'slander can pass for frankness, recklessness for courage, extravagance for copiousness'.[21] Aristotle had added that the same technique can equally well be used not merely to extenuate the vices but also to depreciate the virtues, as when we denigrate the behaviour of a habitually cautious man by claiming that he is really a person of cold and designing temperament.[22]

As Quintilian emphasises, the essence of the technique may thus be said to consist of replacing a given evaluative description with a rival term that pictures the action no less plausibly, but serves at the same time to place it in a contrasting moral light. You seek to persuade your audience to accept your new description, and thereby to adopt a new attitude towards the action involved – either one of increased sympathy or of acquired moral outrage. As Quintilian explicitly adds, this means that strictly speaking we ought not to describe the technique as a case of substituting one word for another. 'For no one supposes that the words prodigality and liberality mean the same thing; the difference is rather that one person calls something prodigal which another thinks of as liberality'.[23] What we are really claiming is that the *res* – the actual behaviour – possesses a different moral character from that which our dialectical opponents may have assigned to it.

Quintilian also explains what makes the use of paradiastolic redescription a perennial possibility. Drawing once more on Aristotle, he reiterates that this is due to the fact that many of the vices are 'neighbours' of the virtues. Cicero had already put forward the same explanation in his *De Partitione Oratoria*. 'Cunning imitates prudence, insensibility imitates temperance, pride in attaining honours and superciliousness in looking down on them both imitate magnanimity, extravagance imitates liberality and audacity imitates courage'.[24] So many of the vices, in short, stand in 'neighbourly relations' with the virtues that a clever orator will always be able to challenge the preferred evaluation of any action whatsoever with some show of plausibility.

One of the distinctive achievements of Renaissance culture was to revive and reassess the rhetorical philosophy of the ancient world. This in turn means that, if we wish to see the techniques perfected by the ancient rhetoricians put to work again, we need to turn to the moral philosophy of the Renaissance. Among Renaissance moralists, it was Machiavelli who arguably took the lessons of the ancient rhetoricians most profoundly to heart. Certainly he employs the technique of paradiastolic redescription with unparalleled audacity in challenging the political morality of his age. He first uses the device in chapter XVI of *Il Principe* to question the so-called 'princely' virtue of liberality. Two contrasting rhetorical strategies are at work in this passage. As we have seen, one is the startling suggestion that liberality may not be the name of a virtue, nor parsimony of a vice. But Machiavelli's other strategy depends on assuming that liberality is unquestionably the name of a virtue. While conceding the point, however, he adds that much of the behaviour usually described and commended as liberal ought rather to be redescribed and condemned as *suntuosità*, mere ostentatiousness.[25] His next chapter questions the princely virtue of clemency in exactly the same way. He begins by acknowledging that cruelty is of course a vice.[26] But he insists that many of the actions usually celebrated as instances of clemency ought rather to be redescribed in much less favourable terms. The avoidance of cruelty for which the Florentines congratulated themselves when they refused to punish the leaders of the uprising at Pistoia ought really to be recognized as an instance of *troppa pietà*, mere over-indulgence.[27] Likewise, the clemency for which Scipio

Africanus came to be so widely admired was really an example of *sua natura facile*, his laxity of character.[28]

I have frequently referred to Machiavelli as a pioneer in recognising the power of paradiastolic redescription in moral debate. But perhaps the most emphatic tribute to the technique is owed to Nietzsche, a deep student of Machiavelli and of the ancient theorists of rhetoric on whom he had relied. Nietzsche's main account of how, within European history, one set of moral evaluations was successfully displaced by another and incommensurable one can be found in his opening essay in *The Genealogy of Morality*. The passage is a famous one, but Nietzsche's commentators appear not to have noticed that the technique he illustrates is precisely that of paradiastolic redescription. He begins by asking whether anyone would like 'to have a little look down into the secret of how *ideals are fabricated* on this earth':

> What's happening down there? Tell me what you see, you with your most dangerous curiosity – now *I* am the one who's listening. –
>
> – 'I cannot see anything but I can hear all the better. There is a guarded, malicious little rumour-mongering and whispering from every nook and cranny. I think people are telling lies; a sugary mildness clings to every sound. Lies are turning weakness into an *accomplishment*, no doubt about it – it's just as you said.' –
>
> – Go on!
>
> – 'and impotence which doesn't retaliate is being turned into 'goodness'; timid baseness is being turned into 'humility'; submission to people one hates is being turned into 'obedience' (actually towards someone who, they say, orders this submission – they call him God.) The inoffensivenes of the weakling, the very cowardice with which he is richly endowed, his standing-by-the-door, his inevitable position of having to wait, are all given good names such as 'patience', which is also called *the* virtue; not-being-able-to-take-revenge is called not-wanting-to-take-revenge, it might even be forgiveness ('for *they* know not what they do – but we know what *they* are doing!'). They are also talking about 'loving your enemy' – and sweating while they do it.'
>
> – Go on! ...
>
> 'But enough! enough! I can't bear it any longer. Bad air! Bad air! This workshop where *ideals are fabricated* – it seems to me just to stink of lies.'[29]

It is Nietzsche's contention, in short, that the slave morality of the Christians succeeded in overturning the moral world of antiquity by rhetorically redescribing a number of vices as their neighbouring virtues.

For a contrasting example of how a virtue can come to seem a vice, consider a case recently discussed by Ian Hacking: the fact that what may appear as wholesome discipline in the rearing of children in one generation may appear as child abuse in the next. Nothing in the conduct of adults towards children need in the intervening period have changed. What will have changed, if the new evaluation is accepted, is the sensibility of a community. A number of practices previously taken for granted will come to seem morally intolerable. This is not of course to say that the process is one of coming to see things as they really are. As before, it is merely a matter of substituting one social philosophy for another, both of which may have been rationally defensible at different times.

It might appear, however, that in talking in this way about rhetorical redescription we are precisely *not* talking about conceptual change. I certainly agree that a number of philosophers have been somewhat too ready to say that such disputes arise because each party 'has a different concept' of (say) what constitutes child abuse. But if the disputants are genuinely arguing, they must have the same concept of what constitutes child abuse.[30] The difference between them will not be about the meaning of the relevant evaluative term, but merely about the range of circumstances in which they think it can appropriately be applied.

This caution strikes me as correct and important, but the fact remains that the outcome of such debates will nevertheless be a form of conceptual change. The more we succeed in persuading people that a given evaluative term applies in circumstances in which they may never have thought of applying it, the more broadly and inclusively we shall persuade them to employ the term in the appraisal of social and political life. The change that will eventually result is that the underlying concept will come to acquire a new prominence and a new salience in the moral arguments of the society concerned.

It is true that, as Palonen remarks, I have again been less interested in these long-term changes than in the kind of epiphanic moments dramatized by Nietzsche. But I acknowledge, of course, that if we are interested in mapping the rise and fall of particular normative vocabularies, we shall have to devote ourselves to examining the *longue durée*. So I am not unhappy with Palonen's concluding proposal that my own research-programme might even be regarded as an aspect of the vastly more ambitious one pursued by Koselleck.

Koselleck is interested in nothing less than the entire process of conceptual change; I am chiefly interested in one of the means by which it takes place.

But the two programmes do not strike me as necessarily incompatible, and I hope that both of them will continue to flourish as they deserve.

Notes

1   Thomas Hobbes, *Leviathan*, ed. Richard Tuck (Cambridge: Cambridge University Press, 1996), 31.
2   [Note: the text referred to is Kari Palonen, 'Rhetorical and Temporal Perspectives on Conceptual Change: Theses on Quentin Skinner and Reinhart Koselleck', *Finnish Yearbook of Political Thought*, 3 (1999), 41–58.]
3   Palonen (1999), 41.
4   Ibid., 41–2.
5   John L. Austin, *How to do Things with Words*, ed. James O. Urmson (Cambridge: Harvard University Press, 1962).
6   Palonen (1999), 42.
7   Thomas D. Weldon, *The Vocabulary of Politics* (London: Penguin Books, 1953).
8   Richard M. Hare, *The Language of Morals* (Oxford: Clarendon Press, 1952).
9   Arthur Lovejoy, *The Great Chain of Being: A Study of the History of an Idea* (New York: Harper and Row, 1960), esp. 3–4, 15–17.
10   [Note: see Dietrich Busse, 'Conceptual History or a History of Discourse? On the Theoretical Basis and Questions of Methodology of a Historical-semantic Epistemology' (chapter four in this volume) for a further discussion of applications of Wittgenstein's theories to the study of concepts.]
11   See especially Melvin Richter, 'Begriffsgeschichte and the History of Ideas', *Journal of the History of Ideas*, 48 (1987), 247–63.
12   Melvin Richter, *The History of Social and Political Concepts: A Critical Introduction* (Oxford: Oxford Universtiy Press, 1995).
13   See Quentin Skinner, 'The State', in *Political Innovation and Conceptual Change*, eds Terence Ball, James Farr, and Russell L. Hanson (Cambridge: Cambridge University Press, 1989), 90–131; and Quentin Skinner, 'Hobbes and the Purely Artificial Person of the State', *The Journal of Political Philosophy*, 7 (1999), 1–29.
14   Quentin Skinner, *Liberty Before Liberalism* (Cambridge: Cambridge University Press, 1998).
15   On this point see John Dunn, *Political Observation in its Historical Context* (Cambridge: Cambridge University Press, 1980), esp. 13.

16 Niccoló Machiavelli, *Il Principe e Discorsi spora la prima deca di Tito Livio*, ed. Sergio Bertelli (Milano: Feltrinelli, 1960), 66–8.

17 Baldassare Castiglione, *The Courtyer of Count Baldessar Castilio*, trans. Thomas Hoby (Imprinted at London: By wyllyam Seres at the signe of the Hedghogge 1561), Sig. E., ii^r. [Note: recent edition: Baldassare Castiglione, *The Book of the Courtier*, ed. Daniel Javitch, trans. Charles S. Singleton (New York: W. W. Norton & Co., 2002).]

18 Quintilian, *Institutio Oratoria*, IV.II.75, vol. 2, trans. and ed. H. E. Butler, 4 vols (London: Heinemann, 1920–22), 90. Here and below, translations from classical texts are my own.

19 Quintilian (1920–2), IV.II.76–7, vol. 2, 90.

20 Quintilian (1920–2), IV.II.77, vol. 2, 90–2.

21 Aristotle, *The 'Art' of Rhetoric*, trans. and ed. John H. Freese (London: Heinemann, 1926), I.IX.28–9, 96–8; cf. Quintilian (1920–2), II.XII.4, vol. 1, 284.

22 Aristotle (1926), I.IX.28, 96.

23 Quintilian (1920–2), VIII.VI.36, vol. 3, 322.

24 Cicero, *De Partitione Oratoria*, trans. and ed. H. Rackhman (London: Heinemann, 1942), II.XXIII.81, 370.

25 Machiavelli (1960), 66.

26 Ibid., 68.

27 Ibid., 69.

28 Ibid., 71.

29 Friedrich Nietzsche, *On the Genealogy of Morality*, trans. Carol Diethe and ed. Keith Ansell-Pearson (1887; Cambridge: Cambridge University Press, 1994), 30–1. [Note: '*Sprechen Sie aus, was Sie sehen, Mann der gefährlichsten Neugierde – jetzt bin ich der, welcher zuhört. – "Ich sehe Nichts, ich höre um so mehr. Es ist ein vorsichtiges tückisches leises Munkeln und Zusammenflüstern aus allen Ecken und Winkeln. Es scheint mir, dass man lügt: eine zuckrige Milde klebt an jedem Klange. Die Schwäche soll zum Verdienste umgelogen werden, es ist kein Zweifel – es steht damit so, wie Sie es sagten." – Weiter! – "und die Ohnmacht, die nicht vergilt, zur 'Güte'; die ängstliche Niedrigkeit zur 'Demuth'; die Unterwerfung vor Denen, die man hasst, zum 'Gehorsam' (nämlich gegen Einen, von dem sie sagen, er befehle diese Unterwerfung, – sie heissen ihn Gott). Das Unoffensive des Schwachen, die Feigheit selbst, an der er reich ist, sein An-der-Thür-stehn, sein unvermeidliches Warten-müssen kommt hier zu guten Namen, als 'Geduld', es heisst auch wohl die Tugend; das Sich-nicht-rächen-Können heisst Sich-nicht-rächen-Wollen, vielleicht selbst Verzeihung ('denn sie wissen nicht, was sie thun – wir allein wissen es, was sie thun!'). Auch redet man von der 'Liebe zu seinen Feinden' – und schwitzt dabei." – Weiter! – ... "Aber genug! genug! Ich halte es nicht mehr aus. Schlechte Luft!*

> *Schlechte Luft! Diese Werkstätte, wo man* Ideale fabrizirt – *mich dünkt, sie stinkt vor lauter Lügen.*", *Nietzsche Source*, Digital Critical Editon, Paolo D'Irio (ed.), based on the *Kritische Gesamtausgabe Werke*, Giorgio Colli and Mazzino Montinari (eds) (Berlin: Walter de Gruyter, 1967ff) <http://www.nietzschesource.org/#eKGWB/GM-I-14> (accessed 10 June 2015).]

30 On this point see Quentin Skinner, *Meaning and Context: Quentin Skinner and His Critics*, ed. James Tully (Princeton: Princeton University Press, 1988), esp. 125–8.

Part III

Translations of Concepts

Jörn Leonhard has been Friedrich-Schiller Professor of West European History at the University of Freiburg, Germany, since 2006. From 2007 until 2012, he was co-director of the School of History at the Freiburg Institute for Advanced Studies (FRIAS). In addition to historical semantics, Leonhard has written extensively on war and peace and on empires and nation-states.

Jörn Leonhard's *Liberalismus – Zur historischen Semantik eines europäischen Deutungsmusters* (2001; 'Liberalism – On the Historical Semantics of a European Interpretive Scheme') is the first major study to take conceptual history beyond the focus on a single language and to focus on transfers and translation instead. His further publications include *Constitutions, Civility and Violence in European History: Mid-Eighteenth Century to the Present* (2008), *Comparing Empires: Encounters and Transfers in the Long Nineteenth Century* (2012) and *Die Büchse der Pandora: Geschichte des Ersten Weltkriegs* (2014; 'Pandora's Box: History of the First World War'). Leonhard has contributed to Rolf Reichardt's *Handbuch politisch-sozialer Grundbegriffe in Frankreich, 1680–1820* ('Handbook of Basic Political and Social Concepts in France 1680–1820').[1]

In the article presented here, Leonhard differentiates Koselleck's concept of *Sattelzeit* ('saddle period', a metaphor which points to the character of the period between 1760 and 1840, which had a leg on each side of the great transformative processes). Leonhard points out that these processes have to be read both in a nation-specific context and with attention to the interaction between nations. This leads him to develop a model for the diachronic analysis of concepts moving between different languages and contexts.

---

[1]See Rolf Reichardt, 'For a socio-historical semantics as a middle course between "lexicometry" and "conceptual history"' (Chapter 3).

6

Translation as Cultural Transfer and Semantic Interaction: European Variations of *Liberal* between 1800 and 1830

Jörn Leonhard

(1) Avoiding the Semantic Nominalism of Political Languages – Translation and Comparative Semantics

Ideologies, Clifford Geertz once remarked, are cognitive maps 'of problematic social reality'.[1] The semantic variations of political and social key concepts in particular contexts represent, like a map, different historical landscapes, based on specific experiences of the past and expectations of the future. Maps imply travel, and travelling in the landscape of ideologies implies contact between speakers, the transfer of interpretative knowledge and hence the semantic transformation of concepts as they are used in arguments. All these elements underline the importance of translational processes for any understanding of semantic change. Every translation involves a conceptual movement between the translatable and the translated, and indeed translation can be described not only as a metaphor, but as a method of semantic analysis. Translations from that perspective have both a diachronic and a synchronic dimension: they stand behind conceptual changes over time, from past past to past present, but they also represent the synchronic export and import of concepts and of their semantic structure between languages and vocabularies, thus reflecting the transfer of hermeneutic knowledge needed to articulate them in discourse.[2]

A comparative history of concepts brings together both dimensions of translation by stressing the diachronic change over time and the synchronic variations of semantic structures. The former points to translations in one national language community, the other to contact and translation within and between different national languages. If taken together, the comparison not only focuses on isolated conceptual histories, but also on processes of semantic transfer and interaction as well as conceptual overlapping.

Two hermeneutical problems are involved here, which the semantics of *liberal/liberalism* can help to illustrate. First, many comparative studies still tend to equate the meaning of the ideological semantics of *liberalism* in different countries, so as if it meant basically a similar canon of ideas, or movements, or parties. They do not take into consideration the distinct contemporary meanings of *liberal* in different historical contexts. The neglect of this semantic aspect results in a trap of semantic nominalism, i.e. the unconsidered transfer of a concept's semantics from the contemporary political language of one country to the political discourse of another. This implicit equating of contemporary meanings in different contexts conceals an important focus of experiences and expectations, in other words the possibility of replacing the category of universal European liberalism with a spectrum of distinct histories of contemporary meanings of *liberal*. This is in contrast to a traditional history of ideas approach which would point to the singular of *European liberalism*, quasi 'distilled' from the realm of ideas to which *liberalism* could be applied *avant la lettre*, i.e. before the concept actually existed in contemporary political discourse.[3] Yet the semantics of political concepts are not the same in different countries. Different contexts point to the problem of how distinct experiences of the past and past expectations of the future were translated into distinct political and social discourses, and how that process was stimulated by the import, export, and translation of foreign concepts and their semantic fields. In other words, it is not possible to sum up the meaning of French *libéralisme*, German *Liberalismus*, Italian *liberalismo* and English *liberalism* in a universal concept of *European Liberalism*. Behind linguistically 'equal' or 'similar' words lie essentially different experiences, interests and expectations.

Second, there is what may be called a translational circle. The results of a comparative semantic analysis need to be re-translated into a language. Theoretically a researcher in such a situation would need a meta-language in order to avoid this problem of *Rückübersetzung*, such as a meta-theory which in other comparative analyses serves as a *tertium comparationis*, for example modernization theories in social history. However for comparative semantics, there is no such meta-language. Since there is no easy solution to this problem, the historian needs at least to be aware of it.[4]

Against this background this paper seeks to illustrate the importance of translational processes for comparative semantic analyses in two parts: first, two ideal-type models are presented, which have been developed on the basis of the semantics of *liberal/liberalism* in European comparison, one focusing on the semantic transformation of concepts, the other concentrating on translation as a selective export and import of interpretative knowledge. Secondly, some exemplary elements of the translational processes that influenced the emergence of *liberal* as a political key concept in early nineteenth[-century][5] Europe are analysed in order to illustrate the importance of translations for semantic change.

(2) Differentiating the *Sattelzeit*: Stage-Models on Semantic Transformation and Translation

From the basis of such a comparative analysis of semantics it is also possible to differentiate Reinhard Koselleck's concept of the saddle epoch (*Sattelzeit*).[6] According to this model a universal semantic change, based on such processes as democratization of concepts, took place between 1750 and 1850 and resulted in modern concepts in political and social vocabulary. However in this paper it is argued that only the comparison allows identifying the specific rhythms of conceptual change and thus the life-cycle of concepts in different countries. There was no single period in which the European vocabularies became modern, but rather particular paths with different connections, relations and overlapping between the semantics of key political concepts. Both models try to take these premises into consideration. The first describes the diachronic transformation of a concept's semantics, consisting of four stages. Its function is to identify the moment when translations can actually influence conceptual change and semantic transformation.

1 The pre-political stage of semantics: In the case of *liberal*, this is the stadium dominated by the pre-1789 uses of *liberal* or *liberality* in the different contexts. As in the case of Immanuel Kant's '*Liberalität der Denkungsart*'[7] or Sieyès' '*education libérale*'[8] of the Third estate in France the concepts reflected an enlightened educational ideal without a fixed political or social meaning.

2 A fermentation of traditional and new semantic elements, caused by new political, social and cultural experiences, newly articulated interests and new expectations: Pre-political and politicized meanings were now beginning to overlap. This process started with the invention of the *idées liberals* in France in 1799 and their subsequent translation into *liberale Ideen* in Germany and *idee liberali* in Italy,[9] but also with the emergence of *liberales* and *serviles* as party names in Spain and the export of this nomenclature to other European countries.

3 The politicization of concepts as controversial through changing connotations of traditional concepts and the development of new concepts: In this phase the speakers attempted to structure the

semantic field by canonical definitions and semantic clarity, relying on a number of key experiences and expectations. This is the stadium in which the import of concepts such as the French *idées liberals* created a framework for the articulation of new experiences and stimulated conceptual debates, thereby testing the semantic field.

4 The ideological polarization and development of bipolar or multi-polar semantic structures: The focus was now on an antagonistic structure of semantics, resulting in a wider field of political and social nomenclatures and their use in arguments. In the case of liberal, the semantic field became defined by symmetric counter-concepts such as *radical, conservative* or later *socialist.*

Translational processes between national languages played a fundamental role in the second and third stages, when the semantic structure of a concept is still relatively fluid and open. In this phase the transfer of concepts and their translation served as a stimulating catalyst for politicized discourses. A very good illustration of this constellation is Rolf Reichardt's reconstruction of a virtual library of French-German

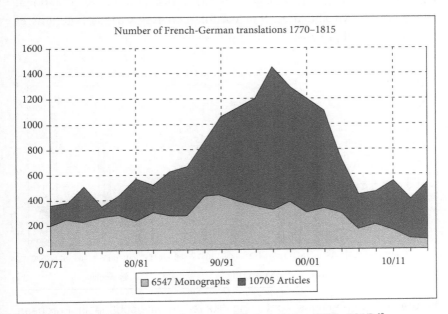

Figure 6.1 A Franco-German Library of Translations, 1770–1815.[10]

Source: Martin Burke and Melvin Richter, *Why Concepts Matter: Translating Social and Political Thought* (Leiden: Brill, 2012), 97.

translations between 1770 and 1815, a quantitative analysis which documents the importance of translations in the politicization of German concepts and discourses through the translation of French texts. It also underlines the growing importance of journal and newspaper articles in this context, especially during the 1790s. (See Figure 6.1)

Conceptual translations presuppose a cultural transfer of concepts that have gained at least a certain degree of universal meaning, before they can be integrated into national discourses. That was the case with the French political connotation of *libéral* and the Bonapartist *idées libérales* after 1799 in particular. The export of *libéral* and its translation became a dominating feature in early-nineteenth-century German and Italian political discourses. The following table shows the number of monographs containing *liberal* in the main or sub-title between 1801 and 1880 in European comparison. Again the quantitative analysis underlines the pioneering role of France as a laboratory of political and social language in early nineteenth century. The export of French concepts and semantic fields to other continental societies was a dominating feature before 1830, especially with regard to the German and Italian states.

Following from this merely quantitative analysis, the second model tries to identify different stages in the translation between national languages and vocabularies, thereby differentiating various functions of the translational process:

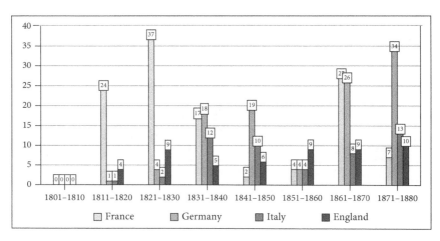

Figure 6.2 Monographs containing 'liberal' in title/subtitle in European comparison, 1801–1880.[11]

Source: Martin Burke and Melvin Richter, *Why Concepts Matter: Translating Social and Political Thought* (Leiden: Brill, 2012), 98.

1 Imitating translation of characteristic French expressions or texts taken from newspaper articles, essays or entries from contemporary dictionaries: This translation usually reflected the direct impact of foreign impressions on a speaker, for instance a German writer travelling to revolutionary Paris and reading political journals there. In this early stadium, there was a characteristic lack of differentiating commentaries which could relate foreign concepts and their semantics directly to the speaker's own political or social context. German Jacobins travelling to Paris translated *principes libéraux* as *liberale Prinzipien*, but focused on the contemporary French context, not on the possibility of applying the concept to the German political situation.[12]

2 Adapting translation: On the basis of imported foreign concepts, selected semantic elements were applied to a different social and political context. In this phase, the selection of semantics is directed by the specific experiences, interests and expectations of the perceiving speakers. Although it still reflected the foreign origins, the concept's original connotation changed. The French *idées libérales* were not only imitated by *liberale Ideen* or *idee liberali* but the translation was applied to the political experiences and constitutional as well as national expectations in Germany and Italy.

3 Discursive integration: In this phase concepts and their semantic structures, which were now applied to the different political and social contexts of the importing society, were integrated into a society's discourse. This is documented by the emergence of encyclopaedic entries of *liberale Ideen*, for instance in the Brockhaus edition of 1817, without any reference to its French origin but with particular references to the German political and constitutional context.[13]

Many objections against such evolutionary types and organic patterns can also be directed against both models. But their primary function is to have a heuristic instrument in the analysis of a particular concept. What is intended here as well is a stimulus for a broader debate about ways to differentiate Koselleck's paradigm of a *Sattelzeit* between 1750 and 1850. From that perspective we may also ask whether parts of these models can be applied to other processes of conceptual change. The aim should be to overcome isolated national histories of concepts by a focus on cultural transfer and semantic interaction between political languages, an entangled history which reflects the synchronic variations of the past.[14]

(3) Universalization and National Application: Translating *Liberal* in Early-Nineteenth-Century Europe

The importance of translational processes for conceptual change can be illustrated by the comparative semantics of *liberal* in the early nineteenth century. On the European continent, the Napoleonic expansionism led to a direct confrontation with the French *idées libérales* as Napoleon's programmatic formula of the results of 1789. In his Proclamation of the eighteenth Brumaire 1799, justifying the coup d'état, Bonaparte's *idées libérales* originally stood for a defensive strategy to safeguard the revolution's legacy by ending both political instability and social anarchy: '*Les idées conservatrices, tutélaires, libérales, sont rentrées dans leurs droits par la dispersion des factieux qui opprimaient les conseils, et qui, pour être devenus les plus odieux des hommes, n'ont pas cessé d'être les plus méprisables.*'[15] Napoleon's invention of the *idées libérales* became part of his short-lived but influential imperial ideology. As the '*héro des idées liberals*' he proclaimed to be both the only legitimate heir of 1789 and the only *garant* of the revolution's positive achievements, as incarnated by the *Code Civil* and the idea of the nation's sovereignty.[16] By referring to the imperial understanding of the *idées libérales*, Napoleon thus claimed to fulfil the revolution's original and legitimate objects. On the other hand, turning the transpersonal principle of the *idées libérales* against Napoleon's military despotism after 1810 integrated the opposition of the *libéraux* around Benjamin Constant and Madame de Staël.[17] This explained why the *idées libérales* could survive the Emperor's defeat in 1815. By discursive export and penetration, by 1815 the *idées libérales* had become a universal concept for continental authors. In Germany and Italy it was possible to distance them from the Napoleonic origin and use them to articulate new constitutional, social and national expectations.

Whereas the English denomination of parties had originated in the seventeenth century and immunized English political discourse against continental imports, which meant that *liberal* was only slowly and reluctantly integrated into an already existing political nomenclature, in Germany the semantic import of *liberal* coined by the French Revolution and Napoleon was essential. In the member states of the Confederation of the Rhine a new language policy was directed by the French authorities, by which the *idées libérales* and the *constitution libérale* found their way to German journals and newspapers. The *idées libérales*, first formulated by Bonaparte in his proclamation of the eighteenth Brumaire 1799, and after 1815 translated into *liberale Ideen* now indicated the overall demand for both national unity and constitutional progress in Germany. German authors looked at French debates, but their translation changed from a mere imitation of the concept to its application to the particular German situation. An excellent example in this context is Johann Christoph von Aretin's adapting translation of a contemporary French article on *Les idées libérales* published in 1815.[18] In his translation Aretin applied the French concept to his own German background and the political and national situation of the German states at the end of the Napoleonic Wars.[19] He gave particular attention to the constitution as the incarnation of a new balance between monarchy and people. But whereas the French text spoke of *civilisation* as the main criterion behind liberty, Aretin used the German *Bildung* which had a much more socially exclusive meaning. Also, the concept of *nation* had very different connotations in France and Germany at that time. Whereas French semantics oscillated between the nation's revolutionary sovereignty and the nation as represented by the constitutional monarch, the German expectation was to establish a constitutional nation-state which by 1815 already existed in France:

Eine Verfassung ist liberal, wenn sie der Nation nicht nur alle Gattungen von Freiheit gewährt, deren ihr Bildungsstand fähig ist, sondern auch die Freiheit unter den Schutz der edlen und großmächtigen Gesinnungen stellt. Wesentliche Bestandtheile einer solchen Verfassung sind daher gegenseitiges Zutrauen der Regierung und der Regierten, ehrenvolle Auszeichnung des Verdienstes und des Talents, Wohlwollen gegen alle Menschen ohne Unterschied des Standes und des Bekenntnisses.[20]	*Une constitution libérale non-seulement donne à une nation tous les genres de liberté que son état de civilisation admet, mais elle met encore la liberté sous la sauvegarde des sentiments nobles et généreux. La confiance mutuelle du gouvernement et du peuple, les égards dus au talent et à la vertu, la bienveillance envers les nations étrangères, font parties de toute constitution libérale.[21]*

Similarly different connotations lie behind the concept of *gouvernement/ Regierung*. Whereas the French author explicitly acknowledged the existence of an institutionalized opposition in parliament, Aretin could only focus on public opinion as a source of political legitimacy and an instrument with which to counterbalance the dangers of despotic rule. Here the different constitutional developments and experiences in both societies became obvious:

> Eins der ersten Kennzeichen einer liberalen Regierung ist, daß sie öffentliche Verhandlungen über die den Staat und das Volk zunächst angehenden Gegenstände gestattet. Mit der Verhandlung wird auch der Widerspruch zugelassen. Jede liberale Regierung erlaubt also die Kritik ihrer Verfügungen: ja sie wünscht sie sogar, einmahl weil die freie Discussion allein dem Volke seine politische Freiheit beweist, und dann, weil sie die Regierung von dem Zustand der Volksstimmung unterrichtet, und ihr Gelegenheit giebt, jene ungeheure moralische Kraft, genannt öffentliche Meinung, zu leiten und in Bewegung zu bringen; ein Vortheil, den der Despotismus gänzlich entbehrt.[22]

> Un des premiers caractères d'un gouvernement libéral, c'est de provoquer une discussion publique sur toutes les questions qui intéressent l'État et la nation. Mais admettre la discussion, c'est admettre la contradiction; or la contradiction habituelle, en fait de politique, est ce qu'on nomme opposition. Tout gouvernement libéral admet donc une opposition; il y a plus, il la désire, d'abord parce que l'existence bien manifeste d'une opposition peut seule constater l'existence de la liberté politique, ensuite parce que les débats entre les ministres et l'opposition signalent les erreurs où les premiers ont pu tomber, éclairent le gouvernement sur la situation de l'esprit public, et fournissent l'occasion de diriger, d'exciter et de mettre en mouvement l'opinion, cette force morale incalculable dont le despotisme se prive lui-même.[23]

The import of the new concept also provoked resistance, reflecting the change from politicization to ideological polarization: For Metternich and the German Confederation this concept could only denote a revolutionary direction. Public confidence in the 'Liberalität der Regierung',[24] the government's liberality, for instance during the Prussian reform era or in the South German constitutional states of Baden, Württemberg and Bavaria, became more and more disillusioned after the reactionary change in the political atmosphere following the murder of August von Kotzebue and the Carlsbad Decrees in 1819/20. When it became clear that there would be no further constitutional progress and no parliaments in the single German states, *liberal* changed into an opposition-label, thus defining the progressive and backward forces in society. Now the use of the term reflected the deepening gap between state and society, for which there was no equivalent in the history of the English concept *liberal*. At the end of the 1820s, *liberalism* in Germany signified an uncontested belief in the progress of reason while the restorative governments represented but backwardness and out-dated forces in history. The *liberal party* stood for a *movement party (Bewegungspartei)* – a symbol of natural progress in history.[25]

Translations from French to German in that period meant an ongoing, implicit confrontation with France. In contrast to the optimistic self-estimation of what *liberal* should stand for, early definitions of *liberal/ liberalism* in Germany reflected a specific uncertainty about the political and social implications of a concrete program. According to most contemporaries, *wahrer Liberalismus* (true liberalism) had to be defended against radical forces in the tradition of the French revolutionary terror.[26] At least until the French July Revolution of 1830 the history of *liberal* in Germany was at the same time a history of interpreting the French Revolution and its consequences in the German states. In Britain on the other hand the delayed and reluctant import of the new concept pointed back to the experiences of the seventeenth century and the existence of pre-modern party names, at least until the early 1830s. In the British case one is confronted with the complex translation from *Whig* to *liberal*.[27] From this point of view the history of *liberal* also stood for the different duration of distinct *Ancien régimes*, reflecting different *Sattelzeiten*. In France, Germany and Italy this was directly or indirectly marked by the period between 1789 and 1815, whereas Britain's *Ancien régime* only came to an end in the course of the 1830s.

France was not the only birthplace of the new concept: Again it was through a complex process of translations that Spanish *liberales* influenced the modernization of other European vocabularies. The political meaning of *liberal* as a party denomination originated from the first Spanish constitution of 1812. The adherents of this new constitution called themselves *liberales* and spoke of their opponents who supported the principles of absolute monarchy as *serviles*.[28] It was with regard to the political situation in Spain that the new political adjective *liberal* found its way into the English political vocabulary. The British example illustrates the limits of translations and the factors that shelter a political discourse against conceptual export from outside: The British import of the Spanish concept was a negative semantic adaptation. In 1816 Lord Castlereagh thought of a purely revolutionary party in the tradition of the French Jacobins when he spoke of the Spanish *liberales*, although their origin had been the fight against French occupation during Napoleon's reign.[29] Until 1818/19 English authors made use of the new political concept *liberal* very often in the foreign spelling to describe the domestic political situation of continental countries, thereby underlining the un-English origin of the new political concept. But when speaking of British politics, authors continued to refer to the historical party names *Whig* and *Tory* or *radical* which had originated from the seventeenth and eighteenth century.

The British example illustrated an imitating, not an adapting translation, which postponed discursive integration for a long time. The continental context dominated the meaning of *liberal* when being used in English political texts until the period after 1815. Only very reluctantly did *liberal* appear after 1815 indicating a changing tone in British politics. In 1816 Robert Southey spoke for the first time of the '*British "liberals"*', thus mixing the Spanish spelling of the party name with an application to the English political scene and stigmatizing the political opponent by the use of the continental adjective.[30] For many Tory authors, *liberal* served as a negative label with which they could relate their opponents to the revolutionary experiments in France, Spain, Italy or Greece. For them *liberal* represented Jacobin terror and Napoleonic despotism under the guise of an apparently progressive label. The import of *libéral* or *liberales* in the British case for a long time meant a confrontation with continental revolutionary experiences and thus provoked discursive resistance.

Only reluctantly the un-English connotation of *liberal* was overcome, making the semantic application of the new concept to English politics possible. An important catalyst for the integration of *liberal* into the English political vocabulary was the founding of Leigh Hunt's Journal *The Liberal, or Verse and Prose from the South* in 1822, the short-lived but influential literary journal of the Byron-circle which contained articles by Byron and Shelley, often in a critical if not opposing tone, not only dealing with the political developments in the South of Europe but also criticizing the politics of George III and Lord Castlereagh. The title already anticipated the program: The South of Europe with its revolutionary movements for national independence and political liberty, such as in Greece, constituted the background, but Leigh Hunt in the preface of the first edition also pointed to the traditional meaning of *liberal* in the context of classical education, thus relating the political implications to the ideal of Roman and Greek literature as the framework of humanity and political liberty.[31] It is significant that in the course of the public controversy about the new journal the opponents reacted to the title by publishing a satirical antidote: *The Illiberal, or Verse and Prose from the North.*[32]

The end of the Napoleonic wars in 1815 marked the end of the internal political abstinence in British politics. The blockade of an open and public debate about reform, defended until 1815 because of the necessary concentration of the national forces in the fight against France, was lifted. The shift of political attention from foreign affairs to domestic problems began to provide a fertile ground for the semantic transformation of *liberal* from an apparently un-English adjective with revolutionary and continental implications into an integral concept of the English political language, especially for the reform-oriented Whigs inside and outside parliament. That included a new context in which the foreign concept's translation helped to develop a new framework for political reform discourses. The changing atmosphere of public opinion, now considered an important factor in the nation's political life, was reflected by the slow adaptation of the imported concept *liberal*. A quotation from Robert Peel's letter to John Wilson Croker in 1820 exactly marks this moment of the semantic process:

> Do not you think that the tone of England – of that great compound of folly, weakness, prejudice, wrong feeling, right feeling, obstinacy, and newspaper paragraphs, which is called public opinion – is more liberal – to use an odious but intelligible phrase, than the policy of the Government? Do not you think that there is a feeling, becoming daily more general and more confined – that is independent of the pressure of taxation, or any immediate cause – in favour of some undefined change in the mode of governing the country?[33]

In 1827, Henry Brougham, a leading member of the moderate Whigs among the Edinburgh Reviewers, reflected on the 'State of parties' since the beginning of the 1820s. He made extensive use of *liberal* to denote a new principle in British politics. Behind the progress of *liberal opinions* he identified a new concept of foreign policy, advocating national independence abroad and opposing the restorative objects of the Holy Alliance. Already before the transformation of the traditional party names *Whig* and *Tory* into *Liberal* and *Conservative* – a long-term semantic process which was not completed before the 1840s – Brougham concluded that the main ideological antagonism in British politics could no longer be expressed by traditional political labels. These party names had either originated from the seventeenth century and thus reflected the factions of the Civil War (*Court* versus *Country*), the political antagonists of the Glorious Revolution (*Whig* versus *Tory*) or they indicated the aspirations of the Stuarts (*Loyalist* versus *Jacobin*) during the eighteenth century or, pointing to the continent, the new party names coined in the course of the French Revolution:

> A new casting also of political sects has taken place; the distinctions, and almost the names, of Loyalist and Jacobin, Whig and Tory, Court and Country Faction, are fast wearing away. Two great divisions of the community will, in all likelihood, soon be far more generally known; the Liberal and the Illiberal, who will divide, but we may be sure most unequally, the suffrages of the Nation.[34]

Unlike most continental party names which originated from the post-1789 period, *liberal* as a post-revolutionary concept in Britain can only be interpreted with regard to the ideological polarization since the absolutist experiments of the seventeenth century, pointing to the distinct British *Sattelzeit*. This was reproduced in the subsequent pre-modern party-names which did not have any equivalents in continental discourses.

(4) Conclusion: Translation as Cultural Transfer and Semantic Interaction

The French stimulus of the *idées libérales* was fundamental for the development of new political and social concepts in Germany and Italy in the 1820s and early 1830s. In addition, the intensified debates about the French *Charte Constitutionnelle* of 1814 as a *constitution libérale* and the polarization between *ultra* and *libéraux* popularized the new concepts well beyond France. Translations of the French import in Germany and Italy changed from imitation over application and adaption to discursive integration.

In contrast to Germany or Italy, where the direct import of the *idées libérales* resulted first in translations and direct applications of the French concept to identify and formulate the demands for national unity and constitutional reforms after 1815, the confrontation with the new concept in Britain took a different path: Regarding the Spanish *liberales* or the French *libéraux*, the new political adjective was used to describe the political situation in continental countries for a long period. Only after 1815 the Tories' use of *liberal* as a derogatory label for their political opponents and the Philhellene movement contributed to a wider diffusion of *liberal*. However, for a long time *liberal* retained an un-English tone because it represented political movements and groups in countries other than Britain. Only after 1820, when the reform oriented Whigs of the *Edinburgh Review* accepted the new concept as a term with which to label their own position and political strategy, *liberal* for the first time became a positive and progressive semantic indicator in English political language, replacing the traditional semantic oppositions between *Court/Country*, *Whig/Tory* and *Jacobin/Loyalist*.

A focus on comparison and transfer makes the different *Sattelzeiten* of European concepts and vocabularies more visible, reflecting distinct rhythms and cycles of past experiences and expectations as they were stimulated and catalysed by the export and import of foreign concepts. These experiences and expectations could not easily be translated, but rather led to complex confrontations with otherness. Translations reflected processes of selective perception stimulating cultural transfers and allowing the articulation of new political and social premises. For the historian translations serve as a seismographic indicator of how past contemporaries articulated their past pasts and their past futures. Friedrich Nietzsche once stated that a concept which contained in itself a whole history, evaded definition – *'definable is anything that has no history'*.[35] However, history necessarily implies translation, whether diachronic or synchronic. The historian, who starts travelling in the landscapes of past experiences and expectations, is well advised to remember that as a traveller he will be dependent on translations. Hermeneutic dictionaries must be part of his vade-mecum, if he does not want to become lost in translation. Travelling implies contact and confrontation, comparison and change of perspectives. Uncertainty leads to questions not asked before.

(Translation: Joy Titheridge)

Notes

1   Clifford Geertz, 'Ideology as a Cultural System', in idem, *The Interpretation of Cultures: Selected Essays* (New York: Basic Books, 1973), 193–233, here: 220.

2   See Jörn Leonhard, 'Von der Wortimitation zur semantischen Integration: Übersetzung als Kulturtransfer', *Werkstatt Geschichte*, 48 (2008), 45–63.

3   See Jörn Leonhard, *Liberalismus. Zur historischen Semantik eines europäischen Deutungsmusters* (Munich: Oldenbourg, 2001), 47, 66 and 83; and idem, 'From European Liberalism to the Languages of Liberalisms: The Semantics of *Liberalism* in European Comparison', *Redescriptions. Yearbook of Political Thought and Conceptional History*, 8 (2004), 17–51.

4   See Reinhart Koselleck, Ulrike Spree and Willibald Steinmetz, 'Drei bürgerliche Welten. Zur vergleichenden Semantik der bürgerlichen Gesellschaft in Deutschland, England und Frankreich', in *Bürger in der Gesellschaft der Neuzeit*, ed. Hans-Jürgen Puhle (Göttingen: Vandenhoek & Ruprecht, 1991), 14–58, especially 22; and Javiér Fernández Sebastián and Juan Francisco Fuentes, 'Conceptual History, Memory, and Identity: An Interview with Reinhart Koselleck', *Contributions to the History of Concepts*, 2/1 (2006), 99–127, here: 111–12; see also *Vocabulaire européen des philosophies. Dictionnaire des intraduisibles*, ed. Barbara Cassin (Paris: Sueil, 2004).

5   [Note: missed word in the original text, correction made by the editors.]

6   Reinhart Koselleck, 'Richtlinien für das Lexikon politisch-sozialer Begriffe der Neuzeit', *Archiv für Begriffsgeschichte*, 11 (1967), 81–99; idem, 'Einleitung', in Otto Brunner, Werner Conze and Reinhart Koselleck (eds), *Geschichtliche Grundbegriffe. Historisches Lexikon zur politisch-sozialen Sprache in Deutschland*, vol. 1 (Stuttgart: Klett, 1972), xiii–xxvii; for a general overview on the perception of 'Begriffsgeschichte' see Willibald Steinmetz, 'Vierzig Jahre Begriffsgeschichte – The State of the Art', in Heidrun Kämper and Ludwig M. Eichinger (eds), *Sprache – Kognition – Kultur. Sprache zwischen mentaler Struktur und kultureller Prägung* (Berlin: de Gruyter, 2008), 174–97.

7   Immanuel Kant, 'Kritik der Urtheilskraft, 1. Theil: Kritik der ästhetischen Urtheilskraft', in Königlich Preußische Akademie der Wissenschaften (ed.), *Kant's gesammelte Schriften*, vol. 5 (Berlin: G. Reimer, 1913), 268.

8   Emmanuel Sieyès, *Qu'est-ce que le tiers état? (1789), précédé de l'Essai sur les privilèges. Édition critique avec une introduction par Edme Champion* (Paris: Au siège de la Société, 1888), 42.

9   See for example Paolo Vergani, *Le Idee Liberali. Ultimo Rifugio dei Nemici della Religione e del Trono* (Genova: Stamperia Pagano, 1816).

10   Martin Burke and Melvin Richter, *Why Concepts Matter: Translating Social and Political Thought* (Leiden: Brill, 2012), 97.

11   Ibid., 98.

12   See for example Konrad Ferdinand Oelsner's letter dated 10 May 1797, quoted in: Klaus Deinet, *Konrad Engelbert Oelsner und die Französische*

Revolution. Geschichtserfahrung und Geschichtsdeutung eines deutschen Girondisten (Munich: Oldenbourg, 1981), 285.

13   Friedrich A. Brockhaus (ed.), *Allgemeine deutsche Real-Encyclopädie für die gebildeten Stände. Conversations-Lexicon*, vol. 5, 4th edn (Leipzig: Brockhaus, 1817), 674–5.

14   See Steinmetz (2008), 175–7.

15   Napoleon Bonaparte, ' "Proclamation du général en chef Bonaparte". Le 19 brumaire, 11 heures du soir', *Le Diplomate. Numéro xvi, Tridi 23 Brumaire, an VIII de la République française* (13 November 1799); see also Philippe J. B. Buchez and Pierre C. Roux, *Histoire parlementaire de la Révolution française ou journal des assemblées nationales depuis 1789 jusqu'en 1815*, vol. 38 (Paris: Paulin, 1838), 257. [Note: 'The ideas of preservation, protection and freedom, immediately resumed their places in the dispersion of the faction who wished to oppress the councils, and who, in making themselves the most odious of men, never cease to be the most contemptible.' *The Annual Register, or, A View of the History, Politics, and Literature for the Year 1799* (London: T. Burton, 1801), 253.]

16   Louis Antoine Fauvelet de Bourrienne, *Mémoires de M. de Bourrienne, ministre d'état; sur Napoléon, le directoire, le consulat, l'empire et la restauration*, vol. 3 (Paris: Ladvocat, 1829), 28.

17   See Xavier Martin, 'Libéral/Illibéral. Sur l'emploi de ces mots dans les *Travaux préparatoires du Code civil* (1801–1804)', in *Dictionnaire des Usages socio-politiques (1770–1815), vol. II: Notions-concepts* (Paris: Klincksieck, 1987), 45–53.

18   'Les Idées libérales', *Le Nouvelliste Français ou Recueil Choisi de Mémoires No. XII* (Pesth: 1815), 273–82.

19   Johann Christoph Freiherr von Aretin, 'Was heißt Liberal? Zum Theil mit Benützung eines französischen Aufsatzes in dem *Nouvelliste francais*', *Neue Allemannia*, 1 (1816a), 163–75.

20   [English translation by the editors: 'A constitution is liberal when it not only permits a nation all the types of freedom that the nation's education level is capable of harnessing, but also puts freedom under the protection of the noble and powerful dispositions. Key elements of such a constitution are therefore mutual trust between the government and the governed, honourable recognition of merit and talent, and goodwill towards all people regardless of class and denominations.']

21   von Aretin (1816), 170; 'Les Idées libérales' (1815), 278–9.

22   [English translation by the editors: 'One of the first characteristics of a liberal government is that it permits public discussion about fundamental matters concerning the state and the people. Opposition is also allowed to be voiced in these discussions. Every liberal government allows criticism of its decrees: the government in fact even welcomes the criticism. Firstly,

because open discussion shows its political freedom to the people, and then, because the criticism informs the government of the state of the public sentiment. Furthermore, it gives the government the opportunity to lead and to bring into motion that tremendous moral strength called public opinion; an advantage that the despotism completely goes without.']

23 von Aretin (1816a), 171; 'Les Idées libérales', 279–80.

24 Johann Christoph Freiherr von Aretin, 'Über Völkerbestimmung', *Neue Allemannia*, 7 (1816b), 51–2.

25 See for example Theodor Mundt, *Moderne Lebenswirren* (Leipzig: Reichenbach, 1834), 33.

26 See Wilhelm Traugott Krug, *Der falsche Liberalismus unserer Zeit. Ein Beitrag zur Geschichte des Liberalismus und eine Mahnung für künftige Volksvertreter* (Leipzig: Kollmann, 1832).

27 Jörn Leonhard, ' "True English Guelphs and Gibelines": Zum historischen Bedeutungs- und Funktionswandel von *whig* und *tory* im englischen Politikdiskurs seit dem 17. Jahrhundert', *Archiv für Kulturgeschichte*, 83 (2002), 175–213.

28 See Juan Francisco Fuentes and Javier Fernández Sebastián, 'Liberalismo', in eidem (eds), *Diccionario político y social del siglo XIX espanol* (Madrid: Alianza, 2002), 413–28.

29 Speech of 15 February 1816, in: Thomas C. Hansard (ed.), *The Parliamentary Debates from the Year 1803 to the Present Time, First Series (1803–1820)*, vol. 37 (London: Hansard, 1820–9), 602.

30 Henry, Lord Brougham, *The Life and Times of Henry, Lord Brougham*, vol. 2 (London: Blackwood, 1871), 325.

31 Leigh Hunt, 'Preface', in idem, *The Liberal, or Verse and Prose from the South* (London: Hunt, 1822), viii–ix.

32 William Gifford, *The Illiberal! Verse and Prose from the North!! Dedicated to My Lord Byron in the South!! To be Continued Occasionally!! As a Supplement to Each Number of 'The Liberal'* (London: T. Holt, 1822).

33 Letter of Robert Peels to John Wilson Crocker, 23 March 1820, in Lewis J. Jennings (ed.), *The Correspondence and Diaries of the Late Right Honourable John Wilson Crocker*, vol. 1 (New York: C. Scribner's Sons, 1884), 155–6.

34 Henry Brougham, 'State of Parties', *Edinburgh Review*, 46 (1827), 431.

35 Friedrich Nietzsche, 'Zur Genealogie der Moral, Zweite Abhandlung: "Schuld", "schlechtes Gewissen", Verwandtes', in idem, *Sämtliche Werke. Kritische Studienausgabe*, vol. 5, ed. Giorgio Colli and Mazzino Montinari (1967), 3rd edn (Munich: Deutscher Taschenbuch Verlag, 1993), 317.

Kari Palonen is an internationally renowned Finnish political scientist. After attaining his PhD in 1975, Palonen began his career in the field of political science. In the 1980s, his attention turned increasingly to the conceptual history of politics, and since the late 1990s he has been actively involved in various international projects on conceptual history. Kari Palonen is professor of political science at the University of Jyväskylä, Finland, as well as Academy Professor of the Academy of Finland. Since 2006, he serves as the director of the Finnish Centre of Excellence in Political Thought and Conceptual Change (PolCon).

Among Palonen's publications are titles such as *The Struggle with Time: A Conceptual History of 'Politics' as an Activity* (2006), *Re-thinking Politics: Essays from a Quarter-century* (2007), *The Politics of Limited Times: The Rhetoric of Temporal Judgment in Parliamentary Democracies* (2008) and *Parliamentarism and Democratic Theory* (co-editor; 2015). Kari Palonen is the founding editor-in-chief of *The Finnish Yearbook of Political Thought*, renamed *Redescriptions* in 2003.

A central aim in the work of Palonen is to bring the traditions of conceptual and intellectual history into a fruitful dialogue. In the article presented here, he deals specifically with the subject of translation in conceptual history. This deepens and expands the debate already encountered in Leonhard's text in the previous chapter.

7

Translation, Politics and Conceptual Change

Kari Palonen

'Any translation into one's own present implies a conceptual history', writes Reinhart Koselleck.[1] With this ambitious thesis, he attributes both a first rank significance to the understanding of the process of conceptual change and suggests that we reconsider the act of translation as a dimension of conceptual history. Koselleck's qualification that we should speak only of translations 'into our own present' is only relative, for in a strict sense any translation is a movement in time, a move between the translatable and the translated.

In this essay I take up the issue of conceptual changes due to translations. I will first present my reflections on the politics of translations, illustrated with historical examples. I will then present fragments of what I would like to call a political theory of language and translation, based on a Weberian nominalistic perspective. Comments on recent retranslations of Max Weber offer me a representative anecdote (in the sense of Kenneth Burke's *A Grammar of Motives*[2]) for a preliminary discussion of analysing conceptual changes through translation. At the more concrete level of the politics of translations, I shall elucidate my argument by examining conceptual changes that are present in translations between different languages. For this purpose, I will explore translation strategies and neglected alternatives from the context of the formation of Finnish political vocabulary during the nineteenth century. Finally, I shall return to the general implications of the politics of conceptual change through translation as a primary source of inspiration.

(1) The Omnipresence of Translations

In this essay, I shall speak of 'translation' in a broad and etymologically literal sense. The Latin verb *transferre* can be counted among the expressions, which originally had the concrete spatial meaning of conveying something, but later served as basis for the shift to a more abstract temporal meaning.[3] We can easily understand how a translation is always a 'transport' or 'transfer' between different contexts. The point of the translation of concepts lies in their selectivity, in the fact that in a transfer between contexts there always is the possibility that something else and unintended creeps into the concept. The intention of translation marks a move that intends to regulate, although by no means always to eliminate, this 'something else'.

My specific point of departure is to insist that a translation between individual speakers is always required, on the simple basis that there are no two human beings that would have exactly the same context when speaking, listening or reading. I consider a 'methodological individualism' of this kind as a condition for understanding the insight that in the use of language the need for translation is omnipresent. Between two individuals there is always an 'existential' distance that renders a spontaneous understanding impossible. Simultaneously, such existential distance indicates the presence of a political dimension in inter-individual relationships, in the sense of both a *Spielraum*[4] for alternative translations as well as a built-in conflict between the users of the 'original' and those using a translation.

From this perspective there cannot be any spontaneous 'linguistic common sense' that would be shared by all 'normal human beings'. This point is directed against the reliance on a Habermasian type of 'ideal speech situations' as well as against the tacit ideology of elementary language teaching, both which are based on the assumption of a correspondence between translatable and translated. My main point is, however, to understand the contingent and controversial, that is, the political dimension in the inter-individual and inter-linguistic relationships of translation which always involves conceptual change. To specify this political dimension, we have to realize that translation does not refer to exceptional situations, but, on the contrary, forms an omnipresent procedure of interpretation of the relation between speakers and audiences in two different contexts.

Translation does not merely signify a relationship between different so-called natural languages but is, in the sense of Koselleck's remark, a general procedure to render intelligible conceptual changes. Translation is no exceptional situation but a rule in our daily linguistic actions.

This does not necessarily imply radical alterations in our linguistic practices, only an inversion of the understanding of what kinds of speech acts we are using when translating. In most cases, translation obviously relies on shared conventions and is quasi-automatic. I simply want to claim that it remains, and we frequently encounter situations in which this automatism does not work and conventions break down. Conceptual changes are actualized in a situation in which we have to stop our linguistic action to reflect on the meaning and point of a concept, but it can also take place as the unintended consequences of linguistic actions. For translation we have to consider both types of situations.[5]

We can speculate about the various grounds for an internal conceptual history that enables us an inversion of perspective on translation. My source of inspiration is Max Weber's famous article 'Die "Objektivität" sozialwissenschaftlicher und sozialpolitischer Forschung'[6] of 1904, in which Weber, above all, defends the perspectivist character of all knowledge in *Kulturwissenschaften*.[7] Behind Weber is the work of Friedrich Nietzsche, and behind this aspect of Nietzsche's perspectivism are the ancient rhetoricians and Sophists, as it has only recently been made clear with the publication of Nietzsche's lectures on ancient rhetoric.[8]

To trace the implications of perspectivism on the omnipresence of translation, I want to insist on three theses. My main nominalistic contention is that all use of language is based on the human acts of naming, not on the 'nature of things'. For example, the entities called 'men' and 'women' are contingent results of certain modes of naming and classifying things, which can always be replaced by others. This means, secondly, that even long-lasting historical consensus about such naming remains contingent, and such established names rather indicate a success in political struggles to exclude alternatives, but one day even such a success may evaporate. Today a growing number of people already experience difficulties in locating themselves through the public and largely 'statistical' categories of men and women, and we can imagine that it will not be long before the universal and unreflected use of that categorical dyad will decline. Thirdly, conceptual changes are omnipresent expressions of the controversiality of concepts, of rhetorical moves in such controversies and of their unanticipated consequences. Just as Tuija Pulkkinen[9] has recently thematized the conceptual and rhetorical history of the concept 'woman', I think that we have now reached a point at which an allegedly 'anthropological' or 'metahistorical' category (to use Koselleck's[10] terms, partly to opposed conclusions that he himself has drawn) has been replaced by a historical and political concept.

It is in this sense we can also better understand Koselleck's thesis that every translation, as an act in time, involves a conceptual history of the movement between the translatable and translated. We could even speak, with Koselleck,[11] of translation as a 'method' of conceptual history, not just as a metaphor, but as a procedure that renders conceptual changes from past to the present as well as the inevitable use of contemporary language in the analysis of such changes intelligible.[12] Indeed, the competent translation presupposes a readiness to regard the translatable as something alien that deserves a paraphrase or an interpretation in order to be intelligible to the present-day audience.[13] You have to treat a word, a concept or a phrase as something that can be transferred to an audience only through an explication of its point and significance. Hence it is no wonder that Koselleck also uses the Brechtian figure of *Verfremdungseffekt*[14] to redescribe the procedure of conceptual history.[15]

(2) The Politics of Translations

A further political implication of the contingency of translations is that a number of alternative translations for a text, a passage or a concept, can always be provided. None of them is perfect, but each of them indicates a different perspective on the transfer between the concepts as well as on the changing styles or fashions of doing so. All of these aspects are accentuated in the politically and historically controversial translations of concepts.

How do the various alternatives achieve or legitimize a conceptual change through translation? Here we have to shift the discussion from single moves to conventional entities, such as languages. My point is, however, not to apply the linguistic criteria of the formation of 'natural' or 'technical' languages to politics. On the contrary, I want to understand all languages as historical and political entities, of which the so-called natural languages are only one specific type.

A metaphorical use of political languages was mentioned already in the early twentieth century. It seems, however, that it was more systematically introduced by John Pocock in his *Politics, Language and Time*,[16] and has since become a commonplace. With Anthony Pagden's edition of the book *Languages of Political Theory in Early Modern Europe* (1987),[17] the metaphor has even been taken so seriously that certain languages have been named, as if they would be entities independent of the context and specific problematic of each scholar. I think this leads, already in the book edited by Pagden, to questionable quasi-naturalizations of definite political languages that could also engage us in rather fruitless debates about the borders and separateness of languages.

Moreover, such a quasi-naturalization of languages tends to provide the political languages with a similar status of quasi-autonomous entities rather than the 'natural languages' that we have in everyday use. It is, however, eminently political whether Serbian and Croatian have now become separate languages or remain politically conditioned dialects of Serbo-Croat with either a Latin or Cyrillic orthography. The example shows, however, that even so-called natural languages are political constructions (with linguists acting as part-time politicians).

Speaking of political languages as loosely related but historically relatively distinct theory complexes has an obvious advantage towards the more common use of 'isms'. This can be found also in academic literature, where 'isms' are discussed as if they would be real things instead of historical constructions, mainly of the nineteenth-century 'Liberalism', for example, can be defended with a number of opposed political languages,[18] and it is often more fruitful to replace the 'isms' by more specific political languages, such as contractarianism or evolutionism. This was a difference that provoked politically significant theoretical differences among the 'liberals', the understanding that contractarian 'liberals' and 'socialists' might have more common than with their party colleagues believing in an evolutionist philosophy of history.

We should, however, use political languages and the divisions between them only in thematically and rhetorically specified manners, making different classifications for different purposes. Thus, we must be cautious when speaking about contractarianism, as if there would be a single language from Hobbes to Rawls. There can be cases in which the common assumptions may be thematized critically, but in others the contractual basis of a polity remains of secondary importance, and the variations between types of contracts and the utilization of contractarian arguments may play a contextually highly different role.

Accordingly, I shall treat the so-called natural languages in the manner of political languages and not vice versa. By this move I do not merely intend the elementary insight that 'natural' languages have been politically constructed, some in more explicit forms than others. I would rather underline the fact that the fluid, diffuse, historical and always comparative character of political languages also holds true for the political dimensions of so-called natural languages. In this sense, there is no difference in principle to compare, for example, republican and contractarian languages than to compare the French and German languages.

In the Weberian mode of proceeding, all types of languages, whether 'natural', technical or political, can be considered as specific, although flexible and historically contingent complexes of '*Chancen*'.[19] All of them contain a limited but complex repertoire of resources for action that consist of a profiled distribution of certain shares of power. What is easily possible in one language cannot be done so easily in another, whereas there may be some inbound implications favouring certain uses and not favouring others and so on. Such limits change historically and may be altered by political moves.

My next move is to distinguish between different aspects of language. To simplify matters, we can distinguish between the resources in vocabulary, in references to reality and in conceptualization. For the study of conceptual change, the vocabulary as well as the modes to refer to non-linguistic events and processes form a way through which 'natural languages' and 'real history' can intervene in the conceptual discussions, in so far as they are conducted in different political languages. What Koselleck calls '*Sache*',[20] namely, the modes by which the events or processed are referred to and the facticities of the situation are established, I will rename as referential languages, avoiding recourse to non-linguistic instances. The facticity of the events and processes is, in other words, always mediated by and interpreted through referential languages.

The description of events is never given, but usually not problematic. Hannah Arendt quotes Georges Clemenceau as remarking about future historians' views on the outbreak of World War I: 'I know for certain that they will not say Belgium invaded Germany.'[21] However, we have to understand that this is just a statement of facticity, and although we do not dispute its validity, the significance and the point of it is always disputable. Or, to put it in terms of speech acts: the strictly locutionary mention of a 'fact' is at the same time only a possibility among the numerous illocutionary modes of *doing* so.[22]

I sometimes call sociology a discipline in which 'nothing happens', that is a discipline in which no names, dates, persons or events are either mentioned at all or referred only in a symptomal manner. More generally, in massive systems of concepts à la Rawls or à la Luhmann, interventions due to the diversity of vernacular languages and to the acuteness of historical events referred to tend to be regarded as disturbances. As opposed to this, conceptual history, as a mode of studying politics, should be keenly interested in names, dates, persons and events. For an understanding of conceptual change, contingent interventions into referred events, proper names of individual agents and the use vernacular languages appear as challenges.

Studying the politics and history of conceptual changes does not mean a study of the competition between a small and finite number of political languages. It forms, rather, a process of mixture, dissolution and formation of such languages, including constant interventions of both the vocabulary of 'natural' languages and of references to the historical events and processes. If we, with Koselleck,[23] understand concepts as 'pivots' around which the language turns, they mark singularizing breaking points in the fluent use of the languages. Actualization of a key concept, such as power, democracy or politics, occurs in a speech act that actualizes a break with the fluent use of language, as an occasion to revise the conceptual horizon or its relations to other linguistic dimensions of the situation.

To sum up, translating refers to a singularizing speech act that is related to a horizon of the concepts. The three levels – 1) the vocabulary of 'natural' languages, 2) the theorizing in political languages, and 3) the modes of referring to the facticities – serve as mediating contextual instances modifying both the conditions and the modes of reconceptualization-by-translation.

It is certainly uncommon to understand translation as an occasion for reconceptualization, using the contextual instances as mediating layers. The 'normal' situation for EU translators, for example, is, rather, to avoid such a reconceptualization. My point is that due to the tacit presence of such contextual instances, unintended conceptual changes are frequently introduced. This is by no means to be avoided at all costs, rather they should be closely analysed with specific cases and with varying types of conceptual alterations.

(3) Translating Max Weber

In a recent issue of *Max Weber Studies*, several contributions dealt with the recent retranslations of Weber's *Protestantische Ethik*.[24] The only existing translation of the famous text was done by Talcott Parsons in 1930. It has been known for some time that Parsons' translation is severely misleading and shaped by his own ideological preferences, which at key points were opposed to those of Weber.[25]

Peter Ghosh has gone further and reconsidered the point of translation of classics, such as Weber. Ghosh claims that translation is primarily not a 'linguistic act' but 'a historical and conceptual act'. He consequently insists on the principle that a linguist should not translate a work on German 'social and political theory', but that it is the task of an historian. According to Ghosh, 'the only properly equipped historian is an historian of ideas, who is familiar not only with Weber's conceptual world, but more or less the entire tradition of German social and political thinking to which Weber has reference'. Only by dispensing with an historical *Bildung*[26] (education) can we have any chance 'that the full range of meaning attaching to concepts can be revealed and explored'.[27]

Although Ghosh does not speak about conceptual history, he clearly has insight into the general historicity and contextuality of the concepts and the need, to use Quentin Skinner's[28] old expression, to avoid the 'mythology of prolepsis'. In addition, Ghosh is also clearly aware of the singular character of Weber's mode of using concepts – which, in my view, causes him to practice a variant of *Begriffsgeschichte*[29] *avant la lettre* in several respects.[30] Ghosh thus proposes the following procedure for the translation of *Die protestantische Ethik*:

> Thus, in Weber the translation of concepts is more important than the translation of any other word; and any attempt to calibrate a set of translations

of Weber's most celebrated work should proceed in the first instance not from the translation of selected passages ... but from a sample mapping in English of the conceptual lexicon of the PE.[31]

Now we can better understand Koselleck's point about the presence of conceptual history in any translation. In order to render intelligible both Weber's contextual horizon and his singularizing speech act in using a certain concept, a comprehensive 'lexicon' of Weber's own conceptual map would be required, in the best case one which takes into account both the *Werkgeschichte*[32] (history of the works) of both Weber's oeuvre and of the writings in question.

Perhaps we could recommend that Weber translators take the indexes of the *Geschichtliche Grundbegriffe* as their point of departure to better understand what were 'key concepts' of that time and how Weber's work was related to them. Weber was, however, a post-*Sattelzeit*[33] thinker and has not been analysed in detail in most of the GG[34] articles, which sometimes tend to miss Weber's singularity as theorist and practitioner of conceptual change.[35] A second step would be to write a lexicon of the Weberian *Grundbegriffe*. The glossaries, which are used in new translations (such as Lassman's & Speirs's in *Political Writings* 1994[36]), could be understood as minimal versions of such lexica, attempting to reconstruct Weber's singular conceptual horizon in order to then understand his specific 'moves in argument'[37] in the conceptual act of translation. Such lexica already exist for several classics and they are, of course, themselves controversial both in their mode of composition and in their content of interpretations. Such author-specific conceptual lexica could also serve as a critical instance for general conceptual lexica, including the *Geschichtliche Grundbegriffe*.

(4) Translation of the Political Vocabulary

After this speculation, I now arrive to the translation of concepts dealt within political theories as a move between languages. More specifically, I shall discuss the topic of turning new vernacular languages, such as the Finnish of the nineteenth century, into written and academic languages, in which both fluent everyday political activity and independent political theorizing became possible.

What differentiates political languages from technical ones is the insight that modern European political languages have largely retained the old Greek or Roman vocabularies for speaking about contemporary political phenomena. The words we use for politics, citizenship, democracy, republic, society, public and private sphere and so on can be traced to either Greek or Roman origins. Of course, there are such concepts as state, representation and parliamentarism, which are of later origin, but it is rather astonishing just how far the ancient vocabularies have been retained, even if they are now used in an entirely different political and conceptual world.

Reinhart Koselleck[38] has suggested that we can detect a divide between the modern languages in so far as the Romanic languages and the English have retained much more of this ancient vocabulary than the Germanic ones, while the Slavic ones are still farther from the classical political vocabulary. In other words, the vernacularization has added to these languages further instances of revising, intentionally or not, the conceptual commitments bound to the vocabularies. Through such unintended conceptual revisions something of the theoretical commitments and referential connections, which are retained in the 'more ancient' languages, will be lost.

While regarding this geography of language, as Koselleck puts it, as a valuable hypothesis, I think its significance should not be overrated. The remarkable thing is that conceptual horizon shifts have been achieved by retaining the old vocabulary. Koselleck himself has paradigmatically shown this with the formation of *die Geschichte*[39] as a collective singular noun that took place between 1760 and 1780.[40] My own work during the last twenty years has been shaped by the insight that we can hardly speak about the activity of politics before the year 1800 in German, French or English. It is a new concept of politics, politics-as-activity, that has been formed, and I have explicated what is done by this conceptualization around a number of different, part competing, part overlapping topoi. This process has been obliged to struggle with linguistic remnants of the old vocabularies, for example by using the English noun politics in plural, or the unavailability of a single word for politicking in languages such as French, German or Swedish.[41]

The recourse to the 'original' Greek or Roman sense of the concepts would be an impossible claim, neglecting the changed world of references and the corresponding opportunities to reconceptualization. Still, which word has been chosen as a linguistic sign of a concept for the modern European languages is interesting in several respects. Why has for example the word *polites* vanished of the *polit*-vocabulary in favour of *citoyen* in French, *citizen* in English and *Staatsbürger* in German, while otherwise the polit-vocabulary has largely been retained?[42] This has led, already in the United States of the late nineteenth century, to the opposition of good citizens to bad politicians.[43] I think here a revision of vocabulary would still be possible, and an interesting suggestion is offered by Max Weber with the expression *Gelegenheitspolitiker* [44,45] which, in a sense, makes of all citizens politicians, the ones rather occasionally, the others professionally. With the depoliticizing inflation of the citizenship vocabulary, I think the Weberian alternative could be singled out when speaking of anyone acting politically, an alternative open also to those 'displaced persons' who have lost their citizenship.

When translation is understood as a 'conceptual act', as Ghosh says, it leaves space for a number of alternatives strategies or translation styles. Taking the Finnish as an example of a language, for which an academic and political vocabulary was created mainly in the middle decades of the nineteenth century, I will speculate with the question of which types of translation strategies are available to people to introduce the political concepts into their own vernacular language?

By retaining the distinction between the international vocabulary used in established 'natural' languages, as well as in existing political languages, and the resources of the vernacular languages we can propose at least five ideal typical alternatives:

1   Adopting the international word as an untranslated loan-word into the vocabulary. For example *Realpolitik* is used in many languages in this manner, or the French expression *raison d'Etat* in English.
2   Adopting the international word but formulating it according to the grammar and pronunciation of the language in question, as for example *politiikka* in Finnish.[46]
3   Adapting the resources of the vernacular language to the meaning of an international word, for example turning the Italian *lo stato* into *l'Etat* in French, *state* in English, *der Staat* in German, *en stat* in Swedish.
4   Adapting the meaning of an international word into the resources of the vernacular language. This is an interesting, although rather anachronistic case, but for example in the older Finnish usage of *valta* (power), there are clearly such tendencies that have then been replaced by conceptions closer to the contemporary academic languages.[47]
5   Creating a neologism that would take into account both the concepts in the international vocabulary and the linguistic resources of the vernacular language, such as *valtio* for the state in Finnish.[48]

Thus, the result of judging *a posteriori* the political vocabulary as it has been adopted in a language, such as Finnish, is a contingent combination of all those strategies. Initially, the 'Fennoman' language politicians set up a program to replace the international vocabulary by a 'native' one. Such attempts were not easily realized, and proposals for translations remained successful only in a few cases, such as *valtio* or *kansalainen* for citizenship. In other cases, however, it became increasingly clear that the use of Finnish concepts has been adapted to international political languages. For example a number of neologisms, based on state or government vocabulary were suggested in the nineteenth century in order to replace politics. However, they never gained a wider usage outside programmatic documents, such as dictionaries. Although there was a definite difference in the frequency of the polit-vocabulary between Swedish- and Finnish-speaking Finns around the parliament reform of 1906, the Finnish-speaking Finns have learned to use *politiikka* as well as their Swedish-speaking co-citizens use *politik*.[49]

The intentions of the creators of a 'political Finnish' were, to considerable extent, pedagogical. They wanted to render journals capable of reporting on the world events surrounding 1848, and to mediate an already existing sense of the international vocabulary to Finnish readers. To understand themselves as political agents was, of course, not an easy task for the academics, journalists and state officials in the Finnish Grand Duchy, even after the reopening of the Estate Diets in 1863. The creation of Finnish political vocabulary surely was a translation strategy that improved the chances to understand the possibility of a 'citizen' to act politically. Later, it was no longer important whether the word used was of Finnish or foreign origin. For example the word *kansan valta* (people's power), as Matti Hyvärinen[50] has illustrated, has recently more or less been replaced by *demokratia*, using the international word in a fashion that is even closer to the ancient Greek than the corresponding word in other modern languages.

Similarly, the downplaying of political controversies is expressed in some of the key political concepts. One of them is the name of the Finnish parliament, *eduskunta* – approximately, *house of representatives*, a term already used for the four-estate Diet after 1863. In writing a conjectural conceptual history, advocated by Terence Ball,[51] I have speculated whether a retranslation would be possible that could do better justice to the character of the parliament as a deliberative space using speech (including voting) as a medium of contestation and decision. My proposal is *puhekunta* – roughly: house of speakers – that would connect to the etymology of *parlare, parler* or parliament, as a specific *locus* of a politics of speech. The Estate Diet was, of course, not such a deliberative space, and in the debates of the Finnish parliament reform committee of 1906 the name of the parliament was not evoked. The phase of creating neologisms for political concepts had already passed. Still, the retention of the old name is an indicator that the new unicameral parliament elected by the universal male and female suffrage, was more considered to 'represent' the people than to deliberate and decide about politics.

The vocabulary that was adopted for political concepts in Finnish in the second half of the nineteenth century remained a highly contingent matter. In certain respects, the contextual origins of the specific Finnish translation remain in contemporary Finnish, largely in a harmless manner, but sometimes containing, as I have indicated, questionable depoliticizing tendencies.

My proposal to replace *eduskunta* by *puhekunta* is, of course, mainly a proposal intended to evoke the historical contingencies of the translation policies in Finnish. I hardly harbour the illusion that after our volume *Kasitteet liikkeessa* (Concepts in Motion, as Matti Hyvarinen has translated the title) is published with my postscript on translations,[52] that an MP would put forward the corresponding motion to change the name of the Finnish parliament. However, it would be enough if there would be an increasing consciousness in the Finnish politico-academic debates that speaking in a parliament is one of the pre-eminently political acts. It is my impression that, in Finnish political culture, the distinction between speaking and doing, between rhetoric and reality, between verbal games and the seriousness of politics has been even harder to overcome than elsewhere. Perhaps this is also the reason why the 'rhetorical turn' has, after all, played a prominent role in Finnish political science of the past two decades.

(5) Shares of Conceptual Power in Translations

It is not uncommon to consider the concepts used as in a certain sense as 'determined' by the language used. Surely nobody denies the constraining role of language in political thought, action and judgment. Some system theorists or structuralists may even celebrate this as a healthy limit to 'anarchistic' tendencies. Others would rather claim that for this reason we have to get rid of 'conceptual thinking', for example in favour of a narrative one,[53] or distinguishing à la Sartre[54] between rigid *concepts* and flexible, multi-dimensional and historical *notions*.

There are certainly tendencies to connect concepts with the magic of words, to capture things by 'knowing their names' or by giving names that are so suggestive that the phenomena named appear in a thing-like fashion. Such tendencies are especially strong when concepts are connected with a strong normative colour of positive or negative colour. For example, the German Christian Democrats once used the electoral slogan *Freiheit statt Sozialismus*,[55] combining a magical positive value with a magical negative value, thus claiming to obtain mutually exclusive concepts. Something of this magical tendency to refuse to distinguish between the word, the meaning and the normative colour of a concept is still present in normative political theory: for Rawls or Habermas, concepts such as justice, freedom or democracy appear to be valuable 'as such', independent of their history and controversies surrounding their interpretation.[56]

The normative project of conceptual history is directed against such essentialist tendencies of speaking about concepts. We could speak about *Entzauberung der Begriffe* (demystification of concepts), when they are understood as instruments (Weber) or as tools (Wittgenstein) in human activities and in the understanding of these activities. In this sense we can also understand Quentin Skinner's claim to treat concepts from the perspective of their 'uses in argument'[57] or as dimensions in 'linguistic action'.[58] Indeed, Koselleck has also subscribed to a nominalistic perspective, in which the formation and reconceptualization of concepts gain over modification through reception.[59]

Translations are a good illustration of the case that even minor differences in vocabulary may sometimes be politically significant, whereas in other cases the vocabulary remains subordinated to conceptual debates. In this sense, we can regard conceptual variation and alternative strategies to use them as strategic resources for linguistic action.

My first conclusion is to affirm that concepts can serve well as power shares for political action. They should be interpreted in a strictly nominalistic manner, not bound to fixed 'networks' or 'discourses' but closely connected to politics-as-activity. However, concepts are above all significant in 'theory politics', in that which is considered to be possible, realizable, legitimate and so on, but not in the facticities of actual political decisions and taking responsibility for them.

'Weighing the significance' of instances is hopeless to do in general terms, independent of the situation and constellation. For students of conceptual history, there is no more reason to declare that concepts are 'most important' phenomena than for a pacifist must declare her faith on the superior efficiency of peaceful means over violent ones. When concepts are used as political instruments, the power of concepts does not indicate any idealism, for example regarding World War I as one between Descartes and Kant.

Still, if we wage an attempt to assess the role of concepts as power shares in strictly Weberian terms, we can relate them to two further types of power shares, the number (*Zahl*) of the adherents and the recourse to violent means. Interestingly enough, Max Weber[60] considers both of them to be the *ultima ratio* in politics. I think the *ultima ratio* of *Gewaltsamkeit*[61] should be regarded as a limit-situation for politics in a modern state characterized by the monopoly of violence. The *ultima ratio* of the number serves as the specific criterion of a modern parliamentary democracy, in which the monopoly of violence is controlled by a parliament elected by universal suffrage.

The power of concepts, within this Weberian conceptual horizon, does not transcend these criteria marking the limit-situation of the regime. It concerns the question of what is possible within the horizon of accepting these criteria as *ultima ratio* within democratized states. In his polemics against the Prussian tripartite electoral system, Weber[62] regarded as the great advantage of democracy that votes are counted and not weighed. This by no means makes the use of concepts meaningless, but rather increases their role as instruments of legitimating past or future moves in both parliamentary deliberations and electoral campaigns.

Historicity, controversiality and contingency of concepts also indicate resources in the struggle with other kinds of shares of power. It is the power of alterability that characterizes the power of concepts, as opposed to fixed conceptual commitments in 'gallup-democratic' interpretations of the power of numbers. It is the omnipresent possibility to contest any interpretation of a concept concerning the naming, meaning, range of reference or normative colour of a concept that serves as a power share in the political struggle. And it is the contingency of politics-as-activity that always enables us not to regard concepts as definitions that close the situation, but as a complex of chances. The views of a majority have no authority but can at any time be delegitimized in their conceptual commitments that may play a role both in parliamentary deliberations and in the chances of political alteration in next elections.

In the Weberian perspective the rhetorical power of the concepts can thus be, in the first instance, a power-share in the politicking of oppositions, minorities and of competent individual politicians to reduce the simple numerical power of the governmental majority. All of them can use conceptual reflections and revisions as instruments illustrating the weaknesses of the policy of the government, in constructing alternatives to them as well as introduce new questions or new dimensions in the old ones into the political agenda.

Perhaps more interestingly we could claim, with Weber,[63] that the power of concepts using their historicity and contingency is a power of politicians subjected to competition in parliaments, elections and parties, as opposed to the bureaucracies (in state, party and business). Bureaucracy is ideally an atemporal order, based on stability and continuity Its use of the power of concepts tends to be characterized by a reliance on clear and unchanging definitions, which are from time to time replaced by others, but not understood as historical and controversial themselves. As opposed to this, the main advantage of the experience of politicians in parliamentary democracies is the temporality of the regime. This concerns not only the alternation in government through elections but also the plural temporalities of parliamentary control and procedure.[64]

Thus, conceptual history is an approach that is poorly understood by bureaucracies, and it is a vain hope to expect it to find its way to the numerous documents of planning and administration, for example at the level of the European Union. Nonetheless, I claim that the temporal condition of politicians is much better than that of the bureaucrats suited to the understanding the contingency, historicity and controversiality of concepts.

Notes

1   'Jede Übersetzung in je eigene Gegenwart impliziert eine Begriffsgeschichte', Reinhart Koselleck, 'Sozialgeschichte und Begriffsgeschichte', in Wolfgang Schieder and Volker Sellin (eds), *Sozialgeschichte in Deutschland*, vol. 1 (Göttingen: Vandenhoek & Ruprecht, 1986), 90. English: Reinhart Koselleck, 'Social History and Conceptual History', *Politics, Culture, and Society*, 2/3 (1989), 309. [Note: see Reinhart Koselleck, 'Social History and Conceptual History' (chapter two in this volume).]

2   Kenneth Burke, *A Grammar of Motives* (Berkeley: University of California Press, 1969).

3   Cf. Reinhart Koselleck, 'Über die Theoriebedürftigkeit der Geschichtswissenschaft', in Werner Conze (ed.), *Theorie der Geschichtswissenschaft und Praxis des Geschichtsunterrichts* (Stuttgart: Klett, 1972b), 10–28.
4   [Note: leeway.]
5   Cf. Quentin Skinner, *Reason and Rhetoric in the Philosophy of Hobbes* (Cambridge: Cambridge University Press, 1996), 7–8.
6   [Note: Max Weber, 'The "Objectivity" of Knowledge in Social Science and Social Policy', in idem and Sam Whimster (ed.), *The Essential Weber: A Reader* (London: Routledge, 2004), 359–404.]
7   [Note: social sciences.]
8   Friedrich Nietzsche, *Werke: Kritische Gesamtausgabe*, 2/4, eds Giorgio Collio and Mazzino Montinari (Berlin: de Gruyter, 1995).
9   Tujia Pulkkinen, 'The History of Gender Concepts; The Concept of Woman', *History of Concepts Newsletter*, 5 (2002), 2–5.
10 Reinhart Koselleck, 'Historik und Hermeneutik', in idem, *Zeitschichten* (Frankfurt am Main: Suhrkamp, 2000), 97–118.
11 Reinhart Koselleck, 'Einleitung', in idem, *Geschichtliche Grundbegriffe*, vol. 1 (Stuttgart: Klett, 1972a), xii–xxviii. [Note: see Reinhart Koselleck, 'Introduction (Einleitung) to the Geschichtliche Grundbegriffe' (chapter two in this volume).]
12 Reinhart Koselleck, 'Begriffsgeschichtliche Probleme der Verfassungsgeschichtsschreibung', *Der Staat*, supplement 6 (1983), 7–21.
13 Cf. also Quentin Skinner, 'Conventions and the Understanding of Speech Acts', *The Philosophical Quarterly*, 20 (1970), 118–138; idem, 'A Reply to My Critics', in James Tully (ed.), *Meaning and Context* (London: Polity, 1988), 231–88.
14 [Note: estrangement effect.]
15 Cf. Koselleck (1972a).
16 [Note: John G. A. Pocock, *Politics, Language and Time* (Chicago: University of Chicago Press, 1989).]
17 [Note: Anthony Pagden (ed.), *Languages of Political Theory in Early-Modern Europe* (Cambridge: Cambridge University Press, 1987).]
18 Cf. Jörn Leonhard, *Liberalismus. Zur historischen Semantik eines europäischen Deutungsmusters* (München: Oldenbourg, 2001).
19 In principle, the political treatment can be extended also to 'technical' languages, such as computer programs. Today we can, for example, explore the majority languages of the PC party, the minority languages of the Mac party, the computer Esperanto of the RTF and the computer Latin of Microsoft Word and other programs applicable to both PC and Mac parties. Between the majority and minority we can detect an asymmetric conceptual opposition: every Mac computer contains a

inter-party translation program, such as MacLinkPlus, whereas the PC remains monolingual and upholds the (vain) hope of extinguishing the Mac party. The lingua franca of Microsoft also allows translations only to the RTF Esperanto, but not to Mac languages (such as Apple Works). In this sense, the PC party tends towards hegemonic monolingualism, whereas the adherents of the Mac languages clearly admit and accept the plurality of languages and the omnipresence of translation. [Note: opportunities.]

20   Koselleck (1972a). [Note: thing.]

21   Hannah Arendt, *Between Past and Future* (Harmondsworth: Penguin 1977), 239.

22   Cf. Quentin Skinner, 'On Performing and Explaining Linguistic Actions', *The Philosophical Quarterly*, 21 (1971), 1–21.

23   Reinhart Koselleck, 'A Response to Comment on the Geschichtliche Grundbegriffe', in Hartmut Lehmann and Melvin Richter (eds), *The Meaning of Historical Terms and Concepts. New Studies on Begriffsgeschichte* (Washington: German Historical Institute, 1996), 59–70.

24   [Note: Max Weber, 'Die protestantische Ethik und der Geist des Kapitalismus', in idem, *Gesammelte Aufsätze zur Religionssoziologie I* (Tübingen: J.C.B. Mohr, 1920), 1–206; English translation: Max Weber, *The Protestant Ethic and the Spirit of Capitalism*, trans. Talcott Parsons (London: George Allen & Unwin, 1930).]

25   Cf. for example Stephen Kalberg, 'The Spirit of Capitalism Revisited. On the New Translation of Weber's Protestant Ethic (1920)', *Max Weber Studies*, 2 (2001), 47.

26   [Note: education.]

27   Peter Ghosh, 'Translations as a Conceptual Act', *Max Weber Studies*, 2 (2001), 60.

28   Quentin Skinner, 'Meaning and Understanding in the History of Ideas', *History and Theory*, 8 (1969), 3–53.

29   [Note: conceptual history.]

30   Cf. Kari Palonen, 'Die Umstrittenheit der Begriffe bei Max Weber', in Gunter Scholtz (ed.), *Die Interdisziplinarität der Begriffsgeschichte* (Hamburg: Meiner, 2000), 145–58.

31   Ghosh (2001), 61.

32   [Note: history of works.]

33   [Note: see the introduction to Jörn Leonhard, 'Translation as Cultural Transfer and Semantic Interaction: European Variations of Liberal between 1800 and 1830' (chapter six in this volume) for a discussion of Koselleck's concept of the 'saddle period'.]

34 [Note: Palonen refers to Otto Brunner, Werner Conze and Reinhart
    Koselleck (eds), *Geschichtliche Grundbegriffe: Historisches Lexikon zur
    politisch-sozialen Sprache in Deutschland*, 8 vols (Stuttgart: Klett-Cota,
    1972–97).]
35 Cf. Palonen (2000).
36 [Note: Peter Lassman and Ronald Speirs (eds), *Max Weber. Political
    Writings* (Cambridge: Cambridge University Press, 1994).]
37 Skinner (1988).
38 Reinhart Koselleck, 'Begriffsgeschichte, Sozialgeschichte, begriffene
    Geschichte. Reinhart Koselleck im Gespräch mit Christof Dipper', *Neue
    politische Literatur*, 43 (1998), 187–205.
39 [Note: history itself.]
40 Cf. already Reinhart Koselleck, 'Historia Magistra Vitae. Über die
    Auflösung des Topos im Horizont neuzeitlich bewegter Geschichte', in
    Hermann Braun and Manfred Riedel (eds), *Natur und Geschichte. Karl
    Löwith zum 70. Geburtstag* (Stuttgart: Kohlhammer, 1967), 196–219.
41 Kari Palonen, 'Conceptualizing the Activity of Politics. A History of the
    Construction of a Temporal Concept' (forthcoming). [Note: the book the
    author refers to is Kari Palonen, *The Struggle with Time: A Conceptual
    History of 'Politics' as an Activity* (Münster: Lit Verlag, 2006). His
    argument is further elaborated in his recently published book *Politics and
    Conceptual Histories: Rhetorical and Temporal Perspectives* (Baden-Baden:
    Nomos, 2014).]
42 Cf. Dolf Sternberger, *Die Politik und der Friede* (Frankfurt am Main:
    Suhrkamp, 1986).
43 Cf. Moisei Ostrogorski, *Démocratie et les partis politiques* (Paris: Fayard
    1993).
44 [Note: casual politician.]
45 Max Weber, 'Politik als Beruf', in idem, *Max-Weber-Studienausgabe* 1/17,
    eds Wolfgang J. Mommsen and Wolfang Schluchter (Tübingen: Mohr,
    1994), 41.
46 Cf. Kari Palonen, 'Transforming a Common European Concept into
    Finnish: Conceptual Changes in the Understanding of "Politiikka"',
    Finnish Yearbook of Political Thought, 5 (2001), 113–53.
47 Cf. Matti Hyvärinen, 'Fictional Versions of Valta (Power). Reading Aleksis
    Kivi, Arvid Järnefelt and Juhani Aho Conceptually', *Finnish Yearbook
    of Political Thought*, 2 (1998), 203–40; idem, ' "The People's Power"
    (Democracy) as an Argument in Finnish Party Manifestos', *Redescriptions*,
    7/1 (2003), 36–67.
48 Cf. Tuija Pulkkinen, 'Valtio – On Conceptual History of the Finnish State',
    Finnish Yearbook of Political Thought, 4 (2000), 129–58.

49   Cf. Palonen (2001).

50   Hyvärinen (2003).

51   Terence Ball, 'Confessions of a Conceptual Historian', *Finnish Yearbook of Political Thought*, 6 (2002), 11–31.

52   Kari Palonen, 'Eurooppalaiset poliittiset kasitteet suomalaisissa pelitiloissa' (European Political Concepts on Finnish Playground), in Matti Hyvärinen et al. (eds), *Käsitteet liikkeessä* (Tampere: Vastapaino, 2003), 569–87.

53   Olivia Guaraldo, *Storylines. Politics, History and Narrative from an Arendtian Perspective* (Jyväskylä: SoPhi, 2001).

54   Jean-Paul Sartre, 'Sur "L'idiot de la famille"', in idem, *Situations X. Politique et autobiographie* (Paris: Gallimard, 1976), 91–115.

55   [Note: freedom instead of socialism.]

56   Cf. Kari Palonen, 'The History of Concepts as a Style of Political Theorizing. Quentin Skinner's and Reinhart Koselleck's subversion of normative political theory', *European Journal of Political Theory*, 1 (2002), 96–111.

57   Skinner (1988).

58   Skinner (1996).

59   Cf. especially Koselleck (1983); idem (1996).

60   Max Weber, 'Wahlrecht und Demokratie in Deutschland (1917)', in *Max-Weber-Studienausgabe* 1/15, eds Wolfgang J. Mommsen and Wolfang Schluchter (Tübingen: Mohr, 1988), 155–89; idem, 'Politik als Beruf (1919)', in *Max-Weber-Studienausgabe* 1/17, eds Wolfgang J. Mommsen and Wolfang Schluchter (Tübingen: Mohr, 1994), 35–88.

61   [Note: violence.]

62   Weber (1988), 155–89.

63   Max Weber, 'Parlament und Regierung im neugeordneten Deutschland (1918)', in Mommsen and Schluchter (1988), 202–302.

64   Cf. Giesela Riescher, *Zeit und Politik* (Baden-Baden: Nomos, 1994); for a detailed description of the nineteenth-century British practices cf. Josef Redlich, *Recht und Technik des Englischen Parlamentarismus* (Leipzig: Duncker & Humblot, 1905).

Lydia Liu is the Wun Tsun Tam Professor in the Humanities and Professor of Chinese and Comparative Literature at Columbia University, New York. She also holds a position at the School of the Humanities and Social Sciences at Tsinghua University, Beijing. Her research focuses on cross-cultural exchanges in modern history, particularly the movement of words, ideas and artefacts across national boundaries. She works on the history of political thought in translation as well as the evolution of writing, textuality and technology.

Among Lydia Liu's publications are titles such as *Tokens of Exchange: The Problem of Translation in Global Circulations* (editor and contributor; 1999), *Translingual Practice: Literature, National Culture and Translated Modernity – China 1900–1937* (1995) and *The Freudian Robot: Digital Media and the Future of the Unconscious* (2010).

The article 'The Question of Meaning-Value in the Political Economy of the Sign', taken from her *Tokens of Exchange*, represents Liu's understanding of translation as critical to modernity. By combining linguistic theory with economic theory and thus reintegrating the category of power to language, Liu seeks to go beyond post-colonialism and post-structuralism. She reads translation as an interaction that reveals the material and intellectual conditions under which meaning and reciprocity are created or denied, focusing on phenomena like shared authorship, circulation, contestation and unequal exchange.

8

The Question of Meaning-Value in the Political Economy of the Sign[1]

Lydia H. Liu

Chapter Outline

Troubled by the uncertainty of commensurability among languages, translators and their critics have a tendency to approach the issue as if the problem resided in the *inherent* properties (value) of individual languages. This seems to suggest a level of intuitive comprehension of value in languages and cultures, although such intuition seldom succeeds in discouraging people from pursuing the possibility of equivalence, finding common ground or achieving optimal pairing of meanings and so on. But before dismissing it as harmless intuition too quickly, we might benefit from a heightened awareness that the persistence of this way of thinking has, as a rule, prevented an otherwise fruitful discussion of the dynamic process of meaning-making that often takes place *between* or *among* languages as well as within a single language. If meaning is thus studied as a problem of exchange and circulation, not entirely bound to the evolutionary process of a homogeneous language or culture, we must, then, raise some new questions about language and translatability. For instance: *Can the achieved or contested reciprocity of languages be plotted as the outcome of a given economy of historical exchange?*

Questions like this can, perhaps, take us a step further toward overcoming the circularity of commensurability and incommensurability in translation theory. At the least, the theorist will be less inclined to insist on the plenitude of meaning and begin to articulate the problem of translation to the political economy of the sign. As I have argued elsewhere, Walter Benjamin's 'Task of the Translator'[2] and Derrida's reading of the same in 'Des Tours de Babel'[3] are among the few bold attempts in the twentieth century to rethink the problem of meaning outside the purview of semantics and structural linguistics. Their notion of complementarity, which refuses to privilege the original over the translation, enables a powerful critique of the metaphysical ground of traditional semantics that has long dominated the translation theories of the West. Derrida's attack on Western metaphysics, in particular, has helped clear the philosophical ground for useful critical work, but one of the questions on which the notion of complementarity remains vague is how hypothetical equivalence is established, maintained, or revised among languages so that meaning, which is always historical, can be made available or unavailable to the translator. I wonder whether hypothetical equivalence does not already inhabit the idea of complementarity itself in a subtle but potent form.[4]

Hence, I would like to sketch out a number of intersecting areas for a preliminary rethinking of the production of meaning as value in circulatory relationship with other meanings (as no value can exist by itself). This tentative reworking of meaning-value may lead us to see that the much contested notion of translatability is often a displaced global struggle (displaced onto metaphysics) over the reciprocity of meaning-value among historical languages. I have suggested in the introduction[5] that there are at least two basic questions we need to think about in order to resist such metaphysical displacements and pursue a fruitful study of translatability as a theoretical and historical problem. First, how does the circumstantial encounter of cultures produce and contest the reciprocity of meaning-value between their languages? Second, how does reciprocity become thinkable as an intellectual problem when predominantly unequal forms of global exchange characterize the material conditions of that exchange? Inasmuch as the historical (re)distribution of meaning-value constitutes a major aspect of global circulation, it is of paramount importance, I argue, to pay attention to the granting and withholding of reciprocity of meaning-value by one language vis-à-vis another.[6] (This struggle is proverbial in bilingual situations where a bilingual speaker always learns to deploy the languages he or she knows strategically under varying circumstance. He or she then becomes one of the physical sites of the processes I am trying to describe in this essay.)

One interesting consequence of recent world history is that we can afford *not* to marvel at the miracle of universal communicability. The argument of untranslatability need not contradict this description, because the suspicion of the circulation of meaning and anxiety to exert control over it may be yet another way of endorsing translatability and the plenitude of meaning. Moreover, such posited translatability among the world's languages is never simply a linguistic matter. Like many of the other events that have shaped the modern world, global translatability has inhabited the same order of universalistic aspirations as the invention of the metric system, modern postal service, international law, the gold standard, telecommunication and so on. The significance of this event is yet to receive the kind of attention it deserves. The fact that we do not normally perceive things in this light goes to show that the mutual intelligibility of languages has been naturalized more than anything else by common dictionaries, repeated acts of translation and received theories of language that are conceptually and structurally incapable of comprehending the monumental significance of this recent happening. The first step toward reconceptualizing translatability as a historical event is, therefore, to integrate the problem of translation into the general interpretation of so-called civilizational encounters and their intellectual and material outcomes.

From Counterfeit to the Colonial Legacy of Value

Let us examine briefly a moment of 'civilizational encounter' in the early eighteenth century, when the modern notion of forgery was still in the process of forging a historical bond between published writing and minted coin. Evidently, fake writing and counterfeit money were widely engaged in the production and circulation of value between Europe and the other civilizations at this time, but, in the business of forgery, no one could beat the record of George Psalmanazar (1679–1763), the notorious imposter of his time or any time. Psalmanazar fabricated a native Formosan (Taiwanese) identity for himself in toto in exchange for patronage by the Church of England.[7] In deciding to 'go native' through his writing and other performances, he anticipated the modern anthropologist long before the invention of the discipline itself. A curious prefiguration of the problematic of value, the Psalmanazar story raises some fascinating questions about the meaning of authenticity, parody and colonial identity, and, more importantly, the circulation of not just silver, tea, silk and porcelain but of *meaning as value* between East and West.

Psalmanazar arrived in London in 1703 in the company of Alexander Innes, chaplain to the Scots regiment at Sluys, who introduced him to Bishop Compton as a native of Formosa.[8] The story he and his accomplice Innes told to their new friends in London was that, as a child, Psalmanazar had been abducted by some evil Jesuits from Formosa to Europe. (Psalmanazar was a pseudonym and his real name was well hidden, even after his death.) Their plot worked instantly. Despite the fact that Psalmanazar had authentic Caucasian looks, blond hair and blue eyes (as this episode occurred before the rise of the scientific racism in Europe), the physiognomic evidence proved less persuasive that his extraordinary gift of the tongue and extravagant performance mimicking the so-called cannibalistic behaviour of the native barbarians of the remote island.[9]

The British public bought Psalmanazar's story because their imagination had fed on nothing less than the similarly extravagant accounts given by the missionaries, sea captains and merchants about exotic lands outside Europe. So when Psalmanazar claimed 'We also eat human Flesh, which I am now convinc'd is a very barbarous custom, tho' we feed only upon our open Enemies, slain or made captive in the field', the sensational description merely confirmed what the British reader had been consuming all along thanks to the European colonial exploitation abroad and the rise of the popular book market at home.[10] For a period of four years, Psalmanazar was a resounding success. He was even invited by Oxford University to study a variety of subjects and give lectures on Formosan practices, including human sacrifice. When Father Fontenay, a Jesuit missionary who had just returned from China, confronted him at a public meeting of the Royal Society, Psalmanazar effectively rebutted his accusation of imposture.[11]

Had Psalmanazar's subsequent conversion and confession not abundantly redeemed his youthful sins, time and death would have absolved him of the remaining moral stigma attached to his imposture. Twentieth-century scholars take much less interest in establishing who this man really was than how his extraordinary career helps us glimpse the meaning of authenticity, authorship, ethnographic writing and the European book market in the eighteenth century.[12] One cannot but be struck by Psalmanazar's uncanny understanding of the power of words and their purported face value. His best-selling book, *A Historical and Geographical Description of Formosa* (1704; 1705), attacked the order of what Saussure would call the signifier and signified to fabricate a society for which there was no referent. Even the pseudonym, Psalmanazar, has no corresponding real name that we know of. He took his pseudonym from 2 Kings 17:3 – Shalmaneser, one of a line of Assyrian kings by this name – and presented himself to British society as a Formosan pagan converted to Christianity.

More fascinating than the infinite regression of names and referents is Psalmanazar's invention of a fictitious Formosan alphabet and an equally fictitious Formosan currency of which he gives meticulous illustration and description in his book (see figures 1 and 2).[13] The fake alphabet and fake money stand forgery on its head by exploiting the materiality of the sign whose value is the face value on paper (signifying Formosan alphabet and Formosan currency, respectively) and nothing more. The so-called referent turns out to be a phantom called up by Psalmanazar's writing.

Within the fabricated textual universe of his book, Psalmanazar the forger rivals Psalmanazar the plagiarist. For the textual sources Psalmanazar relied on in writing his book had been culled from contemporary popular travel literature and the Jesuits' accounts of the Orient, including authors such as George Candidius, an early-seventeenth-century Dutch missionary to Taiwan and the French Jesuit Louis le Comte, who was sent to China in the same year (1688) as Father Fontenay by Louis XIV.[14] Candidius's 'Short Account of the Island of Formosa' was a major source of Psalmanazar's encyclopaedic knowledge of that island.[15] Like Defoe's best-selling novel, *Robinson Crusoe*, which appeared fifteen years later, Psalmanazar's imaginative book *Historical and Geographical Description of Formosa* was written in the form of a first-person narrative that strove to cover the whole gamut of familiar ethnographic data about the exotic island: geography, climate, costume, architecture, religion, burials, language and social customs and organizations. Susan Stewart observes that this book 'fulfilled an ultimate Enlightenment dream – the dream of animation where logical consistency can itself produce a referent, a world engendered by reason alone, unencumbered by history, materiality or nature'.[16] But it seems to me that Psalamazar's elaborate work reads more like a caricature of the Enlightenment dream and a parody of ethnographic imagination than their fulfilment.[17]

Psalmanazar is a supreme parodist. His originality consists in casting himself as a native informant who testifies as he speaks and who goes so far as to use his adopted voice of authenticity to contest the reliability of Candidius's own text calling the latter a forger. For instance, when some people objected that his extravagant description of human sacrifice in Formosa could not be substantiated by Candidius' report, Psalmanazar wrote in the preface to the second edition of his book that those sacrifices were not as strange as Candidius's own statement that women pregnant before their thirty-seventh year had their bellies stomped until they miscarried.[18] This turning of the tables on Candidius not only reverses the order of authenticity and forgery, referent and sign, true value and face value, but raises some fundamental questions among *meaning as face value* and *writing as parody of other writing*. Michel de Certeau once suggested in a different context that the act of making the sources one's own renders 'the general process of fabrication visible; the interlinkage of the imaginary and the collection, in other words the labor of fiction within the library. That invention haunts the "sources" is everywhere indicated by the citations, from the moment one opens the book. It is the law of the other in the narrative.'[19] Psalmanazar's mock narrative inadvertently reveals to us to what extent the original text, Candidius's own 'Account of the Island of Formosa', might have already produced *meaning as face value* and *writing as parody of writing* in the manner of Psalmanazar, who copied him in an ingenious and subversive way.

Psalmanazar's extraordinary career as forger, plagiarist, ethnographer and native informant reminds us that the study of meaning in the political economy of the sign needs to be grounded in the actual history of the global circulation of meaning-value. That history is a history of colonialism whose exploitation of exotic difference has erected major obstacles against a historical understanding of difference. Like Psalmanazar, missionaries and orientalists have fabricated powerful fictions about other cultures and their languages. Those fictions, as Edward Said's critique of the Western philological construct of the Orient has made clear, have long inhibited a historical reassessment of the colonial encounter of languages and cultures.[20] The global romanization of the indigenous languages and dialects by missionaries and linguists in the eighteenth and nineteenth centuries was designed to do precisely what Psalmanazar's alphabet had envisioned for the Formosan language.[21] These universalist translations have produced 'cultural difference' on the world map as an already translated fact and pretend to speak for that difference in a universalizing idiom.

The articulation of difference as value within a structure of unequal exchange thus simultaneously victimizes that difference by translating is as *lesser value* or *non-universal value*. To overcome this conceptual barrier, I propose that we substitute the notion of competing universalism for cultural particularity to help understand the modes of cultural exchange and their genealogies beyond the existing accounts of colonial encounter. The ahistorical dialectic of the universal and the particular may, then, be understood as a recent historical manifestation of the will to the universal. As the studies contained in this volume moments of competing universalisms deserves more scholarly attention than they have heretofore received.

The imperatives of competing universalisms demand that we reconceptualize the ways in which meanings circulate *meaningfully* from language to language and culture to culture. As a migrant deixis of potential value, meaning acquires value in the process of exchange between actual signs. The circumstantial encounter of one sign with another (in a sentence) or another language (in translation) decides the manner *in* which the actualization or sabotage of meaning takes place. Thus, an original text may be 'rewritten', 'parodied' and 'manipulated' but not 'distorted' by its being translated from text to text any more than Candidius's Formosa was 'distorted' by Psalmanazar's Formosa. Derrida's critique of the myth of the transcendental signified can be evoked to undo the common-sense understanding of translation as a transfer of the transcendental signified (authentic value) from one language system to another.[22]

An alternative formulation of meaning would do well by rejecting the metaphysics of signifier and signified on philosophical ground, though one needs to remain vigilant about the deconstructionists' projection of a self-sufficient intellectual realm of Western metaphysics and their possible recuperation of an imperial view of value and global circulation.

William Pietz's study of the problem of the fetish, among other similar works, is an important intervention in that regard. His research demonstrates convincingly that the circulation of the notion of the fetish as 'false value' (parodied verbatim by our Psalmanazar) in Western philosophical discourse is rooted in its own colonial past. In a series of fine studies of the discourse of the fetish, Pietz analyses the mercantile cross-cultural spaces of transvaluation among material objects of radically different social orders on the coast of West Africa in the sixteenth and seventeenth centuries. He writes:

> The mystery of value – the dependence of social value on specific institutional systems for making the value of material things – was a constant theme in transactions on the Guinea coast during this period. The problem was especially expressed in the category of the trifling: European traders constantly remarked on the trinkets and trifles they traded for objects of real value [gold] (just as the socio-religious orders of African societies seemed to them founded on the valuing of 'trifles' and 'trash').[23]

Always initiated and formalized by the moments of translation, these instances of colonial exchange are significant not because they exemplify an earlier moment of civilizational encounters, but because they articulate the condition of possibility of colonial history. Pietz goes on to show how the earlier processes of colonial exchange set the stage for the Enlightenment discourse about value and the fetish, as, for example, when Kant formulated his aesthetic explanation for African fetish worship in 1764, deciding that such practices were founded on the principle of the 'trifling' (*läppisch*), the ultimate degeneration of the principle of the beautiful.[24]

Kant's transcendental philosophy is profoundly indebted to the colonial regime of anthropological knowledge. Emmanuel Chukwudi Eze's recent study points out that, despite his cosmopolitan leanings, Kant never left his home-town Konigsberg in his professional career and gathered his information about distant lands exclusively from seafarers and traveling merchants and from reading books such as Captain James Cook's *Voyages*. Out of this vast conglomerate of accumulated anthropological evidence, or 'the labor of fiction within the library' in the words of Certeau, Kant derived a philosophical doctrine of 'human nature' and assigned the 'essence' of humanity to the self-image of eighteenth-century Europe: 'white', European and male.[25] (Psalmanazar was a mere caricaturist, not a philosopher; rather, he enacted the farce of what would be the philosopher's ethnographic 'evidence'.)

The tautology of the anthropological 'evidence' turned out to circumscribe both Kant's doctrine of 'human nature' and his aesthetic explanation of African fetish worship as the 'trifling'. Whereas the latter's 'superstitious' understanding of *causality* was held responsible for the 'false' estimation of the *value* of material objects in African societies, the discourse of fetishism also articulated a colonial mercantile view of value that caused Europeans to conclude that non-Europeans tended to assign false value to material objects and, therefore, false objective value to their own culture. From this view, according to Pietz, there 'developed a general discourse about the superstitiousness of non-Europeans within a characteristically modern rhetoric of realism, which recognized as "real" only technological and commercial values'.[26]

It bears pointing out, of course, that the circulation of meaning involves a great deal of coauthorship and struggle among the dominant and dominated groups over the meaning and distribution of universal values and civilizational resources. In order for the process of circulation to take place at all, the agents of translation on each side start out by hypothesizing an exchange of equivalent meanings, even if the hypothesis itself is born of a structure of unequal exchange and linguistic currency. What this means is that we need to investigate further how a particular sign or object is made into an equivalent of something else during the process of circulation and how, theoretically speaking, this act of translation articulates the condition of unequal exchange.

The Question of Equivalence and Translatability

To study meaning as value is to place the problem of translation within the political economy of the sign. Contrary to forcing a parallel argument about verbal exchange in terms of its monetary counterpart, the linguistic and the economic – as well as their theoretical articulations – have long evoked each other and inhabited each other. In the *Grundrisse*, Marx draws an interesting comparison between translation and monetary transaction for the purpose of theorizing the problem of the universal equivalent that concerns both:

Language does not transform ideas, so that the peculiarity of ideas is dissolved and their social character runs alongside them as a separate entity, like prices alongside commodities. Ideas do not exist separately from language. Ideas which have first to be translated out of their mother tongue into a foreign language in order to circulate, in order to become exchangeable, offer a somewhat better analogy; but the analogy then lies not in the language, but in the *foreign quality* of language.[27]

Global Conceptual History

This is an important insight. The foreign quality (*Fremdheit*) of language describes a shared process of circulation in translation and in economic transaction, which produces meaning as it produces *value* when a verbal sign or a commodity is exchanged with something foreign to itself. (Here, the mutual articulation of the linguistic and the economic seems to suggest more than an analogous relationship between two separate spheres of activities. Marx's own analysis testifies against the fiction of a pure theory of political economy untouched by other social considerations. By the same token, we can no longer imagine a pure theory of linguistic exchange uncontaminated by economic models of exchange. See my discussion of Saussure below.)

Marx's insistence on the foreignness (*Fremdheit*) of language is central to his working out of a meaningful connection between linguistic estrangement (*Entfremdung*) and monetary alienation (*Entäußerung*) in *Capital*. As Marc Shell has pointed out, this move derives from Marx's preoccupation with the historical transformation of the commodity gold first into coin and then into paper money. 'The act of monetary exchange, like the act of linguistic translation, depends on a socially recognized (*gültige*) universal equivalent, which seems to homogenize everything, or to reduce everything to a common denominator.'[28] Gold became the universal equivalent by a social act (*Tat*) when this commodity began to assume the power to measure or purchase all the others. In *this* process, the foreignness of the other must be conquered in order for the other to assume exchange-value in the marketplace. (In that regard, the English language of the late twentieth century would be the closest analogue to the gold of the preceding era.) But exactly how does Marx elaborate the problem of equivalence and exchange-value?

When considering the equation '1 quarter of corn = x cwt of iron' in *Capital*, Marx begins by asking: What does this equation signify?

> It signifies that a common element of identical magnitude exists in two different things, in 1 quarter of corn and similarly in x cwt of iron. Both are therefore equal to a third thing, which in itself is neither the one nor the other. Each of them, so far as it is exchange *value*, must therefore be reducible to this third thing.[29]

What is this third or common denominator that equates 1 quarter of corn to x cwt of iron or a potentially infinite number of commodities? The answer lies in abstract labour that produces exchange-value. Marx determines this exchange-value as a quantity of socially necessary labour-time (SNLT) required to produce one unit of any given commodity.

As we know, Marx's labour theory of value was a critical response to classical political economy, which takes 'the economy' as a self-regulating market structure and constructs 'trade' as an exchange of equivalents among individual traders. Marx considers the trading of commodities as a trade of 'labour time'. His notion of SNLT demystifies the notion of equal exchange by introducing human activity and its objectification into the analysis of commodity exchange in capitalist society. Because the SNLT is merely an average and not the quantity of actual labour time necessary for the production of the unit of the commodity being exchanged, there is no guarantee that such trade involves equal magnitudes of actual labour time. Such is the theoretical problem Marx raises and tries to resolve in *Capital*. As Jack Amariglio and Antonio Callari have pointed out:

> In fact, these are trades of unequal magnitudes of *actual* labor time. But this inequality notwithstanding, for commodity circulation to take place, trade must be conceived by the agents of circulation – by individuals – as an exchange of equivalents. There is thus a contradiction: the same process of circulation is at once both an unequal exchange of quantities of actual labor time and an exchange of equivalents.[30]

In other words, Marx derived an account of the exploitation of labour (extraction of surplus-value) by capital from an analysis of SNLT and, in so doing, reveals a fundamental inequality in 'equal' exchange in capitalist economy.

Here we are less concerned with Marx's labour theory of value than with the significance of his formal analysis of commodity exchange which is not limited to the economic behaviour of capitalist society. After all, Marx is centrally concerned with the problem of economic *value* as social *value*, that is, a problem of signification that overflows the exclusive realm of commodity production and exchange.[31] This is precisely where theorists of critical semiotics of our own time intervene to recast the study of the sign as a critique of the political economy of the sign. The problem of inequality in 'equal' linguistic exchange also bears directly on our concerns with the reciprocity of meaning as value between historical languages in translation processes. But let us reflect more on the crucial connections that exist between the exchange of commodity and that of the sign in Marx.

In *Capital*, Marx argues that value 'does not have its description branded on its forehead; it rather transforms every product of labour into a social hieroglyphic. Later on, men try to decipher the hieroglyphic.'[32] The word hieroglyphic is interesting because it evokes 'foreignness', 'impenetrability' and 'primitivity' typically associated with non-European cultures. Does this figurative turn of language comment on the situation of commodity exchange in colonial conditions? Marx does not ponder the question here, because he is more interested in explaining the abstract relationship between use-value and exchange-value than in the question of language, which he elaborates elsewhere. 'As a use-value', he writes, 'the linen is something palpably different from the coat; as [exchange] value, it is identical with the coat [*Rockgleiches*], and therefore looks like the coat [*sieht daher aus wie ein Rock*]'.[33] The process of transformation that causes different things (the linen and the coat) to *look alike* is an abstraction process that eliminates difference or use-value for the commodities to become commensurate as exchange-value and be exchanged on that basis. Exchange-value is to political economy what simile, metaphor, or synecdoche is to the linguistic realm of signification, as both involve the making of equivalents out of non-equivalents through a process of abstraction or translation.

This is by no means a fortuitous rhetorical exercise in the service of theory, because the problem of signification within political economy is fundamentally connected with the economy of exchange within the linguistic realm.[34] As Thomas Keenan's rhetorical analysis of *Capital* shows convincingly, for Marx, exchange is 'a matter of signification, expression, and substitution'.[35] The process of signification and substitution (abstract labour for actual labour, etc.) is what allows commodities to be exchanged not as things but as values for other values, as amply illustrated by Marx in the classic case of how the linen becomes 'coat-like or -identical' (*Rockgleiches*) in the exchange process. Not surprisingly, Marx uses the term *der Warensprache* or the 'language of commodities' to talk about this process, and we are supposed to take his word figuratively and literally. In *der Warensprache*, the commodity form, of which money is a pure form of general equivalent, bears out the mutual penetration of the problem of signification within political economy and of the economy of exchange within the linguistic realm. Marx chose to verbalize the former in terms of the latter.

Saussure did the converse. If exchange is a matter of signification and substitution, it is entirely possible to bring the economic system of signification within the fold of parallel systems of signification such as language and other semiotic systems. After all, both use-value and exchange-value signify aspects of social value where a ground of 'figurative equivalence' among different articulations of value, be it commodity value, linguistic value or other, can be abstracted and theorized. In formulating a structural linguistics, Saussure pursued this ground of figurative equivalence in a direction very different from that of Marx. Although like Marx he understood political economy and semiology as mutually embedded systems of value and signification, Saussure reversed the order in which Marx had conceptualized the economic and the linguistic.

In *Course in General Linguistics*, Saussure begins by characterizing language as a social institution and conceives of semiology (language, symbolic rites, customs, etc.) as a science that studies the role of signs as part of social life. (Lévi-Strauss's important reconceptualization of social institutions and structures as communication systems drew inspiration directly from this formulation.) As a social institution, language must be analysed with the same degree of rigor as is practiced in other sciences such as law and economics and in the history of political institutions.

Saussure emphasizes, in particular, the proximity of political economy and linguistics because, 'as in the study of political economy, one is dealing with the notion of value. In both cases, we have a *system of equivalence between things belonging to different orders*. In one case, work and wages; in the other case, signification and signal.'[36] This comes very close to the way Marx analyses exchange-value in *Capital*. Whereas for Marx exchange-value can be analysed and quantified in terms of abstract labour and labour time, Saussure sees an entirely arbitrary relationship between the signifier and the signified. Linguistic value remains for him a matter of internal relations within a linguistic community. 'A community is necessary in order to establish values', says Saussure, and 'values have no other rationale than usage and general agreement. An individual, acting, alone, is incapable of establishing a value.'[37]

According to Saussure, two basic conditions are necessary for the existence of any value and these are paradoxical conditions that require (1) something *dissimilar* that can be exchanged for the item whose value is under consideration and (2) *similar* things that can be *compared* with the item whose value is under consideration. To illustrate this point, Saussure goes on to consider the value of money by analogy:

> To determine the value of a five-franc coin, for instance, what must be known is: (1) that the coin can be exchanged for a certain quantity of something

different, e.g. bread, and (2) that its value can be compared with another value in the same system, e.g. that of a one-franc coin, or of a coin belonging to another system (e.g. a dollar). Similarly a word can be substituted for something dissimilar: an idea. At the same time, it can be compared to something of like nature: another word. Its value is therefore not determined merely by that concept or meaning for which it is a token. It must also be assessed against comparable values, by contrast with other words. The content of a word is determined in the final analysis not by what it contains but by what exists outside it. As an element in a system, that word has not only a meaning but also – above all – a value.[38]

In short, linguistic value expresses a horizontal relationship whose existence depends on the simultaneous coexistence of other values within the same system. Just as the signified, or the conceptual part of linguistic value is determined by relations and differences with other signifieds in the language, so the signifier or the material counterpart of linguistic value such as sound pattern, also relies on phonetic contrasts to allow us to distinguish among words and semantic units. When considered by itself, sound is merely something ancillary, a material the language uses. The arbitrary and differential relations of the sound pattern within a language are what assign linguistic value to a given sign. 'It is not the metal in a coin which determines its value', argues Saussure. 'A crown piece nominally worth five francs contains only half that sum in silver. Its value varies somewhat according to the effigy it bears.' This structural understanding of value leads to Saussure's most uncompromising opposition to essentialism: 'Linguistic signifiers are not in essence phonetic. They are not physical in any way. They are constituted solely by differences which distinguish one such sound pattern from another.'[39]

Saussure makes a distinction between what he calls 'conceptual aspects' (signified) and 'material aspects' (signifier) of linguistic value. In this scheme of things, the meaning of a word is assimilated to the conceptual component of the sign that belongs to the vertical order of the signified and signifier as set out in his famous diagram of the sign (see Figure 8.1). But how does meaning or a concept operate in relation to linguistic value, which, according to Saussure, must be determined in horizontal relationship with other values in the same system? The answer is that a 'particular concept is simply a value which emerges from relations with other values of a similar kind. If those other values disappeared, this meaning too would vanish.'[40]

Saussure's constant recourse to on-the-spot 'translation' and simultaneous failure to theorize his textual operation creates a logical impasse for

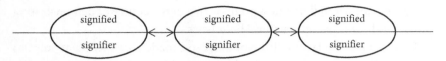

Figure 8.1 The diagram of the sign, from Ferdinand de Saussure, *Course in General Linguistics*.[41]
Source: Ferdinand de Saussure, *Course in General Linguistics*, translated from the French by Wade Baskin (London: Peter Owen, 1964), 115.

structural linguistics. This causes no small degree of confusion when he tries to introduce some levels of distinction between meaning and value.

In the quote above, Saussure equates meaning with value by saying that a 'particular concept is simply a value which emerges from relations with other values of a similar kind. If those other values disappeared, this meaning too would vanish'. In the same space, however, he contradicts himself by arguing that value and meaning are not synonymous terms, one representing the horizontal order of differential relations with coexisting values and the other (meaning) comprising the concept along the vertical arrows of the signified and signifier.

A famous example he uses is the French word *mouton* and its English counterpart 'sheep'. By way of translation, Saussure decides that the two words may have the same meaning but do not share the same value. The difference in value, he argues, hinges on the fact that in English there is also another word, 'mutton', for the meat, whereas mouton in French covers both. The differential relation of 'sheep' and 'mutton' in English, therefore, assigns a different value to each word that does not exist in French.

But if value is different, can meaning remain the same? Why should meaning be a fixed category a priori when the sound pattern and other properties of language are subject to the law of differential relations? How do we know that the French word mouton has the same meaning as the English 'sheep' until we equate them through *selective translation* and vice versa? Is the reciprocity of meaning always guaranteed between the languages? Saussure treats meaning in translation as a given and deduces from it a radical theory of value but a very conventional theory of meaning based on intuitive translation.[42] His mode of analysis, which is ubiquitous translation, participates directly in what he says about signs and structural linguistics but is not registered as such. Saussure simply finds it expedient to utilize his vast knowledge of French, English, German, Greek, Latin, Portuguese, Czech and even Sanskrit to illustrate a point or two in the course of demonstrating the general concepts of structural linguistics.

Recognizing the lacuna, Roman Jakobson made a deliberate attempt to integrate translation and translatability into his theory of semiotics. For Jakobson, translation exemplifies *equivalence in difference* that is operative in all semiotic and literary situations. In 'On Linguistic Aspects of Translation', Jakobson argues:

> Equivalence in difference is the cardinal problem in language and the pivotal concern of linguistics. Like any receiver of verbal messages, the linguist acts as their interpreter. No linguistic specimen may be interpreted by the science of language without a translation of its signs into other signs of the same system or into signs of another system. Any comparison of two languages implies an examination of their mutual translatability; widespread practices of interlingual communication, particularly, translation activities, must be kept under constant scrutiny by linguistic science.[43]

Translation thus becomes the structural principle whereby signs are equated with other signs within the same code or between codes. This is a tantalizing thought, and could be used to explain Saussure's own mode of operation and bring some degree of self-consciousness into semiotic considerations of language. The observation that 'any comparison of two languages implies an examination of their mutual translatability' possesses the best potential to develop into a major theoretical argument about translation.

Although that potential is eclipsed by the subsequent anecdotes Jakobson tells about translation, it is interesting to note that the majority of his anecdotes focus on grammatical gender as a point of comparison and translatability. For example, he points out that the Russian painter Repin was baffled by German painters' depiction of Sin as a woman because Repin was apparently unaware that 'sin' is feminine in German (*die Sünde*); it is masculine in Russian *(грех)*. Jakobson goes on to observe that a Russian child, while reading a translation of German tales, was astounded to find that Death, obviously a woman *(смерть, fem.)*, was pictured as an old man (German: *der Tod*, masc.). These anecdotes are well told and could be multiplied ad infinitum. But what do they tell us about translatability? Are we brought back to the argument that gender does not travel well across linguistic codes and that translation is impossible? If so, how do we translate gender into a non-inflected language where this grammatical category is not available from the viewpoint of Indo-European languages?

Let us consider the gendering of the third-person pronoun in modern written Chinese to test this argument of untranslatability based on a synchronic comparison of linguistic difference. The original form of the written Chinese character for the third-person pronoun *ta* contains an ungendered *ren* radical (denoting 'human'). For millennia, the Chinese had lived comfortably with the ungendered written form *ta* and other ungendered deictic forms, until the need to translate the feminine pronoun from European languages was suddenly thrust upon their attention in the early years of this century.[44] Chinese linguists and translators proceeded to invent a written character that would be capable of translating the 'equivalent' pronouns in the European languages. After many experiments, they settled on a character that replaced the radical *ren* in the ungendered *ta* with the radical *nü* denoting 'woman' to form a new feminine pronoun in the language. That word has since become an inseparable part of the mainstream vocabulary of modern Chinese.

This process is fascinating in that the appearance of the feminine pronoun simultaneously converts the original ungendered *ta* into a *masculine pronoun*, even though the written form of the latter has not undergone the slightest morphological change and is still written with the same radical *ren*. Through the circumstantial contact with the Indo-European languages, the generic radical that denotes 'human' now proclaims a masculine essence. In other words, the presence of a gendered neologism in the linguistic system has forced the originally unmarked pronoun to assume a masculine identity retroactively that is, nevertheless, contradicted by the etymology of its otherwise ungendered radical *ren*.[45]

Saussure would probably find in this a perfect example of structural differentiation, because the feminine and masculine pronouns in modern written Chinese have emerged in relation to each other as differential values. I am inclined to think, however, that translation played a pivotal role in the dual process of both introducing the structural differentiation of gender into the deictic category and making up equivalents where there had been none with reference to the gendered pronoun in Indo-European languages. Grammatical gender acquires translatability precisely in this limited, historical sense. Of course, my point is not to argue with Jakobson about the translatability or untranslatability of grammatical gender but to reflect on the historical making of hypothetical equivalence that is capable of producing shifting grounds of comparison and translatability.

Baudrillard's Quarrel with Saussure

Contemporary theorists attribute the theoretical impasse of Saussure's structural linguistics to a metaphysical conception of language.[46] Baudrillard, for example, re-examines the double condition of Saussure's theory of value and meaning as discussed above: '(1) the coin can be exchanged for a certain quantity of something different, e.g. bread, and (2)…its value can be compared with another value in the same system, e.g. that of a one-franc coin, or of a coin belonging to another system (e.g. a dollar).' Saussure sees a given coin as exchangeable against a real good of some value (bread in condition 1) while at the same time relating it to all the other terms in the monetary system (one franc or a dollar in condition 2). The economic exchange clearly evokes the distinction of the use-value and the exchange-value of the commodity. Although Baudrillard has no problem with the analogy of the economic and the linguistic, he questions the unexamined notion of meaning and its referent in structural linguistics on the one hand and that of use-value in Marx on the other:[47]

> As if articulating theory of exchange-value, Saussure reserves the term *value* for this second dimension of the system: every term can be related to every other, their relativity, internal to the system and constituted by binary oppositions. This definition is opposed to the other possible definition of value: the relation of every term to what it designates, of each signifier to its signified, like the relation of every coin with what it can be exchanged against. The first aspect corresponds to the structural dimension of language, and the second to its functional dimension. Each dimension is separate but linked, which is to say that they mesh and cohere. This coherence is characteristic of the 'classical' configuration of the linguistic sign, under the rule of the commodity law of value, where designation always appears as the finality of the structural operation of the langue. The parallel between this 'classical' stage of signification and the mechanics of value in material production is absolute, as in Marx's analysis: use-value plays the role of the horizon and finality of the system of exchange-values. The first qualifies the concrete operation of commodity in consumption (a moment parallel to designation in the sign), the second relates to the exchangeability of any commodity for any other under the law of equivalence (a moment parallel to the structural organization of the sign). Both are dialectically linked throughout Marx's analyses and define a rational configuration of production, governed by political economy.[48]

Baudrillard attempts to unpack Saussure's notion of the signified in the same manner as Marx analysed the commodity in *Capital*, although both Saussure's notion of the signified and Marx's idea of use-value come under attack.[49] He grapples with Saussure and Marx to develop a theoretical vocabulary that can explain the process whereby social privilege and domination are no longer defined exclusively by the ownership of the means of production but also by the mastery of the process of signification whereby equivalences and a hierarchy of values are established and maintained.[50]

The critique of the magical copula in sign production, or 'the equal sign in "A = A"' in Baudrillard's theory, merits special attention because this is where 'metaphysics and economics jostle each other at the same impasses, over the same aporias, the same contradictions and dysfunctions'.[51] The ideological form that traverses both the production of signs and material production, he argues, often comes with a logical bifurcation theorized in terms of use-value versus exchange-value on the one hand and signified versus signifier on the other. Baudrillard calls this double bifurcation magical thinking.

The binary thinking casts 'use-value' and 'signified' in the role of content, a given, need and transcendental value, thus sealing them off from further inquiry and analysis, because the analyst has confined formal value and formal analysis to the domain of 'exchange-value' and 'signifier' alone. Marx has worked out a critique of political economy at the level of exchange-value but has not extended his theoretical rigor to a similar critique of naturalized use-value. For their part, Saussure and Benveniste have established that the sign presents itself as a unity of discrete and functional meaning, the signifier referring to a signified and the ensemble to a referent.[52] Baudrillard argues, however, that 'the separation of the sign and the world is a fiction, and leads to a science fiction. The logic of equivalence, abstraction, discreteness and project of the sign engulfs the [referent] as surely as it does the [signified].'[53] Furthermore, he points out that the homology between the logic of signification and the logic of political economy rests entirely on this shared fiction. The latter exploits the reference to needs and the actualization of use-value as an anthropological horizon and, in so doing, precludes a consideration of their 'formal' intervention in the actual functioning and operative structure of political economy. Of its linguistic homologue, Baudrillard writes:

> Similarly, the referent is maintained as exterior to the comprehension of the sign: the sign alludes to it, but its internal organization excludes it. In

fact, it is now clear that the system of needs and of use value is thoroughly implicated in the form of political economy as its completion. And likewise for the referent, this 'substance of reality', in that it is entirely bound up in the logic of the sign. Thus, in each field, the dominant form (system of exchange value and combinatory of the [signifier] respectively) provides itself with a referential rationale (*raison*), a content, an alibi, and, significantly, in each this articulation is made under the *same metaphysical 'sign'*, i.e., *need or motivation.*[54]

Before we consider the interesting implication of this critique for a theory of translation and global circulation, let us dwell further on Baudrillard's attack on the received communication theory as a part of his criticism of metaphysics.

Roman Jakobson's famous model of verbal communication serves as a point of departure for Baudrillard's reconsideration of the sequence of transmitter (encoder)-message-receiver (decoder).

The universal sequence was originally schematized by Jakobson as shown in Figure 8.2. Baudrillard regards this 'scientific' construct as rooted in a *simulation* model of communication that allows neither reciprocal relation nor simultaneous mutual (especially conflictual) presence of the two terms. The artificial distance installed between encoder and decoder seals the full and autonomized 'value' of the message, excluding, from its inception, the reciprocity and antagonism of interlocutors, and the ambivalence of their exchange. According to Jakobson's model, 'what really circulates is information, a semantic content that is assumed to be legible and univocal. The agency of the code guarantees this univocality, and by the same token the respective positions of encoder and decoder.'[56]

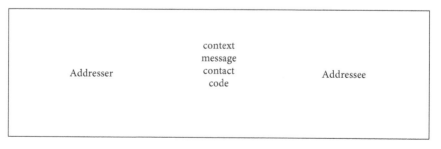

Figure 8.2 Jakobson's model of verbal communication, from 'Linguistics and Poetics'.[55]

Source: Roman Jakobson, *Language in Literature* (Cambridge, Mass.: Belknap, 1987), 66.

This critique of the simulation model of communication and structural linguistics brings Baudrillard to the point of a radical break with the received notion of linguistic exchange among his generation of French theorists. The idea of sign exchange-value, in particular, seems to offer a genuine possibility. Nevertheless, like Saussure before him, Baudrillard has excluded the problem of translation from the overall picture of sign exchange and theorizes the circulation of signs as if the world spoke a lingua franca of value and reciprocity. If the long history of mutual borrowing among the European languages and the hegemony of the metropolitan languages in the former colonies are somewhat responsible for his blind spot, it does not sufficiently explain why he reads Saussure the way he does.

Baudrillard takes Saussure to task for holding onto a metaphysical notion of meaning but fails to elaborate to what extent Saussure's modus operandi might be responsible for producing this metaphysics. Let us recall that in *Course in General Linguistics* Saussure renders the meaning of a sign *self-evident* independently of its history and of the translator's own selective appropriation of its meanings through a foreign equivalent. In Saussure's analysis of *mouton* and 'sheep', the linguist adopts a circular procedure of glossing the meaning of 'sheep' with that of mouton and vice versa, and decides that the two words have the same meaning but not the same value. That which his circular move fails to register, however, is an act of translation that actively produces the 'same meaning' between the two words just as easily as it could have produced a different meaning in a different context (which Saussure has no way of explaining except by separating meaning from 'value') to allow *mouton* to mean 'mutton' and not 'sheep'. Due to the polyvalent etymology of these signs, the French *mouton* does not always have the same meaning as the English 'sheep' until one has equated them through *selective* translation and already eliminated the other possibility, 'mutton' and vice versa. Moreover, the etymology of the English 'mutton' indexes another level of historicity having to do with the original translingual figuring of class relations between the French and the Anglo-Saxons after the Norman conquest of England. As Saussure's textual operation amply demonstrates, the talk of difference and equivalence hardly makes sense until the languages in question are brought together in a reciprocal, differential and antagonistic relationship by translation, etymology and history.

Baudrillard's engagement with Saussure and Marx suggests a parallel to what Pierre Bourdieu does with his own categories of symbolic goods, symbolic capital, habitus, field, symbolic power, cultural production and so on.[57] As we know, Bourdieu also emphasizes an integrated understanding of the economic as a symbolic process and of the cultural as a material process. The mutual embeddedness of the economic and the cultural results in an extraordinary degree of interchangeability of linguistic and economic tropes in his language, which in turn feeds back into his understanding of the linguistic sign. Bourdieu writes:

> Linguistic exchange – a relation of communication between a sender and a receiver, based on enciphering and deciphering, and therefore on the implementation of a code or a generative competence – is also an economic exchange which is established within a particular symbolic relation of power between a producer, endowed with a certain linguistic capital, and a consumer (or a market), and which is capable of procuring a certain material or symbolic profit.[58]

Bourdieu might not find himself operating in a world of metaphors, because the linguistic and symbolic are just as real as the economic and material. The strength of his position lies in his refusal to define the linguistic and symbolic as any less material than the other forms of capital. But when he goes on to speak of the *value* of utterances as regulated by the market and characterized by a particular law of price formation, there appears to be a curious tautological functionalism.[59] The *functional* problem of how a dominant language confers social distinction on the user of that language becomes the self-same point of departure and arrival of his reasoning. (Let us recall how Marx elaborated the problem of signification and with what rigor he went about the whole analysis.) Bourdieu asserts that all verbal expressions

> owe some of their properties (even at the grammatical level) to the fact that, on the basis of a practical anticipation of the laws of the market concerned, their authors, most often unwittingly, and without expressly seeking to do so, try to *maximize the symbolic profit* they can obtain from practices which are, inseparably, oriented towards communication and exposed to evaluation.[60]

That argument produces some extraordinary circular statements about capital, value and exchange that cannot possibly go wrong because they participate in, and derive from, the perfect closure of Bourdieu's conceptual system.[61]

What we need to know is just how the value of an utterance functions with respect to market prices and how meaning gets generated in the process of symbolic exchange *within* a relation of power. The closure of Bourdieu's system prevents him from giving a sustained look at the givenness of each of these articulations with the kind of theoretical rigor exemplified by Marx in *Capital* or Saussure in *Course in General Linguistics*. Saussure's elaboration of the meanings of *mouton* and 'sheep' is taken by Bourdieu to be a mere theoretical argument about the arbitrariness of the sign and dismissed offhand, whereas we have seen that Saussure's own analysis is much more nuanced and deserves serious critical engagement.[62]

Reciprocity and Power in Cultural Translation

Translation need not guarantee the reciprocity of meaning between languages. Rather, it presents a reciprocal *wager*, a desire for meaning as value and a desire to speak across, even under least favourable conditions.[63] The act of translation thus hypothesizes an exchange of equivalent signs and makes up that equivalence where there is none perceived as such. The invention of the third-person feminine pronoun in modern Chinese is a case in point. Like the thousands of loanwords and neologisms I have documented and analysed elsewhere, the existence of this word captures the invention of equivalents in a relation of unequal exchange between Chinese and European languages, and that exchange is further complicated by the changing power relations between Chinese and Japanese caused by the presence of the Western powers in Asia.[64] In contrast, English and the metropolitan European languages have not experienced a similar need in modern times to adapt to the formal characteristics of the other languages by eliminating, for example, one of its gender categories in a reverse mode of operation. The point I am trying to make here is not merely contrastive or comparative. In thinking about translatability between historical languages, one cannot but consider the actual power relations that dictate the degree and magnitude of sacrifice that one language must make in order to achieve some level of commensurability with the other.

In colonial conditions of exchange, commensurability of meaning can sometimes be instituted and kept in place by law and brute military force. As my study of the missionary-Chinese translation of international law in 'Legislating the Universal'[65] shows, the so-called Chinese contempt for European 'barbarians' arose out of a set of unique circumstances in which the

British insisted on the translation of the word *yi* as 'barbarian'. The equating of the meanings of the two words by Britain's official translators became the cognitive ground on which a xenophobic Chinese 'mentality' was first erected and then condemned, even though we know very well that the word *yi* had been previously rendered in English as 'foreigner' or 'stranger' in the eighteenth century and early nineteenth century.[66] After establishing the first level of commensurability between *yi* and 'barbarian', the British felt insulted by the Qing government's use of that word in diplomatic communications and remonstrated against such 'unequal' treatment of the British representatives by the Chinese official establishment. As the numerous dispatches between the two governments before the Opium War well testify, the linguistic crusade against the word *yi* became a counteroffensive led by the British to fight the Chinese government's prohibition of the opium trade. In the 1830s–1840s, the British protest against the Chinese use of *yi* escalated into a major diplomatic event and began to be centrally and thoroughly embroiled in the gunboat policy during the Opium War.[67] After the war had lifted the Chinese ban on opium trade, the British lost no time in banning the word *yi* from diplomatic communications by specific treaty provisions. The legal ban was so effective that it has made the word literally disappear from the languages of today's Chinese-speaking world.

The episode of the linguistic crusade against 'barbarian' and the invention of the feminine pronoun in modern Chinese each tell a fascinating story about the politics of linguistic exchange and demonstrate that, in this general economy of meaning-value, (in)commensurability can be a contentious affair and impact the course of historical events. The reciprocity of meaning in the case of *yi* and 'barbarian' simultaneously secures the non-reciprocity between *yi* and 'foreigner', 'stranger' or other earlier terms of equivalence. This process of meaning-making is guaranteed by a colonial regime of knowledge that recognizes as value only that which can help reproduce the colonial relations of power, hence the rhetorical value of *yi* and 'barbarian' for making war. The circulation of other possible values and other meanings is effectively obstructed – they are labelled 'wrong translations' – when these do not otherwise participate in the production and reproduction of colonial relations.

Even as I emphasize relations of unequal linguistic exchange, I do not *wish* to suggest that this situation can be reduced to the mere 'intentions' of the dominator and depict the dominated always as victims of the situation. To do so would be to underestimate the degree of coauthorship that has been going on between the dominator and the dominated. In the case of the neologism of the feminine pronoun, it was the Chinese linguists and translators, not Westerners, who were troubled by the 'lack' of an equivalent pronoun in their own language and proceeded to invent one. The level of commensurability and reciprocity of meaning thus established between modern Chinese and European languages suggests non-reciprocity at yet another level, because few speakers of metropolitan European languages experience a similar need to reform their gendered deixis, except, perhaps, the feminist critics of our own time.

In the West, feminist critics attack the unmarkedness (universal availability) of the masculine pronoun for entirely different reasons from what I have in mind here. The majority of their criticisms borrow strength from the bourgeois discourse of human rights and equality rather than from a theoretical deconstruction of the gendering of deictic markers as a grammatical category. As a result, very few critics are concerned about the presence or absence of gendered equivalents in non-European languages or the possible 'contamination' of those languages by Western forms of gender in the recent past. The poststructuralist critique of the unmarkedness of the masculine pronoun does not prevent the critics from taking the (gendered) grammatical categories of French or English as universal and using them as a philosophical basis for their argument. Interestingly, feminist critics in the Chinese-speaking world have themselves forgotten how the gendering of the pronoun in their own language occurred less than eighty years ago. When some decide to follow the new English way of writing the feminine and masculine pronouns with a slash in between, the gendering of these Chinese pronouns becomes twice universalized. This new moment of coauthorship leads to a foreclosure of the possibility of bringing forth an alternative way of doing feminist criticism in gender studies. The latter would require the feminist critic to grapple with the disjuncture of gendered and ungendered articulations of deictic relationships among different languages of the world, so that a new understanding of the grounds of reciprocity and power relationship among different feminisms could be envisioned.

What we observe in these processes is a powerful *coauthoring* of universal commensurability envisioned by the Chinese translators and the metropolitan theorists of universal language in a relationship of unequal exchange. That is to say, both the dominator and the dominated participate in the making of this miracle of universal communication but determine the outcome of such exchanges differently. In the global circulation of meaning as value, *hypothetical equivalence* is scrupulously and vigorously guarded and only occasionally contested by speakers of one or the other language. Equally worthy of attention is a condition of unequal exchange that produces and reproduces the condition of hypothetical equivalence and the colonial regime of knowledge. This paradox of equivalence and non-equivalence forms the cognitive basis on which cultural difference becomes articulable ('A= A' or 'A ≠A', etc.). Such difference in turn becomes naturalized in our languages through repeated usage in everyday life, in the media and in scholarly writings. The translator is thus able to manipulate difference, to dispense or withhold the reciprocity of meaning-value among the languages to make war or make peace.

Finally, the universalizing tendencies of the modern, which has grown to be the dominant universalism of our world, have worked toward erasing the traces of this recent happening so that we would all agree that modernity is inevitable, universal and available to everyone. Suppose we treat text and textuality as a genuine historical event and not less than that, certainly not the reverse. The ultimate challenge for a new theory of translation would be to account for the philosophical connection between the universalizing logic of modernity and the invention of *hypothetical equivalence* among the world's languages.

Notes

1   [Note: for reasons of copy right, some illustrations have been omitted.]
2   [Walter Benjamin, 'The Task of the Translator', in Hannah Arendt (ed.), *Illuminations*, trans. Harry Zohn (New York: Harcourt Brace Jovanovich, 1968), 62–82.]
3   [Jacques Derrida, 'Des Tours de Babel', in Joseph F. Graham (trans. and ed.), *Difference in Translation* (Ithaca, New York: Cornell University Press, 1985), 165–207.]
4   Sections of this essay were presented at the Comparative Literature Colloquium of Cornell University in April 1998 at an event called 'Borderless Wor(l)ds: A Roundtable on Translation at the Turn of the Millennium'. I thank Emily Apter, Thomas Conley, Brett de Bary and the graduate student organizers of the roundtable for the stimulating conversations that led to the strengthening of my thesis. See my critique in Lydia H. Liu, *Translingual Practice: Literature, National Culture, and Translated Modernity, 1900–1937* (Stanford: Stanford University Press, 1995), 14–16.

5   [Note: author refers to the Introduction of her book *Tokens of Exchange.*
     The Problem of Translation in Global Circulation (Durham: Duke
     University Press, 1999).]

6   James Clifford briefly discusses reciprocity and translation in his recent
     book *Routes: Travel and Translation in the Late 20th Century*. He argues
     that ' "reciprocity" is itself a translation term linking quite different
     regimes of power and relationality. A capitalist ideology of exchange
     posits individual transactions between partners who are free to engage
     or disengage; a Melanesian model may see ongoing relationships in
     which the wealthier partner is under a continuing obligation to share.
     It is important to keep these different practices of reciprocity in view',
     James Clifford, *Routes: Travel and Translation in the Late 20th Century*
     (Cambridge, MA: Harvard University Press, 1997), 175. Here, Clifford
     is more concerned with alternative models of reciprocity than with the
     articulation of the terms of reciprocity (that is, granting and withholding
     of meaning) between a capitalist ideology of exchange and the
     Melanesian model that seems to have enabled his comparison of these
     two in the first place. The articulation of the terms of reciprocity, hence
     comparative relationality, is precisely what troubles me in cross-cultural
     studies.

7   The little we know about the biographical circumstances of this man
     comes from a few scattered contemporary accounts and Psalmanazar's
     own confessions published posthumously in *Memoirs of****, Commonly*
     known by the Name of George Psalmanazar: A Reputed Native of
     Formosa. Written by himself, In order to be published after his Death.
     He was said to have come from France because he spoke Latin with a
     Gascon accent. His education at the hands of the Franciscans, Jesuits,
     and Dominicans gave him a good grasp of Latin, a smattering of
     theology, and a huge fund of general knowledge. For detailed treatments,
     see Susan Stewart, *Crimes of Writing: Problems in the Containment of*
     Representation (Oxford: Oxford University Press, 1991), 33–5. Also see
     Richard M. Swiderski, *The False Formosan: George Psalmanazar and*
     the Eighteenth-Century Experiment of Identity (San Francisco: Mellen
     Research University, 1991); Rodney Needham, *Exemplars* (Berkeley:
     University of California Press, 1985); and Frederic J. Foley, *The Great*
     Formosan Impostor (Rome and St. Louis: Jesuit Historical Institute and
     St. Louis University, 1968) .

8   The first name of Innes has been consistently misquoted as William by
     several generations of scholars. The main source of the error is Sidney
     Lee's article on Psalmanazar in the *Dictionary of National Biography*,
     in which the chaplain Alexander Innes is called William and the date
     of Psalmanazar's will is also given incorrectly. Foley, who did extensive

archival research on the subject in the late sixties, has tried to correct this important detail, but for some reason his work is not read or cited by scholars who came after him. Foley (1968), 6 n. 2; and also Swiderski (1991), 10–11.

9   For example, he would put on a show of eating raw meat and doing other shocking things to prove his authenticity to the public.

10   George Psalmanazar, *A Historical and Geographical Description of Formosa*, 2nd ed. (London: 1705), 112–13. His sensational description of child sacrifice in Formosa gave Swift the famous trope of cannibalism in *A Modest Proposal*, where his name is mentioned as 'the famous Sallmanaazar, a Native of the Island Formosa, who ... told my friend, that in his Country when any young Person happened to be put to death, the Executioner sold the Carcass to Persons of Quality, as a prime Dainty, and that, in his Time, the Body of a plump Girl of fifteen, who was crucified for attempting to Poison the Emperor, was sold ... in Joints from the Gibbet', Jonathan Swift, *A Modest Proposal for preventing the children of poor people from being a burthen to their parents, or the country, and for making them beneficial to the public* (Dublin: Harding, 1729), 10.

11   The Psalmanazar-Fontaney confrontation took place at a session of the Royal Society on 2 February 1704 when Isaac Newton was serving as the president of the Royal Society. Psalmanazar began by asking Fontaney to whom Formosa belongs (because he had previously claimed that Formosa belonged to Japan). China, Fontaney replied. Psalmanazar wanted to know how Fontaney, who had, by his own admission, never been to Formosa, could be sure of this, and so on. For a detailed discussion of this meeting, see Swiderski (1991), 27–35. The most damaging test of Psalmanazar's truthfulness was conducted by the astronomer Edmund Halley, who asked the Formosan, who had already mentioned the houses and chimneys of his native land, how long the sun shone down the chimney flue at certain times of the year. Psalmanazar slipped and was taken to task for having not even the most fundamental awareness of solar events in his 'native' island. See Swiderski (1991), 40–1.

12   The most sophisticated analysis of George Psalmanazar is found in Stewart (1991). See chapter 2, 'Psalmanazar's Others', 31–65.

13   [Note: figure 1, omitted for reasons of copy right, is the illustration 'The Formosan Alphabet' from George Psalmanazar's *A Historical and Geographical description of Formosa*, depicting his fabricated Formosan Alphabet.]

14   Candidius's book and Bernhardus's *Description of Japan* in Latin were the reference books given to him by Innes. See Foley (1968), 21.

15   See George Candidius, 'A Short Account of the Island of Formosa', in
     A Collection of Voyages and Travels, ed. Awnsham Churchill and John
     Churchill (London: 1704), 526–33.
16   Stewart (1991), 54.
17   [Note: in the original text follows Figure 2: The drawing of Formosan
     money, taken from George Psalmanazar's *A Historical and Geographical
     description of Formosa*. It depicts his fabricated drawing of Formosan
     money and had to be omitted for reasons of copy right.]
18   Ibid., 50.
19   Michel de Certeau, *Heterologies: Discourse on the Other*, trans. Brian
     Massumi (Minneapolis: University of Minnesota Press, 1986), 139.
20   Edward Said, *Orientalism* (New York: Random House, 1979).
21   Both Jesuit and Protestant missionaries designed the romanization
     systems for non-European languages and dialects, including Cantonese,
     Vietnamese, Fukienese and indigenous Taiwanese (in spite of
     Psalmanazar's alphabet) to replace and contest the established universal
     script, that is, the written Chinese language.
22   See Jacques Derrida, *Positions*, trans. Alan Bass (Chicago: University of
     Chicago Press, 1981), 20.
23   William Pietz, 'The Problem of the Fetish, I', *RES: Anthropology and
     Aesthetics*, 9 (1985), 9.
24   Immanuel Kant, *Observations on the Feeling of the Beautiful and Sublime*,
     III, as quoted in Pietz (1985), 9.
25   See Emmanuel Eze, 'The Color of Reason: The Idea of "Race" in Kant's
     Anthropology', in idem (ed.), *Postcolonial African Philosophy* (Cambridge,
     MA: Blackwell, 1997), 103–40
26   Pietz (1987), 42.
27   Karl Marx, *Grundrisse: Foundations of the Critique of Political Economy*,
     163, as quoted in Marc Shell, *Money, Language, and Thought: Literary and
     Philosophic Economies from the Medieval to the Modern Era* (Baltimore:
     Johns Hopkins University Press, 1993), 106. Emphasis added.
28   Shell (1993), 107.
29   Karl Marx, *Capital: A Critique of Political Economy*, I, trans. Ben Fowkes
     (New York: Vintage, 1997), 127.
30   See Jack Amariglio and Antonio Callari, 'Marxian Value Theory and the
     Problem of the Subject: The Role of Commodity Fetishism', in Emily Apter
     and William Pietz (eds), *Fetishism as Cultural Discourse* (Ithaca: Cornell
     University Press, 1993), 204. Their discussion of value in this article is
     part of a more extended treatment of how economic rationality, equality
     and private proprietorship articulate the self-identity of individuals in the
     process of exchange.

31   For a juxtapositional reading of Marx's notion of value and contemporary French psychoanalytical theory, see Gayatri Chakravorty Spivak, 'Scattered Speculations on the Question of Value', in idem, *In Other Worlds* (New York: Methuen, 1987), 154–75.

32   Marx (1997), 167.

33   Ibid., 143. The German quotes are from *Das Kapital: Kritik der politischen Ökonomie*, in Karl Marx and Friedrich Engels, *Werke* (1890; Berlin: Dietz, 1984), vol. 23, 66.

34   For a related study, see Donald N. McCloskey, *The Rhetoric of Economics* (Madison: University of Wisconsin Press, 1985). McCloskey's analysis of rhetoric in economics is mainly concerned with how economists use rhetorical means to make arguments to achieve a certain end. This is not what concerns us here. We are talking about a two-way situation where the linguistic and economic penetrate each other at the rhetorical level and at the level of the basic conceptualization of value which is indispensable both to economic theory and to structural linguistics.

35   See Thomas Keenan, 'The Point Is to (Ex)Change It: Reading Capital, Rhetorically', in Apter and Pietz (1993), 174.

36   Ferdinand de Saussure, *Course in General Linguistics*, trans. Roy Harris (La Salle: Open Court, 1983), 80.

37   Ibid., 112.

38   Ibid., 113–14.

39   Ibid., 117.

40   Ibid., 115–16.

41   Ferdinand de Saussure, *Course in General Linguistics, translated from the French by Wade Baskin* (London: Peter Owen, 1964), 115.

42   In this essay, I consider meaning and value together as a problem in the theoretical elaboration of translingual circulation. It is to be distinguished from 'sound value', whose role in translation is not as central as the reproduction of 'meaning value' in the host language.

43   Roman Jakobson, 'On Linguistic Aspects of Translation', *On Translation*, 3 (1959), 233–4.

44   [Note: presumably the twentieth century.]

45   In 1920, an unsuccessful attempt was made to introduce sound differentiation between the feminine and masculine pronouns as well. For a detailed discussion of the gendering of the Chinese pronoun in the larger context of East-West encounters, see Liu (1995), 36–9, 150–79.

46   Both Derrida and Baudrillard launched their respective theories by criticizing Saussure and his metaphysical conception of language. I choose to discuss Baudrillard here because he seems more attuned to what Saussure is trying to do in his own context than is Derrida, who is interested in Saussure's work insofar as the latter serves as a springboard

for his critique of the privileging of the *phoné*, the *glossa* and the *logos* in Western metaphysics. Saussure's other important contributions that deserve serious critique are passed over in silence. For Derrida's critique, see Jacques Derrida, *Of Grammatology*, trans. Gayarti Chakravorty Spivak (Baltimore: Johns Hopkins University Press, 1974), 27–73.

47 Baudrillard calls structural linguistics the 'contemporary master discipline, inspiring anthropology, the human sciences, etc., just as, in its time, did political economy, whose postulates profoundly informed all of psychology, sociology and the "moral and political" sciences'. Jean Baudrillard, *For a Critique of the Political Economy of the Sign*, trans. Charles Levin (St. Louis: Telos Press, 1981), 165, fn. 3.

48 Jean Baudrillard, *Symbolic Exchange and Death*, trans. Iain Hamilton Grant (London: Sage Publications, 1993), 6.

49 Baudrillard (1981), 148. For an informed discussion of Baudrillard's complex relationship to Marxism, see Douglas Kellner, *Jean Baudrillard: From Marxism to Postmodernism and Beyond* (Stanford: Stanford University Press, 1989).

50 Baudrillard sometimes uses the word 'sign value' interchangeably with the word 'meaning value'.

51 Baudrillard (1981), 71.

52 Saussure locates the arbitrariness of the sign between the signified and the signifier. Benveniste modifies this schema by relocating the arbitrariness between the sign and that which it designates. 'What is arbitrary', says Benveniste, 'is that a certain sign, and not another, is applied to a certain element of reality, and not to any other. In this sense, and only in this sense, it is permissible to speak of contingency, and even in so doing we would seek less to solve the problem than simply to pinpoint it in order to set it aside provisionally.... The domain of arbitrariness is thus left outside the comprehension (logical intention) of the linguistic sign'. Emile Benveniste, *Problems in General Linguistics*, as quoted in Baudrillard (1981), 151. See Roger Hart's discussion of Derrida's critique of Benveniste in Roger Hart, 'Translating the Untranslatable: From Copula to Incommensurable Worlds', in Liu (1995), 50–2.

53 Baudrillard (1981), 152.

54 Ibid., 153.

55 Roman Jakobson, *Language in Literature* (Cambridge, Mass.: Belknap, 1987), 66.

56 Ibid., 179.

57 In Bourdieu's earlier Algerian studies, structural linguistics was still very much part of his vocabulary as he was trying to develop a new set of analytical categories for anthropological work on a non-European society. For example, he would speak of the Kabyles' 'grammar of honor'

in a good old structuralist fashion when describing their elaborate code of honor. The 'grammar of honor' is a linguistic trope, and much more. Within the specific theoretical context of Bourdieu's fieldwork, it acquires an ontological status and becomes the *conceptual equivalent* for what structural linguists and anthropologists take to be the totality of a social structure. Thus, 'when they spontaneously apprehend a particular line of conduct as degrading or ridiculous', says Bourdieu, 'the Kabyles are in the *same* position as someone who notices a language mistake without being able to state *the syntactic system* that has been violated' (emphasis added). Saussure's linguistic model resonates loudly in the form of a simile and conceptual closure. See Pierre Bourdieu, *Algeria 1960: The Disenchantment of the World, the Sense of Honour, the Kabyle House or the World Reversed*, trans. Richard Rice (Cambridge: Cambridge University Press, 1979), 128.

58   See Pierre Bourdieu, 'The Production and Reproduction of Legitimate Language', in ed. John B. Thompson (ed.), *Language and Symbolic Power*, trans. Gino Raymond and Matthew Adamson (Cambridge, MA: Harvard University Press, 1994), 66. This chapter was originally published as 'La production et la reproduction de la langue légitime' in Bourdieu, *Ce que parler veut dire: L'économie des échanges*. The original French title of this book, emphasizing the economy of exchange, more directly spells out the theoretical emphasis of the author than does J. B. Thompson's English edition.

59   Ibid., 67.

60   Ibid., 77. Emphasis added.

61   Another good example of this tautology is found in the following: 'When one language dominates the market, it becomes the norm against which the prices of the other modes of expression, and with them the values of the various competencies, are defined. The language of the grammarians is an artefact, but, being universally imposed by the agencies of linguistic coercion, it has a social efficacy in as much as it functions as the norm, through which is exerted the domination of those groups which have both the means of imposing it as legitimate and the monopoly of the means of appropriating it' in Pierre Bourdieu, 'Economics of Linguistic Exchanges', *Social Science Information* 16/6 (1997), 652.

62   See Bourdieu (1994), 53.

63   The term 'reciprocal wager' is taken from Baudrillard out of the immediate context of his discussion of the art auction. See Baudrillard (1981), 116.

64   See Liu (1995).

65   [Note: referring to another chapter in this chapter's original publication. Lydia H. Liu, 'Legislating the Universal: The Circulation of International

Law in the Nineteenth Century', in eadem (ed.), *Tokens of Exchange: The Problem of Translation in Global Circulations* (Durham: Duke University Press, 1999), 127–64.]

66   For a critical analysis of *koutou* and other related constructions of Chinese contempt for the foreigner before and after the Opium War, see James Hevia, *Cherishing Men from Afar* (Durham, NC: Duke University Press, 1995), 229–37.

67   See Dilip Basu, 'Chinese Xenology and Opium War', paper presented at the conference 'Empire and Beyond' (University of California at Berkeley, 1997).

Andrew Sartori holds a professorship in South Asian history at New York University. While colonial Bengal is his main region of expertise, his main research interests revolve around the relationship between concept-formation and political economy. Sartori aims to move beyond the notions that transfers and translations have been behind the co-occurrences of many concepts across different languages. In search of a different kind of explanation, Sartori focuses instead on the development of global capitalism as a common base which accounts for similarities.

Andrew Sartori's publications include *From the Colonial to the Postcolonial: India and Pakistan in Transition* (co-editor; 2007), *Bengal in Global Concept History: Culturalism in the Age of Capital* (2008), *Global Intellectual History* (co-editor; 2013) and *Liberalism in Empire* (2014). He co-edits the journal *Critical Historical Studies* published by the University of Chicago Press and serves on the editorial board of *Modern Intellectual History*.

In his early text 'The Resonance of "Culture": Framing a Problem in Global Concept-History', Sartori traces the global concept of 'culture'. He seeks to uncover the concept's European origins from Enlightenment onward in order to better understand the global appearance of the concept. Intra-European semantic continuities and developments are shown along with examples of global resonance. Sartori's point of departure is allowing for autonomous agency in a concept that emphatically includes multiple specificities of time and space.

9

The Resonance of *Culture*: Framing a Problem in Global Concept-History

Andrew Sartori

In the course of the nineteenth and twentieth centuries, *culture* achieved the status of a truly global concept. We find discourses of *culture* emerging to prominence in the German-speaking world during the second half of the eighteenth century (with the closely associated linguistic areas of the Netherlands and Scandinavia rapidly following suit); in the English-speaking world starting in the first half of the nineteenth century; in Eastern Europe, East Asia and South Asia starting in the second half of the nineteenth century; and just about everywhere else in the course of the twentieth century. *Culture* began to circulate far beyond the European sites of its modern genesis, sometimes through the direct transfer of lexical items from Western European languages (e.g. Russian *kul'tura*; the use of *kalcar* in various South Asian languages); and more often through the construction of new translative equivalencies with pre-existing words or concepts most often signifying purification, refinement, or improvement (e.g. Japanese *bun-ka*; Chinese *wen-hua*; Bangla and Hindi *sanskriti*; Urdu *tamaddun*).[1]

However creatively deployed in however divergent a range of contexts, the power, resonance and usefulness of any conceptual vocabulary must surely derive from the denotative and connotative baggage accumulated in the course of the history of its prior deployment. Any attempt to understand the global dimensions of the dissemination and circulation of modern cultural discourses must proceed, then, from some initial understanding of what was being disseminated and circulated. Without for a moment thinking that a global concept-history could be reducible to its Western origin, we nevertheless might well wonder what the history that preceded the culture-concept's journey beyond the narrower confines of Western Europe might tell us about the logic of its global dissemination. What was this concept, *culture* that people in these disparate places were adopting? Proceeding from the recognition that this particular concept was found powerful, resonant and useful in numerous and diverse historical contexts as the appropriate thought-form for certain kinds of social analysis and critique, this paper sets out first of all to challenge the disaggregative instincts of contemporary intellectual historians by identifying a single, broadly pan-European modern culture-concept that has traversed the boundaries of the specific discourse-formations of pedagogy, aesthetics, anthropology and so on. This culture-concept, I suggest, has articulated a claim about the *fundamental underdetermination of human subjectivity*, and has done so fairly consistently since its emergence into philosophical importance in the eighteenth century. From the perspective of this analysis, the global dissemination of the culture-concept consequently becomes susceptible to a more systematic historical analysis than is suggested by fragmentary histories of the transmission of intellectual influences or the reproduction of discursive apparatus. Reading the global history of the culture-concept as the dissemination of a category of *autonomous agency* does not foreclose the investigation of the specific conditions of its reception in particular times and places; rather, it forms the starting point for an investigation into the ubiquitous centrality of discourses of *culture* to critiques of alien bureaucracy, of colonial domination and of the anarchic and anomic tendencies of commercial society.

I

Matthew Arnold's well-known espousal of the term 'culture' in the 1860s immediately identified him in the eyes of his contemporaries as a spokesman for what the Victorians termed 'Germanism'.[2] 'Culture' and 'cultivation' were two mostly synonymous English words that were closely bound throughout the nineteenth century to two German words, *Kultur* and *Bildung*, which at least until the end of the eighteenth century still had fuzzy enough contours to be sometimes used interchangeably: Immanuel Kant, for example, used them more or less interchangeably, while Moses Mendelsohn's pragmatic juxtaposition of the two terms was necessarily self-conscious.[3] *Bildung* began its career as a translation from Latin: *Bild* = *imago* (*dei*). In the course of the eighteenth century, however, it shed its Pietist roots and instead came to signify the process of active self-cultivation envisioned by the philhellenist neohumanists.[4] The term *Kultur* was assimilated into German from an earlier French usage (*la culture*), which also had an early English offshoot (culture), all of which were in turn ultimately derived from Latin (most famously, Cicero's stoic conception of *cultura animi*). In early usage, 'culture' was typically accompanied by a genitive phrase ('of the spirit', 'of the mind', 'of literature' or even 'of the body') in keeping with its foundation in the agricultural metaphor. But from as early as the late sixteenth century, we find it gradually emerging as a freestanding concept. Samuel Pufendorf's juxtaposition of a *status naturalis* and a *status culturae* (identified in turn with the *status civilis*) may be the first important instance of such a usage; and this early formulation of the nature/culture opposition already seemed to presage the later importance of the concept.[5]

Culture has had a long and intimate relationship with the more expansive concept of *civilization*, a term that emerged in mid-eighteenth-century French (and English very soon thereafter) with the aspiration to unite the disparate themes of *police, politesse, civilité* and *doux commerce* under the single heading of an overarching social process.[6] To say *Kultur* in German has most often meant implicitly to translate *civilisation* (or its English twin); for *Kultur* was most often understood on a collective scale to name the degree to which some specific people or nation had progressed in overcoming their subjection to Nature – in other words, the overcoming of scarcity, the development of technical capacities, the institution of a rule of law and/or rational administration, the progress of knowledge and the softening of manners that were at the core of the various narratives of 'civilization'.[7] Conversely, both the British and the French would translate the word *Kultur* as 'civilization' wherever the usages seemed consonant, including in some rather prominent instances: Burkhardt's *Die Kultur der Renaissance* was translated into English as *The Civilization of the Renaissance* and into French as *La Civilisation de la Renaissance* soon after its publication in 1860; and Freud's 1930 essay *Das Unbehagen in der Kultur* became *Civilization and Its Discontents* and *Le Malaise dans la Civilisation*.

But the concept has also been slipperier than such an easy translative equation might suggest. 'The German word *Kultur*', explained W. D. Robson-Scott in a footnote to his 1928 translation of Freud's *Future of an Illusion*, 'has been translated sometimes as "culture" and sometimes as "civilization", denoting as it does a concept intermediate between these and at times inclusive of both'.[8] In fact, *culture* could be distinguished from *civilization*, to begin with, through a simple juxtaposition of part (the spiritual, intellectual and moral dimensions of human development) to whole (the total process of social development). However, to disembed *culture* in this way could already be the first step to making a more radical claim about the autonomous activity of the human subject within or against the objective historical processes of civilizational development, which could in turn be figured in broadly Rousseauvian terms as a corruptive descent back into external or material determinations (selfish interest, materialistic desire, structures of social interdependence). The *Bildungsideal* assumed its centrality in German intellectual discourse in the late eighteenth century precisely as a critique of Enlightenment rationalism's reduction of human beings to functional utility within a (bureaucratic) division of labour, from the standpoint of the natural self's 'unconditional right to self-determination'.[9] Anthony La Vopa's emphasis on the role of 'poor students' in this discourse echoes, even as it complicates, Norbert Elias' classic sketch of the origins of the modern German culture/civilization dichotomy in the exclusion of the middle-class intelligentsia from the (francophone) courtly society of the eighteenth century.[10] Elias' longer *durée* history must of course be tempered with the recognition that the famous *lexical* opposition between the terms *Kultur* and *Zivilisation* was essentially a product of the late nineteenth century, and that the specifically nationalistic understanding of this lexical opposition became commonplace only from around the period of World War I.[11] Yet in the end, Elias' analysis was seeking to derive the later emergence of the lexical opposition from an earlier, eighteenth-century *conceptual* opposition between external institutions and inner life that was the precondition for nationalistic homologies.[12] In any case, it is quite clear that from the 1870s at least, German writers like Heinrich von Treitschke were increasingly matching stereotypes of France's glossy and formalistic show of *civilisation* with critiques of Britain's allegedly sudsy conception of 'civilization', and German academics were beginning to grapple with conceptual oppositions that substantially prefigured the later, more systematic lexical opposition of *Kultur* (authentic subjectivity free from the material determinations of utility and self-interest) and *Zivilisation* (the material progress of human beings).[13]

Conversely, writers in English, drawing directly on these German intellectual influences, would adopt the words 'culture' or 'cultivation' whenever a distinction from 'civilization' was implied.[14] Thus, in 1829, Samuel Coleridge, erecting his political theory on a solid foundation of German classical idealism, had already identified 'the permanent *distinction*, and the occasional *contrast*, between cultivation and civilization', adding the observation that 'a nation can never be too cultivated, but may easily become an over-civilized race'.[15] Arnold himself would echo this formulation forty years later when opposing culture (the 'idea of perfection as an inward condition of the mind and spirit') to 'the mechanical and material civilization in esteem with us'.[16] Similarly, while the French might commonly translate *Kultur* as *civilisation*, they could also, working under German intellectual influences that were at least as powerfully felt in nineteenth-century France as in nineteenth-century Britain, reinvigorate the marginalized term, *culture*, where a lexical distinction from *civilisation* was called for, as for instance during the reception of Nietzsche in the 1890s.[17] In fact, francophone authors had already in the eighteenth century developed their own terminological opposition between 'true' and 'false' civilization, the latter being characterized by the superficialities of *civilité*, lacking any real underlying moral substance.[18] This was a theme that would be further elaborated in the early nineteenth century, as the eminent philosopher Victor Cousin worked to establish philosophically, and cultivate practically, the efficacious integrity of a *moi* grounded in the power of volition. Through a critique of the sensationalist doctrines of Locke and Condillac, which threatened to dissolve the self into discrete moments of sense-perception, Cousin sought to elaborate a 'self-possessed' form of personhood capable of rational reflection and moral responsibility against the relatively 'unselved' form of personhood that functioned merely as the passive instrument of 'spontaneous suggestions of consciousness'.[19]

Even in the French intellectual world, then, the distinction between inner and outer development had been significant since the eighteenth century.

For a liberal like François Guizot, the distinction between the moral and material dimensions of human progress, while clearly conceived, was nonetheless contained within the larger process of *civilisation*, which was the higher synthesis of its two equally necessary subordinate elements.[20] This French faith in the coherence of a unitary civilizational narrative synthesizing both moral and material progress could fairly be described as the norm in both English and German for most of the modern era.[21] In fact, the culture-concept has never been incompatible with liberal thought, even when that liberalism grounded itself in the objective historical processes of civilizational development. *Culture* could supplement the more classically liberal, negative conception of *emancipation from* the illegitimate exercise of State authority, with the positive conception of subjective freedom as a *capacity to*. John Stuart Mill, for instance, shared with other liberals the belief in individual liberty both on grounds of principle and general social utility, and he was hardly eccentric in linking the historical emergence of a liberal society to major transformations in the structure of economy, society and polity. But what Mill added to the framework of his liberal and utilitarian forebears was the notion that such freedom from external constraint was justified not only because it allowed for the generalized pursuit of material pleasure (Bentham's *happiness*) that underpinned the logic of political economy; but also because it provided the opportunity for the cultivation of each individual's innate potential through the pursuit of the 'higher pleasures' of the spirit or mind.[22] Here, the positive freedom that was at the core of the culture-concept was being nested within a liberal conception of negative freedom.

Yet one can see how easily this kind of liberal culturalism could slip into a culture/civilization opposition: while Mill would on the one hand posit *liberty* and *culture* as mutually reinforcing and complementary principles, he could also call for the cultivation of higher virtues on the part of university elites to *counter* the dangerous levelling effects of the democratized mass-society that *civilization* had called forth.[23] It was broadly the same argument that Arnold would make in his manifesto for a 'better liberalism' that would eschew 'the pedantic application of certain maxims of political economy in the wrong place' in favour of the cultivation of a '*best self*'. By bringing men into harmony under the guidance of an impersonal 'right reason', 'culture' would provide a 'principle of authority' to 'counteract the tendency to anarchy which seems to be threatening us'. That principle directly implied 'the idea of *the State*', that is the 'organ of our collective best self, our national right reason', 'entrusted with stringent powers for the general advantage'.[24] At such moments, we see *culture* becoming entangled in a wider project that would use the idea of disinterested self-cultivation to construct an 'extrapolitical, extraeconomic space' homologous with the universal collective interest represented ideologically by the State.[25] But what this in turn meant was that the ethical State was being positioned, through the language of *culture*, as the preeminent organ of the nation's collective spiritual life, so that it served as a force antithetical to the material determinations of petty self-interest that drove *civilization*.[26] In the end, even though *culture* could be posited as a complementary or even metonymically subordinate moment of *civilization*, wherever the progressive course of history was understood to entwine human subjects heteronomously in ever-tighter networks of materialistic desire and instrumentalization, *culture* could always be invoked as a Rousseauvian counter-principle of internality, authenticity and autonomous self-formation.

II

Seen from this wider perspective, we might suggest that the culture-concept enjoyed a precarious universality within the European cosmopolis constituted by the heritage of Latin cosmopolitanism and the subsequent history of modern vernacular interpenetration. Yes, this universality was shot through with different emphases, degrees of prominence, discursive functions, homological transformations and ideological implications within particular national and linguistic arenas. And of course, the instabilities of two centuries of usage render any single and exhaustive definitional generalization outrageous at a strictly lexical level. Yet in the end it seems undeniable that the concept's major fault-lines have followed less the contours of different languages than certain *internal* semantic differentiations.

The well-known 'review' of the history of the culture-concept undertaken by Alfred Kroeber and Clyde Kluckhohn identified two of the most prominent of these semantic fault lines. To begin with, the distinction between culture and civilization in Germany seemed, they not unreasonably noted, to correlate with 'the spirit-nature dichotomy – *Geist und Natur* – that so deeply penetrated German thought from the eighteenth to the twentieth century'.[27] But the exact nature of this correlation was, they observed, fraught with ambiguity. It might seem obvious to those familiar with the discourses of German and English cultural criticism that *culture* would line up unproblematically with *Geist*. Yet, as Kroeber and Kluckhohn observed, some forms of usage also suggested the very opposite alignment. *Kultur* had often been used, since the late eighteenth century, to refer to the development of man's technical capacities to control nature, much in keeping with the agricultural metaphor at the etymological core of the concept. In contrast to the instrumentalism of *Kultur* then, it would be *Zivilisation* that would bear the burden of both moral and social improvement. This would seem to align *culture* with nature, and civilization with spirit. It would also seem to imply that the nineteenth-century usage of the term *Kultur* was so puzzlingly broad as to encompass conceptual polarities.

'*Civilization*', explained Wilhelm von Humboldt, Kroeber and Kluckhohn's most important exemplar of this alternative tradition, 'is the humanization of peoples in their outward institutions and customs, and the inner attitudes pertaining thereto. *Culture* adds science and art to this refinement of the social order'.[28] Yet only a certain lexical literalism could have led Kroeber and Kluckhohn to ignore the fact that, despite this apparent downgrading of *Kultur* in a definitional passage ripped from its context, Humboldt was indeed still working from within a more familiar form of the culture/civilization dichotomy. He did so, however, by contrasting both *Zivilisation* and *Kultur*, as 'outward' forms, to *Bildung*, the kind of cultivation that is 'something at the same time higher and more inward, namely the disposition that, from the knowledge and feeling of the entire mental and moral endeavour, pours out harmonious upon temperament and character'.[29] *Zivilisation* names the social interconnections that link human beings with each other – 'in their *outer institutions and customs* and in their inner attitude *pertaining thereto*'. It has no *necessary* connection with inner cultivation, but can be a wholly external imposition.[30] Inner cultivation, on the other hand, begins with the subordination of an inchoate creative energy to organic form:

> Even in his earlier circumstance, man transcends the *present* moment, and does not remain sunk in mere sensual enjoyment. Among the roughest tribes we find a love of adornment, dancing, music and song, and beyond that forebodings of a world to come, the hopes and anxieties founded on this, and traditions and tales which commonly go back to the origin of man and of his abode. The more strongly and brightly does the *spiritual power*, working independently by its own laws and forms of intuition, pour out its light into

this world of the past and future, with which man surrounds his existence of the moment, the more purely and variously does the mass [of his creative energy], simultaneously, take shape. Thus do *science* and *art* arise, and the goal, therefore, of mankind's developing progress is always the fusion of what is produced independently from within with what is given from without, each grasped in its purity and completeness, and bound into the subjection which the current endeavour by its nature demands.[31]

For Humboldt, 'contact with the *world*' and 'communication of outer exertion and inner perceptions' turn out to be irreducibly necessary for the actual '*formation of character*' that *Bildung* names.[32] Neohumanists like Humboldt understood *Bildung* to be, in La Vopa's words, a form of 'self-cultivation [that] throve on constant and ever varied interaction between the subject and objective reality. Subjectivity acquired substance for its inner articulation in its very self-projection into external forms'.[33] This in fact positions *Kultur* – the technical capacity to subordinate nature to inner force that Humboldt himself defined through a direct reiteration of the terms 'science and art' in the definitional passage with which we began – as the necessary outward expression of the free and spontaneous agency that characterizes human consciousness.[34] The distinction between *civilization* and *culture* can thus be understood as a distinction between human beings embedded in relationships with other human beings, and human beings in their relationship with (inner and outer) nature. It is in their relationship with nature rather than with each other, Humboldt seems to be saying, that human beings are able to give practical expression and meaning to subjective freedom. Yet, as the truly proto-anthropological passage cited at length above makes abundantly clear, this alignment has never precluded the relationship to nature being understood at the level of the collectivity, so long as collectivity is grasped organically rather than in terms of individual interaction.

Humboldt's emphasis on *Kultur* as the practical expression of subjective freedom was fundamentally inspired by Kantian idealism. Kant himself had defined *Kultur* as the process of '[p]roducing in a rational being an aptitude for purposes generally (hence [in a way that leaves] that being free)', where such 'aptitude for purposes generally' included both 'man's aptitude in general for setting himself purposes' and his aptitude 'for using nature (independently of [the element of] nature in man's determination of purposes) as a means [for achieving them] in conformity with the maxims of his free purposes generally'.[35] Such a practice of *culture* necessarily founded humanity's acquisition of technical prowess ('*skill*') upon a prior 'culture of discipline' that served to constitute a rational 'will' capable of casting off the 'despotism of desires' (which might otherwise condition or limit the freedom of rational thought to select the ends to which a human being might direct such skills).[36] Kant had read too much Rousseau to confuse culture with a mere denatured artifice, though: 'The ideal [*Idee*] of morality belongs to culture', he famously declared; 'its use for some simulacrum of morality in the love of honour and outward decorum constitutes mere civilization [*Civilisierung*]'.[37] Culture was not, then, the mere artificiality of human sociality, which would ultimately have to derive from the element of nature (specifically, desire and self-love) in man's determination of purposes. Rather, it specifically named those forms of nature-commanding activity that expressed the rational self-determination of the human subject.

Culture in this usage might seem, as Raymond Geuss has argued, a profoundly individualized, and even utterly asocial, category.[38] Yet Kant made it clear in his writings on education that it is the pedagogical application of discipline (*Disciplin, Zucht*) that, by making possible the subsequent internalization of self-discipline, lays the foundation for the regular exercise of subjective freedom (i.e. skill directed to freely and rationally chosen ends). Unlike the beast, 'man requires his own reason. He has no instinct, and must himself construct the plan of his own behaviour. Since he is not however immediately capable of doing this ... others must do it for him ... *One generation educates the other*'.[39] Culture is, in other words, something that is formed *within* the realm of the social, and always tends towards the construction of a social framework that encourages conduct in accordance with the moral principles of practical reason.[40] In fact, if the passage of human history can be seen as a transition from 'an uncultured, merely animal condition to the state of humanity, from bondage to instinct to rational control – in a word, from the tutelage of nature to the state of freedom' – then it was the role of culture to 'bring about such a development of the dispositions of mankind, considered as a *moral* species, as to end the conflict between the natural and the moral species ... until such time as finally art will be strong and perfect enough to become a second nature' and thus complete 'the genuine education of man as man and citizen'.[41]

Seen from this perspective, the relationship between what Kroeber and Kluckhohn identified as 'contrary' currents of usage appears much less opaque: both Kant and Humboldt agreed that technical prowess could be the logical extension of the critical constitution of the self as a self-determining (autonomous) subject. Even when it seemed to name an instrumental relationship to *res extensa*, *culture* ultimately and crucially retained its affiliation with the 'spirit' side of the classic antinomy. But more importantly, we can already identify in these most proto-Hegelian (but still ultimately subject-centred) moments of Kant's philosophy the key problematic that has consistently defined the culture-concept: the practical realization of free subjectivity.

III

Kroeber and Kluckhohn, however, viewed this first genealogical puzzle as an anachronism that could be largely consigned (as, in their opinion, 'mainly an episode in German thought') to the pre-history of the 'scientific' culture-concept that was at the heart of their concerns.[42] This previous (apparent) inconsistency in nineteenth-century usage remained firmly within what they termed a 'humanistic' understanding of culture – that is, the individual or collective cultivation (understood as either a process or an achieved state) of the 'human' or 'spiritual' or 'rational' or 'higher' or 'universal' qualities, and extending from there to include the objectified results of such cultivation (literature, art, etc.). This was, of course, the older usage, and for most of the culture-concept's history it remained the more commonplace. Yet it is true that there has long been an alternative set of meanings to culture that would seem to exceed the terms of the discussion above – what is commonly referred to as the 'anthropological' understanding of the concept. Where the humanistic concept would appear to express an achieved *degree* of emancipation from natural determinations ('the despotism of desires'), anthropological *culture* would instead accord to all human collectivities the fundamental characteristic of self-determining agency – 'a set of attributes and products of human societies, and therewith of mankind, which are extrasomatic and transmissible by mechanisms other than biological heredity'.[43]

Analytically, then, it would be quite straightforward to assume, as so many have, that the humanistic and anthropological conceptions are in a straightforward sense definitionally distinct. 'Culture', in other words, was simply a homonym. But a *historical* investigation cannot afford to leap directly to this analytical premise, without first lingering over some important questions: Why have these two analytically distinct dimensions of the culture-concept been so ubiquitously *conflated* in actual usage (hence provoking the need for recurrent analytical clarifications, of which Kroeber and Kluckhohn's own review merely stands as the best known)? And if the humanistic meanings of the word 'culture' long predate its ethnological meanings, what was it about that earlier usage that made the word available for its new role as the foundational concept of an emergent discipline of 'cultural anthropology'?

Genealogies of anthropological *culture* most commonly begin with German Romanticism, and more particularly with Herder's pluralistic organicism as the antithesis of Kant's abstract universalism. They all too rarely take stock of the fact, however, that Herder's pluralism revolved around the concept of *Volk*, not *Kultur*.[44] The latter term occurs exclusively in the singular. Each people had its own distinct instantiation of 'culture', but *culture* itself remained a process of unfolding the inner propensities of each people, who were in turn bound within the single world-historical process of the organic development, as the ultimate end of human nature, of a unitary principle of 'humanity' – that is to say, *'reason and equity in all conditions, and in all occupations of men'*, defined 'not through the will of a sovereign, or the persuasive power of tradition, but through natural laws, on which the essence of man reposes'.[45] 'Every addition to the useful arts secures men's property, diminishes their labour, extends their sphere of activity, and necessarily lays therewith the foundations of farther cultivation and humanity ... [L]et us thank the Creator, that he conferred *understanding* on mankind, and made *art* essential to it'.[46] Thus, while Herder embraced the diversity of peoples, this pluralism seems to have been inextricably bound to his providentialist attachment to a broadly Kantian understanding of culture. 'God made man a deity upon Earth; he implanted in him the principle of *self-activity*, and set this principle in motion from the beginning, by means of the internal and external wants of his nature'.[47] This attachment to a universalistic conception of 'humanity' was equally characteristic of other late-eighteenth-century romantics like Adelung, who sought to extend the semantic range of *culture* to include a properly *social* meaning: 'Culture is the transition from a more sensual and animal condition to the more closely knit interrelations of social life', and 'consists of the sum of defined concepts and of the amelioration and refinement of the body and of manners'.[48] Such moments underline once again the continuity between – indeed, the near coevality of – humanistic usages and usages that even Kroeber and Kluckhohn were able to recognize as proto-anthropological.

Whether used in the singular as a horizontal conceptual distinction within social process or as a vertical distinction between different social groups, anthropological *culture* has always taken plurality and diversity as its defining object. One can in fact trace through the course of the nineteenth century the gradual 'reification' of the culture-concept, along with the word's consequent pluralization.[49] But while the term's assimilation as a constitutive element of new historical and ethnological discourses in the second half of the nineteenth century represented a significant moment in the evolution and extension of the concept, we need to beware of overstating the degree to which the consequent extension of its range of reference constituted a real break in its history. Of course, one might well suspect Kroeber and Kluckhohn themselves of having something of a disciplinary interest in trying to demarcate such a sharp break: they were seeking to ground the integrity of a specifically 'cultural' anthropology in a creation myth that would prophylactically seal its core concept from the sullying touch of its pre-disciplinary, humanistic past. But anthropological *culture* enjoyed no immaculate conception. As George Stocking has observed, despite Kroeber and Kluckhohn's nomination of E. B. Tylor as the Zeus to anthropological *culture*'s Athena, 'the history of the culture idea in English and American anthropology suggests that it did not leap full-blown from Tylor's brow in 1871'. On the contrary, 'close consideration of Tylor's definition in the context of his work and time does in fact suggest that his idea of culture was perhaps closer to that of his humanist near-contemporary Matthew Arnold than it was to the modern anthropological meaning'.[50] For Tylor, *culture* named the progressive evolution of human moral, intellectual, and technical capacities in society, *in contrast to custom*, which could include regressive holdovers of the past. It is quite clear that, as a concept that named the gradual emancipation of human life from the despotism of nature, Tylor's *culture* remained firmly within the humanistic tradition, even as that tradition was being stretched to incorporate a relatively new object of investigation. In other words, 'knowledge, belief, art, law, morals, custom and any other capabilities and habits acquired by man as a member of society' (all categories long-established in the study of human societies) were now being re-conceptualized, re-articulated and re-defined as a 'complex whole' that, in so far as it represented a progressive agent of the emancipation of human subjectivity, could be called 'culture'.

Whether we are talking about *culture* as such, or the various 'cultures' that differ from one another, the category has emerged as a term of social analysis in constitutive contradistinction to objective determinations. Freud, for instance, would define both functions of *Kultur* – 'to protect men against nature and to adjust their mutual relations' – in terms of the imposition of the restriction and sublimation of the primordial instinctual drives of the individual.[51] If his interpretations of the actual symbolic fabric of consciousness were in terms of its over- rather than under-determination, this was *in spite of* culture's effectivity, the result of the irremediable incompleteness of a cultural process that could never truly eliminate the element of nature from man's determination of purposes. Of course, *culture* can be defined to include *all* elements of a social organization, but it names the elements of such an organization specifically as forms distinct from direct biological determinants, at least in the very minimal sense that, even if *culture* were understood as a form of animal behaviour, it must remain a form of *learned* behaviour whose most obvious index would be variability within a biologically homogeneous species. The Boasian adoption of the culture-concept served precisely to assert the autonomy of even 'primitive' systems of social action and meaning (what Kroeber and Kluckhohn called the 'superorganic') from racial and biological determinations.

Alternatively, *culture* has been analytically juxtaposed to other dimensions of the social that are organized by what are understood to be objectively necessary abstract laws, such as the *economy* or *society*. Adam Kuper has persuasively argued that Talcott Parsons' tripartite anatomy of the structure of social action was not only central to laying the foundations for anthropology's claims to disciplinary autonomy, but that in so doing it further underwrote the autonomy of *culture* itself as a distinct determination of social action.[52] Even that notorious arch-determinist Claude Lévi-Strauss used the concept of *culture* to mark out an autonomous function for the intellectual process of transforming percepts into signs, radically distinguishing the logic of classificatory systems from the 'social' determinations of infrastructural 'praxis' and demographic change.[53] From this perspective, the critique of structuralist *culture* as a reification that effaces individual human agency (following the terms of the structure/agency debate) assumes secondary importance to a more fundamental (and thoroughly Kantian) move to establish the intellectual process of meaning-making as a self-positing agency constitutive of, rather than constituted by, structures of practice; for as a relatively autonomous sign-system, *culture* is a form of subjectivity whose only determinations (inflexible as these may be) are 'cultural'.

Following from such substantive contrasts between collectively constituted subjectivity and objective structures of social organization, anthropological *culture* can also by extension be opposed as a theoretical or methodological category of analysis to the 'brute and disinterested objectivism' of sociological abstractions, providing a richer subjectivistic emphasis on the 'rich description' of 'human thought, achievement, consciousness, pain, stupidity and evil' that, precisely because of its irreducibility to objective structures of determination, 'cannot be anticipated on the basis of some theoretical premise'.[54] This is, of course, nothing other than a restatement of the anti-reductionist tradition stretching from Dilthey into American cultural anthropology.[55] This methodological dimension of the culture-concept emerged in late-nineteenth-century German thought as a direct reaction against the rise of positivistic science, and after something of a lull in the concept's centrality during the period of Hegelianism's intellectual ascendancy.[56] It needs to be positioned, then, in the context of the resurgence of a neo-idealist defence of subjectivity from reductionist determinism in later nineteenth-century philosophy and social inquiry – alongside, in other words, the neo-Kantian turn in epistemology that culminated in Heinrich Rickert's re-definition of the *Geisteswissenschaften* (a term which could include the deterministic knowledge of law-like regularities characteristic of psychology, for example) as the *historische Kulturwissenschaften*[57] (a term that specifically designated a form of knowledge that applied to unique phenomena the significance of whose singularity was grounded simultaneously in the value-orientations of historical actors and in the historian's own subject-centred judgments of value).[58]

The issue is not then, as Stocking sometimes seems to imply, one of shifting the moment of the transition from humanistic to anthropological conceptions of *culture* from Tylor in the later nineteenth century to Boas in the early twentieth. For Kroeber and Kluckhohn, the key issue on which the difference between anthropological and humanistic 'cultures' turned was value-neutrality. But while the shift from viewing *culture* as a condition achieved through a history of human improvement to viewing it as a universal condition of human social existence is certainly of great significance for the history of the social sciences, the two 'cultures' are still defined by a single problematic. Anthropological *culture* still indexes the relative autonomy of human subjectivity from 'natural' or 'objective' determinations. This is not to deny, of course, that there can be a theory of *culture* that attempts to identify forms of social or biological determination. On the contrary, Malinowski's analysis of 'basic needs' is just one eminent attempt within the modern anthropological tradition to identify such forms of determination. But for the object of such an analysis to be initially identifiable as *culture* is what first requires historical explanation. While culturalism – that is, a discourse that assumes the *standpoint* of culture as a category of human underdetermination – was required for the identification of certain kinds of objects or practices (e.g. custom, symbolic representation) as *culture*, once the identification of such objects as forms of *culture* was disciplinarily conventionalized, *culture* itself became immediately susceptible to analysis in terms of external determinations, whether in terms of needs, interests or practices. Yet the deeper history of the constitution of the 'cultural' object of knowledge remains evident symptomatically even in the writings of an ethnologist with such distinctly reductionist leanings as Malinowski. In *Argonauts of the Western Pacific*, for instance, he used *culture* as a standpoint from which to attack the stereotype of the 'Primitive Economic Man', the fabricated projection of classical political economy who was 'prompted in all his actions by a rationalistic conception of self-interest'. Even 'man on a low level of culture', Malinowski sought to demonstrate, was driven to 'work and effort' – far beyond the merely necessary, and, indeed, even as 'an end in themselves' – 'by motives of a highly complex, social and traditional nature, and towards aims which are certainly not directed towards the satisfaction of present wants, or to the direct achievement of utilitarian purposes'.[59] The Trobriand Islander was, as a 'cultural' subject, necessarily underdetermined by the despotism of desires – that is, by his immediate wants, needs or self-interest. The collective *culture* of the Islanders thus became for Malinowski the medium through which basic needs were fulfilled while at the same time releasing human beings from their immediate subjection to the demands of merely organic existence.

The anthropological conception of *culture*, stripped of its implication of evolutionary improvement so as to accord underdetermined subjectivity to all social collectivities, replicates the Kantian understanding of human subjectivity at a collective level – and in all the more Kantian a spirit for its radically universal attribution of *culture* to all human societies. In other words, *culture* still names the emancipation of human reason (now grasped as variable systems of meaning-making, but still constituted subjectivistically in keeping with Kant's 'Copernican revolution') from the natural determinations of utility maximization or biological necessity ('the despotism of desires'). The community thus comes to stand in as the arena for the realization of human worldly agency ('skill') that this fundamental freedom is supposed to ground.[60]

IV

None of this is to say that these different forms of cultural discourse, anthropological and humanistic, are simply 'the same'. After all, the specific modalities in which subjective autonomy has been conceived – as a characteristic of the individual or the social, the community or the state – must surely be significant when we turn our attention to particular historical contexts. My point is rather to suggest that, from a historical standpoint, the proliferation of meanings should be considered within a single, internally differentiated conceptual history structured by a single, more-or-less internally consistent, modern understanding of human subjectivity as underdetermined and thus self-positing. *Culture*, humanistic and anthropological, has with remarkable regularity operated within a repertoire of homologous antinomies: inside-outside, authenticity-appearance, content-form, organism-mechanism, mind-body, meaning-thing, subject-object, freedom-necessity, autonomy-heteronomy and spirit-nature. As a method of investigation, it will be indisputably important to *specify* the historical transformations the concept has undergone at *particular* points in time and space. It is in fact only because this concept has been assimilated into diverse discursive fields to diverse ends that the recognition of an underlying regularity becomes historically and theoretically meaningful. Such contextualization is, in the end, the only way to proceed to an understanding of this conceptual regularity as in any sense historically determinate. This in turn is what might make it possible to analyse in a historically determinate manner the changing ways in which free subjectivity has been construed in different temporal and spatial locations. Yet it will simply not do to *dissolve* this remarkable regularity into the pluralized discursive formations connected to particular institutional practices – to deny that *culture* is a concept that has exceeded its articulation as a specific form of discourse within particular institutional contexts. Such a strategy will get us no closer to understanding the central antinomic logic – the 'deep structure', if you will – that has with such remarkable consistency marked the concept across its different major forms of usage. The Foucauldian emphasis on the embeddedness of discourse within regimes of practice should instead serve to impel us to recognize that 'intellectual history', narrowly conceived either in terms of a chain of influence or in terms of the intertextual context of intellectual production, is far too narrow a framework within which to make sense of these deeper regularities across time and space.

A concept that is historically *modern* cannot be derived from metaphysical Truth; not, at least, without explicitly addressing the question of why an eternal verity had to wait so long for a systematic elaboration. Recognizing this has driven many intellectual historians to critique the more traditional 'history of ideas' from the standpoint of a 'genealogical' approach to the history of discourse formations. Yet it remains unclear whether the explanatory power and compelling plausibility of any concept to which can be ascribed the kind of universality that *culture* has enjoyed within the modern European tradition (in the dual sense of the regularity of its reproduction across centuries and its disregard for geographical and linguistic boundaries) can be plausibly derived from the specific institutional contingencies of discursive practice. The Foucauldian argument has certainly been made. Ian Hunter has argued that British cultural discourse in the second half of the nineteenth century took its significance from the pedagogical arrangement of the classroom: the presentation of the teacher as a model for ethical emulation shifted cultural discourse from its earlier valence of reflexive self-formation to a form of power-knowledge whose normalizing function was strategically directed to the production of a manageable population. For Hunter, then, the history of cultural discourse is not a 'tradition' of thought, but rather a discourse-formation generated 'piecemeal' out of an 'ensemble of historical surfaces and forces' that was a 'purely contingent and provisional configuration or "programme"', whose emergence is not governed by any overarching historical purpose or theoretical goal' such as might be figured by the concept of 'man'.[61] Yet the only way to sustain this kind of argument is to radically disaggregate discourses of culture into their particular institutional contexts. Such a turn to concrete repertoires of practice seeks to unveil the process of the hypostatization of historically determinate concepts; but in the process, it leaves the larger regularities and the eminently transmissible nature of the culture-concept ultimately unmotivated.

David Lloyd and Paul Thomas share Hunter's suspicion of the figure of 'man' at the heart of cultural discourse, but they balk at this crypto-positivist reduction of discourse to institutional contingency.[62] They instead argue that cultural discourse is an ideology whose 'regulative idea' is that of the 'modern state', which is as much as to say, the state not 'as a contingently linked assemblage of institutions which have emerged over time in *ad hoc* response to political and social pressures' on the Foucauldian model, but rather 'as the fully developed and unifying representative of a national people'. Culture, in the terms of this discourse, serves to 'mediate between a disenfranchised populace' who represent fractious interests, and 'a state to which they must in time be assimilated' because it represents a truly universal interest that must sublate the competing fractious interests within the nation.[63] In the hands of ideologues like Matthew Arnold and John Stuart Mill, *culture* was constituted as an 'extrapolitical, extraeconomic space' beyond the limits of civil society and thus homologous with the state.[64] This is an ideological project, Lloyd and Thomas have suggested, that far exceeds the limitations of discipline-formation with which Hunter was concerned, for literary education might be an 'instrument' of cultural ideology, but it was certainly not coterminous with the 'concept' itself.[65]

Yet surely the devastating critique that Lloyd and Thomas direct at Hunter could just as easily be laid at their own feet. Does the fact that the ideological project of Victorian state-consolidation appropriated a discourse of *culture* (as they convincingly demonstrate it did) necessarily mean that the concept itself can be derived from or reduced to such functionality? In this sense, Hunter as well as Lloyd and Thomas fundamentally fail to come to terms with one of the core insights of the classic text against which they have commonly positioned their own arguments. In *Culture and Society*, Raymond Williams had sought to show, in a thoroughly non-functionalistic manner, how the concept of *culture* had emerged in modern British thought 'as an abstraction and an absolute'. The delineative axis of the concept's significance was grounded in 'the recognition of the practical separation of certain moral and intellectual activities [and ultimately, these conceived in turn as 'a whole way of life'] from the driven impetus of a new kind of society' – which is as much as to say, the positing of a peculiarly modern subject-object dichotomy, and its subsequent alignment with a culture-society dichotomy. The second, evaluative axis then involved 'the emphasis of these activities, as a court of human appeal, to be set over the processes of practical judgment and yet to offer itself as a mitigating and rallying alternative' – which is as much as to say, the assumption of cultural subjectivism (individual or collective) as the standpoint for a critique of the abstract, coercive and destructive forces of modern industrial society.[66] Lloyd and Thomas' critique of Williams' fundamental inability to recognize the historical complicity of the cultural trope of 'man' with Victorian statist ideologies seems fair. But they fall short of the deeper insight of Williams' text. For Williams located the emergence of the culture-concept in a specifically modern experiential bifurcation (admittedly only posited rather than really analysed or explained) of two zones of social existence: one constituted by subjects inhabiting meaningful life-worlds, the other constituted by an abstract field of heteronomous forces. He thereby generated a framework that, by eschewing functionalistic explanations for the culture-concept's importance, remains the most promising starting-point for developing a truly *historical* account of the constitution of the concept itself, as distinct from its deployment within any particular discursive apparatus.

Yet Williams was, of course, writing about modern Britain, which leaves wide open the larger question of what such a non-functionalistic historical account would look like when considered at the level of the global dissemination and circulation of the culture-concept as a category variously of colonial cosmopolitanism, anti-colonial nationalism, pan-Asianism and anti-Western anticapitalism. Whatever else may be said, if we wish to follow the travels of the culture-concept beyond the borders of industrial Britain – even so far as to the eighteenth-century German-speaking world where the concept first rose to prominence – we will necessarily have to begin by displacing the problematic of 'industrial society' from the conceptual primacy accorded to it in Williams' own account. There are, I would suggest, good reasons for doing this even on the basis of the British materials that Williams himself analysed. Carlyle's critique of 'Laissez-faire', 'Supply-and-demand' and 'Cash-payment as the sole nexus' aspired not to the dissolution of industrial society, but to the liberation of the 'rational soul' of labour from its subjection to the 'Brute-god Mammon'.[67] Arnold's culturalism, on the other hand, explicitly targeted not the growth of industry itself, but rather the threatening new tendency of the proletariat to join a free-for-all pursuit of 'doing as one likes'.[68] In the light of such cases, the critique of 'industrial society', so explicitly central in Ruskin and Morris, is better understood as the logical extension of a broader (and older) critique of 'civil' or 'commercial' society – a social order characterized in terms of the generalized pursuit of individual self-interest, the one-sided development of individuals through over-specialization, the instrumentalization of human beings and human relationships, individual social isolation and anarchic and anomic socio-economic energies.

The emergence of an assertive culturalist politics in colonial Bengal followed the broad contours of the British juxtaposition of subjective agency to the heteronomy implicit in objective structures. While direct critiques of Western industrial production were in circulation in the late nineteenth century, Bengali critics like Bankimchandra Chatterjee more generally focused on the deleterious characterological, ethical and political consequences of the absorption of Indian bureaucratic and clerical functionaries into the structures of civil society: the reduction of society to a 'giant marketplace' where effeminate, hypocritical, verbose and ineffective '*babus*', reciting '*mantras* from Adam Smith's *puranas* and Mill's *tantras*', lived a travesty of 'independence' in the practical reality of a mere 'habit of heartless isolation'.[69] Conceiving a stark dichotomy between either debasing oneself through the bestializing pursuit of material self-interest, or debilitating oneself through an otherworldly pursuit of spiritual detachment, Bankim would draw from British cultural criticism to elaborate a third way: a 'doctrine of culture' according to which the cultivation of innate capacities through non-desirous practice (*nishkam karma*) would give birth to a new model of humanity capable of disavowing slavery to material attachments at the same time as enhancing the (this-worldly) rational agency of both the individual and collective-national subject.[70] In Bengal, Bankim's intervention marked the beginning of a vibrant culturalism that would flourish throughout the twentieth century in a variety of forms: a nationalist political discourse that pitted a developmentalist national state grounded in the ethical and spiritual practices of Indian culture against the shallow materialism of Western civilization; a communalist political discourse that pitted cultured Hindus against a Muslim tenantry who were slaves to the baser instincts of selfishness, lust and atavistic fanaticism; and an aesthetico-literary discourse (associated most famously with the Nobel laureate Rabindranath Tagore) that pitted self-realization through free creativity as an end in itself against everyday utilitarian activity driven by practical necessity or material self-interest.[71]

This pattern was not confined to Britain's colonial territories. Starting in the later nineteenth century, the concept of culture was widely adopted to challenge Western civilizational domination through an identification of authentic indigenous tradition as the practical and intellectual foundation for the recuperation of an autonomous subjectivity from slavish imitation. In the 1850s, Ivan Kireevsky was clearly in search of a concept with which to articulate a distinction between Europe's alleged propensity for rationalist formalism and Russia's Christian commitment to the 'higher and living unity' of 'inner wholeness'. His contrast turned on the difference between Western and Russian *prosveshchenie* (enlightenment), a term that evokes quite powerfully the notion of a subjectivity liberated from heteronomous constraint, but whose usage in this context to express the notion of discrete value-orientations stretched its conventional meaning to the limits of intelligibility.[72] By the 1860s, Nicolai Danilevsky had found a better term with which to articulate the autonomy of Russian values and institutions from the superficial universalistic judgments of Western civilization: *kul'tura*.[73] Just as Bankim was identifying 'the principle of culture' as the foundational doctrine of a revived Hinduism, so too would Konstantin Leontiev identify the 'love of culture' as the 'central idea' of 'true Slavophilism'.[74] Meanwhile, 'civilization and enlightenment' (*bunmeikaika*[75]) were the watchwords of the Meiji project to overthrow the burden of the past and establish Japan as a viable and independent national subject in the modern world order.[76] But some Japanese and Chinese intellectuals were already in the 1870s juxtaposing the formalism and materialism of Meiji reformist thought to the authentic cultivation of subjective autonomy. To this end, they adapted the concept of *wen* (writing) – the classical antithesis of *wu* (military force) and the basis for what would become the Chinese and Japanese translative equivalents of civilization (*wen-ming, bunmei*) and culture (*wenhua, bunka*) – as a key platform from which to 'organize an opposition to the present', that is, to the 'tide of Westernization [that] promised to flood Japanese society with immoral and inhuman practices like "economy"'.[77] In both Japan and China, *national culture*, a concept that condensed both humanistic and ethnographic discursive functions, would become a fundamental element of state-building and empire-building ideologies; while the idea of the global redemptive mission of 'eastern' or 'Asian civilization' would sweep through East and South Asia well before the East Asia Co-Prosperity Sphere appropriated its rhetoric.[78] It is of course true that these ideological projects would as often ride under the banner of *civilization* as *culture*, but this was explicitly understood to be a specifically 'Eastern' or 'Asian' form of *civilization* – a 'cultural' or 'spiritual' civilization antithetical to the materialism of *Western civilization*, formally recapitulating the twentieth-century German understanding of the relationship between *Kultur* and *Zivilisation*.[79]

I am not of course trying to conflate the mere *identification* of such formal regularities across cultural discourses with an *explanation* for the global dissemination of the culture-concept. This paper undertakes a more modest task: to emphasize the unity of *culture* as a global conceptual field in order to frame a starting-point from which a more substantial historical investigation of the significance of this modern thought-form might proceed. The distinction I have been trying to draw between the conceptual content of the culture-concept and its specific discursive and ideological deployments challenges any straightforward reduction of the globalizing movement of the concept to the heterogeneous contingencies of the concrete institutional or intellectual vehicles of its dissemination. After all, the remarkably consistent tendency of the concept to global dissemination over the past two and one-half centuries in itself seems to militate against an account that depends solely on the specificity of contingent historical conjunctures. An emphasis on structural continuity over contingency and heterogeneity and conceptual content over discursive effectivity, flies in the face of the conventional disaggregative wisdom of contemporary intellectual history, whether of the Foucauldian or Skinnerian varieties. Yet the approach I am suggesting here does not necessarily have to abandon the considerable insights of this literature in the dubious cause of flattening the historical process of the globalization of the concept into a homogeneous monocausality; for it allows for the possibility that *culture* arrived in specific locations embedded in specific discursive frameworks, serving potentially quite different concrete functions in the hands of quite different historical agents intervening in quite different historical contexts and conceptualizing the appropriate agent of subjective autonomy in quite different ways. Nonetheless, I submit that there seems to be a deep coherence to the history of the culture-concept, and recognizing this could form the working hypothesis from which further historical investigation into its global dissemination and circulation might begin. Such an investigation could do worse than to broadly follow Williams in proceeding from a question quite different from the kind normally asked in the history of ideas: *Under what circumstances has the problematic of subjective autonomy come to assume such global resonance in the modern age?* If the culture-concept has indeed consistently articulated a claim about the underdetermination of human subjectivity, its movement might well track the dissemination of a more fundamental problematic: the definitively 'modern' problematic of subjective autonomy itself. It is the historical conditions for the global emergence of this problematic, rather than the history of ideas or of the transfer of discursive-institutional apparatus from metropole to periphery, which should form the basic material for a truly global history of the culture-concept.

Notes

1   For a discussion of the formation of 'translative equivalents' as an object of specifically *historical* study that goes 'beyond the deconstructionist stage of trying to prove that equivalencies do not exist' and instead looks 'into their *manner of becoming*', see Lydia H. Liu, *Translingual Practice: Literature, National Culture, and Translated Modernity. China, 1900–1937* (Stanford: Stanford University Press, 1995), 16 [Note: a chapter of this

book is part of the present volume: Lydia Liu, 'The Question of Meaning-Value in the Political Economy of the Sign' (chapter eight in this volume).]

2   The prominent English Comtean, Frederic Harrison, for instance, wrote good-humouredly of Arnold's 'fiddlestick, or sauerkraut, or culture (call it as you please)', in 'Culture: A Dialogue', *Fortnightly Review*, 2 (July–Dec. 1867), 603–14.

3   In his essay *Über Pädagogik* (Langensalza: Hermann Beyer and Sons, 1883), Kant refers in §1 to '*Unterweisung nebst der Bildung*', and in §7 to '*Kultur (so kann man die Unterweisung nennen)*'. Mendelssohn's contrastive definitions in his essay, '*Über die Frage, was heisst aufklären?*' are cited in Rudolph Vierhaus, 'Bildung', in Otto Brunner, Werner Conze and Reinhart Koselleck (eds), *Geschichtliche Grundbegriffe: Historisches Lexikon zur politisch-sozialen Sprache in Deutschland* (Stuttgart: Ernst Klett, 1972), vol. 1, 508.

4   See Anthony La Vopa, *Grace, Talent, and Merit: Poor Students, Clerical Careers, and Professional Ideology in Eighteenth-Century Germany* (Cambridge: Cambridge University Press, 1988), especially chapter 9; Rudolph Vierhaus, '*Bildung*', in Brunner et al. (1972), vol. 1, 508–51.

5   Jörg Fisch, 'Zivilisation, Kultur', in Otto Brunner, Werner Conze and Reinhart Kosellek (eds), *Geschichtliche Grundbegriffe: Historisches Lexikon zur politisch-sozialen Sprache in Deutschland* (Stuttgart: Klett-Cotta, 1992), vol. 7, 685, 700–3; Philippe Bénéton, *Histoire de mots: Culture et civilisation* (Paris: Presses de la Fondation nationale des sciences politiques, 1975), 30. The *OED* cites Wordsworth's *Preludes* (1805) as the earliest example of this stand-alone usage in English, but one could certainly find significantly earlier examples.

6   Lucien Febvre, '*Civilisation*: Evolution of a Word and a Group of Ideas', in Peter Burke (ed.), *A New Kind of History* (New York: Harper and Row, 1973), 219–57; and Emile Benveniste, 'Civilization: A Contribution to the History of the Word', in idem, *Problems in General Linguistics* (Coral Gables, FL.: University of Miami Press, 1971), 289–96.

7   Cf. Fisch (1992), 679.

8   Sigmund Freud, *The Future of an Illusion*, trans. W. D. Robson-Scott (London: Hogarth Press, 1943), 7, fn. 1.

9   La Vopa (1988), 264–78.

10   Norbert Elias, *The Civilizing Process* (Oxford: Blackwell, 1994), 3–28.

11   Fisch (1992), 681–2, 714–15, 722, fn. 246, 749–52; Bénéton (1975), chapters 4–5.

12   In fact, it is worth noting that Elias himself began his discussion with the more nuanced recognition that 'the function of the German concept of *Kultur* took on a new life in the year 1919', but that in doing so it was reactivating and re-appropriating an older conceptual antithesis that had

its 'concrete point of departure' in the 'significantly different' historical context of the late eighteenth century. See Elias (1994), 7. This was a nuance to which Herbert Marcuse was also drawing attention more or less contemporarily, and without at all reducing the concept to its nationalistic homology: 'Although the distinction between civilization and culture may have joined only recently the mental equipment of the social and cultural sciences, the state of affairs that it expresses has long been characteristic of the conduct of life and the *Weltanschauung* of the bourgeois era'. Herbert Marcuse, 'The Affirmative Character of Culture', in idem, *Negations: Essays in Critical Theory* (Boston: Beacon, 1968), 88–133. On the other hand, Timothy C. W. Blanning has recently restated the importance of the conceptual opposition between Frenchness and Germanness in his *The Culture of Power and the Power of Culture: Old Regime Europe 1660–1789* (Oxford: Oxford University Press, 2003), 232–65.

13   David Blackbourn has briefly but suggestively linked the emergence of *cultural* discourses in late-nineteenth-century Germany to the economic instability of the Great Depression of 1873–1896, and thereby helped to locate the specificities of these discourses within an international frame, in 'The Discrete Charm of the Bourgeoisie: Reappraising German History in the Nineteenth Century', in David Blackbourn and Geoff Eley (eds), *The Peculiarities of German History: Bourgeois Society and Politics in Nineteenth-Century Germany* (Oxford: Oxford University Press, 1984), 206–21. On the role of Treitschke in leading the shift in German attitudes toward England from the 1870s, see Charles E. McClelland, *The German Historians and England: A Study in Nineteenth-Century Views* (Cambridge: Cambridge University Press, 1971), part IV. Fritz Ringer has given the best-known account of the German academy's renewed emphasis on the culture/civilization dichotomy in the later nineteenth century, in Fritz Ringer, *The Decline of the German Mandarins: The German Academic Community, 1890–1933* (Hanover, N.H.: Wesleyan University Press, 1990).

14   Raymond Williams has provided the classic account of the English tradition of cultural criticism in *Culture and Society: 1780–1950* (New York: Columbia University Press, 1983).

15   John Morrow (ed.), *Coleridge's Writings, Volume 1: On Politics and Society* (Princeton: Princeton University Press, 1991), 176.

16   Matthew Arnold, *Culture and Anarchy* (Cambridge: Cambridge University Press, 1963), 48–9.

17   Bénéton (1975), 56–9, 73–6.

18   Jean Starobinski, *Blessings in Disguise; or, The Morality of Evil* (Cambridge, Mass.: Harvard University Press, 1993), chapter 1.

19   See Jan Goldstein, 'Mutations of the Self in Old Regime and Postrevolutionary France', in Lorraine Daston (ed.), *Biographies of Scientific Objects* (Chicago and London: University of Chicago Press, 2000), 86–116. Cousin, Bénéton notes (Bénéton (1975), 56–7), was also instrumental in introducing the French public to the philosophies of Fichte, Schelling and Hegel.

20   See Francois Guizot, *General History of Civilization in Europe from the Fall of the Roman Empire to the French Revolution* (New York: D. Appleton, 1928).

21   Alfred L. Kroeber and Clyde Kluckhohn, *Culture: A Critical Review of Concepts and Definitions* (New York: Vintage, 1963), 29–30.

22   John Stuart Mill, *On Liberty*, ed. Leonard Kahn (Peterborough, Ontario: Broadview, 2015); and see also Wilhelm von Humboldt, *The Limits of State Action* (Cambridge: Cambridge University Press, 1969).

23   John Stuart Mill, 'Civilization', in idem, *The Collected Works of John Stuart Mill, Volume XVIII: Essays on Politics and Society* (Toronto, Buffalo, and London: University of Toronto Press and Routledge and Kegan Paul, 1977), 117–47.

24   Fraser Neimann (ed.), *Essays, Letters, and Reviews by Matthew Arnold* (Cambridge, Mass.: Harvard University Press, 1960), 105; Arnold (1963), 75, 82, 95–7.

25   See David Lloyd and Paul Thomas, *Culture and the State* (New York and London: Routledge, 1998).

26   Stefan Collini has written persuasively concerning the ubiquity of anxieties about the social consequences of the generalized pursuit of self-interest in Britain in the second half of the nineteenth century, noting Victorian social critics' 'obsessive antipathy to selfishness' and their 'constant anxiety about the possibility of sinking into a state of psychological malaise or anomie, a kind of emotional entropy assumed to be the consequence of absorption in purely selfish aims', in Stefan Collini, *Public Moralists: Political Thought and Intellectual Life in Britain, 1850–1930* (Oxford: Clarendon Press, 1991), 65.

27   Kroeber and Kluckhohn (1963), 26.

28   Wilhelm von Humboldt, *On Language: On the Diversity of Human Language Construction and Its Influence on the Mental Development of the Human Species*, ed. Michael Losonsky, trans. Peter Heath (Cambridge: Cambridge University Press, 1999), 34; Kroeber and Kluckhohn (1963), 26–9.

29   Humboldt (1999), 34–5.

30   Ibid., 35.

31   Ibid., 30.

32   Ibid., 23, 30–1.

33 La Vopa (1988), 272.

34 Humboldt (1999), 34.

35 Immanuel Kant, *Critique of Judgment*, trans. Werner S. Pluhar (Indianapolis: Hacket, 1987), §83, 319, translator's interpolations.

36 In the first critique, Kant had juxtaposed discipline and culture as negative to positive: the restraint and extirpation of our natural inclination to contravene the dictates of reason, versus the acquisition of skills that can be used to any given end, which may or may not be in accordance with reason. Immanuel Kant, *Critique of Pure Reason*, trans. Norman Kemp Smith (1781; Houndmills, New York: Palgrave Macmillan, 2003), 575 (A 709–10, B 737–8). The formulation just cited from the third critique, however, recognizes that an aptitude is only *culture* (i.e. a properly *human* aptitude) if it is grounded in the 'culture of discipline', that is in the free subjectivity of a rational will.

37 Immanuel Kant, 'Idea for a Universal History from a Cosmopolitan Point of View', in Lewis White Beck (ed.), *On History: Immanuel Kant* (New York: Macmillan, 1963), 21.

38 Raymond Geuss makes this claim in '*Kultur, Bildung, Geist*', in idem *Morality, Culture and History: Essays on German Philosophy* (Cambridge: Cambridge University Press, 1999), 33–4.

39 Immanuel Kant, *Über Pädagogik* (Königsberg: Friedrich Nicolovius, 1803), § 3–4, my emphasis.

40 Cf. Robert B. Pippin, *Idealism as Modernism: Hegelian Variations* (Cambridge: Cambridge University Press, 1997), chapters 3 and 4; Allen W. Wood, *Kant's Ethical Thought* (Cambridge: Cambridge University Press, 1999); and Yirmiahu Yovel, *Kant and the Philosophy of History* (Princeton: Princeton University Press, 1980).

41 Immanuel Kant, 'Conjectural Beginning of Human History' in Lewis White Beck (ed.), *On History: Immanuel Kant* (New York: Macmillan, 1963), 60–3.

42 Kroeber and Kluckhohn (1963), 29.

43 Ibid., 284. Proceeding from this anthropological universalization of *culture*, the older part-whole relationship of *culture* and *civilization* could be reversed, so that *civilization* could specify that subset of 'cultures' that had achieved certain levels of technical advancement. See for example Robert Redfield, 'Civilizations as Things Thought About', in Margaret Park Redfield (ed.), *Human Nature and the Study of Society: The Papers of Robert Redfield*, vol. 1 (Chicago: University of Chicago Press, 1962), 367–71.

44 Raymond Williams appears to be partly responsible for the ubiquity of this misrepresentation. See Raymond Williams, *Keywords: A Vocabulary of Culture and Society* (New York: Oxford University Press, 1983, rev. edn), 89.

45 Johann Gottfried von Herder, *Reflections on the Philosophy of the History of Mankind* (Chicago and London: University of Chicago Press, 1968, abr. edn), 100–1; and cf. Fisch (1992), 708–12.
46 Herder (1968), 110–11.
47 Ibid., 84, my emphasis.
48 Kroeber and Kluckhohn (1963), 35–8.
49 Fisch (1992), 746–8.
50 George W. Stocking Jr., *Race, Culture and Evolution: Essays in the History of Anthropology* (New York: Free Press, 1968), 72–3.
51 Sigmund Freud, *Civilization and Its Discontents* (New York, London: W. W. Norton, 1961), 36–50.
52 Adam Kuper, *Culture: The Anthropologists' Account* (Cambridge, Mass.: Harvard University Press, 1999), chapter 2. In the developmentalist discourse of the 1950s and 1960s, the construction of *culture* as the residual determinant after social and ideological factors were subtracted often led to a negative characterization of cultural subjectivity as an obstacle to the 'natural' process of economic growth. Cf. Carl Pletsch, 'The Three Worlds Concept and the Division of Social Scientific Labor, Circa 1950–1975', *Comparative Studies in Society and History*, 23 (1981), 565–90.
53 Claude Lévi-Strauss, *The Savage Mind*, trans. John Wightman and Doreen Wightman (Chicago: University of Chicago Press, 1966), 66–70, 130–1.
54 Roy Boyne, 'Culture and the World System', *Theory, Culture & Society*, 7/2–3 (1990), 57–62.
55 Cf. Elman R. Service, *A Century of Controversy: Ethnological Issues from 1860 to 1960* (Orlando: Academic Press, 1985), chapter 16.
56 Geuss (1999), 36–7; Kroeber and Kluckhohn (1963), 47; Ringer (1990).
57 [Note: misspelling corrected.]
58 Heinrich Rickert, *Science and History: A Critique of Positivist Epistemology* (Princeton, New Jersey: D. Van Nostrand, 1962). See also Andrew Arato, 'The Neo-Idealist Defense of Subjectivity', *Telos*, 21 (1974), 108–61.
59 Bronislaw Malinowski, *Argonauts of the Western Pacific: An Account of Native Enterprise and Adventure in the Archipelagoes of Melanesian New Guinea* (London: Routledge, 1922), 60–2.
60 Of course, this transformation of the subjectivistic standpoint from the individual to the collective level may not be admissible in the strictly *philosophical* terms of Kant's argument, but this should not blind us to the deeper homology in the structure of argumentation.
61 Ian Hunter, *Culture and Government: The Emergence of Literary Education* (London: Macmillan, 1988), 262.
62 Lloyd and Thomas (1998), 16–20.
63 Ibid., 3–5.

64 Ibid., 15.

65 Ibid., 118.

66 Williams (1983a), xviii.

67 Thomas Carlyle, *Past and Present* (Cambridge: Riverside Press, 1965), 38, 191, 207; Thomas Carlyle, 'Signs of the Times', in idem, *Critical and Miscellaneous Essays* (London: Chapman and Hall, 1899), vol. 2, 56–82.

68 Arnold (1963), 80–1; and cf. Stefan Collini, *Arnold* (Oxford: Oxford University Press, 1988), 78–81.

69 Andrew Sartori, 'Emancipation as Heteronomy: The Crisis of Liberalism in Later Nineteenth-Century Bengal', *Journal of Historical Sociology*, 17/1 (Mar. 2004), 56–86.

70 Bankim first broached this argument in an 1877 essay, '*Manushyatva ki?*' (What is humanity?), in Dr. Vishnu Basu (ed.), *Bankim racanabali: Sahitya samagra* (Calcutta: Tuli-Kalam, 1393 BS (*c.* 1986 A.D.)), 374–6. His most detailed statement followed in his 1880s dialogical treatise, 'Dharmmatattva: Anushilan' (The essence of religion: Culture) – see the new translation by Apratim Ray: *Bankimchandra Chattopadhyay's Dharmatattva* (Oxford: Oxford University Press, 2003).

71 See Andrew Sartori, 'The Categorial Logic of a Colonial Nationalism: Swadeshi Bengal, 1904–1908', *Comparative Studies of South Asia, Africa and the Middle East*, 23/1–2 (2003), 271–85; Joya Chatterji, *Bengal Divided: Hindu Communalism and Partition, 1932–1947* (Cambridge: Cambridge University Press, 1994), chapter 4; and Niharranjan Ray, *Krishti, kalcara, samskriti* (Calcutta: Jijnasa, 1979). I am currently working on a book manuscript that will present a more detailed substantive and theoretical consideration of the culture concept's history in Bengal. [Note: the author probably refers to his book *Bengal in Global Concept History: Culturalism in the Age of Capital* (Chicago: University of Chicago Press, 2008).]

72 Boris Jakim and Robert Bird (trans and eds), *On Spiritual Unity: A Slavophile Reader: Aleksei Khomiakov and Ivan Kireevsky* (Hudson, N.Y.: Lindisfarne Books, 1998), 187–8, 213.

73 Kroeber and Kluckhohn (1963), 53–4; Frank Fadner, *Seventy Years of Pan-Slavism in Russia: Karazin to Danilevskii, 1800–1870* (Washington, D.C.: Georgetown University Press, 1961), 314–38; Andrzej Walicki, *The Slavophile Controversy: History of a Conservative Utopia in Nineteenth-Century Russian Thought* (Notre Dame, Ind.: University of Notre Dame Press, 1989), chapters 12 and 13.

74 In Walicki (1989), 529, where the author himself cites Williams to draw a direct parallel between Slavophilism and the British tradition of cultural criticism.

75 *Bunka* was widely understood in the Meiji period to be an abbreviation of *bunmeikaika*. By the 1920s, however, it had been clearly established as the

translative equivalent of *Kultur*, and (on the model of *Kultur/Zivilisation*) it could be opposed to *bunmei*, or the material civilization with which the Meiji era was associated. In China, the character (*kanji*) used in Japan for *bunka* was then 'translated back' into its classical Chinese equivalent, *wen-hua*, to allow the classical term to do the new work of translating the concept of *culture*. See Douglas Howland, *Borders of Chinese Civilization: Geography and History at Empire's End* (Durham and London: Duke University Press, 1996), 294, fn. 37; Liu (1995), 32–34, 239.

76 Tessa Morris-Suzuki, 'The Invention and Reinvention of "Japanese Culture"', *Journal of Asian Studies*, 54/3 (1995), 762–3.

77 Howland (1996), 65.

78 Prasenjit Duara, 'The Discourse of Civilization and Pan-Asianism', *Journal of World History*, 12/1 (2001), 99–130; Stephen N. Hay, *Asian Ideas of East and West: Tagore and His Critics in Japan, China and India* (Cambridge, Mass.: Harvard University Press, 1970); Liu (1995); Morris-Suzuki (1995).

79 Cf. Duara (2001); Morris-Suzuki (1995), 762.

Ilham Khuri-Makdisi teaches Middle Eastern history, world history and urban history at Northeastern University in Boston. Her research interests include Mediterranean urban life during the late nineteenth and early twentieth centuries as well as transregional movements of people and ideas. Her current research focuses on the growth of migrant networks among intellectuals, dramatists and workers. She also investigates the roles of such networks in the spread of radical ideas between Beirut, Cairo and Alexandria.

Ilham Kuri-Makdisi's publications include 'Projecting Beirut': CD-Rom by Harvard University's Graduate School of Design (1997), 'A Mediterranean Jewish Quarter and Its Architectural Legacy: The Guidecca of Trani, Italy (1000–1550)', *Traditional Dwellings and Settlements Review* 14/2 (2003) and *The Eastern Mediterranean and the Making of Global Radicalism, 1860–1914* (2010).

In her article 'The Conceptualization of *the Social* in Late Nineteenth- and Early Twentieth-Century Arabic Thought and Language', Ilham Khuri-Makdisi traces the semantic contestation around 'the social' by Arab intellectuals in the Ottoman Arab world. Taking up Reinhart Koselleck's approach of concepts as both indicators and factors of change, she traces the concept's future-oriented impetus towards social and political transformations.

10

The Conceptualization of *the Social* in Late Nineteenth- and Early Twentieth-Century Arabic Thought and Language

Ilham Khuri-Makdisi

Between 1860 and 1914, the Ottoman Arab world underwent tumultuous change in the political, social, economic and cultural realms. For intellectuals, political and material change was accompanied by a heightened perception that their world was changing in profound ways, but also that they had a part to play in reconfiguring and strengthening it. For thinkers based in Beirut and Cairo (two of the major cities of the Ottoman Arab world in the period under study), this was the moment to rethink, and to think anew, the relationship between state and society. Specifically, it was the moment to conceptualize *society* – what it is that constitutes it, what kind of future society is envisioned, the steps needed to reach this ideal society, the relationship between the social and natural resources, the relationship between the various categories within *society* and, finally, the connection between *society, civilization* and the *nation*. This is not to suggest that political and material change linearly triggered (or forced) the emergence of new categories of investigation, or led unquestionably to new conceptualizations and conceptual ruptures that merely reflected 'tangible' changes; indeed, the point is to follow Reinhart Koselleck's approach to *Begriffsgeschichte*, which

> does not assume that the concepts it tracks are epiphenomenal, mere reflections of more profound political, social, and economic transformations. Language ... changes at a different speed than do events, forms of government, or social structure, all of which language sometimes shapes and directs, and sometimes only registers. But even such linguistic recording indicates how significant political and social alterations were perceived by those experiencing them.[1]

In other words, concepts not only shape the perception of change, but also suggest the path for action when they are future-oriented, and simultaneously (and in complex ways) are deeply connected to social and political transformations and events.[2]

This chapter investigates how *the social*, and concepts that at various times had been attached to it or had competed with it (*civilization, political economy, progress, reform, revolution, socialism*), were conceptualized in the writings of Arab intellectuals as they appeared in dictionaries, encyclopaedias, in major periodicals and in the writings of opinion-makers published in the two afore-mentioned cities. Through an analysis of these writings, the chapter seeks to shed light on the multiplicity of meanings attached to *society* and *the social*. It also seeks tentatively to identify conceptual tensions between various interpretations of *the social* as well as other dominant concepts; to determine the semantic fields associated with *the social* at certain pivotal times; and to identify major moments of conceptual tensions, ruptures and turning points. This includes identifying the moment at which 'the social' became a basic concept, that is, 'an inescapable, irreplaceable part of the political and social vocabulary' in which *the social (al-ijtima'i)* became a dominant and widespread concept and thus 'crystallize[s] into a single word or term'.[3]

Specifically, I focus here on certain authors, articles and publications that occupied a central place in the production of knowledge and concepts. These authors were influential; they were relatively widely read by fellow intellectuals and were representative of, or were generators of, not only intellectual networks but intellectual trends. My contribution here does not claim to be comprehensive. Many important networks and schools of thought are barely covered in the chapter (most glaringly, that of seminal Islamic modernists such as Abduh and Rashid Rida), while others are perhaps over-scrutinized. The thinkers and texts I focus on here can be roughly (perhaps problematically) labelled 'secular' many of them being Arab Christians based in Beirut or Cairo, whose writings, especially in the form of periodical articles, circulated between the two cities and were read and discussed by their intelligentsia. Within this group I pay special attention to three authors, Butrus al-Bustani, Shibli Shumayyil and Salama Musa, the latter two of whom were socialists. In the process of focusing on these intellectuals' conceptualization of *the social*, I will also discuss competing interpretations and conceptualizations formulated by other groups of thinkers.

The State of the Ottoman Arab World between 1860 and 1914, the *Nahda* and the Making of Arab Intellectuals

Before analysing how *the social* was conceptualized in the period under study, I will briefly chart the major events and transformations that marked the second half of the nineteenth-century Ottoman Arab world. It is no exaggeration to say that, by 1860, the pre-existing social order that had regulated life within the Ottoman Empire for all its subjects was coming to an end. Starting in the 1830s, but increasingly in the late 1850s, the *Tanzimat* (the reordering, or restructuring of the Ottoman state) ushered in tremendous changes, including new land laws, accessibility to land and the abolition of the juridical and social distinctions between Muslims and non-Muslims that for centuries had been an ordering feature of Ottoman Arab societies. Accompanying such monumental change was the full integration of the eastern Mediterranean into the capitalist world economy, starting in the 1870s and gathering further pace in the 1890s. Such integration was particularly visible in cities such as Beirut, Cairo and Alexandria. It triggered profound social change, as many sectors of the economy, especially manufacturing, faced tremendous competition from European industries. At the same time, it meant large infrastructural projects (port expansions, railway construction) that required unprecedented concentrations of labour. The progressive disappearance of various professions, coupled with an exponential enlargement of the labour market, peasant migration and general labour flux, led in the 1890s to the emergence of new methods of social contestation, in the form of strikes.

Linked to all this was the lengthening military, political and economic shadow of the European powers, as well as the increasing realization, by statesmen and intellectuals alike, of the need to reform and modernize not only the state, but institutions, societies, economies and individuals in order to catch up with Europe and be able to defend the empire against European hegemony.[4] This became an even more urgent matter after 1880, with the British occupation of Egypt in 1882, France's control over Tunisia and Morocco, respectively in 1881 and 1912, and Italy's invasion of Libya in 1911. For thinkers from Beirut and its hinterland, reflecting on society and social order had an added urgency after the peasant uprisings of 1858–60 and the civil war of 1860. What had kept society together before that trauma, and what would allow this fractured society to recompose itself and to forge a bond that would prevent it from fracturing all over again, was a driving question for anybody reflecting upon the state of the empire and of society.

The social, as it was conceptualized starting in the 1860s, was inextricably linked to an obsession with and sense of the urgency of reform, a term that became a central concept and something of a mantra during the late nineteenth and early twentieth century, a period of intellectual effervescence known as the *nahda* (renaissance or reawakening). A conscious articulation of the urgency of reform by thinkers belonging to a variety of networks, groups, institutions and intellectual traditions, the *nahda* was not interpreted monolithically; however, there were significant shared concerns and interests between *nahda* thinkers that allowed for the formulation of a cohesive world view – and simultaneously allowed opposition to that world view to emerge. Most central, perhaps, was the fact that reform was conceived of as a total project.[5] This all-encompassing reform included modernizing religion and looking for ways to purge certain of its elements deemed incompatible with the present age's needs and realities; curbing the authority of both local and foreign religious institutions over communal affairs; reforming education – either by secularizing it, or by modernizing traditional Islamic schools; and promoting female education. The reform project included an agenda for political reform, underlining the need for constitutional politics (after the abolition of the short-lived Ottoman constitution in 1878) and advocating an end to absolutist power, while simultaneously underlining the need for individual reform through self-improvement. For many reformists, a major *sine qua non* of reform was to examine, engage with, explain and popularize European concepts, events and institutions that seemed to be at the core of European civilization and societies and seemed to constitute their strength. The fact that many of the reformists could read French and/or English allowed them to mine the contents of British, French and American journals and books, and extract that which they deemed useful from them.

The social was also intimately connected with the emergence and construction of a new class: that of intellectuals – usually members of the middle class who had gained access to a specific kind of education deemed 'novel' and modern, and who had anointed themselves chief reformists and public intellectuals. These intellectuals (who very often were also members of new professions such as journalism, publishing, 'modern/Western' medicine and 'modern' law) had access to institutions and media that appeared in the second half of the nineteenth century and whose synchronicity magnified their impact. These included the periodical, the theatre, municipalities, new educational institutions, reading rooms, masonic lodges and scientific and literary clubs. Accompanying these institutions and spaces was the very rapid proliferation of cultural genres hailed as novel and transformative – the periodical, the play, the novel – which would serve to articulate new notions of the public and conceptualizations of *the social*. It was in such spaces that discussions on what *society* was and how to reform it took place.

Between 1860 and 1914, the concepts and categories of the *intellectual* and of *society*, as they simultaneously emerged, were mutually dependent and symbiotic.

Finally, *the social* as it was being conceptualized in the period under study, like every other concept in the period, entailed an unfailingly comparative element – whether the comparison was diachronic (with the past) or synchronic (vis-à-vis Europe, but also other societies). It was also future-oriented. *Society* and *the social* were not only about past and present, but entailed a work in progress, a constant state of change, which would transform it into a future, perfect society. In general, there was an in-built notion of progress and change associated with all the concepts of the period, and most visibly with that of *society*.

Civilization as a Dominant Concept

In the 1860s and 1870s the notion of society, expressed as the social body/social configuration (*al-hay'a al-ijtima'iyya*),[6] was connected to and subservient to a number of dominant concepts. These included common, shared *benefits* or *public interests* (*sawalih mushtaraka* or *al-maslaha al-'umumiyya* or *al-'amma*); a *people* or *kin* (as in 'nation', but in the pre-nineteenth-century sense – *qawm, jins*); and *civilization* (*tamaddun*). These concepts were articulated and published by a number of liberal (that is, in favour of constitutional government) secular intellectuals, many of them Christians, often belonging to networks that included Muslim reformers as well. In Beirut, Butrus al-Bustani was perhaps this group's most famous intellectual, the founder of the first modern Arabic dictionary *Muhit al-Muhit* (1867–70), of a number of periodicals and of the first modern Arabic encyclopaedia. In his dictionary, Bustani defined *al-hay'a al- ijtima'iyya* as 'the condition that results from the gathering (*ijtima'*) of a people or kinsfolk (*qawm*) who have common benefits/interests (*hiya'l-hala al-hasila min ijtima' qawm lahum sawalih yashtarikun fiha*)'.[7] Other authors of the 1870s expanded on the definition of the social body by underlining collaboration between its various members. In articles published in the handful of periodicals that appeared in Beirut in the 1870s, they linked the social body/*society* even more explicitly to the concept of *civilization*, in fact 'upgrading' the definition of the social body by arguing that its existence and its health were a *sine qua non* of *civilization*. In some of the writings of this period *civilization* and the social body are almost equated, and authors argue that it is the existence of a social body that allows a group of people (for lack of a better word) to evolve from *barbarity* (*hamajiyya*) to *civilization*. Such an idea was expressed in an article on the theatre, a relatively novel institution in the Arab world which subsequently came to be viewed as one of the most vital tools for *progress, civilization* and the formation of a social body. In this article Salim Naqqash, an intellectual close to Bustani and sharing many of his ideas, argued that Europe's early promotion of the theatre was both the reason for and the manifestation of its primacy in the realm of civilization. Naqqash linked the rise of *civilization* to the concept of *collaboration* – that of man's need to work with other human beings to satisfy his basic needs for safety and food. *Collaboration* led to the creation of a social body or a social configuration (*hay'a ijtima'iyya*) whose wellness and health

> was the cause of civilization. Without it [the *hay'a ijtima'iyya*], man would have remained in his savage condition (*al-hamajiyya*). The Europeans knew this before us, and they devised ways to improve it [the social body]. Among these ways [were] theatres.[8]

Without a social body, Naqqash advanced, there could be no civilization. *Civilization* means a language that instils in man the morality of urban dwellers (*akhlaq ahl al-mudun*), and transports him from a state of roughness or lack of refinement (*khushuna*) and ignorance to a state of sociability/ friendly atmosphere (*uns*) and knowledge.

> But this definition does not encompass all that which we mean when we use the term *tamaddun* ... it is a call for the tying of people to works, as well as the reason of their strength and the way to improve their condition. It is also a way to divide their wealth among them with justice (*qust wa 'adl*) ... Suffice it to say that *civilization is the connection of private interest to public interest* (*al-tamaddun huwa irtibat al-maslaha al-khususiyya fi'l-maslaha al-'umumiyya*); that is, man, in his activities, should attend to the interest (*maslaha*) of all the people of his kind (*abna'jinsihi*); where such ties and assistance exist, there will we find civilization, and where we see man tending only to his own interests ... there will there be roughness or barbarity (*khushuna*) and weakness resulting from the love of the self.[9]

Naqqash's definition of *civilization* (*tamaddun*), which was widespread in the 1870s, was clearly influenced by the writings of the fourteenth-century philosopher Ibn Khaldun, and especially his theory of *civilization* and its connection to urbanity. The history of Ibn Khaldun's 'rediscovery' or reinterpretation during the *nahda* remains to be written. In his most famous work, the *Muqaddima* (the Prolegomenon), Ibn Khaldun 'forged the first technical language for a general sociology, as well as a sociology of the Near East', articulating his theory and building on key concepts such as *dawla* (*dynasty, rule, empire, state*) and *ijtima'* (which experts on Ibn Khaldun have translated as sociability rather than society).[10] Ibn Khaldun saw the history and civilization (he used the term *'umran*) of the Arabo-Muslim world as one of constant competition and struggle between two civilizations, that of the rural world and the desert (*badawiyya*) on the one hand, and sedentary urban culture on the other. He argued that the rise and fall of civilizations was cyclical; it occurred every few generations, once the urbanites – merchants and rulers – became lethargic and corrupted through wealth (and education!) and had to appeal to the 'bedouin' (by which he meant the residents of rural areas, as well as nomads) for a renewal of civilization. At the heart of *civilization* lay *ijtima'*, but the problem with it, according to Ibn Khaldun, was that it constantly came under threat from unavoidable rivalry and competition between its members. Hence, every society required a sovereign armed with the authority (*mulk*) to suppress rivalries, in whose hands lay tremendous authority.

Progress and *Civilization*: From Cyclical to Linear Trajectories

Naqqash clearly retained the Khaldunian argument about the cultural and moral superiority of urban dwellers; however, he and others diverged dramatically from Ibn Khaldun. First, they 'shed' the notion of an 'unavoidable' struggle between rural/nomadic and urban/sedentary cultures. Second, any mention of a strong ruler was eliminated. They focused on the individual and his active work towards cooperation with others, transcending the self and 'the linking of private interests to public interests' as a way to building a strong society and civilization. And third, they rejected the idea of cycles in history (that is, the unavoidable rise and fall of civilizations) and adhered to progress and evolution as leading all civilizations towards a future higher realm. This last idea was particularly clearly expressed in Bustani's 1876 preface to the first Arabic encyclopaedia, many of whose entries had been translated from European sources and many of whose terms appeared in both Arabic and French. The author explained that his incentive for compiling an encyclopaedia stemmed from his realization that 'the state and needs of nations varied according to time and place. What was needed now was knowledge (*ma'arif*)', that is, applied knowledge, 'a necessity for the development of agriculture and manufacturing and trade, the mother of inventions, a spring for wealth and strength'.[11] Hence the encyclopaedia's mission: to offer this kind of knowledge to 'Eastern nations [which] have sought to take leaps towards *civilization* (*tamaddun*) and *progress/evolution* (*irtiqa*') on the ladder of knowledge'.[12] Knowledge, to be gleaned from both Arab/Islamic history and civilization and contemporary sources (essentially European books), was necessary in order for contemporary Ottoman Arab civilization, nation and society to prosper, evolve and become modern. The encyclopaedia would provide contemporary knowledge and know-how (*ma'arif hadha'l-zaman*) for this purpose – for a project that was developmental, entailed a final utopian (or ideal) vision, and was future-oriented. These major differences between the way in which *civilization* and *society* was conceptualized by Ibn Khaldun and by others after him, and especially the conceptual break in the perception of time and the move away from the cyclical to the linear and the universal (*progress* and *civilization*), point to a moment of conceptual rupture.

Justice ('Adl), Rights (Huquq) and Jumhur (Republic/Public)

What would determine the level and degree of *civilization*, and what would be the endpoint of reaching the apex of civilization? In his entry for '*Tamaddun*' (with the term 'civilization' also appearing in the tide), Bustani argued that justice – or more precisely, '*adl*, a term which historically had meant 'obeisance of the moral and religious law' according to the *Encyclopedia of Islam*[13] – lay at the core of true *civilization*. '*Adl* is what 'guarantees or insures to [the city's inhabitants] the enjoyment of earthly goods (*al-khairat al-ardiyya*) and that which is most valuable to them: namely their *republican or public rights* (*huququhum al-jumhuriyya*). If [this is not provided], then civilization is [mere] lies and deception (*kudhb wa khida*')'.[14]

However, while acknowledging that this aspect of *civilization* was universal and that there could be no *civilization* outside of '*adl* (justice based on moral and religious law), Bustani questioned whether all civilizations could easily be hierarchically organized on the basis of a shared, singular understanding of justice. He understood justice to be based on specific religious laws and norms, which vary from one civilization to another. Nonetheless, it was still possible to assess the level of progress and the degree of *civilization* of each country or civilization (he jumps between these entities), but using their own index of what their laws determined justice to be.[15] There were competing conceptions of *progress, justice* and *civilization*, in which all thinkers agreed on the abstract endpoint (*civilization*, combined with some understanding of *justice/'adl*), and all agreed on the notion of *progress*; but whether or not the blueprint of *civilization* had to be universal and universalizable was subject to profoundly different interpretations.

Bustani's writings represent a larger trend, one where existing notions of *civilization* and of *justice*, and especially Ibn Khaldun's, were being interwoven with newer concepts of *republican rights* first articulated by the *philosophes* in Europe, and especially in France, in the late eighteenth century. These concepts were constantly debated and revisited by French and other intellectuals. The encyclopaedia was particularly interested in 'updating' its readership on the latest theories and reflections pertaining to notions such as justice, rights, revolutions, and so on, which had been ushered in through the French Revolution. I would argue that this did not yet constitute a moment of rupture: it certainly indicated the injection of new meanings into 'classical' terms and concepts, but in the 1860s and 1870s the dominant approach seems to have been to examine the limits and possibilities of reconciling various interpretations and 'traditions' concerning *civilization, justice* and *rights*. To this already complex bricolage, we should add the fact that Ibn Khaldun himself was in the process of being discovered and rediscovered by European thinkers, most notably French orientalists.[16] It is quite likely that Bustani and his peers' re-readings of lbn Khaldun were mediated through French orientalist readings as well.

Nonetheless, this specific interpretation of *progress* and of *civilization* was not uncontested. For instance, thinkers and authors close to the Jesuits in Beirut, expressing their opinions in conservative, anti-secular periodicals such as *al-Bashir* (the mouthpiece of the Jesuits in Beirut), understood *civilization* – and by extension, *society* and *nation* (*umma*) – to mean very different things. In a series of articles analysing (and deploring) the Paris Commune of 1871, they equated *civilization, nation* and *society* with *order* (especially public order), and with preserving the status quo and respecting authority. The greatest threat to *society, nation* and *civilization* was identified as revolutions and revolutionaries. In the case of the Paris Commune, these were accused of being members of the Socialist International and of wishing to trigger a 'cosmopolitan revolution' and establish a mass or a commoners' republic (*jumhuriyya 'amma*).[17] Nonetheless, despite the existence of competing interpretations of *civilization*, by the end of the nineteenth century the notion that *civilization* was intrinsically linked to progress and reform seems to have become dominant. Up until the 1890s, *civilization* was at the centre of the intellectuals' preoccupations. Connected to *civilization* were the organizing concepts of *nation* (*umma*), *progress* and *evolution* (*irtiqa'*) and *knowledge* (*ma'arif*). The social as noun (*al-ijtima'*) or adjective (*al-ijtima'i/yya*) used alone outside the expression *al-hay'a al-ijtima'iyya* was rare in the 1860s and 1870s; it is not until the 1890s that it starts to be used as a standalone term.

The 1890s as a Turning Point and the Emergence of 'the Social'

The period between 1860 and the 1880s witnessed the growth of what we would nowadays call civil society. Communal and secular associations (*jam'iyyat*), clubs (including scientific ones) and periodicals started to proliferate, many with self-proclaimed reformist agendas and names. The 1890s represent something of a turning point, however: *the social* starts to stand out, and to stand conceptually on its own. As anecdotal evidence for this, the number of Arabic periodicals appearing in the 1890s and later in the Arab world or in the diaspora whose subtitles included the adjective 'social' or the noun 'society' is an eloquent sign of a shift that seems to last until the 1920s.[18] Several different factors seem to account for this shift: a greater familiarity with and exposure to European conceptualizations of *the social*, by way of educational institutions in the Arab world that were either established by foreigners or modelled after them; the rise of the social sciences as academic disciplines and their popularization; the exponential rise in transportation and communication channels, which effectively meant that news and ideas from the rest of the world made it to eastern Mediterranean cities faster and in greater concentration than ever before; and the expansion of migrant communities linking Syria and Egypt to Europe, and especially to the Americas. Many of the Arab intellectuals who wrote about the 'social' were fluent in European languages (usually French and/or English) and had spent time in Europe or the Americas (as had the authors discussed below, Shibli Shumayyil and Salama Musa), at a time when *the social* was becoming increasingly dominant as a concept there. Furthermore, it was most likely triggered by a loss of faith in the figure of the ruler and in the state's ability to trigger real reform – on the one hand, the Ottoman sultan Abdulhamid's absolutism up until the revolution of 1908, coupled with a state that was increasingly impotent and incapable of defending local society or empire in general against European interests and privileges; on the other, British imperialism in Egypt. Hence, hopes and expectations that reform would be state-triggered and imposed from above were being challenged. They were giving way to notions of *society* as a self-regenerating, living organism, with change being generated by individuals and associations working for the well-being of society, state and empire. This allowed intellectuals and leaders of this 'civil society' to posit themselves as the chief reformists of 'society'.

Shibli Shumayyil, Evolutionary Theory and Society as an Organism

In the 1880s and 1890s, the concept of society was becoming increasingly developed; ways of strengthening the social body were explored and further theorized. Many of the ideas that would gain ground among intellectuals were published in articles in the pages of *Al-Muqtataf*, a self-proclaimed popularizer of modern, especially Western concepts and ideas, and also of scientific ideas.[19] The periodical, first established in Beirut in 1876 by two instructors of science at the Syrian Protestant College, moved to Cairo in the mid-1880s, where it remained highly influential and relatively widely read until the 1950s. Among the authors most involved in formulating new ways of thinking about *society* in the 1880s and up to World War I was Shibli Shumayyil, a doctor and polymath educated at the Syrian Protestant College in Beirut who had settled in Egypt. His article 'Human Society or Civilization' ('*Al-ijtima'al-bashari aw al-'umran*'), published in 1885 in *Al-Muqtataf*, was one of the earliest comprehensive discussions of the concept of *ijtima'*. In this article, Shumayyil made very explicit reference to Ibn Khaldun's concepts and theories, without, however, merely reproducing them. Like other intellectuals of the late nineteenth century, Shumayyil had consciously adapted Ibn Khaldun to the intellectual framework of his time and had bent his concepts of *society* and *political authority* in significant ways.

As with the earlier thinkers previously discussed, most blatant was the elimination of all mention of a sovereign imbued with repressive authority, whom Ibn Khaldun had deemed vital for maintaining *society* together. In an age and among authors enamoured of the notions of a constitution, autocracy held no appeal. A second major shift was the conceptualization of *society* as a living organism, as well as its corollary: the idea that cooperation between the members of the social body was natural, possible and in fact necessary to ensure its proper functioning, which could stem from within rather than being imposed by a ruler. Gone was the idea of rivalry and competition as 'inherent' to human nature. Again, there had been precedents for this idea of cooperation, and the trope of society as an organism can itself be traced back to classical Greece. It was most likely fairly widespread in the Arabo-Islamic medieval world. Nonetheless, it was undoubtedly Shumayyil who gave it its fullest elaboration in the 1880s, with the systematic adaptation and 'injection' of evolutionary and biological concepts from the works of Herbert Spencer, Charles Darwin and Ludwig Büchner. This conception of *society* as a living organism, whose health depended on the health of its every part and on the good functioning of the whole, became central to thinkers of the *nahda*, who called for a social reform that would rid society of various internal as well as external 'diseases' threatening its cohesion. In the place of an ailing society, reformists would build a strong social body, a healthy organism, where the various divisions (including those brought about by wealth disparity and sectarianism) would be eliminated – or at least eroded. Shumayyil returned to Spencer in a second long article in the same year, 'The History of Natural Society' ('*Tarikh al-ijtima' al-tabi'i*', once again published in *Al-Muqtataf*), where Shumayyil introduced and translated terms such as 'physiology of groups' (*fisiologiyat al-ijtima'at*) and *evolution* (*nushu'*) to describe human societies, again emphasizing cooperation as a necessity for social evolution and health.

Society, Reform, Violence and the Public/the Masses

In his articles of 1885, Shumayyil argued that reform was necessary to the health of the social organism, but that this had to be willed by *the public* (*jumhur*) or the majority rather than be imposed by a small vanguard group, otherwise it would be unnatural and artificial (*islah istina'i*). Natural reform was preferable to *revolution* (*thawra*). However, revolutions were sometimes necessary and were not always damaging, contrary to what some historians claimed, as long as they were an expression of the voice of the people. Otherwise, '[they] would turn into evil (*sharr*)'.[20] In the following decades, Shumayyil elaborated on the means to create a healthy social organism, and revisited the notion of revolution and the use of social and political violence. Reflecting on the assassination of US President McKinley by anarchists in a 1901 article entitled 'Social Murder' (*al-qatl al-ijtima'i*), Shumayyil argued that those committing 'high profile' assassinations, especially against heads of states (i.e. anarchists, *al-fawdawiyyun*), were 'useful' because they were consciously committing murder to attract the public's attention to the system's injustices. Progress was achieved thanks to challengers to the status quo who fought for their violated rights. Sometimes this could be done peacefully, but at other times, violence was necessary. Criticizing the fact that the assassination of McKinley had received much more coverage by newspapers than that of 'the killing of the interests of the public/the masses (*masalih al-jumhur*) every day by every government in the world ... even the most reformist ones', he bemoaned the fact that governments in the US, but also in France and England,

> dealt with such attacks by punishing anarchists rather than looking for remedies for society's ailments, or curing them by eliminating their causes, which are greed and injustice ... so that the two strongest powers [that is France and England], who nowadays rule over most of the world, rather than figuring out how to decrease their hubris and improve/reform the conditions of the masses/the public (*al-jamahir*) ... focus on ways to achieve full power and on protecting and empowering society's thieves (*lusus al-ijtima'*) who export ... and accumulate capital (*al-mal*) through perfidy and ruse ... extract and accumulate profits and benefits from projects and businesses while the workers themselves (who provide the labour for these businesses) are barely able to survive. Thieves who are roaming around freely, protected by laws backed by governments ... but there are people, even if they are few in numbers, who have been ... looking into the reasons behind these [gross injustices] ... and this has led *ijtima'iyyin* [not clear whether this refers to sociologists, or communists/socialists] to identify the ailing spots to prescribe the medicine and hasten the cure.[21]

I have dwelled at length on Shumayyil's writings and his conceptualization of *the social*, because his writings were simultaneously symptomatic of a larger conceptual shift yet also deeply constitutive of it. First, his writings indicate that, starting in the 1890s, *the social* occupied discursive centre stage. It became a basic concept, an 'inescapable, irreplaceable part of the political and social vocabulary'.[22] This does not mean that *society* and *the social* replaced *civilization*; *civilization* continued to matter a great deal, and in fact at times seemed to compete with the concept of *society*, and especially with *the social*. Second, as reflected in Shumayyil's writings, part of *the social's* semantic field in the 1890s comprised terms and concepts such as *capital*, *capitalism*, *class*, *labour*, *imperialism* and *exploitation* – the exploitation of *individuals*, *classes*, *natural resources* or *nations*. The way in which these concepts were connected, and the meaning and value judgements attached to each one of them, were all highly contested and hotly debated. Shumayyil's socialist and radical conception of *society* and of the occasional importance of violence and revolution needed to usher in a reformed society were not shared by many, and from that perspective he was atypical (yet influential). The point, though, is that by the 1890s, the aforementioned concepts of *capital*, *labour*, *exploitation* and *society* were starting to become omnipresent. By the end of the first decade of the twentieth century, they (or various matrices made up of a combination of them) had become unavoidable terms and issues for people thinking and writing about *society* and *the social*.

The Public and the Masses

Shumayyil's writings also reflected new understandings of *al-jumhur* (plural *al-jamahir*), a term which Bustani too had used. The term itself originally meant 'a gathering, a crowd, a public'; it could also mean 'public' and 'republic'. During their occupation of Egypt (1798–1801), the French 'used it to introduce themselves in their very first proclamation to the Egyptians, issued "on behalf of the French *jumhur*", and used it frequently thereafter in their communication with the local leadership'.[23] The term spread in the nineteenth century, and by the 1860s *jumhur* and *jumhuriyya* (republic) seem to have been conflated with *democracy*: the two 'were still regarded as broadly synonymous terms, and the same words were often used for both'.[24] The terms *jumhuriyya* and *jumhur* also connoted popular and representative governments rather than republican ones *per se*, and 'it is probably in this sense that the term is used of the Lebanese peasant rebels led by Tanyus Shahin [1858]'.[25] Shumayyil used the term differently, however. He used it to refer to *the masses*, but to the masses whose political, economic and labour rights had been violated by a combination of capitalism, capital, corrupt politics and imperialism. It was the harm done to these masses that he then defined as social theft and social murder. This kind of language was connected with three interrelated phenomena: (1) the development of disciplines such as sociology; (2) an increased familiarity with these disciplines among certain Arab intellectuals, along with an increased interest in them (including the translation of certain 'bestselling' works on sociology and pseudo-sociology and connected fields such as mass psychology and criminology); and, last but not least, (3) the spread of socialist (and anarchist) concepts and vocabularies, in which Shumayyil was a key player.

Socialism

Shumayyil was not the first intellectual to write about *socialism*, to strongly critique *capitalism*, or to use expressions such as 'social theft'. However, he was one of the first to endorse socialism vocally, passionately and consistently. Socialism had first started getting mentioned in Arabic periodicals in the late 1870s, usually not in positive terms. A shift took place in the first decade of the twentieth century, when it started to receive more positive coverage in the pages of objective and supposedly non-partisan periodicals such as *Al-Muqtataf* and *Al-Hilal*.[26] Nonetheless, while by 1914 it had a strong, articulate core of supporters, and while socialist ideas became a lot more prevalent than traditional historiography has claimed, socialism remained confined to a small group of supporters. Second, however, the term used to translate socialism did not become fixed until later. In the first decades, while socialism was mostly translated as *ishtira-kiyya* (from the root *shrk*, which implies common participation), it could also appear as *ijtima'iyya* (socialism; social, sociability). It was sometimes accompanied by the English or French term, in Latin characters and/or transliterated in Arabic characters.[27] Third, the distinction between *communism* and *socialism* was not always evident. The terms designating them were sometimes switched or swapped, and sometimes it is really not clear from the descriptions and definitions of socialism which one of the ideologies the authors are writing about. Four, articles on socialism very often included genealogies built on a kind of 'Best of' or 'Who's Who' logic. These genealogies were fairly canonized and always included Owen,

Fourier, Saint Simon, Proudhon and occasionally (not very often) Marx. Various brands of socialisms were written about and introduced in the Arabic press, depending on the 'informer's' personal trajectory, travels and idiosyncratic interests. Thus by the early twentieth century, the German Social Democratic Party was receiving kudos, Fabianism also was receiving a fairly good press, there was interest in the British Labour Party and what its members read, and even the fact that Japan had a socialist newspaper was taken as a sign of civilization.

By 1914, various long and seminal articles promoting socialism were being published in periodicals, as well as a few books in Beirut and, especially, Cairo, investigating *labour* and its connection to *society*. One such article, penned by Shumayyil and published in *Al-Muqtataf*, embodied the author's ideas concerning *the social* and its connection to natural science, *civilization*, evolutionary theory and *reform*.[28] Socialism, Shumayyil explained, was a way of preserving social harmony by ensuring that everybody got their rightful due for their labour:

> social organization should be such that all people become useful workers, each benefiting according to their merit so that society would no longer have members doing nothing and others duped or aggrieved (*maghbunun*) who will then be damaged and corrupted (*yushawwashun wa yufsadun*).[29]

The author argued that it was to the advantage of all parts of society (or this organism) to rid it of all that would lead to trouble and strife and thus endanger the social body's health. Exploitation posed one such threat, sectarianism another. Significantly, then, in his advocacy for socialism and his efforts to convince his readership of its merits, Shumayyil invoked individual equality and other inalienable rights less than he did the health of society in general, which he knew to be a familiar trope and one of prime concern to his readers – and to himself.

Shumayyil believed that cooperation, rather than exploitation, was the most advanced stage of evolution, and should be society's highest aim. Socialism was therefore the natural, rational application of evolution theory onto human societies. In his view (which was heavily influenced by Büchner),[30] the leading principle of socialism was 'the regulation of work and pay based on one's work; and the non-exploitation of the weak by the strong … hence socialism becomes … a necessary consequence of natural science.'[31] Shumayyil emphasized the rational and scientific process through which this conclusion was reached. He argued that this was a sure proof of socialism's inherent modernity.[32]

Society, the Nation, Nationalism

If *the social* began to stand on its own in the 1890s, another concept that both complemented and competed with it was also being seriously developed in Egypt in this decade. Partly as a consequence of the British occupation of 1882, various intellectuals and political activists were placing the nation at the centre of their concerns, beginning to implement projects that sought to build an Egyptian nation and promote national consciousness among various segments of Egyptian society. A part of building or imagining a nation was imagining and reforming society, especially workers. Zachary Lockman's work has shown how Egyptian, mostly nationalist elites and the bourgeoisie (the *effendiyya*) constructed the working class in Egypt through discursive and material practices. Lockman argues that at the very beginning of the twentieth century:

> through political and ideological contestations involving both workers and non-workers, new representations of society, a new collective social agent (the 'working class'), and a new category of identity (the 'worker') bound up with new social practices were constructed. A key role in this process was played by Egyptian nationalist intellectuals, who, to further their own political project, began to exalt the previously disdained lower classes as the authentic core of the Egyptian nation and to promote a new vision of working-class identity, organization, and activism.[33]

The result was that:

> by the end of this century's first decade, and certainly by the First World War, some (though by no means all) Egyptians had come to regard workers as a distinct social category, to perceive a nascent working class as a component of Egyptian society, and to see class conflict as an indigenous phenomenon.[34]

Whereas the middle classes were depicted as the hope of the nation and its redemption, the lower classes, like the upper classes, were dismissed, the first for their abysmal ignorance, the second for their degenerate habits. For the nationalists, as well as for many middle-class individuals, being part of the nation meant being productive and working for the benefit of the nation: in agriculture or in industry, or as a state civil servant or intellectual. Hence the notion of productivity, and of a normative way of 'being a worker', was formulated by nationalists and by bourgeois reformists as part of a burgeoning, imagined national society – a society 'befitting' the nation.

Political Economy

The idea of *society* as comprising mostly productive elements that would serve the nation coincided, competed and overlapped with various discourses that had begun in the 1890s and peaked around 1908–10. Among these were the demarcation of *the social* from *the civilizational*; the emergence and use of concepts such as *labour, capitalism* and some kind of *class* (and 'masses'); the dissemination of socialist ideas and the publication of articles on socialism; and a greater familiarity with, interest in, and availability of translations of European and American sociological writings.[35] To give a few examples, Gustave LeBon's widely circulated *Psychologie des Foules* was translated into Arabic and published in Cairo in 1909 by Ahmad Fathi Zaghlul as *Ruh al-ijtima'* (The Spirit/ Soul of Gathering),[36] and Durkheim's works, as well as that of American sociologists, were also translated and its ideas introduced by periodicals. And in addition to sociology, another discipline linked to society and *the social* was to generate tremendous interest: political economy (*al-iqtiṣād al-siyasi*).

The term *al-iqtisad al-siyasi* (political economy) started to be used in the 1880s. Before then, the term capturing the Greek concept of *oikonomia* was *tad-bir al-manzil* (household management/administration), a faithful translation of the Greek term (combining the notion of household, *oikos*, with administration or management). This term was used in medieval Arabic philosophical treatises, although in some cases the term *siyasa* (politics) was used as a synonym for *tadbir al-manzil* (most famously in Ibn Sina's treatise on the subject).[37] In Ibn Khaldun's writings,

> political government (*al-siyasa al-madaniyya*) is the administration of a household or of a city (*tadbir al-manzil aw al-madina*) in accordance with the demands of ethics (*akhlaq*) and philosophy (*hikma*) for the purpose of directing the mass towards behaviour that will result in the preservation of the [human] species.[38]

Although the term *iqtisad* was absent from Bustani's dictionary in the late 1860s, the root of the word (*qasada*) was there. This root meant breaking into two and implied moderation in spending. As well as moderation, the idea also contained notions of *'adl* (justice according to moral and religious law). In the 1870s, notions of earthly goods and natural resources were loosely, inconsistently, and sometimes implicitly tied to those of *civilization* and a healthy social body. In the mid-1880s, *Al-Muqtataf,* by then based in Cairo, provided what seems to have been the first batch of articles on political economy. The three main categories within political economy were duly explained – land, labour and capital – as well as the exploitation of natural resources. Political economy was not clearly or consistently linked to society in the 1880s, and these articles fleshed out and explicated the notion of capital and the different kinds of capital – for example, fixed versus circulating capital (suggesting that the authors were drawing on Adam Smith's works on political economy, especially his *Wealth of Nations*,[39] or sometimes directly citing their source as Adam Smith). In one article entitled 'Capital and Wages' (*Al-mal wa'l-ujra*), Smith's argument for unequal wages between holders of different professions was presented and endorsed.[40]

In the last decade of the nineteenth century, the notion of the economy in Egypt became connected to that of wealth and the generation of wealth, itself in turn linked to land production, the expansion of private property, and the circulation of a single commodity, cotton. It was now the landowners who had the power to choose which crops to cultivate.[41] The expansion of private property with the focus on a single commodity required violence (the expropriation and forced evictions of peasants) and triggered resistance. The topics of private property, single crop cultivation and agricultural labour, organization and productivity were analysed in faculties of law (established in the first decade of the twentieth century in Egypt), where they were taught by French and Italian professors.[42] For one group of people, generally middle- and upper-class individuals with links to large agricultural estates, the concept of *political economy* was first and foremost about production and an efficient exploitation of natural resources. Within this conceptualization of *political economy*, 'society' referred to productive members of society. Not much thought was given to class or to the relationship between the labouring classes and economic production – whether this be extraction of natural resources or industrial production. With the onset of strikes and labour unrest in the Egyptian cities in the 1890s, some thinkers – those who were attracted by radical ideas, or those who realized at this early stage that the labouring classes would not be quietly co-opted into the model of political economy they believed in – began to connect the economy and its proper functioning to the concepts of *greater justice* and *division of profits*, an increase in workers' wages and improvement of working conditions. These thinkers explored notions of *cooperation* between owners and workers, or even between workers themselves.

Hence, just as had happened within the concept of *society* in the late nineteenth century, the notion of *cooperation* began to occupy a central role within political economy. However, it took on different meanings in this context. One of *Al-Muqtataf*'s early articles on the topic explained to readers the notion of 'cooperation in work/business' (*al-ta'awun fi'l-a'mal*), a concept that was 'used in the science of economics' (*'ilm al-iqtisad*). Covering negotiations between striking workers and factory and business owners in Britain, France and Germany, the articles approvingly explained how workers had been given a stake in a business or a factory, either through shares or through a share of the profits rather than a fixed salary.[43] Still, in the 1880s and even most of the 1890s, there was no larger discourse about class *per se*, or about society being made up of social classes. The dominant attitude to labour was that it should 'collaborate' with business owners – a kind of solidarist discourse. Labour and labour issues were to be subservient to a larger developmentalist goal: that of building factories and industrializing, of strengthening the country (*al-bilad*) or the nation (*al-umma*) – and, ultimately, being civilized. Unsurprisingly, political economy was first and foremost linked to concepts of *country*, *nation* and *state* rather than *society* in discussions on what the role of the state should be in assisting the development of industries and private enterprise. In fact, even in articles supporting strikers, labour unrest was taken as saying something about the country and the nation (and the unavoidable catchword, civilization). Thus in 1902 (and again in *Al-Muqtataf*) one author sympathetic to strikers argued that the tailors' strike in Cairo indicates the nation's vitality, pointing out that 'we only hear of strikes in nations … which have reached the apex of civilization, such as European nations. We do not hear of strikes among Asian nations, such as India or China, for instance.'[44] Again, it is important to underline here that strikes and labour issues were not then seen as being primarily about society and social relations.

The Connections between *Political Economy*, *Class* and *World Political and Economic Order*

A decade later, there would be greater contestation over the meanings and schools of *political economy*. First, the more enlarged repertoire of ideas on political economy was clearly connected to various intellectual shifts taking place in European economic and political thought, and to the professionalization of the field. The classical economists (Adam Smith and David Ricardo) were no longer the only, or main, political economists with whom Arab intellectuals were familiar. One thinker who seemed to have followers in the Arab and Ottoman world was Charles Gide (1847–1932), the founder in 1887 of the *Revue d'Économie Politique* in Paris. A Christian socialist and a proponent of popular universities for free mass education and agricultural and consumers' cooperatives (and mutual aid), Gide authored a number of books on political economy that gained international fame. His works were translated into virtually every European language, as well as into Ottoman Turkish in 1911, and articles summarizing his ideas appeared in Arabic periodicals.[45] His books were available in French and English at the library of the Syrian Protestant College in Beirut. Gide's ideas were also summarized and cited in *L'Egypte Contemporaine*, an influential social science periodical first published in Cairo in 1909 (to which I will briefly return below).

By 1908 there were thus two (not completely mutually exclusive) camps. One of these still endorsed liberal economic theories and focused on the making of a local bourgeoisie (connected to landowning families) and the accumulation of capital and knowledge about the economy in the hands of local industrialists; and another, more radical, argued for overturning the privileges of landowning families and used a language more or less pertaining to class. Self-proclaimed socialists, obviously, belonged to the second camp; but many of these socialists and radicals called for some kind of alliance between workers and members of the new middle class. It was this alliance which would reverse the 'decrepit' old order represented by the degenerate, incompetent and exploitative elites. Salama Musa, a self-proclaimed Egyptian socialist and writer, was one of the most vocal representatives of this radical camp. In his letter to the editors of *Al-Muqtataf* entitled 'The Nation's Education' (*ta'lim al-umma*), Musa strongly criticized Egyptian nationalists for being backward. He called instead for:

> the liberation of peasants and other workers from Egyptian capitalists which have turned them into animals, through strikes and the spread of socialism; and our liberation from the English, because … their actions indicate bad intentions and an intentional neglect [of our society].[46]

However, a month earlier Musa had penned another article, 'The Evolution of Nations and their Decline' (*irtiqa' al-umam wa inhitatuha*), in which he began with 'the economic cause'. Summarizing a popular theory among English liberals at the time[47] that nations evolved or declined according to the wealth of the country (*bilad*) and the concentration or dissolution and distribution of this wealth, Musa argued that what put Germany and England ahead of other nations civilizationally was the high number of:

> Their averagely/moderately wealthy individuals [i.e. a middle class] [as well as]...the improved conditions of their workers...the presence of such a large class constantly moves the government forward and towards reform, whereas if wealth is concentrated in the hands of the very few...this leads to decline, because the poor who own nothing in this world, would not care whether a government is constitutional or tyrannical...and the indigent themselves will decline (*yanhatt*), and because of their numbers, this will lead to a decline of the nation. And the example of this is: the Egyptian peasant. Activists have worked hard to attract him to the national movement, but he [has not been receptive] and he has all the right [not to be receptive], because his condition is so bad that it cannot get any worse, even under a tyrannical regime.[48]

Musa not only uses a terminology pertaining to class (*tabaqa*) here, he also argues for the necessity of protecting and defending the middle class 'at the expense' of the upper class 'as can be seen in Japan nowadays'. This was to be done through the imposition of an incremental tax in which the poor and the middle classes would end up paying a similar percentage of their income, one which would be much lower than that paid by the wealthy (he argued that Marx advocates a similar policy).[49]

Musa's opinions and terminology were connected to the growing popularity of socialism and to the professionalization of the disciplines of social sciences in Europe, as well as to the burgeoning interest in such disciplines as schools teaching 'Western' disciplines proliferated and as Cairo University was established. It was around that time that the *Société Sultanieh d'Economie Politique, de Statistique et de Législation* was founded in Cairo in 1909; and its mouthpiece, *L'Egypte Contemporaine*, published a number of articles by lawyers, industrialists and sociologists – Egyptian, French and Italian, most of whom were based in Egypt.[50] Many articles examined the changing relations between workers and employers in Europe, bemoaned the lack of legislation in Egypt on this topic, and strategized about ways to introduce legislation regulating such matters.[51] It was within this context of new, 'modern' schools that Muhammad Fahmi Husayn published what he described as the first manual on political economy (*Al-Iqtisad al-Siyasi*) in 1908. The author, a lawyer in the Egyptian native courts (*al-mahakim al-*

ahliyya), explicitly designed his book as a manual for students at commercial schools, describing the science of political economy as 'the most pertinent to commerce'. It was only through such establishments that Egyptians (*al-watani*) could become on a par and compete with foreigners over the control and exploitation of natural resources, Husayn argued. The ultimate goal was for 'nationals (*al-wataniyyun*) to benefit from their country's wealth, which others are enjoying'.[52]

Among the thinkers wishing to promote and increase the role of 'nationals' in expanding their country's wealth, some of the more radical authors began to pen articles that described and denounced the entire edifice on which world trade rested, an edifice which led to world economic inequality and to unfair trade agreements between nations. The solution for these authors was simple: to consume locally produced goods.[53] Not only did these authors promote mutualism and cooperation and the establishment of mutual aid societies, they also provided a remedy to unfair competition. Powerful foreign countries, companies and a general world order that favoured them had triggered local workers' exploitation and gross underpayment, privileging foreign workers and forcing out local businesses. The result was unfair trade, in which countries such as Syria were exporting people, capital and skills and receiving Western knick-knacks in return.[54]

By 1914, *political economy, civilization, labour, society, capitalism*, some form of *economic nationalism* or *localism*, resistance to European economic (if not political) imperialism, along with resistance to the existing political and economic world order – all had become entangled. Not all had the same coordinates: each one of these concepts had multiple and contested meanings, and there were factions and tensions regarding each one of them. However, by around 1908, they were all unavoidable. They had become basic concepts, and what is more, interconnected concepts. For some factions, *the social* was the most important of these concepts; for others, it was *political economy*, and for yet another group, it was *civilization*. However, one would be hard pressed to find pieces written on either one of these topics around 1908 which did not rely conceptually on the other concepts as well. Significantly, even *Al-Mashriq*, a Beiruti pro-Jesuit, conservative periodical, used a very similar terminology. While *Al-Mashriq*'s authors saw religious education as central to *al-hay'a al-ijtima'iyya* and often did not make a distinction between *al-hay'a al-ijtima'iya* and *al-watan* (i.e. between society and homeland), asserting that 'God … [is] the creator of the *ha'ya ijtima'iyya*, and people are its members', they still used the same concepts, and they still used the analogy of the social body as an organism and as the human body.[55] And if *Al-Mashriq*'s contributors were generally in favour of European investments in Syria, praising European investors who 'have helped us exploit our resources (*istithmar khayratina*)', they still insisted that such natural resources belonged to 'us'.

Notes

1   Melvin Richter and Michaela Richter, 'Introduction: Translation of Reinhart Koselleck's "Krise" in Geschichtliche Grundbegriffe', *Journal of the History of Ideas*, 67/2 (2006), 348.

2   According to Richter and Richter, 'as formulated by Koselleck, *Begriffsgeschichte* neither treats concept-formation and language as reflecting the external forces of "real history"; nor regards political and social language as autonomous "discourses" unaffected by reference to anything extra-linguistic'. Ibid., 349.

3   Ibid., 345.

4   Reformists throughout the Ottoman Empire argued that reform had become urgent due to the unequal and exploitative relationship between 'East' and 'West'. See Alain Roussillon, 'Introduction', in idem (ed.), *Entre Réforme Sociale et Mouvement National: Identité et Modernisation en Egypte (1882–1962)* (Cairo: CEDEJ, 1995), 13.

5   Or, to quote Roussillon, 'l'horizon même de toute pensée hic et nunc'. Ibid., 11.

6   The construct *hay'a ijtima'iyya* appears to have been the most widespread way of designating society in the period under study. The term that is presently used to refer to society, *mujttama'* (same root, but different form), while not completely absent in that period, seems to have become dominant in the 1930s to early 1940s.

7   Butrus al-Bustani, *Muhit al-Muhit: Qamus mutawwal li'l-lugha al-Arabiyya* (The Encompasser of the Ocean: an extensive (or Long) Dictionary of the Arabic Language. Or The Ocean's Ocean: an extensive (or Long) Dictionary of the Arabic Language) (Beirut: s. n., 1867–70). Arabic words are all derived from a (usually) three-letter, (seldom) four-letter verb root. The form of the word (its *tvazn*) contains vital information, such as whether it is passive or active, whether the action described in the word is the result of internal mechanisms (that is, it is self-induced), or whether it is a causal reaction to outside events/forces, and so on. The word *ijtima'* is derived from the root *jama'* (to gather). Among the words spanned by *jama'* are *jam'iyya* (association), such as Sufi (Muslim mystical) gatherings and *jami'* (mosque, or gathering place for the congregation).

8   S. Naqqash, 'Al-Jinan (11 August 1875)', in Muhammad Kamil al-Khatib
     (ed.), *Nadhariyyat al-masrah* (Damascus: Manshurat wizarat al-Thaqafa,
     1994), 41.
9   Ibid.; emphasis added.
10   See Ibn Khaldun's *Muqaddima*, as well as Olivier Carré, 'À propos de la
     sociologie politique d'Ibn Khaldûn', *Revue française de sociologie*, 14/1
     (1973), 115–24. [Note: Ibn Khaldun, *The Muqaddima. An Introduction
     to History*, trans. and intr. Franz Rosenthal, ed. N.J. Dawood (Princeton:
     Princeton UP, 1969).]
11   Butrus al-Bustani, 'Muqaddima', in idem, *Da'irat al-Ma'arif* (Compendium
     of Knowledge) (Beirut, 1876), 2.
12   Ibid.
13   On the meaning of *'adl*, see Emue Tyan, 'Adl', in Peri J. Bearman et al.
     (eds), *Encyclopaedia of Islam*, vol. 1, 2nd edn (Leiden: Brill, 1960), 209–10.
     [Note: article online available at <http://www.brillonline.com/>]
14   Butrus al-Bustani, 'Tamaddun' (Civilization), in idem (1876), 214.
15   Ibid., 213.
16   This started in the late seventh century, but reached a peak first in the
     early nineteenth century with Silvestre de Sacy's translation, and then in
     1858 with the complete edition of the *Muqaddima*. Mohammed Talbi et
     al., '*Abd al-Rahman b. Muhammad b. Muhammad b. Muhammad b. Abi
     Bakr Muhammad b. al-Hasan*, in Bearman et al. (2009), 6.
17   *Al-Bashir*, 13 May 1871. See also ibid., 29 April 1871.
18   One example among many is *Al-Manar*, Rashid Rida's famous Cairene
     periodical (1898–1935), whose subtitle was 'a monthly periodical
     investigating the philosophy of religion, and matters pertaining to society
     (*al-ijtima'*) and civilization ('*umran*)'.
19   From 1876 to 1888, *Al-Muqtataf*'s subtitle was 'Journal of Science and
     Industry'. In 1889, it added one more adjective and became a journal of
     'Science, Industry to Agriculture', before adding yet another field between
     1893 and 1898 and becoming a 'Journal of Science, Medicine, Industry
     to Agriculture'. See Nadia Farag, 'Al Muqtataf 1876–1900: A Study of the
     Influence of Victorian Thought on Modern Arabic Thought', PhD thesis,
     Oxford University, Oxford, 1969, 90.
20   Shibli Shumayyil, 'Tarikh al-ijtima' al tabi 'i: al-maqala al-khamisa'
     (History of Natural Society: the fifth article), *Al-Muqtataf* (1885),
     reproduced in Shibli Shumayyil, *Al-Duktur Shibli Shumayyil: Mabahith
     'ilmiyya wa ijtima'iyya* (Doctor Shibli Shumayyil: scientific and social
     essays) (Beirut: Dar Nazir Abbud, 1991), 40–2.
21   Shibli Shumayyil, 'Al-Qatl al-ijtima'i' (Social killing), *Al-Basir* (1901),
     reproduced in Shibli Shumayyil (1991), 147–9.
22   Richter and Richter (2006), 345.

23 See Ami Ayalon, 'Semantics and the Modern History of Non-European Societies: Arab "Republics" as a Case Study', *Historical Journal*, 28/4 (1985), 821–34. See also Rait Khuri, *Modern Arab Thought: Channels of the French Revolution to the Arab East* (Princeton, NJ: Kingston Press, 1983).

24 Bernard Lewis, 'Jumhuriyya' (Republic), in Bearman et al. (2009).

25 Ibid.

26 See Chapter 2 of Ilham Khuri-Makdisi, *The Eastern Mediterranean and the Making of Global Radicalism* (Berkeley, CA: University of California Press, 2010).

27 Malcolm H. Kerr, 'Notes on the Background of Arab Socialist Thought', *Contemporary History*, 3/3 (1968), 145–59; Mourad M. Wahba, 'The Meaning of Ishtitakiyah: Arab Perceptions of Socialism in the Nineteenth Century', *Alif: Journal of Comparative Poetics*, 10 (1990), 42–55; Dagmar Glaß, *Der Muqtataf und seine Öffentlichkeit: Aufklärung, Räsonnement und Meinungsstreit in der frühen arabischen Zeitschriftenkommunikation* (Würzburg: Ergon Verlag, 2004), 557–8.

28 Shibli Shumayyil, 'Al-Ishtirakiyya al-sahiha' (True socialism), *Al-Muqtataf* (1913), reproduced in As'ad Razzuq (ed.), *Hawadith wa khawatir: Mudhakkarat al-duktur Shibli Shumayyil* (Sayings and recollections: the memoirs of Doctor Shibli Shumayyil) (Beirut: Dar al-Hamra, 1991), 106.

29 Ibid.; emphasis added.

30 Friedrich Karl Christian Ludwig Büchner (1824–99) was the author of, amongst others, *Darwinismus und Sozialismus; oder, Der Kampf um das Dasein und die modern Gesellschaft* (Leipzig: E. Gunther, 1894). His work was at that time highly popular among leftist circles in Europe, as part of a trend of thinking on socialism and political economy in general within the context of evolutionary theory, and his theory on the unity of all beings was particularly influential. On Büchner in the Arab world, see Albert Hourani, *Arabic Thought in the Liberal Age* (Cambridge: Cambridge University Press, 1962); and Marwa El Shakry, 'Darwin's Legacy in the Arab East: Science, Religion and Politics, 1870–1914', PhD thesis, Princeton University, Princeton, 2003.

31 Shumayyil (1913), in Razzuq (1991), 106.

32 In Shumayyil's words, 'socialism is a modern teaching, although its roots are ancient'. Ibid., 105.

33 Zachary Lockman, 'Imagining the Working Class: Culture, Nationalism, and Class Formation in Egypt, 1899–1914', *Poetics Today*, 15/2 (1994), 156.

34 Ibid., 157.

35 As a discipline taught at university, *'ilm al-ijtima'* would first appear in 1925 at Cairo University, founded in 1910. See Omnia El Shakry, *The*

Great Social Laboratory: Subjects of Knowledge in Colonial and Postcolonial Egypt (Stanford, CA: Stanford University Press, 2007), 7.

36   [Note: Gustave LeBon, *Psychologie des Foules* (1895; Paris: Presses Universitaires de France, 2013); Ahmad Fathi Zaghlul, *Ruh al-ijtimaʿ* (Cairo: Matbaʾat al-Shaʾb, 1909).]

37   Wilhelm Heffening, 'Tadbir', in Bearman et al. (2009). All of the following information on Tadbir al-Manzil, unless otherwise specified, is from this source.

38   Ibid. See also Yassine Essid, *A Critique of the Origins of Islamic Economic Thought* (Leiden: Brill, 1995); and Ibrahim Oweiss's chapter in George Atiyeh and Ibrahim Oweiss (eds), *Arab Civilization: Challenges and Responses: Studies in Honor of Constantine Zurayk* (Albany: SUNY Press, 1988).

39   'Raʾs al-mal' (Capital), *Al-Muqtataf* (January 1887), 214–7.

40   'Raʾs al-mal waʾl-ujra' (Capital and wages), *Al-Muqtataf* (March 1887), 348–51.

41   Timothy Mitchell, *Rule of Experts: Egypt, Techno-Politics, Modernity* (Berkeley, CA: University of California Press, 2002), 94.

42   Ibid., 85.

43   'Hall mashakil al-ʿummal wa ashab al-aʿmal' (A solution to the problems between workers and capitalists), *Al-Muqtataf* (June 1887), 517–20.

44   'Al-iʿtisab wa hayawiyyat al-umma' (Strikes and the nation's vitality), *Al-Muqtataf* (February 1902), 160–1.

45   His *Principes d'économie politique* was translated by Hasan Hamit, Hasan Tahsin and M. Zühtü. [Note: Charles Gide, *İlmi iktisat dersleri*, trans. Hasan Hamit, Hasan Tashin and M. Zühtü (Istanbul: Kanaat Matbaası, 1911).]

46   Salama Musa, 'Taʿlim al-umma' (The nation's education), *Al-Muqtataf* (October 1910), 1012–13.

47   Musa attributed the theory to John M. Robertson, as it was formulated in his book *An Introduction to English Politics* (London: Grant Richards, 1900).

48   Salama Musa, 'Irtiqa' al-umam wa inhitatuha' (The evolution of nations and their decline), *Al-Muqtataf* (September 1910), 852–5.

49   Musa also clearly believed in eugenics (this appears under 'other reasons' behind the evolution and decline of nations) and expressed a hodgepodge of racist notions and ideas pertaining to survival of the fittest and deterministic notions ('it is self-evident that agriculture in Egypt does not require great mental capacity. By this, I mean that the chances of finding simpletons among peasants are higher than the chances of finding them among lawyers or journalists'). [Note: reference not given by the author but probably referring to note 48.]

50 *L'Egypte contemporaine, Revue de la Société Khédiviale d'Économie Politique, de Statistique et de Législation*, 1 (1910), introduction. See also René Maunier, *Bibliographie economique, juridique, et sociale de l'Egypte moderne (1798–1916)* (Cairo: Imprimerie de l'Institut français d'archéologie orientale, 1918).

51 See for instance M. E. Sainte-Claire Deville, 'La Responsabilité des patrons envers leurs ouvriers et l'assurance collective contre les accidents du travail'; or Edoardo D. Bigiavi, 'Des accidents du travail et de la protection des ouvriers en Egypte', *L'Egypte contemporaine*, 1 (1910).

52 Muhammad H. Fahmi, *Al-Iqtisad al-Siyasi* (Political economy) (Cairo: Matba'at al-Sa'ada, 1908), 7.

53 'Al-Tanafus al-dawli al-iqtisadi' (International Economic Competition), *Al-Muqtataf* (September 1909). 886–7.

54 Khairallah Khairallah, 'Risala fi usul al-'umran' (Essay on the origins of civilization), *Al-Hurriyya* (5 February 1910), 435. The author had also made a similar argument in *Al-Hurriyya* (29 December 1909), 416.

55 K. Edde, Al-madaris wa'l-hay'a al-ijitima'iyya (Schools and the social body), *Al-Mashriq* (September 1908), 000. [Note: no pages given in the original text.]

Katrin Bromber is senior researcher at the Centre for Modern Oriental Studies (ZMO) in Berlin, Germany. She has worked extensively on Swahili language and literature, Tanzania and its press, applied linguistics, twentieth-century African and European history as well as conceptual history.

Bromber's publications include *Kala Shairi: German East Africa in Swahili Poems* (2003), *Globalization and African languages: Risks and Benefits* (2004), *The World in World Wars: Experiences, Perceptions and Perspectives from Africa and Asia* (2012) and *Under Construction: Logics of Urbanism in the Gulf Region* (2014).

In her article '*Ustaarabu*: A Conceptual Change in Tanganyikan Newspaper Discourse in the 1920s', Bromber investigates a period of intense semantic change in the basic Swahili concept of *ustaarabu* through its contestation in a Tanganyikan newspaper. She traces the conceptual transformations through semantic nets and their various entanglements. As one of the pioneers of conceptual history in the African context, Bromber shows not only that a history of concepts in African languages is possible but also how macro and micro perspectives can be combined in a conceptual history analysis beyond the colonizer–colonized dichotomy, focused on the threefold negotiation between Swahili, English and Arabic.

11

Ustaarabu: A Conceptual Change in Tanganyikan Newspaper Discourse in the 1920s

Katrin Bromber

If you ask a European, I do not think he would say that they primarily came to Africa to turn black people into Europeans, no, but into *wastaarabu*, so that they would be equal to other people.[1]

Introduction

The desirability and necessity of 'civilizing the African' in terms of giving him the economic, moral and social ability 'to stand for himself on equality with the other civilized Nations in the struggle for civilization'[2] was by no means propagated by the British colonial administration alone. According to Cecil Matola, the first president of the African Association, African intellectuals and political activists had also declared it one of their principal goals from the early 1930s onwards. Both sides made use of and altered the existing concept of *ustaarabu* in their conceptual work on what 'civilization' means in the East African context.

Ustaarabu, which is generally rendered as 'civilization' and etymologically reduced to 'becoming or being an Arab', has been described and defined by historians and anthropologists from various perspectives and for different places or periods of time. Jonathon Glassman states that in the second half of the nineteenth century *ustaraabu* was, at least in the eyes of the East African urban elite, a way of distancing themselves from the slaves and pagans of the hinterland.[3] In this respect, the term shares some of the features of *uungwana*, an earlier concept that also emphasizes urbanity, freedom and high social standing. Although these features suggest that the social hierarchy was based on 'cultural inferiority',[4] it was in fact frequently 'inferiority grounded in descent',[5] where 'superior' individuals or families claimed Middle Eastern origin, thus implying religious purity and cultural hegemony.[6] Apart from its structural notion, the concept also contained a strong representational inference, which, at the turn of the century, led either to adoption of new consumer goods or integration in urban institutions of public life.[7] The intellectual history of *ustaarabu* is still strongly connected to (religious) education.[8] According to Middleton, this aspect comprises far more than merely acquiring a considerable degree of Islamic knowledge:

> *Ustaarabu* refers to the condition of being wise and aware of divine knowledge, of observing behaviour befitting members of a society ... and knowing how to dress, eat, and comport oneself correctly.[9]

Thus, the term is linked to notions of *usafi* ('purity') and *heshima* ('respectability'). Consequently, Middleton suggests that the derived verb *-staarabu* should be translated as 'to be wise or knowledgeable' and not 'to become or be an Arab'.[10]

The notion of accumulating knowledge in the broadest sense of the word in order to become a *mstaarabu* was the subject of a newspaper debate in the 1920s and is the focus of this paper. I propose to show how the monthly *Mambo Leo* (Current Affairs) contributed to the conceptual alteration of *ustaarabu* to encompass 'Western' ideas on civilization, which were to have a vast influence on East African intellectuals and political activists.

Mambo Leo and *kujibizana*: Place and Form of the Debate

With Germany's defeat in World War I, all press activities in former German East Africa came to a standstill. The subsequent reorganization of the media sector concentrated exclusively on European-style English publications.[11] As early as 1917, however, J.E. Philipps, Captain of the Intelligence Department of the East African E. Forces, drew the Foreign Office's attention to the establishment of a 'native', i.e. Swahili newspaper.[12] Although the need for a Swahili press as an element of British propaganda was clear to both the Foreign Office (FO) and the Colonial Office (CO), particularly with a view to countering 'pan-Islamic' ideas, it took another six years for the first 'native' newspaper to come off the press.[13] *Mambo Leo* was launched by the Department of Education, British Tanganyika, in January 1923.[14] The British Administration had thus created its own mouthpiece to reach the 'natives'. Perceived by the local population as the successor of the once thriving German weekly *Kiongozi* (The Guide), *Mambo Leo* was highly appreciated by its readers. Since the British officials recognized its useful purpose, the Administrative Conference ensured its continuance through a resolution passed in 1924. With a circulation of 9,000 copies, *Mambo Leo* had a wider distribution than any other newspaper in British Tanganyika in the 1930s. Primarily aimed at educating 'Africans', it also published home news, executive announcements and entertaining stories.[15] For the editors, education meant first and foremost the propagation of 'modernity', which comprised economic and administrative progress as well as ideas on 'good citizenship'.[16]

The debate about *ustaarabu*, which disseminated ideas about colonial 'modernity' and the future of East Africa, was shaped in a time-honoured and popular linguistic form known as *kujibizana*.[17] Ann Biersteker defines *kujibizana* as:

> Eliciting answers from each other. It is considered both as a 'formal structure' of Swahili poetry and other texts; i.e. as a scheme ... by which two

individuals answer and ask each other questions or are represented as doing this, and as rhetoric, trope, or figure of meaning ... that enables various, but related senses ... to be metaphors or symbols of social discourse of different types in specific contexts.[18]

Interestingly, *kujibizana* was not only the discursive structure of *Mambo Leo* debates on various issues but also a matter for critique. The first appeared in 1925.[19] The author, S.W. Kizozo from Tanga, reminds readers that they should choose their words more carefully when employing *kujibizana*, which he defines as 'news from questions and answers' (*habari ya maulizo na majibu*). Contributions should be meaningful, beneficial and smooth. Describing *kujibizana* from a historical perspective, he states that the question must be asked in the form of *fumbo* ('riddle', a common element of Swahili poetry) in order to stimulate a response from the audience and thus secure the continuation of the debate. The question should preferably be posed in a joking manner, since only an entertaining conversation would prosper. By emphasizing that *kujibizana* is a means of reducing ignorance, S.W. Kizozo links this popular form of communication to development:

> Don't think that ignorance has now ceased to exist. Certainly not! If we want to lessen it, we have to question and answer in a suitable manner. Disgusting words do not relieve people of their ignorance.[20]

Ustaarabu, or: 'How to Civilize the East African'

Mambo Leo began the discussion on *ustaarabu* in its very first issue. An anonymous author referring to himself as *Mwenyeji wa Inchi* ('a native') set up a column entitled *Afrika ya Kesho* ('Tomorrow's Africa') in which he outlined the overall conceptual framework.[21] Using orientational metaphors, he suggested that *ustaarabu* should have a valuable core (*kiini*), wrapped or protected by a skin (*ganda*). Reaching the inner part requires effort, especially with regard to economic development. Since the 'native population' (*wenyeji wa inchi*) has not yet made such an effort, it permanently lacks the inner part or essence of *ustaarabu* and even the skin.

The editor took up the subject in the next issue and discussed it with regard to trade. By adding that it was crucial to find the key (*ufunguo*) to the door of prosperity (*ustawi*), he not only defined the essence of *ustaarabu* but developed the metaphorical shape of the concept further. He also confirmed the existence of different notions of *ustaarabu*, which he linked to racial categories such as 'African' and 'Indian'. Although maintaining that *ustaarabu* is prerequisite for development, he stresses that not all forms are suitable for achieving it.[22] He compares 'Indian' and 'African' ways of doing business, indicating that the 'Indian' method leads to more profit (*faida*) and, hence, prosperity, while the 'African' way is described as disorganized and wasteful.[23]

Summarizing the discussion at this point, it can be said that *ustaarabu* is conceptualized as having prosperity at its core, which can only be achieved by going beyond the skin via economic development and personal effort. Since there are several (racial) types of *ustaarabu*, it is essential to adapt to those that have proved to be the most effective.

Sales Meissner's letter to the editor, which appeared in the same issue, introduced a slight shift in the discussion from economics to race and education. In order to be accepted as a participant in the discussion, the author begins by asserting his 'native' status.[24] Developing his argument in two steps, he first takes up the conceptual frame and transforms it along racial lines from a historical perspective. Beginning with the general statement that each ethnic group in East Africa had its own form of *ustaarabu* before the European conquest, he emphasizes that they had lost their ability to be considered *wastaarabu* when the African population was enslaved and treated badly by the 'Arabs'. Completely ignoring the fact that the Europeans (*wazungu*) had established their power in East Africa by military means, Meissner states they were kind to 'Africans' and educated them, and were therefore the only ones entitled to be considered *wastaarabu*. He summarizes the first part of his argument as follows:

> As I understand it, the European form of *ustaarabu* is its inner part, while the skin of *ustaarabu* is that of the Arabs and other existing forms.[25]

Thus, accepting their claim to superiority, he propagates the need to co-operate with the Europeans.[26] In the second part of his argument, Meissner discusses *ustaarabu* with regard to professions and work spheres. Contrary to preceding contributions, he considers trade (*biashara*), and especially the 'Indian' method of trading, as an obstacle to rather than a means of achieving *ustaarabu*.[27] Although craftsmanship (*ufundi*) and cultivation (*kulima*) are characterized as useful or even original forms of work (*kazi ya asili*), they do not bring about *ustaarabu*. Reading and understanding are the only acceptable method, since they lead to the indispensable qualities a *mustaarabu* should possess.

> Those who compose and write what is read are the ones to be praised [literally, the qualified ones]; calm people who first respect before they are respected. Many of them love veracity and truth. They are the ones [to be called] *wastaarabu*.[28]

Since reading and writing not only serve the individual but also the wider society, *ukarani* ('clerical work') is, according to Sales Meissner, the only [sic] acceptable profession in achieving *ustaarabu*.

In his reply to Meissner's contribution, *Mwenyeji wa Inchi* tries to balance the discussion with regard to its racial connotation by pointing out that although 'Arabs' enslaved parts of the 'African' population, they were 'people who embraced *ustaarabu*' (*watu waliostaarabu*), and that only the ignorance (*ujinga*) of the 'native' population prevented them from embracing it, too.[29] Elaborating further on the 'Arab' connotation of the term, the author states:

> And this word *ustaarabu*, I did not say it is linked to the Arabs. In Kiswahili, even if you wear European clothes, you are referred to as someone who has embraced the European form of *ustaarabu*. *Ustaarabu* does not mean being an Arab, but being recognized as a human being in the eyes of other human beings.[30]

In order to avoid being misunderstood, *Mwenyeji wa Inchi* makes it clear that *ustaarabu* as little or nothing to do with dress, but with education. Interestingly, he refers to the German colonizers, emphasizing that they even forbade the 'native' population to wear European dress, since they wanted them to embrace European mentality (*akili*) first.[31]

The author introduces the aspect of 'modernization' while addressing the second part of Meissner's argument related to work spheres. He argues that a profession alone is not an indicator of *ustaarabu* but rather the standard of the work in terms of technological development and expert knowledge. In this respect, he continues, the 'Indian' method of doing business is exemplary and should be imitated because it is more advanced and yields more profit.

The immediate and sharp response to Sales Meissner's criticism of the 'Arabs' for maltreatment of the 'African' population and the latter's consequent denial of *wastaarabu* status was not surprising. In their letter to the editor, Abdulrehmani Ismail and H. Mohamed Muhsin remind the readers that even European authors[32] had emphasized the importance of the 'Arabs' in spreading *ustaarabu* in East Africa. Writing from a historical perspective, they describe how 'Arab' immigrants brought economic and cultural development to an almost barbaric 'African' population. *Ustaarabu* was thus defined in terms or urbanity (*-jenga miji*), education (*-fundisha watu*), due respect towards elders (*-kataza kuwachinja wazee*), clothing (*-wauzia nguo*), agriculture (*-panda mchele, mtama, embe na minazi*) and the establishment of administration (*maliwali, maakida*). The essence of their argument reads as follows:

> So we should say that the Arabs are the key to *ustaarabu*, in the sense that even Kiswahili is half Arabic.[33]

A summary at this point indicates a shift in the discussion towards sorting out who brought about *ustaarabu* and therefore possesses the 'key' (*ufunguo*) to it. Although the various authors more or less agreed on the existence of various notions of *ustaarabu*, they tried to position them along racial lines. Interestingly, European and 'Arab' impressions of the concept were discussed more comprehensively, while the 'Indian' notion was merely reduced to trade. References to economy and culture not only incorporated the discourse about modernization and development, but also conceptualized *ustaarabu* as non-static. Furthermore, visual markers such as clothes were not considered as indicators of having achieved *mustaarabu* status.

Three months later, the discussion was taken up again by Akida Waziri Kizozo. In his contribution entitled 'Makumbusho', he defines *ustaabaru* as follows:

> The meaning of this word is to pay attention to our intellect, to protect ourselves from the things which we will see in future, and to present ourselves to our superiors in such a way that they realize we have internalized their teaching fully, and that our purity refers not only to clothing, no but to all features without exception.[34]

By elaborating further on the features (*sifa*) of human principles (*desturi za utu*), comprising honesty (*tuwe waaminifu*), discipline (*watii kwa ufuato wa amri*), patience (*wenyi saburi*) and humility (*wapole kwa jamaa zetu*), the author shifts the meaning of *ustaarabu* from its racial and economic connotation to that of character (*tabia*) and behaviour (*vitendo*).

Although not directly replying to Akida Waziri Kizozo's contributions, *Mwenyeji wa Inchi* takes up the question of character (*tabia*) in his article on the obstacles to Tanganyika's progress, which appeared in the subsequent issue.[35] The author changes the metaphorical representation of the concept here by introducing maritime terminology. *Ustaarabu* is either defined as a harbour (*bandari*) – a safe haven after a difficult journey – or as a wave (*wimbi*) that has already reached the East African shore. In order to state more precisely what hinders and what promotes *ustaarabu*, *Mwenyeji wa Inchi* structures the text in oppositional terms:

1 Gaining the status of *ustaarabu* brings about equality (*kuwa mtu kama watu*), while the lack of it enforces inequality (*kuwa watu duni ya watu*).
2 *Ustaarabu* is achieved by progressive movement (*-kwenda, -kuendelea, -ota, -stawi*) and prevented by regressive movement (*-rudisha, -chelewa*) or standstill (*-simama*).
3 With regard to trade, *ustaarabu* requires saving money for reinvestment (*-weka akiba*) and is hampered by careless waste (*-poteza*).
4 Concerning interpersonal relations, *ustaarabu* means mutual support (*-saidiana*) and respect (*-heshimiana*) and not harassment or bullying of others (*-oneana*).
5 In order to achieve *ustaarabu* one must strive for education (*-soma*) and fight ignorance (*ujjinga*).

All in all, the author defines *ustaarabu* as a project for building the future of the continent (*Afrika ya Kesho*).

In the following year (1924), *Mambo Leo* published two contributions that critically reviewed the discussion and its effects on the readership. In his letter to the editor, M.K.J. Salim from Tanga claim that the adoption of qualities such as honesty (*uaminifu*) and carefulness/self-discipline (*utaratibu*), especially with regard to administrative work spheres, which he qualifies as *ustaarabu kweli* or *ustaarabu haswa* (real or genuine *ustaarabu*), must achieve the substitution of the foreign labour force (*wahini, wagoa*; literally, Indians and Goans) by locals (*wenyeji wa inchi hii ya Africa*).[36] Another author, who remained anonymous, even points out that the various educative series published by *Mambo Leo* had in fact very little effect:

> I think that many readers and those who were read [the newspaper] have not understood these ideas ... They did not get the point about what we can learn from these teachings.[37]

The main reason for this sad situation, according to the author, is the lack of a multiplying effect from those who have already received a 'European' education. He substantiates his argument by pointing to the fact that the education system, which allowed a large part of the population to become literate, is by no means a new phenomenon but has been in existence for almost fifty-five years. Moreover, many Africans went to the European metropolises (Berlin, London and Paris) for higher education. All of them have obviously been unable to transmit their knowledge to the people or even explain what *ustaarabu* meant.[38] Thus, *ustaarabu* is described in terms of cultural capital, as having a good job (*kazi kubwa*), wearing European clothes (*-vaa kizungu*), speaking a European language (*-sema kizungu*) or receiving a high salary (*mshahara kubwa*). Finally, the author expresses his sincere hope that *Mambo Leo* would continue its teaching so that slowly but surely the required understanding of the 'project' is instilled in the minds of the people.

Despite this severe critique, the newspaper did not discuss the issue further along these lines but brought the discussion back to the question of inner part (*kiini*) or essence of *ustaarabu*. The editor began by stating that *ustaarabu* is a 'great' thing (*jambo kubwa sana sana*) and leads to prosperity and the extinction of darkness (*giza*), impurity (*uchafu*), barbarism (*ushenzi*) and contempt (*ufithuli*).[39] While the effort to become a *mstaarabu* should be accomplished individually, he holds that its effects should be felt on the interpersonal level.

> *Ustaarabu* not only concerns the individual, and neither can one be a *mstaarabu* purely to one's own advantage. *Ustaarabu* requires a person to act [for the benefit] of his neighbours and all mankind.[40]

The editor points out that because Kiswahili lacked an appropriate term for this concept of behaviour, it has been necessary to introduce the term *uraiya* ('citizenship').[41] Apart from defining *uraiya* in terms of obligations (*kazi*) such as following government orders (*-tii amri zote za Serikali*) and promoting one's country (*-stawisha inchi yake*), the editor also declares it to be the essence of *ustaabaru*. This verbally established link between *ustaarau*, *uraiya* and *serikali* ('government', here referring to the British colonial administration) was intensified in the next editorial, where the editor emphasized the vital role of government for both *ustaarabu* and *uraiya*[42] and the importance of good citizenship (*uraiya wema*) for the process that eventually leads to *ustaarabu*.[43]

Summing up the discussion at this point, it appears that the editors of *Mambo Leo* aimed at incorporating the concept of *ustaarabu* into the underlying colonial propaganda, implying that 'good citizenship' meant to serve colonial aims. Interestingly, other contributions did not pursue this direction but, once again, emphasized the personal qualities of a *mstaarabu*,[44] thereby verbally strengthening the notion of equality (*kuwa mtu kwa watu*).

In 1926, however, *Mambo Leo* published an article by Zainah binti Mwinyipembe entitled 'Umama wa Ustaarabu', which introduced the gender question as a new aspect to the debate.[45] She begins by asking whether only men can contribute to the future development of Africa[46] – obviously a rhetorical question, as she goes on to give a detailed account of the physical ill-treatment of 'African' women (*wanawake weusi*) by their husbands resulting in a permanent state of fear, the general lack of respect towards women, the fact that (free) females had to work side by side with slaves, the existing dowry custom, polygamy, and the denial of equal education opportunities. While directing her criticism towards men, women and parents alike, her final appeal addresses male readers only:

> Well, gentlemen, if you want *ustaarabu*, you first of all have to educate your wives and daughters, who are the mothers of the *wastaarabu*, so that they will be on the same level as you, even though you are superior. If you manage this, believe me, the quarrels and trouble at home will stop ... Men, you will be happy to see your wives and your wives will be happy to see you.[47]

Despite her verbal acknowledgement of male superiority, Zainah binti Mwinyipembe not only challenges either male and parental authority or patrimonial control, but considers a fundamental change in gender relations as a precondition for bringing about *ustaarabu*.

The first response to Zainah binti Mwinyipembe's contribution came from Ubwa bin Salim. He first of all criticizes her for introducing a religious [sic] topic to a newspaper that had clearly stated it did not support such debates. Despite this critique, Ubwa goes on to develop his argument entirely on religious grounds. He mainly attempts to blame women themselves:

> As you said, all religious demand great respect towards women, but if your souls were not so weak, you would be the saints to your husbands and get the respect you deserve.[48]

Apart from rejecting all of Zainah's arguments, he completely ignores her main issue of education and gender equality as the prerequisite for *ustaarabu*. The only statement left untouched in Zainah's contribution was her appeal to the *Wakuu wa Elimu* (Education Officers), who are allegedly in charge of women's education, which in turn could elevate them to a standard fit for *ustaarabu*.[49] However, Ubwa bin Salim's letter was not the only male response published in *Mambo Leo*. In the same issue,

S.P.T. Kiobia largely agrees with Zainah's arguments and confirms the ill-treatment of women as common knowledge. However, he does point to the foreign roots of her ideas, identifying them as the idealized European/Christian concept of gender relations. He further argues that because of the basic difference between the 'European' and the 'African' character (*tabia*), and the slow implementation of ideas introduced through education, no fundamental change would be achieved within the next fifty years. In addition, great patience would be required on all sides in order not to hurt anyone, especially not the elders.[50]

At this point, the very lively debate on the concept of *ustaarabu* came more or less to a halt. Further contributions used the term merely as a signifier of appropriate behaviour or repeated claims as to whether or not ethnic or racial groups historically deserved the attribute. Whether this particular development indicates that the Department of Education, as decision-maker on the content of the newspaper, dropped the issue altogether is a matter for further research.

Conclusion

This paper has attempted to show how the Department of Education used the existing concept of *ustaarabu* to spread 'Western' ideas on 'civilization' to a wider public. In doing so, it channelled the discussion along the notions of 'good citizenship' and education in its broadest sense to serve the colonial power. The different voices that appeared in its mouthpiece, *Mambo Leo*, in the 1920s more or less emphasized the 'Africanness' of the concept in that they did not establish a link between *ustaarabu* and elite urban coastal life. Instead, *ustaarabu* was described as a project for the future development of Tanganyika's population with reference to all social strata and gender groups. It thus prepared the discursive development that James Brennan described as follows:

> By the 1930s the public employment of *ustaarabu* on the mainland had become geared more towards the language of racial self-improvement than the older meaning of coastal integration, except for those discussions – increasingly rare in print on mainland Tanganyika – specific to Islam.[51]

The newspaper discussion analysed here clearly shows that *ustaarabu* was – and, as I would argue, still is – a heuristic device to conceptualize society. Given the fact that most studies of 'Swahili' culture have described *ustaarabu* as on if its basic concepts, further research should consider the changing notions of *ustaarabu* that have, historically, produced a diversity of meanings.

Notes

1   'Afrika ya Kesho', *Mambo Leo*, 3 (1929), 7: 'Lakini sighani kama ukimwuliza Mzungu haswa atakuambia kuwa wao wamekuja Afrika kuwafanya watu weusi wawe Wazungu, la, illa wastaarabu, wawe watu kama watu.' All newspaper translations are my own. Deviations from standard Kiswahili orthography are due to the fact that it did not exist at that time.

2   Matola to Colonial Secretary, 25 July 1930, Tanzania National Archives, Dar es Salaam (TNA) 18325/2, cited in James R. Brennan, 'Nation, Race and Urbanization in Dar es Salaam, Tanzania, 1916–1976'. PhD thesis, Northwestern University, Evanston Illinois, 2002, 252.

3   Jonathon Glassman, *Feats and Riot: Revelry, Rebellion and Popular Consciousness on the Swahili Coast, 1856–1888* (London: James Currey, 1995), 117.

4   Alamin M. Mazrui and Ibrahim Noor Shariff, *The Swahili: Idiom and Idenity of an African People* (Trenton, NJ: Africa World Press, 1994), 27.

5   Brennan (2002), 255.

6   Glassman (1995), 119.

7   Laura Fair, *Pastimes and Politics: Culture, Community and Identity in Post-Abolition Urban Zanzibar, 1890–1945* (Oxford, James Currey, 2001), 45–55.

8   Randall L. Pouwels, *Horn and Crescent: Cultural Change and Traditional Islam on the East African Coast, 800–1900* (Cambridge: Cambridge University Press, 1987).

9   John Middleton, *The World of Swahili: An African Mercantile Civilization* (New Haven and London: Yale University Press, 1992), 192.

10   Ibid., 224.

11   These were *The Morogoro News* (1916–19), the *Tanganyika Territory Gazette* (1919), *The Tanga Post and East Coast Advertiser* (1919–21), and the *Dar-es-Salaam Times* (1919–25). For further details, see Martin Sturmer, *The Media History of Tanzania* (Ndanda: Ndanda Mission Press, 1998), 48–50.

12   'The German Government in German East Africa maintained two native newspapers [*Kiongozi*, "The Guide" and *Khabari ya Pwani*, "News of the Coast"] containing items of news from each station or district,

compiled by natives for natives under white supervision, with legal articles explaining any legislation, giving general ideas of the development of the country. The papers were published fortnightly and monthly. They had a wide circulation among all classes of literate natives and were a great assistance to the Administration. They were much appreciated by the natives and much regretted when our Administration refused to carry them on. The renewal of these papers would be a valuable measure … since the educated native conveys the ideas contained to his illiterate friends who are as eager as the Athenians to tell or hear some new thing.' (Public Record Office, London (PRO) Foreign Office (FO) 395/64, *Memorandum. 'Africa for the African' and Pan-Islam*, J.E. Philipps to Foreign Office, 15 July 1917, 5–6.)

13   In taking up Philipps' idea, S. Gaselee (FO) suggested a 'picture paper' similar to *El-Hakikat* or *Warta Jang Julus*, which would be produced in London and distributed via Zanzibar. A Swahili newspaper in the strict sense of the word should be locally produced. Here, propaganda 'has to be hidden among the news – very little powder to a great deal of jam, and the news, to interest the people who will see the paper, must be local' (PRO FO 395/64, Minute, S. Gaselee, 22 November 1917, 2–3). Apart from reminding Gaselee of *El-Usbueyah*, a Zanzibari weekly published by the British Administration that could serve as a model for a similar newspaper on the mainland, Major F.H. Smith (CO) urged for an immediate reorganization of the 'native' press to fill the gap created by defunct German newspapers (see PRO FO 395/64, Smith to Gaselee, 13 December 1917, 2–3).

14   It was taken over by the Public Relations Department in 1949.

15   Martin Sturmer, *The Media History of Tanzania* (Ndanda: Ndanda Mission Press, 1998), 51–2.

16   For an excellent discussion of attempts to conceptualise 'modernity' in Africa, see Peter Probst, Jan-Georg Deutsch and Heike Schmidt (eds), *African Modernities. Entangled Meanings in Current Debate* (Oxford: James Currey, 2002).

17   'Mambo yanayozuia Afrika ya Kesho', *Mambo Leo*, 7 (1923), 5: 'Lakini sipendi kuendelea kuandika illa niwape nafasi wenzangu waseme wanavyoona, kama vile nilivyofanya kwanza, maana tamu ya meneno ni kujibizana.' – 'But I don't want to continue [my] writing unless I can ask my fellowmen to state their opinions as I did at the beginning, seeing that the sweetness of words is in [their] exchange.'

18   Ann Bierstecker, *Kujibizana: Questions of Language and Power in Nineteenth- and Twentieth-Century Poetry in Kiswahili* (East Lansing: Michigan State University Press, 1996), 20–1.

19   'Tamu ya maneno ni kujibizana', *Mambo Leo*, 27 (1925), 50.

20   *Mambo Leo*, 27 (1925), 50: 'Msifikiri ujinga umekwisha sasa, la sio, illa, tukitaka kuupunguza tujibizane vizuri. Maneno y karaha hayamtoi mtu ujingani.'

21   'Afrika ya Kesho', *Mambo Leo*, 1 (1923), 2.

22   'Biashara', *Mambo Leo*, 2 (1923), 1: 'Ingawa ustaarabu ni lazima kwa maendelo ya watu, si lazima kila mtu aendelee kwa sababu ya ustaarabu wake tu.' – 'Although *ustaarabu* is essential for the development of the people, this does not mean that each individual makes progress on the basis of his/her method of *ustaarabu*.'

23   For further details on the economic and political role of South Asian immigrants in Tanganyika in the 1920s see James R. Brennan, 'South Asian Nationalism in an East African Context: The Case of Tanganyika, 1914–1956', *Comparative Studies of South Asia, Africa and the Middle East* 29/2 (1999), 25–8.

24   'Sanduku la Posta', *Mambo Leo*, 2 (1923), 14: 'Mimi nihesabikaye miongoni mwa wenyeji wa inchi hii … '.

25   Ibid.: 'Ustaarabu wa kizungu ninavyoona mimi, ndicho kiini cha Ustaarabu na ganda la Ustaarabu ndio ule wa Waarabu na huo mwingine ukao.'

26   Ibid.: 'Jitahijka bidii zetu tuungane nao, tuwe waana kwao na wao wawe Baba kwetu.' – 'We should make an effort to join them. Let us be like children to them and let them be fathers to us.'

27   Ibid., 15: 'Hayaonyeshi kwa wazi kuwa ni Ustaarabu … kuunguzia mwenziwe haiwezi kumwea Ustaarabu, illa kuna lingine badala ya Ustaarabu.' – '[Indian] trade does not really seem to have anything to do with *ustaarabu* … Playing down your fellow country-man does not stimulate *ustaarabu*, quite the contrary.'

28   Ibid.: 'Waliotunga na kuyaandika yasomwayo ni watu wenye sifaa, watuliva walioanza kuheshimu kabla hawajaheshimiwa, wengi miongoni mwao waipenda haki na kweli. Hawa ndio wastaarabu.'

29   Instead of using the term *wenyeji wa nchi/inchi*, he applies the personal pronoun in the first person plural (*sisi, tu-*) or the possessive pronoun (*-etu*).

30   'Majjibu ya Mwenyeji wa Inchi', *Mambo Leo*, 3 (1923), 7: 'Na hili neno la ustaarabu, sikusema kuwa laungana na Waarabu. Kwa lugha ya Kiswahili hatta kama unavaa nguo za kizungu utaitwa umestaarabu kizungu, kustaarabu sio kuwa Mwuarabu, lakini kuwa mtu kama watu.'

31   Ibid.: 'Lakini nguo wa kizungu akawakataza watu wasivae. Kwa kuwa aliona hili si neon la kwanza katika ustaarabu. Wachukue akili za kizungu kwanza, halafu wavae nguo.' – 'But [the German] forbade them to wear European clothes since he considered it unimportant for *ustaarabu*. They [the 'Africans'] should first take up their ideas and then wear their clothes.'

32   In particular, they referred to Sir Harry Johnston and F. B. Pierce.

33   'Majjibu ya Mwenyeji wa Inchi', *Mambo Leo*, 3 (1923), 7: 'Tena, yatupasa tuseme kwamba Waarabu ndio ufunguo wa ustaarabu, maana, hatta lugha ya Kiswahili nussu ni Kiarabu.'

34   'Makumbusho', *Mambo Leo*, 6 (1912), 11: 'Maana ya neno hili adio kuangalia haswa akili zetu, kuhjihifathi na jambo tutakaloona siku zijazo, na kujionyesha mbele za wakuu wetu watuone kwa mafundisho yao yamekamilika kabisa, wala sio usafi wetu uwe juu ya kuvaa tu hapana illa yote yaonekane kwetu sawasawa pasipokuwa hatta sifa moja.'

35   'Mambo yanayozuia Afrika ya Kesho', *Mambo Leo*, 7 (1923), 6–7.

36   'Habari ya ustaabaru (Tanga)', *Mambo Leo*, 13–14 (1924), 23–4.

37   Ibid., 24: 'Nathani wasomaji wengi na wasomewao hawakupata sana maneno haya ... hawashiki kuangalia ya kuwa, nini, na sababu tunafundishwa, tupate nini?'

38   Ibid.: 'Lakini katika hao waliosoma hivi so kufika katika miji mikubwa hii, hapana aliyefanya nia ya kuonyesha kwetu ustaarabu nini ... ' – 'However, of those who received this education or arrived in the metropolises, not a single one made any attempt to show us what *ustaarabu* is ... '

39   'Kiini cha Ustaarabu ni Uraiya', *Mambo Leo*, 32 (1925), 171.

40   Ibid.: 'Ustaarabu haumpasi mtu peke yake tu, tena mtu hawezi kuwa mstaarabu kama anajitafutia faida yake yeye tu. Ustaarabu ni jambo linalowapasa watu tote watendee jirani zan na watu wote.'

41   In fact, the term and concept of *uraiya* has existed since the second half of the nineteenth century and gained particular significance in the legal system of the Sultanate of Zanzibar.

42   'Siku za Kale na za sasa Bora nin nini?', *Mambo Leo*, 33 (1925), 194: ' ... billa Serikali inchi haiwezi kustaarabika, na billa Serikali hauwezi kuwa Uraiya.' – 'Without government there is neither progress to civilization nor citizenship.'

43   Ibid.: ' ... na mpaka watu wote wamekwisha kuamka na kujifunza na kufuata Uraiya Wema, inchi itachelewa kustaarabika.' – 'Unless everyone stands up and learns and internalizes good citizenship, the country will lag behind the civilizing process.'

44   'Ustaarabu, Uungwana, Uhuru', *Mambo Leo*, 33 (1925), 200–1; 'Ustaarabu ni Mali', *Mambo Leo*, 18 (1925), 95.

45   Although, as in other newspapers of the time, women did not have an equal voice, they were not totally neglected. With regard to *Mambo Leo*, see Bromber (forthcoming). [Note: Katrin Bromber, 'Buibui: un débat sur le vêtement porté par le femmes sur la côte du Tanganyika (1929–1934)', in Jean-Luc Vellut (ed.), *Ville d'Afrique. Exploration en histoire urbaine* (Paris: L'Harmattan, 2007), 201–17.]

46 'Umama wa Ustaarabu', *Mambo Leo*, 39 (1926), 331: ' … wanaume peke yao wataweza kuifanukisha Afrika ya Kesho?'

47 Ibid., 332: 'Haya mabwana, mkitaka ustarabu yawapaseni mjitahidi kwanza kuwafunza wake zenu na binti walio Mama wa Wastarabu wawe na daraja moja na ninyi wenyewe, japokiwa Ukubwa ni Wenu. Mkifanya hivi, fahamuni kelele na shari majumbani ztakuwa na mwisho … Wanaume mtaona raha kuwaona wake zentu, na wake watakuwa furahani kuwaona waume zao.'

48 'Majjibu wa Bibi Zainah', *Mambo Leo*, 40 (1926), 362: 'Usemayo dini yoyote imeamuru kuheshimiwa sana wanawake, na lau kama si udhaifu war oho zenu mngekuwa wlii kwa waume zenu na heshima mlizostahili kupewa … '.

49 'Umama wa Ustaarabu', *Mambo Leo*, 42 (1926), 408: 'Wakipatikana wanawake kumi pamoja na mimi wapendao kujifunza Umama wa Ustaarabu, natumaini kwa hisani kwamba Wakuu wa Elimu tutapewa mwalimu aliye wa namna yetu afundishe … kadhalika kwa bidii yetu atatukalisha kitini pa ustaarabu.' – 'If they find eleven women and myself, who want to learn what is necessary for the mothers of the wastaarabu, I believe the education officers will find an appropriate teacher for us … and with our diligence, place us on the chair of *ustaarabu*.'

50 'Majibu – Umama wa Ustaarabu', *Mambo Leo*, 42 (1926), 410: 'Bassi, kwa hivyo nafikiri kwa vema hayo yote yatazamwe polepole mpaka wakati wake utimie watu wote watakapoelimishwa.' – 'Thus, I think it is good to observe things calmly until such time as all people are educated.'

51 Brennan (2002), 262.

Imke Rajamani is a doctoral research fellow at the Research Centre 'History of Emotions' which is part of the Max Planck Institute for Human Development in Berlin, Germany. She studied literature and media, history and musicology at the University of Hamburg, Germany. Currently, Rajamani is working on a project about the 'angry young man' and the conceptual history of anger in popular Indian cinema. This project combines her research interests in South Asian media cultures – in particular Hindi and Telugu cinema – with the theoretical endeavour of integrating methodologies from media studies into conceptual history.

In her article 'Pictures, Emotions, Conceptual Change: Anger in Popular Hindi Cinema', Rajamani advocates studying the changing meanings of concepts in mass media. She uses an approach of conceptual intermediality to argue for the inclusion of visual and other media into conceptual analysis. Her theoretical reflections reference Reinhart Koselleck's own work on political iconography, which has only recently become subject of scholarly debate.

12

Pictures, Emotions, Conceptual Change: Anger in Popular Hindi Cinema

Imke Rajamani

The story of the popular Hindi film *Zanjeer* (1973)[1] reaches its climax with the final confrontation. The young hero, Vijay, stands face to face with the villainous businessman Teja, whose criminal techniques of smuggling, fraud and murder have cost many innocent lives. Representing the common man, Vijay has come to remove once and for all the personified evil and to take revenge in the name of society, morality and justice. As they face each other, Vijay notices the chain with a little horse-shaped pendant around Teja's wrist and recognizes him to be the murderer of his parents. A fanfare with brass and drums marks the beginning of the dramatic climax, which starts with a forty-second sequence of increasingly fast cuts between key shots of the film's story: the chain on Teja's arm, an exploding rocket in the night sky (both the murder and the revenge are set to happen during a Hindu festival), Vijay's narrowing bloodshot eyes that from cut to cut become increasingly surrounded by drops of sweat from his forehead, a black rider on a chained

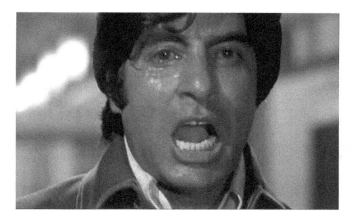

Figure 12.1 *'Kamīne!'*: Amitabh Bachchan as angry Vijay in *Zanjeer.*

white horse from the hero's earlier revealed nightmares, Vijay's mother being hit by the bullet and the young child witnessing his parents' death. The staccato chime of bells from the musical nightmare motif builds into another fanfare that is accompanied by the sound of bullets firing and a horse neighing. Suddenly, the music stops and Vijay cries out Teja's name while the camera brings his bloodshot eyes into focus. With his voice tensed, Vijay reveals his recognition and traumatic memory to the surprised villain. His short monologue is initially supported by a sentimental string theme, which is gradually overtaken by growling synthesizer sounds. The music signifies how the pain of the child's trauma transforms into the action of the angry young man. Shouting the abusive word *kamīne*[2] (rogue, immoral person) Vijay throws his body toward a finally fear-struck Teja and they fight.

This scene encapsulates the essence of the film's narrative key concept, which constantly drives the story and is at the centre of the plot, namely *anger*. Even though the complex concept is not explicitly mentioned in the film dialogue with the word itself, the interplay of visuals, music, sounds, the narrative logic and their references to popular knowledge about and associations with anger (for example, reaction to injustice, heat, tension, eruptive action) invoke an unambiguous interpretation of meaning for the Indian audience in the 1970s. *Zanjeer* marks the birth of the *angry young man* film as a genre in popular Hindi cinema and the emergence of a new audio-visual concept of *virtuous anger*.

This article argues that in the 1970s, a new concept of *anger* became popularized and politicized in urban India through the screen image of the *angry young man*[3] in commercial Hindi cinema. A body of action- and revenge-themed films that were very successful among the mass audience of cinema for almost two decades, created a new concept of *virtuous anger* through narrations that dealt with the pressing social and political issues of the time, such as poverty, corruption and social injustice. The story of a common man or social underdog, like Vijay in *Zanjeer*, who fights against politicians and evil businessmen like Teja, was initially depicted with great psychological depth in the film narratives, before the *angry young man* and his emotional conceptualization became simplified and stereotyped in the 1980s. One reason for the simplification is that the storylines and audio-visual codes of the *angry young man* films shared many features, which became recognized as typical for the film genre. I further suggest that the translation of the pre-existent filmic concept into written language in film magazines and newspapers was one major reason for the simplification and stereotypification of the *angry young man* and his *anger*. I refer to this translation process as linguification. By analysing the concept of *anger* in the film *Coolie* (1983),[4] I demonstrate how the stereotyped image of the *angry young man* builds on the earlier meanings of the concept. I do so by (re-)constructing selected threads of a semantic net that spans different media and layers of time in the history of the concept of *anger*.

No other form of media of the 1970s and 1980s in India is comparable in its outreach and impact on the male urban population of the lower and middle classes as popular cinema. Therefore, it is an established methodology among film scholars and social historians to read films, their stories and their ideologies as a blurred mirroring of the socio-political issues and the idealized common man's experiences in a certain time period.[5] I use this approach as well, but also suggest the need to understand popular cinema in India as an agent of social, cultural and conceptual change in a period that has been perceived as the fiercest economic and political crisis in India's postcolonial history.[6] In popular national ideology and filmic logic before the 1970s, anger had been conceptualized as a bad emotion. By popularizing narratives of *virtuous anger* against injustice due to corruption and inefficiency of governmental institutions, the *angry young man* films reflect the experience of the urban poor in India in the 1970s. They induced conceptual change and therewith initiated public anger management within the framework of popular nationalism. *Virtuous anger*, as mediated through popular Hindi cinema, is a popular political key concept in this time and context. Its audio-visual signifiers serve as meaningful intersections between different discourses and concepts of acute ideological and political relevance.

Within the discipline of conceptual history, the absence of anger words in the *angry young man* films poses a theoretical and methodological challenge.

The established methods are based on a logocentric paradigm and an exclusive positioning of language. Concepts are predominantly researched as words in use. Using the analysis of *anger* in popular Hindi cinema, I suggest a broader understanding of concepts. Significant meanings and processes of conceptual change can also be detected in other non-textual semiotic spheres, such as in pictures and in sounds. In the case presented here, the audio-visual concept of *anger* precedes linguistic discourse in magazines and newspapers. Film magazines and newspapers started using *angry young man* and *anger* at the earliest in 1978, in order to identify a series of successful films produced since *Zanjeer*'s release in 1973 as a coherent genre. The example of the early *angry young man* films shows that the dynamics and process of popularization of *anger* and its conceptual change in this period can only be understood if the multisensory signifiers of the audio-visual discourse and the conceptual intermediality of *anger* are taken into account.

Following Koselleck, this article explores the audio-visual concept of the *angry young man*, specifically his *anger*, not only as an indicator but also as a factor of socio-cultural change.[7] In the first part of the article, I present an analysis of popular print media and selected film scenes. The sources demonstrate how the meaning of *anger* evolved, and its conceptual change occurred in dynamic intermediality. In the second part, I suggest a revision of some theoretical assumptions and methodological practices in order to enable an approach to modern mass media, specifically popular films, as sources for the study of histories of concepts. Understanding conceptual change and the meaning of anger within its semantic net and intermedial interplay does not only allow scholars to account for the multisensory quality of possible historical experiences among the young, urban Indian males in the 1970s, but also to comprehend how the dominant narrative of the history of urban popular culture in India became a history of emotions.

The Cinematic Concept of *Anger* in Indian *Angry Young Man Films*

Historical Context

India was proclaimed an independent, sovereign, democratic and secular republic on 26 January 1950. Since then, an atmosphere of optimism and hope prevailed in public political discourse.[8] The period between 1966 and

1991, however, was marked by intense political upheavals and a notion of crisis in India.[9] The first phase of Indira Gandhi's mandate as prime minister from 1966 to 1977 was marked by the fragmentation and decline of the ruling Congress Party, an economic crisis and the authoritarian governance during the time of National Emergency from June 1975 to March 1977.[10] Starting in the late 1960s, a noticeable rise in political violence and especially communal violence[11] was felt during the growing comprehensive 'crisis of governability'[12] in many regions of India. Poverty, unemployment and various strike movements fuelled the socio-political instability for almost two decades. In this atmosphere of crisis, ideological redirections, populism and radicalizations dominated the political debates. The idea of the ruling Congress Party as representative of India's 'unity in diversity', which Jawaharlal Nehru, Indira Gandhi's father and first prime minister of India, had promoted, seemed to have failed.[13] Radicalizing socialist forces created the strong notion of an 'elite-mass conflict', while market-orientated political factions argued that problems of poverty could only be solved though massive liberal economic reform.[14] The popular idea of India as a secular and moderate socialist democracy was being attacked as an ideology that was compromised too much by radicalized political forces from all directions. After the assassination of Indira Gandhi in 1984, the populist rhetoric of the major political factions cooled down gradually. The liberal economic reforms of 1991 marked the establishment of a shaky political stability on the national level, which remained challenged by communal conflicts. In such a period of destabilization and crisis, the historian can expect to detect a number of concepts in a dynamic process of contestation and change. Indeed, Hindi films reveal a new audio-visual concept of *virtuous anger* against injustice as a key concept in popular political and socio-cultural discourse.

Looking Back on Anger: The History of Indian Cinema as a History of Emotions

The history of long-term trends in popular Hindi cinema has been established in popular and scholarly writing to be a history of emotional trends. The narrative for a history of emotions of the Indian nation-state and its popular Hindi films after 1947 reads as follows: from independence to the mid-1960s, an emotional atmosphere of optimism and hope dominated public discourse in urban India.[15] Thus, the majority of popular films of this period construct their stories and images mainly around romance, love, trust and hope. *Anger*, as a bad emotion and uncontrollable passion, is either sanctioned through narrative logic, used to characterize villains or is simply absent. After 1966, at times of political and economic crisis, 'optimism and hope of the Nehru-era' vanished and soon 'action and violence dispelled love from the films'.[16] In the 1970s the *angry young man* film became the most popular genre and characterized 'Bollywood's angry years'.[17] Growing discontent, disillusionment, and resentment are the words used to describe the emotional atmosphere of the period until the middle of the 1980s.[18] In the 1990s, love and trust regained dominance in popular Indian films, which is usually explained against a background of massive economic and social changes in India, the opening of opportunities for social advancement and again, a general feeling of hope.

I next show how *anger* became recognized as a significant cinematic concept in popular film magazines and newspapers. I argue that *anger* became stereotyped in the process of defining the *angry young man* as the almost exclusive image of the actor Amitabh Bachchan and his films as a genre. It is this simplification of the cinematic concept that gave the *angry young man* and his *anger* the symbolic appeal to serve as a signifier for a period in popular narratives of history.

In popular film magazines and newspapers one can trace how the *angry young man* film became recognized as a coherent genre in the late 1970s. Central to this discourse is the screen image of the star Amitabh Bachchan, whose popularity exploded after his role as Vijay in *Zanjeer* in 1973. Interestingly, the contemporary reviews of the films generally included in the *angry young man* genre do not mention *anger* at all until 1978. It is possible that the hero's anger was considered so obvious as an emotional state and concept that the reviewers did not write about it. The reviews of *Zanjeer* for example, which is today popularly known as the first film of the *angry young man* genre, mainly talk about the 'violence of the kind of Hollywood [sic]'[19] and the outstanding performance of the young actor Amitabh Bachchan.[20] Interestingly, several readers around 1975 seem to bring up the idea of *anger* as an attribute of the genre in letters and readers' reviews by complaining that Amitabh Bachchan would repeatedly play the 'same role', such as 'the angry doctor of "Anand", angry policeman of "Zanjeer", angry executive of "Benaam", angry husband of "Abhiman" and angry smuggler of "Deewaar".[21] For the authors of the middle class targeting magazines *anger* seems to remain a concept belonging to non- popular foreign 'revolutionary' or 'leftist' cinema,[22] until several articles and reviews in 1978 and 1979 start stereotyping the *angry young man* as Amitabh Bachchan's screen image.[23] Tall and lanky and embodying new acting style somewhere between brooding and physical violence, he added a new masculinity to the history of Hindi film heroes, which stood in opposition to the image of the leading male star of 'the '60s, that era of light-hearted romance',[24] Rajesh Khanna. 'Amitabh is as tense, as Rajesh is loose, as cool as he is warm, as angry as Rajesh is easygoing', describes *Filmfare* author Sheela Naheem the oppositional male star images.[25]

In this discourse, Rajesh Khanna becomes the icon of love and romance, while the appearance of Amitabh Bachchan on screen is perceived as the embodiment of the concept of popular *anger*. By the early 1980s, *anger*, *angry*, and *angry young man* are no longer perceived as terms referring to a 'foreign concept'. The English words become frequently used in Indian vernacular languages and usually appear transcribed into the vernacular scripts.[26] The Hindi word *gussā* (anger) is very rare in texts referring to the respective genre films. The verbal concept *angry young man* does not have a vernacular equivalent at all.

The linguistic term *angry young man* has been adapted by film journalists from discourses around the British *new wave*. In this literary

Figure 12.2 A new rough masculinity: Amitabh Bachchan as Vijay in *Deewar*.

and cinematic movement of the 1950s, works in the style of John Osborne's play *Look Back in Anger*, which was made into a film for the first time in 1958, expressed the resentment of the young generation with the lifestyle and hypocrisy of the upper middle classes.[27] In the British context, the concept refers mainly to the young authors themselves but has also come to describe some of their literary and filmic characters. However, the audio-visual concept of the Indian *angry young man* is distinct and gains its connotations and meaning from the logic of the cultural and historic context of 1970s India. The popular Indian films have aesthetically nothing and thematically too little in common with the British *new wave* to call the *angry young man* a conceptual adaption of the British namesake. Granted, the *new wave* reached India as well and generated films that are considered classics of artistic filmmaking among intellectuals, but it never reached the mass audience that made the popular *angry young man* films huge hits at the box office.[28]

In present-day India, *angry young man* is mainly a nickname for the actor Amitabh Bachchan and his screen image, rather than a narrative concept. In the 1970s and 1980s there were only a few attempts to analyse the differences between characters Amitabh Bachchan played in his various films.[29] Violence and action remain the main connections to *anger* in its simplified semantic field. Articles about films with similar plots but with other lead actors do not refer to *anger*. Exceptional is an article titled 'Filmoṁ ke tīn pramukh eṁgrī yaṁgmain' (Cinema's three leading angry young men) in the Hindi film magazine *Madhuri*,[30] which discusses the actor personalities and screen images of Amitabh Bachchan, Shammi Kapoor and Naseeruddin Shah. Naseeruddin Shah, who plays in films with less popular but more social or artistic appeal, is also called 'the real angry young man' by the magazine *Filmfare* for playing the 'fiery revolutionary'[31] in films like *Albert Pinto ko gussa kyoon aata hai*[32] or *Aakrosh*.[33] His anger is 'real', becaused his films bear more resemblance to the aesthetic approach of 'realism' in British *new wave* (or the French *nouvelle vague*) films. The films that depict the struggles of the lower classes but target a middle-class audience are regarded as artistically superior to the mass-orientated *angry young man* films with Amitabh Bachchan.

Looking back upon the 1970s, the narrative that *anger* and action replaced the romantic films of the 1950s and 1960s became common. In the early 1980s, the reviewers used this narrative to announce the next emotional turn, namely 'the return of romance' and 'emotional films'.[34] They argued that the general emotional atmosphere in society has changed to love, hope and contentment, and that the audience had reached its saturation point for *anger* and action films. However, it took filmmakers and the audience almost another ten years to fulfil the reviewers' prophecy, with *angry young man* films remaining the leading genre until the end of the 1980s. Summing up the discourse in film magazines and newspapers, *anger, angry* and *the angry young man* are assigned iconically to the 1970s and labelled conceptual contradictions to the *romance* and *emotion* of the 1960s and 1980s.

The newspapers and magazines quoted above represent one type of media in which *anger* was popularized and stereotyped. Three important things have to be noted here. First, the discourse on *anger* and the *angry young man* begins to appear in the magazines with a considerable delay compared to the releases of films with *anger* at the core of their plot, which are only much later assigned to that genre. The delay in the written discourse, however, cannot be taken as an indicator that the audience did not recognize the filmic concept of *anger*. Second, the most popular film magazines at that time (*Filmfare, Star & Style*, and *Screen*) target mainly a middle-class audience and are written in English. The audience that turned the Hindi *angry young man* films into box office hits despite the bad reviews in the magazines is largely constituted by the lower-class male urban youth. Third, the use of the term *angry young man* and the word *anger* in the magazines does play a role in the processes of popularization and stereotyping of the concept, but the magazines cannot be said to instigate its politicization, which can be observed in the films. Therefore, to understand the popular concept of *anger* as it circulated among the so-called mass audiences of that time, one must turn to an analysis of the films themselves.

The Conceptual Change of Anger: Film Analysis

As an example of how the concept of *anger* gained and changed meanings in Hindi films in the 1970s and 1980s I present an analysis of the film *Coolie* (The Porter), released in 1983. To shed light on how the concept of *virtuous anger* became first popularized, politicized and finally stereotyped, I analyse the meaning of filmic messages of selected scenes by taking their references to earlier films of that genre and other popular knowledge of that time into account. *Coolie*, I argue, marks the stage of conceptual change, in which *anger* became stereotyped and simplified. The implications of that simplification cannot be understood without knowledge of the previous conceptual complexity. Therefore, I see the film as a popular text, whose meaning for the contemporary audience is not only constructed through the interplay of narrative logics, visuals, dialogues and sounds, but also through the layers of time and knowledge that have enabled and are constituting that specific film. I imagine my analysis of *Coolie* as an unravelling of the multiple threads in the semantic net of *anger* that spans the temporal layers of the filmic messages and across the different sign systems of the audiovisual mode.

A New Concept of Anger: From Personal Emotion to Social Virtue

In *Coolie*, the young man Iqbal has many reasons to be angry with the villain Zafar, who is a greedy businessman and corrupt politician. As a child, Iqbal witnesses how Zafar tries to kill his father and abducts his mother. Deprived of his family and home Iqbal grows up working on a railway platform. Over time, Iqbal develops strong anger against injustice and pledges his life to protect the coolies and to defend their rights. The enmity with Zafar becomes not only social cause after he and his business partner Mr. Puri try to cheat the coolies out of their hard-earned money, which was meant to build proper homes for this poor working-class community. The violence done to Iqbal's mother, the destruction of a happy family and home already refers to a section of the semantic net under exploration that weaves its threads through the history of filmic convention and meaning in connection with prevailing nationalist ideologies.

The mother is an established symbol for the Indian nation. Ever since the release of the iconic film *Mother India* (1957),[35] popular films take on that semantic relation. In particular, the genre of the *angry young man* films build their narrative logic of emotions and the moral framework of a national ideology on it. In *Zanjeer* (1973), *Deewaar* (1975),[36] and *Trishul* (1987),[37] to name just a few landmarks of the genre, the angry young hero enacts revenge against injustice or violence done to his mother, which turns out to be a social mission against problems that are addressed in the political discourse of the 1970s, such as poverty and corruption. Therefore, in *Coolie* the transformation of the personal emotions of traumatic pain and anger caused by the sufferings of the mother into a *virtuous anger* with a social cause is taken for granted and requires no further scenes that elaborate the hero's character. *Coolie* builds on earlier films that explicitly contest the idea of *anger* as a bad emotion that needs to be managed in order to create the new concept of *virtuous anger*, which enables understanding the *angry young man* as a hero. Another example from the film *Zanjeer* sheds light on the processes of conceptual change within the semantic net of *anger*:

Vijay's lover Mala is dreaming of marriage and of building a home to start a family. She asks Vijay to forget his anger, hatred and plans of revenge – in other words, to manage his bad emotions. But in his mental state he is unable to live up to the normative standards of a lover and family man. A suggestive shot of his face behind the iron bars of a window shows him to be a prisoner of an unhappy domestic existence. He delivers a monologue that explains the conflict between love and anger, family and corrupted society:

> We will surely build a beautiful home, and we will forget that the world in which this home is built is so ugly, that there is so much oppression, that there is so much injustice. (shouts) We will forget all this. Isn't that what you want?[38]

Mala then understands that Vijay will only be able to love 'properly' and fulfil the role of a good husband, if he can complete the mission of his *virtuous anger* and revenge against the villain, who has caused the deaths of several innocent victims throughout the film: 'I know that there is a volcano inside you. Until it erupts and the lava flows out of it, no lake of sweet water can form there.'[39]

After that dialogue, Vijay's facial expression loses its grimness, his earlier stone-like body gets into action and a soft background music suggest clearly that Mala's selfless support for his angry mission is the way out of the emotional conflict. But for that to occur, the prevailing common sense assumption – that *anger* is a bad emotion that is causing suffering to others – had to be challenged. Still, that meaning is not lost, as Vijay's anger causes suffering to Mala, but at the same time, his anger is the necessary emotional motivation for taking revenge on the villain, which will bring relief and happiness to the whole society and finally to Vijay and Mala's own home.

The emotional conflict exemplified above is typical for the *angry young man* films of the 1970s. Their main characters are psychologically very complex and shady heroes that are balancing between what is morally good and morally bad. In analytical terms, the early *angry young man* films show the contestation of anger as a bad emotion through the concept of *virtuous anger*. With the establishment and stereotyping of the concept of *virtuous anger* in the 1980s, the *angry young man* appears to be a rather simple, idealized working-class hero, like Iqbal in *Coolie*.

Anger and Socialism

It is not only the narrative logics of revenge against social injustice that fit the *virtuous anger* of Iqbal in *Coolie* into a popular socialist-communist ideology that pertains to the political discourses and ideological reorientations in India between the late 1960s and mid-1980s. Several visual, aural, and metaphorical signifiers work as additional ties between *anger* and *socialism* in the semantic net. One is the visual staging of the angry young Iqbal as a working class hero. The physical appearance of the actor Amitabh Bachchan, who played the lead character in Hindi films that are popularly assigned to that genre, are exploited to the highest degree. His already exceptionally tall and lanky body is captured by low-angle shots in the introduction and several fight scenes, adding to his impression of being a larger-than-life character. Stylish music marks the special moment of his entry and accompanies his heroic fights. Unlike the neat and clean middle-class characters of popular Hindi films in the 1960s, the *angry young man*'s dress and body language show him to be belonging to the masses, the common, poor, hard-working people. Therewith, Amitabh Bachchan and his screen image marked a change in the heroic masculinity of Hindi cinema following the popularization of action-oriented films and plots based on *anger* that frequently require the hero to engage in fistfights.

In all *angry young man* films, the hero carries out the major fights with his fists, not with a gun. Most fight scenes actually start with a scene of the hero disarming the villain. The first symbolizes the hero's reliance on his physical strength, ethics of fairness, belief in the justice of his cause, as well as refers to the symbolic meaning of the hand with reference to the working classes. The hero's introductory fistfight in *Coolie* between Iqbal and the son of a member of the railway advisory board ends with Iqbal declaring a strike against the mistreatment and disrespect against the coolies by the wealthy class and the authorities. He grabs a bright red cloth from another coolie's shoulder and flings it onto the ground like a flag. He tears the badge from his upper arm and lets it fall onto the cloth. Shouting *hartāl* (strike), he throws up his fist. The camera zooms onto his sweating face with a wide-open mouth that has blood dripping from the edge and red bloodshot eyes. The picture is frozen into a still and features the name of the star and title of the film – almost twenty-five minutes after its beginning. The stereotyped, iconic angry young man in *Coolie* as a socialist or communist working class hero is again made explicit when in a fight following the demand by the coolies for better housing facilities and the destruction of Mr. Puri's luxurious villa, Iqbal picks up a hammer and a sickle and crosses them in a gesture of attack.

In that context, *Coolie* also employs the metaphor of *bojh uthānā* (shouldering a load or burden), which as a visual metaphor has become a canonized concept, weaving its semantic threads through the history of the film genre. The hero as a child, the hero's mother or the young man and his colleagues are frequently shown lifting heavy objects, such as bricks at a construction site (*Deewaar*), sand and heavy stones in a quarry (*Trishul*) or luggage and goods at the dockyard and railway station (*Deewaar* and *Coolie*). These scenes function as an intense visual metaphor for the lower class having to carry the burden of the system and society, which is recalled in a foot-tapping song in *Coolie*. The refrain, 'Sarī duniyā ka bojh ham uthātemæ haimæ' (We are shouldering the load/burden of the whole world), is accompanied by pictures of physically disabled or malnourished coolies lifting heavy loads of luggage with a smile. The hero is dancing while shouldering heavy suitcases and singing about the necessity of recognizing the human dignity of the hard-working poor ('ham bhī insān haimæ' – 'we are human too'). While earlier *angry young man* films, especially *Deewaar*, thematised the possibility of an emotional conflict deriving from *anger*

Figure 12.3 Iqbal fights with hammer and sickle.

against the gods and one's bad fate for being poor and exploited, *Coolie* uses the metaphor of *bojh uthānā* in favour of conveying a stereotyped *anger* against injustice and working class romanticism. The coolies' *anger* and accusations are not against a divinity or fate, but targeting the injustice by what is perceived as the inefficient system, the corrupt authorities and the evil rich. The sympathy for the poor, honest and hard-working is indeed semantically tied to religious sentiments: In the same song, the coolies are shown taking their rare breaks for collectively performing prayers to Allah and celebrating a procession for the Hindu deity Ganesha. Accordingly, the *anger* of Iqbal does not only gain its virtuousness through his social commitment for the secular community, but also through divine accordance and support.

Virtuous Anger as a Religious Concept

Iqbal is always accompanied by his pet falcon Allah Rakha, whose name literally means 'protected by god'. Whenever the evil characters are about to prevail over the good, the bird executes a divine intervention. It also passes assignments for action to the hero. The bird and its symbolic role are introduced in the film accompanied by a musical leitmotif. The fanfare and dramatically vivid string theme of high recognition value accompany the scenes throughout the film, in which justified and *virtuous anger* is applied by either Allah Rakha or Iqbal. The music is used to mark the conceptual meaning and significance of the respective scenes. It signifies the difference between moments of violent justice and ordinary fight scenes that serve to entertain and are therefore usually accompanied by light rhythmic music and smashing sounds that support the stunt choreography.

Further, Iqbal wears the badge number 786, signifying *Bismillah* (in the name of Allah) in Islamic numerology. Iqbal is not the first *angry young man* to wear this badge number. It evokes the memory of Vijay in *Deewaar*, whose badge number as a dockyard coolie is 786 as well. Vijay's senior colleague is a Muslim and explains that 786 contains 'divine power equal to that of "Om" for the Hindus'. The Hindu Vijay, who has just renounced his trust into the Hindu gods, never forgets his divine talisman on the way to a fight or other dangerous undertaking. In the course of the film, the badge saves him twice from being shot and gets lost just before he is fatally shot. The badge 786 was used frequently in Indian *angry young man* films and, as Amitabh Bachchan said in a recent interview, it became 'a nationwide phenomena' of popular knowledge and belief.[40]

Figure 12.4 Divine anger: A sacred cloth covers Iqbal's chest in the final fight.

In the final fight scene in *Coolie*, which is staged in the Haji Ali Mosque in Mumbai, neither Allah Rakha nor the badge 786 are present to support Iqbal. It is the prayer of his mother that causes a strong wind to blow the red and green cloth with the half moon and star that covered the shrine onto Iqbal's chest. While the hero chases the villain, three bullets hit Iqbal's chest. Wrapped in the sacred cloth and shouting prayers, Iqbal remains strong in the fight until he finally manages to carry out his angry (signified by the iconic facial expression), virtuous (signified by his mother's presence and narrative logic) and divine revenge by throwing Zafar from the minaret. He then breaks down in his mother's arms. The following sequence shows the coolies and other people from the four major religious communities in India – Hindus, Christians, Sikhs and Muslims – offering prayers for Iqbal's recovery. Prayer by prayer, the bullets are removed from his body. In the end, a healed hero thanks the masses for the prayers that saved his life.[41]

In addition to invoking divine support for Iqbal's anger, the religious symbolism in the film refers the audience to the popular ideology of secularism. Secularism here is the idea of a brotherhood between the different religions and stands as a major ideological pillar of national ideology, for example as propagated by the Congress Party. The concept became increasingly challenged in that period by radicalized forces (especially

Hindu nationalists) on political grounds and lost its credibility against the background of increasing communal violence.[42] One significant attempt to support a popular secularism is the characterization of the *angry young man* Iqbal (meaning 'the blessed') as a Muslim. In the previous landmarks of that genre (*Zanjeer, Deewaar, Trishul*) the hero was always a Hindu named Vijay (meaning 'the victorious'). Employing the audiences' previous viewing experience and knowledge of built-up genre conventions, this religious characterization creates a meaningful difference. Moreover, the filmic message of secularism itself is typical for that genre. The visual religious references range from Mary and Jesus as a parallel to a self-sacrificing hero and his mother, to Allah as the protector of the virtuous and faithful fighters, to the Hindu gods Shiva and Durga as traditional patrons of just anger and divine revenge.[43]

Additional threads connecting the concepts of *anger, secularism* and the *Indian nation* are created in *Coolie* by the colour design. The colours of the Indian tricolour are regardless of their actual symbolic meaning also popularly interpreted to symbolize the religions: deep saffron for Hinduism, white for Christianity and green for Islam. Various scenes of the film predominantly feature these colours in the costumes or set designs, with the peculiarity that deep saffron is replaced by intense red.

The Angry Man 'Sees Red' for the Indian Nation

The colour red ties together several concepts within the semantic net of anger in the visual language of popular Hindi cinema. As mentioned above, in the colour design of *Coolie*, red replaces saffron in the Indian tricolour. In scenes with reference to Hindu rituals, sacred vermillion powder is used extensively. Red is the colour of the traditional Indian long shirts that the coolies wear as uniforms. The uniforms visually define the community and provide a link to the symbolic colour for socialism or communism. Conversely, the rich and corrupted villains are dressed in 'cold' colours, such as grey, light blue or white. Their costumes are 'Western' clothes, marking the villains 'un-Indian' in their life-style, and therefore excluding them ideologically from the nation. The colour red also refers to the popular knowledge about the physical state of *anger*. In certain scenes the hero has red bloodshot eyes. His body is shown as sweating from inner heat, sometimes even before the fight. Popular metaphors compare the physical state of *anger* with an inner fire or the *angry man* – as mentioned in a scene from *Zanjeer* – with a volcano. In *Trishul*, the visuals compare Vijay to exploding dynamite. Following up the audio-visual eruption or explosion of *virtuous anger* in the final fight scene and climax of an *angry young man* film, the mise-en-scène never lacks a generous display of bright red blood. It adds to the dramatic and symbolic effect of the screenplay. In *Coolie*, for example, Iqbal is writing an Arabic numeral, which designates the number 786 and the word *Bismillah* (in the name of God), with his own blood on a white pillar of the minaret while he assumes to be dying in his mother's lap. The display or mentioning of blood is also used to refer to family relations, especially between the mother (being allegorically tied to the concept of nation) and the son (as the ideal patriot and citizen). Iqbal's abducted mother, who is subjected to electroshocks by Zafar so that she is not able to recognize her own son, remembers her true identity, family and home only after seeing the bright red blood from a wound on her forehead, caused by a Qur'an falling from a rack in Iqbal's house.

As Iqbal's character in *Coolie* lacks the psychological complexity of the previous angry lead characters, the film can be seen as a landmark in the creation of the stereotyped iconic figure of the *angry young man* as a popular national hero. In the film, Iqbal is encouraged by the coolies to enter the political arena and form a socialist party against Zafar's political ambitions. In 1984 – one year after the release of *Coolie* – the actor Amitabh Bachchan entered politics and became a member of the Indian parliament.

The stereotyped and iconic but highly referential image of the *angry young man* in *Coolie* marks a significant point in the development of the concept of *anger*. The film solidifies the concept of *virtuous anger* with symbolic images that have a popular appeal. At the same time the *angry young man* and *anger* become verbalized and frequently used concepts in memory discourse in the1970s in magazines and newspapers. The process of conceptual contestation and change of *anger* in popular films involved a disputation and modification of the popular national ideology. Films like *Zanjeer, Deewaar* and *Trishul* contested social norms and values by judging some activities of the *angry young man* as virtuous and patriotic according to the logic of the moral film codes, even though they were in fact crimes according to Indian law. The *angry young men* take the law into their own hands. Their tactics of violence, deceit and rudeness become justified when the official institutions and ruling classes are portrayed as inefficient in protecting the society from harm, crime, and immoral actions. This *anger* against injustice due to corruption and inefficiency of governmental institutions pertains to the experience of the urban poor in 1970s India and can be argued to serve a kind of anger management and emotional integration through conceptual change.

Before the 1970s, anger in the popular public sphere had been conceptualized as a bad emotion – an uncontrollable passion that leads its bearers to commit inexcusable crimes against law and morality. In accordance with popular religious and ideological discourse of nonviolence, narratives of popular films suggested that anger had to be transformed, suppressed or 'cooled' in order to make its bearer a good member of Indian society. Within the prevailing atmosphere of rising discontent and anger among the lower classes and urban youth in the 1970s, a continuation of that conceptualization would have implicitly degraded the masses (and paying audiences) to immoral subjects according to the cinematic national ideology. Therefore, the genre of immensely popular *angry young man* films became a space for the gradual establishment of the new concept of *virtuous anger* – a concept with the potential to emotionally reintegrate the disappointed and dispelled masses into a popular national ideology and thereby overcoming anger in favour of contentment. The film magazines added to this cinematic dynamic by further simplifying the concept of *anger* through the linguification, or translation, of the audio-visual concept into language, and the retrospective view from the 1980s onto the 1970s. Characterizing the 1970s as a period of *anger* or identifying *anger* as a concept that signifies social, political, and cultural essence of this time period juxtaposes the angry past against a contented present. Declaring *anger* as outdated according to the emotional trend evokes, stabilizes and reconfirms the end of the crisis. This feel-good mood is finally associated with the new romantic films that emerged parallel to the economic and political developments from the mid of the 1980s on that marked a still tottery political stability after almost twenty years of crisis, and political, economic, social and emotional upheaval.

Multimedia and Conceptual History

The analysis above has shown that popular cinema is an important agent of conceptual change in the political history of *anger* in postcolonial India. The argument for the conceptualization of *virtuous anger* as an audio-visual concept that preceded the linguification of *anger* in the textual sources poses theoretical challenges to some canonized assumptions and methods in the scholarship of conceptual history. I address these challenges by advocating the use of multiple media sources in conceptual history.

From the viewpoint of media studies and contemporary history, conceptual history's preference for written text as opposed to visual and sonic sources seems rather anachronistic. The public sphere and political communication in the twentieth and twenty-first century have been extensively shaped through various forms of modern mass media – and so are concepts. In that context, the study of conceptual meaning and function must take into account the specific modes of mediality through which concepts are shaped in communication. Moving from the established methodology of text analysis toward media analysis, a study of concepts in contemporary history has to acknowledge image and sound as constituents of conceptual meaning. Detaching linguistic components from their larger medial contexts, for example isolating dialogue from the accompanying pictures and sounds, could in many cases distort meaning and sometimes even make the identification of any meaning impossible.[44]

In addition, modern mass media – such as cinema, radio, television and the various forms of digital new media – extends the reach of conceptual history beyond the rarefied scholarly texts that the discipline had favoured in its initial projects, a focus criticized in the German discourse as *Höhenkamm* or *Gipfelwanderungen*.[45] But the argument for increasing the inclusion of non-linguistic sources into conceptual history also holds for the study of earlier periods: Concepts have always been applied in various media, and almost every possible socio-political experience, if understood as located in situations of communication, is multisensory.

Although the *sonic turn* has left no marks in conceptual history yet,[46] the argument for the significance of pictures for the study of categories like historical experience and memory has been made by various scholars in the course of the *pictorial turn*.[47] What is surprising is that pictorial sources have remained underutilized in the practice of conceptual history. Next, I summarize some examples and key arguments for the inclusion of visuals into the study of conceptual history and historical semantics, which leads me to argue for the consideration of conceptual intermediality. I also point out two linked problematic aspects in the practices of interpreting pictures with regard to concepts thus far. The first problem is the approach of reading pictures as 'visual representations' of pre-existing concepts. If pictures are understood as mere representations, they could only function as indicators, never as factors. I argue that Koselleck's claim on linguistic concepts functioning as indicators and factors of historical change also applies to concepts in the visual sphere. The second problem is the practice of justifying the inclusion of pictures by locating emotional and sensual aspects of concepts exclusively in the visual sphere and thereby implying a functional opposition between 'rational' language and 'emotional' image. I argue for an understanding of emotion and reason as inseparable constituents of conceptual meaning in multimedia based communication situations.

Reinhart Koselleck provided us with intriguing examples for studying history through visual sources.[48] But his language-centred *Begriffsgeschichte* and the writings in the name of a 'political iconology',[49] especially his later publications on war memorials and monuments,[50] are usually perceived as different approaches to history. However, while reading his works that deal with pictures and monuments, one cannot deny that they are contributing to an understanding of historicized concepts. For example, Koselleck framed his essay on the Early Modern 'Future Past' with an analysis of the concept of time in the picture *The Battle of Alexander at Issus* by Albrecht Altdorfer.[51] His introduction to the anthology *Der politische Totenkult* (Cult of the dead) suggests that studying monuments enriches the historical understanding of concepts such as *nation, democracy, death* and *the unknown soldier,* and that the changing representations of these concepts are highly relevant to understanding historical experiences and practices of memory.[52] That the English term *concept* is semantically less bound to language than the German word *Begriff* invites inclusion of what Koselleck called 'political iconography' into conceptual history. Moreover, Hubert Locher and Faustino Oncina Coves argue that Koselleck had thought of a 'comprehensive conceptual history' (*umfassende Begriffsgeschichte*). That means an approach that 'needs to account not only for texts, but also for collective actions and images, culminating in a history of symbols'.[53] In other words, Koselleck understood pictures as profoundly shaping thought and memory and therefore considered the 'ideational content of pictures', especially in modernity, as 'political factors' that are closely bound to 'changing conditions of living and spaces of experiences in the respective time and place'.[54]

Opposition to conceptual history's 'ignorance' of pictorial sources has also occurred in the realm of 'political iconography'.[55] For example, Rolf Reichardt, the most adamant advocate for the inclusion of pictures into conceptual history, has argued convincingly that it was not only in modern times of global mass media that 'public communication and collective symbols united in a kind of multimedia process in which texts, pictures and songs frequently worked together'.[56] But as Bettina Brandt has remarked, the relationship between the scholarship of historical semantics and historical visual studies (*historische Bildwissenschaft*) is still rather imbalanced in practice. The value of visuals for the study of historical semantics has been widely recognized,[57] but there have been few attempts to theorize possible ways for image analysis to contribute to conceptual history.[58]

One major reason for this imbalance lies in the approach of reading pictures as representations of pre-existing linguistic concepts. The assumed 'sisterhood of word and image'[59] in constituting the meaning of concepts is still characterized through a subordination of the visual. For example, in his analysis of 'conceptual paintings' from seventeenth-century Dutch art Eddy de Jongh argues that from most pictures no definite meaning could be extrapolated – ambiguity seems to be the nature of the visual sphere. But those visual representations that through their symbolic or iconic quality can be identified as 'painted words and expressions', can be included in the historical semantic structure and become unambiguous.[60] De Jongh's argument implies the assumption that pictures cannot contribute self-contained meanings to historical semantics. The meanings of pictures seem dependent on references to linguistic concepts, while the apparently reasonable language can be taken for granted and interpreted independently. If one follows such argument, selected images only acquire a value in that discipline if they are representing pre-existing concepts; the gains made by the inclusion of pictorial sources into conceptual history seem low compared to the amount of work and risk of fuzziness they can cause in a field known for its theoretical strength and rigorous methodology (*Methodenstrenge*).

It is therefore not a surprise that conceptual historians are either reluctant to take pictures into account at all or tend to carefully select pictorial sources that function as 'fine representations of concepts which were of central importance to the intellectual history'[61] as a kind of useful 'visual supplementation'.[62] The arguments revolve around the representational, iconic, and symbolic function of images. As a result, the *Eigenkraft*, the specific or self-contained meaning of pictures, the existence of visually constituted concepts and their potential to lead to reinterpretations or challenge textual sources, are neglected.[63] Two observations made by Koselleck on political iconology to support this claim. First, in processes of perception, experience and memory pictures can precede words. In that case, it is not the picture that represents a linguistic concept, but the word that represents the visual concept. My discussion of *anger* in popular Hindi cinema and print media has shown that this not only pertains to individual thought processes, but also to larger public discourse. Second, he observes an 'emancipation of the picture from the word' in modernity. The 'wordless picture' (*das wortlose Bild*), its independent meaning, its sense and the specificity of its aesthetic effects, has been increasingly used in political communication.[64] Instead of treating pictorial sources as supplements to textual sources, the potential meaning of their *Eigensinn* (their self-contained significations) should be considered in the analysis of conceptual meaning and change. However, acknowledging the specificities of textual and visual sources should not imply that both should be studied separately or that exclusive, separate functions can be assigned to either the textual or the visual sphere.

Reichardt observes that pictures 'increased the social effectiveness of the concepts by symbolizing, emotionalizing and popularizing them'.[65] He repeatedly emphasizes the simplification of concepts down to their core meanings and a 'sensualisation' (*Versinnlichung*) through emotionalisation as a significant and specific agency of pictures in the process of enabling 'collective experience' among the common people.[66] By giving abstract concepts recognizable shapes, he argues, pictures generally contribute a great deal to the popularization of concepts by increasing their 'appellative potential' (*appellative Potenz*).[67] Even though distinct functions can be convincingly assigned to pictures in certain cases, and Reichardt's analysis of certain pictorial sources are most convincing, they should not be generalized. Such attribution creates the distinction between more so-called hard-wired and complex functions of logical reason and meaning, on the one hand, and more so-called soft and simple cultural functions of 'emotionalisation' or 'sensualisation', on the other hand, locating the former in the linguistic sphere and the latter in the visual sphere. This is despite Reichardt remarks that not only the meanings of pictures, but also that of 'central key concepts' always remain ambivalent or ambiguous.[68] This binaristic separation through exclusively assigned functions is unfortunately common sense among many scholars. For example, Brandt justifies the importance of studying pictures with the argument that they form the cultural space for 'sensual perceptions, feelings and memories' ('sinnliche Wahrnehmung, Gefühle und Erinnerungen') and in her analysis of visual representations of politics, pictures are highlighted as the main agent of the emotionalisation.[69] Koselleck too, in his recent political iconography work emphasized the *politische Sinnlichkeit* (the political sensuality) of pictures.[70]

The example of the conceptual change of *anger* in popular Hindi films as analysed in this article refutes the understanding of different sign systems having a priori fixed functions in the process of conveying meaning.

The most obvious argument is that the filmic message and meaning is constituted through the interaction of pictures, sounds, dialogs and script in the audio-visual mode. A more complex argument concerns the conceptual intermediality of *anger*: The initial significant meaning of the *angry young man's anger* derives from the audio-visual and narrative logic of the popular films in the 1970s. The simplification of the complex audio-visual concept is initiated by its translation into language in magazines and newspapers, starting in 1978. The simplification of *anger* and the stereotypification of the *angry young man* in the linguistic discourse of the 1980s enable the stereotypical character in *Coolie* and the rather simple and symbolic audio-visual presentation of his emotional constitution. Hence, the meaning of *anger* and the processes of its conceptual change are produced through a dynamic intermediality and in the intersection of the semiotic spheres.

Conclusion and Further Challenges

For a prolific use of modern mass media in conceptual history two assumptions have to be overcome. First, that language is the exclusive medium of negotiating conceptual meaning. Some concepts acquire meanings of primary relevance through their application beyond language, for example in pictures and sounds. Second, that emotion and reason are separate spheres that are located in distinct sign systems, namely pictures and language. Emotions can be understood as cultural concepts of political relevance. The analysis in the first part of this article has exemplified that *anger* in popular Hindi films of the 1970s and 1980s is tied to concepts of *nation, socialism* and *secularism*. Through these ties the concepts determine each other's meanings. Pairing rather than polarizing emotion and reason discloses meaningful discursive overlaps and semantic ties in the history of concepts, such as the identification of *virtuous anger* as an audio-visual key concept in the framework of a popular national ideology in India in the 1970s and 1980s. Instead of assuming a concept's meaning and change exclusively in the linguistic sphere of written texts I have emphasized the importance of considering conceptual intermediality. The concepts of *anger* and the *angry young man* in magazines and newspapers gained their meaning only with reference to the visuals and narratives from the popular movies, while the simplification and stereotyping of the cinematic concept was initiated by its linguification in the print media.

The semiotic complexity of audio-visual media and the amount of relevant information retrieved through media analysis pose further practical and theoretical challenges. Project resources need to be balanced between thorough analysis of singular sources and the research on sequenced material that represents a certain period. Therefore, a more elaborate theoretical basis and methodological toolbox would be desirable. To meet the specific challenges that popular films pose to conceptual historians writings from film semiotics might offer intriguing ideas for dealing with the generation of meaning in the complex audio-visual mode.[71] The understanding of film as a language holds the potential to bring theoretical ideas from film semiotics and conceptual history together.[72]

A convenient starting point for the development of suitable methodologies might be the understanding of conceptual meaning as a multidimensional semantic net, the threads of which are woven through different media, sign systems, discourses and temporal layers of meaning.[73] In this semantic net, the visual and sonic entities are not subordinate to the linguistic ones. They are assumed to have equal potential in constituting concepts that shape the experience and memory of a certain event or period in history. The *angry young man* films served as an emotional integration for the masses into the Indian nation and shaped the experience and memory of the 1970s as an era of *anger*.

Notes

1   *Zanjeer* (The Chain), directed by Prakash Mehra (1973; Mumbai, India: Prakash Mehra Productions, Eros Entertainment, 2007), DVD. (Film titles are given according to their official release names, using Latin alphabet.) see <www.historyofconcepts.org/anger>.

2   The transliterations of film dialogues, concepts, and texts that are originally in Hindi follow the system adapted by Ronald Stuart McGregor, *Oxford Hindi-English Dictionary* (Oxford/Delhi: Oxford University Press, 1993).

3   The English *anger* and *angry young man* are the common linguistic signifiers for the audio-visual concepts in this article. The phrase *angry young man* has no vernacular equivalent. The Hindi word *gussā* (anger) is rare in this context.

4   *Coolie* (The Porter), directed by Manmohan Desai (1983; Mumbai, Delhi, India: M.K.D. Films and Aasia Films Pvt. Ltd., Time N Tune Delhi, 2005), DVD.

5   See, for example, Ashis Nandy, 'Indian Popular Cinema as a Slum's Eye
      View of Politics', in idem (ed.), *The Secret Politics of our Desires: Innocence,
      Culpability and Indian Popular Cinema* (New Delhi: Oxford University
      Press, 1998); Madhava Prasad, *Ideology of the Hindi Film: A Historical
      Construction* (New Delhi: Oxford University Press, 1998).

6   Sudipta Kaviraj, 'Indira Gandhi and Indian Politics', *Economic and
      Political Weekly*, 21/38 and 39 (20–27 September 1986); see the chapter
      on democracy between 1967 and 1984 in Sunil Khilnani, *The Idea of India*
      (New Delhi: Penguin, 2004), 42–55; see also Ramchandra Guha, *India
      after Gandhi* (London: Macmillan, 2007), 416ff.

7   Reinhart Koselleck, *Vergangene Zukunft: Zur Semantik geschichtlicher
      Zeiten* (Frankfurt am Main: Suhrkamp, 1979), 120, English: idem, *Futures
      Past: On the Semantics of Historical Time* (New York: Columbia University
      Press, 2004).

8   Atul Kohli, *Democracy and Discontent. India's Growing Crisis of
      Governability* (Cambridge: Cambridge University Press, 1990), 4. The
      propagation of good emotions can also be interpreted as an emotional
      regime in order to drown the 'trauma of partition' of India and Pakistan in
      1947.

9   For the various notions of experiencing the 1970s as crisis, see for example
      Rajni Kothari, *State Against Democracy* (Delhi: Ajanta Publications, 1988),
      98: 'For some it is basically a crisis of economic performance, for others, a
      crisis of leadership, for still others, a crisis of character.'

10   Yogendra K. Malik and Dhirenda K. Vajpeyi (eds), *India: The Years
      of Indira Gandhi*, International Studies in Sociology and Social
      Anthropology Series, vol. 47 (Leiden: Brill, 1988).

11   Guha (2007), 431.

12   Kohli (1990).

13   On Nehru's idea of India as an integrative nation based on the peaceful
      coexistence of differences, see Khilnani (2004).

14   Guha (2007), 385ff.; Kohli (1990), 297–300.

15   Kohli (1990), 4.

16   Rekha Kamath Rajan, 'Popularisierungsstrategien: Die Bombay-
      Filmindustrie und Hollywood' (Strategies of Popularization: The Bombay
      Film Industry and Hollywood), in Gereon Blaseio, Hedwig Pompe and
      Jens Ruchatz (eds), *Popularisierung und Popularität* (Popularization and
      Popularity) (Cologne: DuMont, 2005), 283.

17   Nikhat Kazmi, *Ire in the Soul: Bollywood's Angry Years* (New Delhi: Harper
      Collins, 1996).

18   Guha (2007), 432–3.

19   'Zanjeer: Amitabh Stars in Languishing Role', *Pune Herald* (29 May
      1973).

20 'Zanjeer', *Screen* 22/37 (25 May 1973), 4; S. J. Banaji, 'Zanjeer: Busted Copper', *Filmfare*, 22/11, 35.

21 Avinash Garg, 'Reader's Letter: Same Angry Role', *Filmfare*, 24/5 (7 March 1975).

22 Bikram Singh, 'Mockery Is More Effective Than Anger', *Filmfare*, 23/2 (22 March 1974); Bharat Dogra, 'Look Back in Anger at the Oppressors', *Filmfare*, 26/25 (9 December 1977), 12–13.

23 See, for example, 'Trishul: Gorgeous Dress for Formula Theme', *Times of India* (14 May 1978); Shekar Hattangadi, 'Limits to Anger: Amitabh Bachchan and the Mechanics of Anger', *Filmfare*, 27/20 (16 November 1978); R. Raja Rao, 'The Angry Amitabh, a Dangerous Infection?', *Star & Style*, 28/23 (16 November 1979), 50–1.

24 Sucharitaa Saha, 'Return of Romance, Heart to Heart', *Filmfare*, 39/7 (1 July 1990).

25 Sheela Naheem, 'Amitabh Bachchan: Violence without Apology', *Filmfare*, 29/3 (1 February 1980): 17ff.

26 For the vernacular use of the terms, see the Amitabh-cartoon on anger in the Hindi film magazine *Madhuri* (25 March 1977), 32, or the article 'Apnā zāmāna apnā raṁg. Filmoṁ ke tīn pramukh eṁgrī yaṁgmain' (Our time/world, our color/style: Cinema's three leading angry young men), *Madhuri* (8 February 1980), 7–8.

27 *Look Back in Anger*, directed by Tony Richardson (1958; UK: MGM Home Entertainment 2001), DVD.

28 For information on the influence of the *new wave* on Indian arthouse and documentary cinema see Aruna Vasudev, *The New Indian Cinema* (Delhi: Macmillan India, 1986).

29 A rare exception is Naheem (1980).

30 *Madhuri* (1980).

31 'The Real Angry Young Man', *Star & Style*, 30/6 (20 March 1981).

32 *Albert Pinto ko gussa kyon aata hai* (What makes Albert Pinto angry?), directed by Saeed Akhtar Mirza (1980; Delhi, India: NFDC) FTII film database.

33 *Aakrosh* (Cry of the wounded), directed by Govind Nihalani (1980; Delhi, India: NFDC) FTII film database.

34 Sucharitaa Saha, 'Return of Romance', *Filmfare*, 39/7 (1 July 1990), 28–34.

35 *Mother India*, directed by Mehboob Khan (1957; New Delhi, India: Mehboob Productions, Moser Baer, 2008), DVD.

36 *Deewaar* (The wall), directed by Yash Chopra (1975; Mumbai, India: Trimurti Films, Eros Entertainment, 2007), DVD.

37 *Trishul* (Trident), directed by Yash Chopra (1987; Mumbai, India: Trimurti Films, Eros Entertainment, 2008), DVD.

38 'Ham zarūr ek khubsūrat ghar banāeṁge aur ham bhūl jāeṁge ki yah
ghar jis duniyā meṁ banā hai vah kitnī badsūrat hai, vahāṁ kitnī zulm
hai, kitnī beinsāfi hai. Ham yah sab bhūl jāeṁge. Yah chāhtī ho na tum?'
Translation by the author.

39 'Maiṁ jāntī huṁ tumhāre aṁdar ek jvālāmukhī hai. Jab tak vah pategā
nahiṁ, lāvā nikhlegā nahiṁ, vahāṁ mīthī pānī ke jhīl ban nahīṁ saktī.'

40 'Coolie, Deewaar, Zanjeer, Agneepath – Amitabh Bachchan, Down the
Memory Lane', video, interview with Amitabh Bachchan by Faridoon for
Bollywoodhungama, <http://www.youtube.com/watch?v=g3TQFR8LvpI>
accessed 2 June 2015.

41 The scene blurs fiction and reality in a special way. During the shooting
of the film the actor Amitabh Bachchan was seriously injured. Being the
major super star of Hindi cinema at that time, his fans offered prayers
for his recovery publicly. The original script was changed from Iqbal's
death to his recovery, so that the actor could thank his fans for their
support.

42 See the chapter on Indian secularism in Sumit Ganguly and Rahul
Mukherki, India Since 1980 (Cambridge: Cambridge University Press,
2011), 141–66.

43 References to Sikhism are very rare and as yet I have not come across any
reference to other significant religions in India, such as Buddhism.

44 See the critique of German media linguist Werner Holly on the sectioning
of multimedia for the sake of methodology and his example of the
mediation of meaning through interlocking words and pictures. Werner
Holly, 'Der Wort-Bild-Reißverschluss: Über die performative Dynamik
der audiovisuellen Transkriptivität' (The Word-Visual-Zip: On the
performative dynamic of audio-visual transcriptivity), in Helmut Feilke
and Angelika Linke (eds), Oberfläche und Performanz (Surface and
performance) (Tübingen: Niemeyer, 2009), 389–406.

45 See Rolf Reichardt, 'Einleitung, III – Für eine sozialhistorische Semantik
als Mittelweg zwischen "Lexikometrie" und "Begriffsgeschichte"' (For
socio-historical semantics as middle course between 'Lexicometry' and
'Conceptual History'), in Eberhard Schmitt (ed.), Handbuch politisch-
sozialer Grundbegriffe in Frankreich, 1680–1820 (Handbook of political
and social key concepts in France) (Munich: Oldenbourg, 1985),
22–47, [Note: extract included in Rolf Reichardt, 'For a socio-historical
semantics as a middle course between "lexicometry" and "conceptual
history"' (chapter three in this volume)]; Dietrich Busse, Historische
Semantik, Sprache und Geschichte (Historical semantics, language and
history) (Stuttgart: Klett-Cotta, 1987), 58. For a secondary discourse
on the 'excursions of the heights' and focus on 'highflying literature'
see Faustino Oncina Coves, 'Memory, Iconology and Modernity: A

Challenge for Conceptual History', in Javier Fernández Sebastián (ed.), *Political Concepts and Time* (Santander: Cantabria University Press, 2011), 304, fn. 4.

46   Albrecht Riethmüller has analysed the semantic field of the concepts of sound in German philosophical and scholarly discourses, albeit without referring to any sonic sources or transcriptions of sounds, such as notations of music. Albrecht Riethmüller, 'Ton alias Klang. Musikalische Elementarterminologie zwischen den Disziplinen' (Tone, also known as sound: elementary terminology for music between the disciplines), in Gunter Scholtz (ed.), *Die Interdisziplinarität der Begriffsgeschichte* (The inderdisciplinarity of conceptual history) (Hamburg: Meiner, 2000), 73–84.

47   See, for example Rolf Reichardt, 'Historical Semantics and Political Iconography: The Case of the Game of the French Revolution (1791/92)', in Iain Hampsher-Monk, Karin Tilmans and Frank van Vree (eds), *History of Concepts: Comparative Perspectives* (Amsterdam: Amsterdam University Press, 1998), 191–226; Bettina Brandt, 'Politik im Bild? Überlegungen zum Verhältnis von Begriff und Bild' (Politics in the picture? Thoughts about the relationship of concepts and pictures), in Willibald Steinmetz (ed.), *Politik: Situationen eines Wortgebrauchs* (Frankfurt am Main: Campus, 2007), 41–74.

48   On Koselleck's engagement with visual sources as 'political aesthetics', 'visual semiotics' or 'political iconology', see Coves (2011), 305–44.

49   Hubert Locher recently showed that Koselleck's theoretical considerations on a historical program of 'political iconology' can be traced back to unpublished texts by Koselleck as early as 1963. Hubert Locher, 'Denken in Bildern: Reinhart Kosellecks Programm *Zur politischen Ikonologie*' (Thinking in pictures: Reinhart Koselleck's program of political iconology), *Zeitschrift für Ideengeschichte*, 3/4 (Munich: C. H. Beck, 2009), 81–96.

50   This is mainly referring to Koselleck's works on war memorials; for example Reinhart Koselleck, *Zur politischen Ikonologie des gewaltsamen Todes: Ein deutsch-französischer Vergleich* (On the political iconology of violent death: A German-French comparison) (Basel: Schwabe, 1998); idem, 'Kriegerdenkmale als Identitätsstiftungen der Überlebenden' (War memorials: identity formations of the survivors), in Odo Marquardt and Karlheinz Stierle (eds), *Identität* (Munich: Fink, 1979), 255–76.

51   Koselleck, 'Vergangene Zukunft der frühen Neuzeit', in idem (1979b), 17–37.

52   Reinhart Koselleck, 'Einleitung', in Michael Jeismann (ed.), *Der politische Totenkult: Kriegerdenkmäler in der Moderne* (Cult of the dead: war memorials in modernity) (Munich: Fink, 1994), 9–20.

53 Coves (2011), 307.

54 Locher (2009), 94.

55 Brandt (2007), 43.

56 Reichardt (1998), 224.

57 For an overview, see Martin van Gelderen, 'Between Cambridge and
    Heidelberg: Concepts, Languages and Images in Intellectual History',
    in Hampsher-Monk, Tilmans and van Vree (1998), 227–38. Similar to
    Koselleck's *Grundbegriffe* (key concepts) are Aby Warburg's *Schlagbilder*
    that function as key images of the political everyday communication. See
    Michael Diers, *Schlagbilder, Zur politischen Ikonographie der Gegenwart*
    (Key images, on the political iconography of the present) (Frankfurt am
    Main: Fischer, 1997).

58 Brandt (2007).

59 Eddy de Jongh, 'Painted Words in Dutch Art of the Seventeenth Century',
    in Hampsher-Monk, Tilmans and van Vree (1998), 167–89, especially 174.

60 Ibid., 172–3.

61 Van Gelderen (1998), 227. The author interprets late sixteenth-century
    glass windows in churches in Wassenaar and Gouda as representations
    of political concepts that 'dominated the political literature of the Dutch
    Revolution.'

62 Brandt (2007), 44, 50.

63 On the 'self-contained potency of words' to convey meaning (*Eigenkraft
    der Worte*) see Koselleck (1979b), 107; on the potency of 'self-contained
    signification in visuals' (*Eigensinn des Bildes*) see Rolf Reichardt, 'Bild- und
    Mediengeschichte' (History of pictures and media), in Joachim Eibach and
    Günther Lottes, (eds), *Kompass der Geschichtswissenschaft* (Compass for
    historical science) (Göttingen: Vandenhoeck and Ruprecht, 2002), 219–30,
    especially 221.

64 Unpublished note on political iconology by Koselleck, recently presented
    as facsimile in Locher (2009), 83.

65 Reichardt (1998), 224.

66 Ibid.; see also Reichardt (2002), 229.

67 Rolf Reichardt, 'Wortfelder – Bilder – semantische Netze: Beispiele
    interdisziplinärer Quellen und Methoden in der Historischen Semantik'
    (Lexical fields – pictures – semantic nets: examples of interdisciplinary
    sources and methods in historical semantics), in Gunter Scholtz (ed.), *Die
    Interdisziplinarität der Begriffsgeschichte* (Hamburg: Meiner, 2000), 122.

68 Reichardt (2002), 229.

69 Brandt (2007), 57, 60.

70 Locher (2009), 96.

71 For an overview of different approaches and schools in the study of
    meaning in films, I recommend Robert Stam, Robert Burgoyne and Sandy

Flitterman-Lewis, *New Vocabularies in Film Semiotics: Structuralism, Post-Structuralism and Beyond* (New York: Routledge, 1992).

72 Christian Metz, *Film Language: A Semiotics of the Cinema*, trans. Michael Tylor (New York: Oxford University Press, 1974; First published as *Essais sur la signification au cinema* in 1971).

73 For some basic thoughts about the semantic net as a methodological tool for including pictures, but also practices, rituals, or other symbolic entities into the study of historical semantics, see Reichardt (2000), 126ff. See also Brandt (2007), 41.

Part IV

Outlook

Willibald Steinmetz, who wrote his PhD dissertation under Reinhart Koselleck, has been Professor of Modern Political History at Bielefeld University since 2003. From 2001 to 2012, he served as spokesperson of the Collaborative Research Centre 'The Political as Communicative Space in History' at Bielefeld University. Focusing mainly on Great Britain and Germany between the eighteenth and twentieth centuries, his research interests include the interactions between language use and political action in various institutional settings. In the field of conceptual history, Steinmetz goes beyond the study of single concepts to a focus on their anchoring in structures of argumentation. More recently, he has been working on facets of nineteenth-century European history as well as comparative historical semantics.

Willibald Steinmetz's publications include *Das Sagbare und das Machbare: zum Wandel politischer Handlungsspielräume – England 1780–1867* (1993; 'The Say-able and the Do-able: On the Change of Political Scopes of Operation – England 1780–1867'), *Begegnungen vor Gericht: Eine Sozial- und Kulturgeschichte des englischen Arbeitsrechts 1850–1925* (1999; 'Encounters at Court: A Socio-cultural History of English Labour Law 1850–1925'), *Political Languages in the Age of Extremes* (as editor and contributor; 2011) and *Writing Political History Today* (as editor; 2013).

In 'Forty Years of Conceptual History – The State of the Art', Willibald Steinmetz reflects on the current state of conceptual history and the trajectories and challenges for future development. Steinmetz shows the discipline's vitality in its methodological and geographical spread. He argues for a conceptual history more engaged with linguistics, advancing a perspective of entangled history of global multilingualism and translation. According to Steinmetz, conceptual history should continue to move beyond its traditional spatial and temporal frames and engage with the breadth of global history.

Forty Years of Conceptual History – The State of the Art

Willibald Steinmetz

Chapter Outline

1. New Fields of Research: From Conceptual History to Historical Semantics

Taking stock of current practice and open questions in conceptual history is only worthwhile if it has a future as a research discipline. This was recently denied it by one of its prominent champions of the older generation, Hans

Ulrich Gumbrecht. Sitting at his desk, his gaze resting on the epic conceptual history studies stacked up on the shelves – the *Historical Dictionary of Philosophy*, the *Fundamental Concepts in History*, the *Handbook of Fundamental Political and Social Concepts in France*, the *Fundamental Concepts of Aesthetics* – Gumbrecht speaks of an 'ossification of the once lively study of conceptual history'.¹ The major lexical projects in which he was personally involved now seem to him 'pyramids of the mind', 'records from a closed epoch in the history of the humanities'.² Is conceptual history, then, a realm of the dead?

The monumental lexical works may have somewhat clouded Gumbrecht's judgement. Whatever the case, the vigorous activity taking place in conceptual history scholarship, particularly also outside Germany, appears to have escaped his notice. Conceptual history can no longer be regarded as 'a specifically German preoccupation and project',³ nor has this been the case for a good ten years.

Anyone who has taken part in one of the annual conferences hosted by the 'History of Political and Social Concepts Group' since 1998 will contest to this.⁴ The focus of discussion at these events is historiographical conceptual history as conceived by Reinhart Koselleck and developed by Rolf Reichardt and others. Philosophical conceptual history in the context of the *Historical Dictionary of Philosophy*, on the other hand, has inspired few outside the German-speaking world.⁵ This may well be due to the fact that it is less firmly anchored in general social and political history and the history of mentalities. As can be observed at the conferences of the international and interdisciplinary research network that is the 'History of Concepts Group', conceptual history following Koselleck is one of the few products of German humanities scholarship to currently receive worldwide attention and continue to be critically developed. Its international acceptance is reflected in a range of very different publications. In addition to the venerable *Archiv für Begriffsgeschichte* (since 1955) and the *Cahiers de Lexicologie* (since 1959), which are oriented more towards lexical history than conceptual history, there are two new English-language journals with international editorial boards. Both provide a specific forum for discussion of the theory and methods of conceptual history and publish empirical articles. They are the yearbook, edited in Finland, entitled *Redescriptions. Yearbook of Political Thought and Conceptual History* (since 1997)⁶ and the journal *Contributions to the History of Concepts* (since 2005), coordinated in Brazil.⁷ Interconnected research groups are involved in conceptual history research from a national, comparative and transfer history perspective for numerous countries and language groups. This takes the form of monographs and collections of essays or larger lexical projects which are modelled on the *Fundamental Concepts in History* and the *Handbook of Fundamental Political and Social Concepts in France*, though prudently kept to more modest dimensions. There are for instance a large number of monographic and smaller case studies on concepts and concept clusters for the Scandinavian countries, some of them from a comparative perspective.[8] Larger collected works for France, Spain and the South American countries are in preparation.[9] For many years now, a research group in the Netherlands has been studying the history of fundamental Dutch political and social concepts and its relationship to the three key neighbouring languages (French, German, English) and to the common Latin tradition.[10] The debates between German and Russian conceptual historians have also recently been reflected in first publications; not for long, it seems, will Eastern Europe as a whole remain a *terra incognita* from a conceptual history point of view.[11] At the latest conference of the above-mentioned 'History of Political and Social Concepts Group' in Uppsala (2006), the appropriation and re-semantization of western concepts in China and Korea in the nineteenth and twentieth centuries was discussed.[12] Similar issues surrounding the translation and translatability of western social concepts of description and classification (*class, caste, citizen*) into the languages of the Indo-Islamic world (and vice versa) in the colonial and post-colonial era have also been the subject of research in recent years.[13]

As we can see from this brief overview, conceptual history is very much alive internationally, with heavy German involvement. It is also testimony to the liveliness of activity in this field that the above-mentioned research groups do not merely transfer the paradigm of lexical-semasiological conceptual history established in Germany onto hitherto unexplored countries and languages. Instead, they examine it critically, adapt it and raise new questions. In particular, the conceptual history issues, which Gumbrecht quite rightly spoke of as unsolved, acquire greater relevance the more international conceptual history becomes. The frequent lack of directly equivalent concepts in other languages raises the pressing issue of how we can seek articulations that are on the one hand metaphorical but also colloquial and visual, of world perceptions which are not yet or no longer conceived conceptually.[14] Similarly, the problem of the conceptualization of the interdependency of usage, concept formation and material history is still more complex if we are to draw comparisons and examine processes of translation between different speech communities.[15] The challenges facing conceptual history in the wake of its internationalization are among the most exciting fields of research anywhere in the historical sciences. It goes without saying that they can only be addressed in cooperation with linguistics and other neighbouring disciplines.

Conceptual history is not only continuing to develop internationally. In the German-speaking world too, it is turning to new areas of research, exploring new periods and employing new methods. For example, one new field currently attracting particular attention in the historical sciences is that of religious terminology. A Bochum research group led by Lucian Hölscher is studying the verbal expressions of religious community creation in Europe since the early modern era.[16] Research ranges from the history of the concept of religion itself and the history of the reciprocal identification of self and other by religious groups to the designations for religious institutions and practices (*church, piety, faith*). In view of the increase in religious conflicts in today's world, this conceptual history research into religious semantics is increasingly also assuming a political and educational dimension.

With regard to periods that have yet to be explored, the twentieth century in particular has received only cursory treatment from a historical point of view.[17] This is due to the acknowledged concentration of the lexicon *Fundamental Concepts in History* on what is known as the *Sattelzeit*, or 'saddle period'. From a linguistic perspective, on the other hand, extensive studies have been published on language in the public sphere following 1945, some in lexicographical form.[18] All further studies need to take their cue from these, whether they proceed in the manner of conceptual history in the narrower sense[19] or are founded on a broader understanding of historical discourse analysis in the tradition of Michel Foucault or other theorists.[20] Besides the work of Koselleck and Foucault, Niklas Lumann's studies on the relationship between social structure and semantics have proved seminal for research into contemporary trends, such as the 'semantics of the welfare state'.[21]

In addition to the twentieth century, pre-modern Europe also remains largely unexplored territory from a conceptual history point of view. This long epoch from the end of the Western Roman Empire to the mid-eighteenth century is both challenging and fascinating for conceptual historians. In societies throughout Europe, multilingualism within a single territory – with social and functional distinctions – was the norm. The difficulty of artificially isolating 'national' speech communities is even greater for this period than it is for the modern age. [22] At the very least, the continual translations and back-translations between the Latin (written) language of the scholars and vernacular (oral, increasingly transcribed) practice in politics, church, the administration of justice and other fields of activity must be considered systematically and not merely sporadically. From the seventeenth to the early nineteenth century there was also a similar linguistic interrelation between use of the vernacular language, which was often fairly unelaborated, and an elite communication conducted in a foreign language: principally French but also German or other languages in northern and eastern European countries, for instance Swedish in Finland.[23] But there is a lack not only of conceptual historical case studies on translation processes between the language of scholars, the language of the elite and the vernacular, for these long phases of European multilingualism. There is also a need for an analytical frame of reference. Much like the 'saddle period' hypothesis introduced by Koselleck for heuristic purposes, such a framework would give direction to research in this field.[24]

Those of the elites who read, spoke and wrote in more than one language were faced by a challenge during these centuries of transition to more nationally homogenous speech communities. They continually had to switch languages in everyday life, constantly adjusting and aligning the meanings of words. Conversely, this also gave them greater leeway to 'play' with the meanings of words, which were not yet very rigorously defined. This was subsequently restricted when endeavours to standardize the language in France, Germany and other countries began to enjoy some success. The late Middle Ages were characterized both by an explosion of documents written in the vernacular and the gradual impact of attempts to provide at least temporary definitions of words in monolingual, bilingual or multilingual dictionaries. A tentative hypothesis could thus be put forward that meanings in the respective vernaculars were marked, as a rule, by a permanent instability or even obscurity. This significantly complicates conceptual history. Appropriate methodological tools to deal with this problem have yet to be developed in historical semantics. One thing is clear: any method proceeding purely semasiologically, based on individual words, would seem less promising here than it ultimately proved to be for the 'saddle period' (despite legitimate criticism of the concept underlying the *Fundamental Concepts in History*).

With regard to the 'Latin' Middle Ages in the narrower sense, that is, the centuries until around 1200, when written communication was exclusively or very predominantly conducted in Latin, it is somewhat easier to follow the classical conceptual historical paradigm.[25] Studies on political, social and – inextricably linked to these – religious usage between late antiquity and the High Middle Ages can also benefit from the fact that a large portion of the canonized theological and political theory texts are available in digital form. This makes it immensely easier to find references for simple matters such as determining the shifting contexts in which words are used. The benefits will be even greater as existing computer-based lemmatization and collocation analysis techniques continue to improve.[26] However, corpus linguistics and text technology, which have been heavily focused on synchronic analyses of present-day language, must first understand the importance of diachronic studies and be encouraged to develop appropriate methods of recognition, differentiation and analysis for use in historical research. By the same token, this requires that historians adapt their terminology and methodology to linguistic standards of accuracy. If this does not happen, it will be very difficult for historical semantics to profit at all from the advantages of the new technologies.[27]

These few remarks on new fields of research should suffice to refute Gumbrecht's impression that conceptual history was dead. Perhaps such an assumption could be valid if one believed that the research programme set out forty years ago by Reinhart Koselleck and others, and developed ever since, had been fulfilled with the completion of the encyclopaedic *Fundamental Concepts in History*. Koselleck himself would have been the last to concede this. The longer the work on the lexicon dragged on, the more unsatisfied he became with the practical realization of his theoretical concepts. He was fully aware of the disadvantages that were attributable to the specific dictionary form of presentation. He spoke of the 'theoretical straitjacket' imposed by his chosen format.[28] The encyclopaedic work was for him only an initial step on the way to a historical semantics that also included the aspect of language pragmatics.

In its conventional incarnation, conceptual history concentrates on the nodal points in the diachronic semantic change of individual words, drawing on a relatively narrow base of references from dictionaries, political theory texts and other scattered sources. These references are largely removed from the communicative situation and context of action in which they were used. This approach will remain worthwhile, albeit primarily as an aid in the formulation of hypotheses on broader processes of semantic change. Regarded thus, as a sub-discipline of a historical semantics that is increasingly dedicated to the investigation of broader semantic fields, sentence patterns, discourses or 'languages' in John Pocock's sense, and considers also the shifting manners and situations in which these occur, 'old-school' conceptual history is by all means still valuable. It is a method that leads relatively quickly to verifiable results.[29] 'Historical semantics', on the other hand, is an appropriate umbrella designation to encompass all of the branches of research which are concerned with processes of semantic change in the broadest sense. The emphasis may be placed on different aspects of semantic change. Historical semantics as it is understood here comprises research into shifts in the regular use of linguistic (and other) signs, in the relationship of these signs to cognitive correlates (concepts) and in the reference of these signs to extra-linguistic circumstances.[30]

2. An Open Question: Possible Explanations for Semantic Change

Both older conceptual history studies and more recent discourse-historical research have developed sophisticated bodies of tools and methods to describe semantic change. When it comes to explaining it, however, they are often at a loss. In both cases, the main reason for this problem seems to be that speech acts at the microdiachronic level are neglected. Appropriate models for the explanation of semantic change can only be developed – such is my view – by incorporating the aspect of language pragmatics and observing verbal interaction within short periods of time and in specific areas of activity. The fact that neither conceptual history nor historical discourse analysis can provide satisfactory results here is linked to their respective epistemological assumptions and the human interests that inform their findings.

In the case of discourse analysis in the tradition of Michel Foucault, the difficulties in conceptualizing semantic change stem from a persistent reluctance to permit as explanatory factors two things: the strategic action of subjects on the one hand and, on the other, extra-linguistic constellations that can be (re-)constructed through historical research. From an epistemological point of view, this reluctance is based on the assumption of the insubversibility of language as the medium of our own and every previous constitution of reality. Subjective intentions (rational choice) and extra-linguistic constellations are excluded from discourse analysis – not because it is believed they do not exist but because they cannot be identified with absolute certainty.[31] If we accept this as the common basis of all varieties of the 'linguistic turn', all that remains by way of context to explain verbal manifestations in the past are other surviving documents. Ruling out the strategic action of subjects and extra-linguistic factors (for e.g. the spatial positioning of subjects or the availability of certain media) as drivers or motivations for semantic innovation places the entire burden of explanation on intralinguistic, anonymous, and, from the perspective of the participants, contingent shifts in the aggregate of what may be said in a given situation. Questions of causation then become almost pointless to ask and virtually impossible to answer. Foucault himself, and the discourse historians he inspired, have accordingly concentrated on identifying such shifts in the utterable. They were primarily concerned with demonstrating *that* – in Foucault's terminology – the rules governing the occurrence of statements between moment *a* and moment *b* changed. Analysis of the circumstances of and reasons for the transition from *a* to *b* were secondary. At most, they may mention identifiable breaks, slips of the tongue, contradictions and interferences of other discourses in the textual fabrics. These are cited as indications that individual speakers always have leeway to say things in a manner other than that prescribed by the rules.[32] However, why and how certain variations or breaches of the rules prevailed at the supra-individual level and in the long-term, while others did not, remains unanswered.

Reinhart Koselleck and the conceptual historians following him generally had less scruples about explaining semantic change by referring to material history independent of verbal records or to strategic action on the part of individual speakers. It is not because of fundamental epistemological reservations that practical application of the lexicon *Fundamental Concepts in History* tends to describe, rather than explain, semantic change. This is due rather to a preference for the diachronic perspective and a primarily referential understanding of 'meaning'. The primary objective of lexicographical conceptual history was initially to illuminate the temporal dislocations between the use of certain words, the concepts expressed with them, and a 'material history' of political and social conditions that was reconstructed using other methods. The main subject was – to use Koselleck's terminology – the 'convergence' or divergence between the 'real' history on the one hand and the history 'understood' by contemporaries on the other.[33] The emphasis was on identifying moments in which certain words first assumed or assimilated the abstract meanings with which they have been associated since the 'saddle period'. The conceptual histories provided in the lexicon are designed above all to show when older meanings became incomprehensible or fell into oblivion; when the modern meanings with which we are familiar became established; and, finally, whether this semantic change occurred in unison with the 'real' history, subsequently, or in anticipation of it. Koselleck spoke in this context of 'semantic surpluses', of 'anticipations' of future history, and of different rates of semantic and social change.[34] And this is presumably what he initially meant by his much-cited remark that conceptual changes can be both 'indicators' for changing social, political, economic conditions as well as 'factors' in the change of these very conditions.[35] When Koselleck spoke of concepts as 'factors' of historical movement, he was at first thinking mainly of the special case of the 'anticipation' of future history. In other words, he was referring to the many concepts that have been politicized, ideologized, democratized and temporalized since the Enlightenment and have thus unleashed expectations that determined how people thought and acted. All of these early remarks by Koselleck viewed conceptual history on the one hand and 'real' or social history on the other as two largely unrelated sequences of events. How and why semantic changes occurred in the interaction between social conditions and language usage was barely addressed in the *Fundamental Concepts in History*. This accounts for the fact that 'meaning' was primarily understood in the lexicon in terms of the reference to extralinguistic circumstances or cognitive correlates (concepts) and only as a rare exception in terms of regular usage in communication.

The objectives formulated in the lexicon's introduction can be understood in hindsight as a response to the situation in which the discipline of historical science found itself at the time of conceptual history's emergence. The early phase of conceptual history, that is the period from the late 1960s to the mid-1980s, coincided with the rise of the structural or social history paradigm in historical science. Broadly speaking, social historians were concerned with the reconstruction of social macrostructures (for example social classes) and the historical distribution of power among them. They investigated this on the basis of sequences of sometimes quantified data gathered from various sources: statistics on income, taxes paid, inheritances, circles of potential spouses, family size. The historical 'reality' of the social structures and collective subjects reconstructed in this manner was not a matter for discussion. Likewise, the historical 'reality' of economic trends reconstructed in a similar manner and political history investigated using traditional methods was undisputed. The constructivist perspective that is prevalent today, and the doubts this entails about such an uncritical understanding of historical reality, only established themselves in German historical science since the mid-1980s. During the initial conception and early evolution of conceptual history, too, doubts about the reality of social historical reconstructions played virtually no role.

But ever since the advent of the linguistic and constructivist turn, Koselleck and others around him turned their interest to the 'how' and 'why' of the linguistic constitution of reality.[36] There was an increasing awareness of the fact that all kinds of social 'structures' (from groups, classes, communities and institutions through to states, peoples and nations) constantly (have to) reproduce themselves in the act of communication, that is, through speech acts or symbolic acts, and are therefore in a permanent state of reconfiguration.[37] This view is now generally considered common sense in the historical sciences. For conventional social history as espoused by Jürgen Kocka and Hans-Ulrich Wehler, however, it initially represented a considerable provocation. It now became apparent that the supposedly stable collective subjects that had hitherto figured as subjects in representations of social history were essentially highly unstable constructs which were created by language and in a constant state of renewal. For conventional conceptual history, this new perspective brought about a shift in focus from long-term diachrony to micro-diachrony. Connected to this was a replacement, or at least supplementation, of the referential understanding of meaning by an understanding which focused on the analysis of meaning as continually recreated through speaking and understanding (or misunderstanding). In the context of the *Fundamental Concepts in History* and other major encyclopaedic works, this paradigm shift could only be effected to a limited degree. This was dictated by their very presentation and design.[38] This explains Koselleck's increasing dissatisfaction, mentioned above, with the original concept for the *Fundamental Concepts in History*. Diachronic conceptual history, referring to long periods of time and presented in encyclopaedic format, remains indispensable for the formulation of hypotheses. However, it is ill suited to explaining the constant fabrication of social, political, legal, economic and other structures and conditions through speech acts, and – conversely – to offer explanations as to why the actors spoke as they did in given circumstances.

Specific processes of semantic change, of the accumulation, shift or displacement of meaning, can be better observed with the methods of micro-diachrony. Only by observing verbal interactions in actual situations is it possible to recognize how and why speakers/writers used certain words in one way in one case and differently in another, and how and why listeners/readers understood them in one way or another. One problem that arises from this narrowing of focus to micro-diachrony is that reducing the period under investigation and increasing the different varieties of text to be analysed leads to greater complexity. The broad, linear narratives of older conceptual history tend to dissolve into numerous small stories of situation-specific usage which no longer appear to follow any general patterns.

Is it possible, nevertheless, to identify recurring (or indeed typical) patterns of interaction between semantic change and social change? This is an open question, for which only abstract hypotheses can be tentatively proposed here. Three typical scenarios present themselves as possible explanations of semantic change: (1) change caused by a loss of plausibility of words or manners of speech as a result of unexpected events and upheavals; (2) change caused by an increase or decrease in the strategic utility of words or manners of speech in recurrent communicative situations; (3) change caused by disturbance of the lexical and semantic balance of a language through words imported from another language.

The first explanatory model – change brought about by the *loss of plausibility* of former manners of speech – is borne out by many historical examples. The classic case is of sudden, 'unheard-of' events that are irreconcilable with previous experience. The available vocabulary is no longer equal to the task of conceptualizing the 'unheard-of' aspect of the new. Early modern historian Andreas Suter illustrated this process with a good example, the linguistic responses of those involved to the Swiss peasant war of 1653. When the peasant revolts began, the authorities in the Swiss cantons were unruffled; they believed it was one of the usual 'revolts', episodes of 'unrest' or 'acts of insubordination' with which they were familiar and for whose suppression they had developed routines. When the revolt spread to large parts of Switzerland, however, the authorities were seized with panic. They now saw themselves faced with 'methods and extremities ... that we could never have imagined'.[39] And precisely in this situation, when something happened that they could previously 'never have imagined', the authorities now began to describe the 'unrest' differently, namely as an 'all-out conspiracy' or – and this was a conceptual innovation even for Europe – as a 'revolution'.[40] Suter goes on to demonstrate that over the course of the various Swiss revolts, the revolting peasants also found new linguistic and symbolic forms to give voice to their demands.[41] These processes of re-semantization, Suter believes, can be explained by experiences of failure or, to be more precise, by the experience of 'falsification of semantic systems and concepts, whether this is because the act of attribution no longer succeeds, or because the procedures derived from such attributive acts no longer produce the expected results'.[42] This is an example of semantic change brought about by a loss of plausibility. To generalize and put it very simply: something unexpected occurs; it is ascertained that existing manners of speech neither capture the new circumstances nor permit effective action in the new situation; and manners of speech are altered.

However, this model does not provide an adequate explanation for the specific new choice of words that replaces the old. Why was the word 'revolution' used and not some other, to articulate the newness of the experience of the Swiss peasant war? This brings me to the second of the above-mentioned (and complementary) explanatory models. Loss of plausibility is one possible explanation for the decline or displacement of former manners of speech,[43] but this alone does not explain the emergence and spreading of specific new manners of speech.

This is where the second model comes in, that of semantic change caused by an increase in strategic utility in the communicative situation. Put very simply, it comes down to the fact that certain words gain currency because they facilitate effective speaking and acting – whatever 'effective' may mean in the individual case; that depends on the situation. I lack the empirical expertise to say with certainty in what the added value of the word 'revolution' actually consisted as against the older designations 'unrest', 'revolt', etc. in the case of the Swiss peasant war. Generally speaking, I suspect that the greater degree of abstraction contained in the image of the *revolutio* was one reason for the choice of this particular (metaphorical) expression. In still more general terms: words achieve greater utility value in political communication when they possess the ability to express the greatest possible number of disparate experiences. In political communication, abstract expressions that can be used in many different contexts to mean many different things are of particular advantage. Insofar as a political actor is dependent on the assent of others – periodically confirmed – it is in his or her interests to use words which leave a number of options open. Opportune expressions include those which make it possible to inconspicuously do away with untenable positions without necessitating a change of terminology. Collective designations which make it possible to form broad alliances, that is, are as inclusive as possible, are also advantageous. The same is true, conversely, of designations which concede as little substance and meaning as possible to that which is contrary and to be excluded. All of this explains the great appeal of abstract and, in extreme cases, even 'empty' signifiers in politics.[44] The usage of strategically favourable words can be explained without appealing to intentionality. However, I see no reason to exclude this as an explanation in cases where it is clearly revealed by explicit remarks in parallel sources.

One example of semantic change brought about by an increase in strategic utility is the use of certain terms to describe social phenomena in nineteenth-century parliamentary discussions on electoral reform.[45] The remarkable proliferation of the designations *classes moyennes* in the French and *middle classes* in the English electoral debates during the first half of the nineteenth century can be explained in this way. By appealing in parliament to the *classes moyennes* or the *middle classes*, by maintaining that the middle classes were on their side, politicians indicated that their own position enjoyed broad support among the population. However, these expressions left open which specific professions and interest groups were actually meant. And precisely this semantic openness of words (in the referential sense) was – and is – an advantage in political communication. In non-political communicative situations, for instance in legal communication in court, the opposite is true. Here, a person will be at a disadvantage if he or she is unable to translate his or her personal case into the precise specialist jargon required for the judge's legal decision. Hence no general rules can be given for the utility of words and manners of speech but only ones which are specific to a particular situation. And of course these situation-specific rules also vary historically in tandem with the institutionalised or established forms of communication themselves, for instance election campaigns and parliamentary and legal proceedings.

The two explanatory models for semantic change which we have looked at thus far, namely changes to the choice of words due to a loss of plausibility and an increase in utility in the particular situation, have a common basis. Both stem from the fact that speakers have experiences and expectations for which, whether purposefully or gropingly, by trial and error, they seek appropriate verbal means of expression. Both explanatory models require actors with certain identifiable interests. This requirement need by no means imply that the speech behaviour of those involved is instrumental. Deliberate endeavours to find the 'optimal' choice of words in the given situation, or deliberate tabooing of a certain usage, appear to be the exception.[46] The choice of words is generally guided instinctively by intimations of success or failure in everyday communication. It is more complicated, however, to explain semantic change without appealing to actors and their desire for effective speech acts. I can currently conceive of only one mode of semantic change that functions without presupposing a desire for effective speech acts. This is the third explanatory model: semantic change brought about by *disturbance as a result of words imported* from one language into another.

As we have seen, multilingualism was the norm in many European territories until sometime into the nineteenth century. It was therefore not uncommon – this may be confirmed by even a cursory glance at any written documents from the early modern period – for words from a foreign language (Latin, French) to enter into the native (written and spoken) language as 'foreign' words with often only very vague definitions. How these word imports and exports were transmitted, by which media, and instigated by whom, is a field of historical-semantic research in itself. Very little progress has been made in this field to date, with the exception of the subdiscipline of historical translation studies.[47] The fact is that words imported from foreign languages can trigger semantic shifts. Similar disturbances can be brought about by words imported from technical languages; we need only think here of computer terminology. The foreign words, initially only vaguely defined, are in a sense raw material that can be put to many different uses. For instance, certain negative connotations of a semantically related word in one's own language can be supplanted onto a foreign word, creating a semantic distinction that had previously not been possible in this form. A classic example is the negative connotation of the French word *bourgeois* in German since Marx (if not earlier), as a result of which the German word *Bürger* acquired a positive ring even without any additional, positive adjectival or nominal modifiers. Another example, which is described by Ingrid Schierle and Walter Sperling, is the introduction into Russian of the foreign word *politics* (*politika*). Schierle and Sperling demonstrate how the Russian political vocabulary initially diversified after it was introduced through translations. Later, in the course of the struggles for participation in late Tsarist Russia, it underwent a transformation from marginal, pejorative term to uncontested battle cry.[48] A third example, cited by Koselleck, is Luther's translation of the biblical word *berith* with the German word *Bund* (covenant). This translation process invested the term *Bund*, which until then had been purely secular, with a religious meaning which it retained into the nineteenth century.[49] Newly introduced foreign words thus admit of processes of semantic differentiation. However, this also does not take place quasi-autonomously within the system of language. Once the foreign words have been imported, the desire of nameable actors for effective speech acts also plays a crucial role here. In this respect, the third explanatory model for semantic change complements the two others.

3. Conceptual History at a Transnational Level: Translation Processes and the Problem of the Translatability of Concepts

The projects mentioned above of a historical semantics with a comparative or histoire croisée[50] approach are concerned with societies dominated by a multilingualism which was distinguished according to functional, social, ethnic, religious or other criteria. In the colonial societies, this multilingualism also went hand in hand with a considerable imbalance of power between speakers. In medieval Iran since the beginning of the dynasties founded by Turkish warriors, for instance, Turkish was the language of the rulers and the military, while Persian was the language of culture and administration and Arabic that of religion and law.[51] This power, however – which is founded on extra-linguistic factors but maintained by linguistic means – of privileged communication partners and 'their' language over others, is typical of situations of multilingualism within a single territory in non-colonial societies, too. Every historical semantic study taking a histoire croisée approach must therefore consider the prevailing balance of power.[52]

However, there are no universal rules according to which political, military, economical or any other form of dominance by a particular section of the population or the rule of conquerors/colonizers must necessarily lead to the dominance of their language over the language of the subordinate section of the population, the conquered/colonized. To be sure, there are numerous cases where the languages of European colonial powers from the sixteenth to the twentieth century have exerted a massive pressure for change on the languages of colonized populations or semi-colonial powers (India, China, Japan). This has resulted in loan translations and re-semantizations of local terms or even the adoption of entire institutional systems of values and norms. There are likewise numerous examples of the transfer of Western concepts in drawn-out processes of modifying appropriation. The transferral of the categories of the German Civil Code to Japan is one striking instance of this.[53] Another is the establishment of the originally European (Portuguese) term 'caste' in nineteenth-century India.[54] From a historical point of view, however, the reverse also exists: a pressure for change on the language of the conquerors, even to the extent of its complete transformation. The classical example of this is the linguistic Romanization, associated with the religious Christianization, of the Germanic conquerors of the Western Roman Empire. Generally we can probably speak of an overlapping of the languages and hybridity of the speakers over a long period of time. It is chiefly nominal elements and cultural words that are transferred to and fro.[55]

Beyond empirical studies on processes of transferral and translation, the fundamental question remains of the translatability of concepts. There are three distinct aspects here: (1) the problem of equivalence at the synchronic-comparative level, (2) the problem of equivalence in diachrony, and (3) the problem of the Eurocentrism, or modern bias, of the metalanguage we require in order to be able to communicate with each other about equivalence and translatability.

The first problem, that of equivalence (both in the sense of usage and in the referential sense) at the synchronic-comparative level, is particularly virulent in modern Europe in the case of concepts which are closely linked to a specific national culture and the relevant institutions. We may ask, for instance, whether there existed contemporary concepts in other European languages, evincing at least a somewhat similar range of meanings and applications, for the concepts perceived even by contemporaries as specifically 'German' – *Bildung* (education, culture), *Staat* (state), *bürgerliche Gesellschaft* (civil society), *Kultur* (culture)? This problem of synchronic equivalence is central not only to comparative historical-semantic research but also to the study of social, cultural and political history. If we answer the question of equivalence in the negative, the concepts concerned can only be used as analytical categories for comparisons after they have been very carefully defined. One possible way of answering this question is to observe previous attempts at translation. However, what we then frequently encounter is nothing but a history of misunderstandings, or, in more neutral terms, of reinterpretations and adaptations to different cultural and institutional contexts. For example, as Fania Oz-Salzberger demonstrates, German recipients of eighteenth-century Scottish moral philosophy often translated the English terms *community, polity* and *nation* with *Staat* (state, nation). Their classical republican meaning, in particular in the work of Adam Ferguson, was thus not only lost but radically transformed into an almost pro-government sentiment.[56] Less massive, but still considerable, are the differences in meaning when it comes to terms whose root derives from the common European Latin tradition – as in the case of the party and ideological designation 'Liberalism'.[57] The study of attempts at time-delayed or contemporaneous translation offers no foolproof guide to solving the question of equivalence.

Onomasiological studies could present an alternative. They would need to be designed in such a way that open test questions are directed at texts from comparable previous communicative situations such as debates on the right to vote and political participation. In this way, it may be possible to identify central terms with similar strategic utility, that is, terms with equivalent 'significance' in the speech act theory sense. In the context of electoral debates, then, one could ask how the social groups described themselves who at a particular period of time called for recognition, inclusion, the right to have a say. Similarly, one could search for designations imposed extrinsically on the groups desiring recognition, inclusion and the right to have a say. Furthermore, one could investigate the competing names for the desired form of wanting to have a say and the legitimizing formulae used to support or reject the demands. Two conditions must be met if this onomasiological procedure is to be practicable: comparable and roughly contemporaneous communicative situations must exist. And categories for the formulation of the test questions must be available which are applicable across cultural and national divides. Both of these conditions are more easily met for a historiography that looks only at the Western and Central European context, than for a global historiography.

The second problem – equivalence in diachrony – shall only be touched upon here. It is of only minor relevance for ethnologists, sociologists and linguists if they are concerned primarily with foreign, or their own, contemporary societies and language within short periods of time. In historical science, on the other hand, it is present everywhere. With regard to research and presentation, the problem of diachronic translation chiefly arises in connection with the question whether modern concepts can also serve as analytical categories for the historical representation of earlier epochs. The classic case, which remains a point of contention in mediaeval studies today, is the question of whether we may speak of *states*, *constitutions* or at least *statehood* in the context of the Early and High Middle Ages. The problem of diachronic equivalence, or, to be more precise, the danger of using anachronistic analytical terminology, was a key motivation for the development of conceptual history, in particular as conceived by Otto Brunner.[58] This is why good conceptual histories for the countries and language groups being examined must be in place before we can even begin to think about historical semantic studies with a comparative or transfer history approach.

The third problem – the danger of the Eurocentrism, or modern bias, of the 'metalanguage' (Koselleck) of academic communication – is becoming increasingly significant as historical semantics as a discipline moves beyond the European-Western world and expands to encompass global history.[59] We could almost ask whether the Eurocentrism trap can be avoided at all. Can there be 'neutral' analytical terms that structure representations of historical or cultural phenomena, without judging the 'foreign' culture by concepts native to one's own? Should we not avoid this danger by drawing instead on concepts from contemporary sources in the foreign culture being studied? South Asia historian Margrit Pernau discusses this problem in relation to India under British rule. She asks whether one may speak in this context of an Indo-Muslim *Bürgertum* (≈ middle class, bourgeoisie)[60] or *middle class* and of a *civil society*.[61] She concludes that the use of non-Western terms from the source language is not only a hindrance to understanding but also implies a fundamental, essential 'otherness' of the indigenous cultures and must therefore also be regarded as Eurocentric. Pernau sees no other alternative in histories intended for a Western readership than to use terms with which Western readers are familiar. However, she proposes enriching these semantically, as it were, with a very precise explanation of the differences in meaning. Then, when reading the word *Bürger*, readers can also imagine an Indian *sharif* wearing a turban. If this advice were to be followed, Historical Semantic studies with a comparative and histoire croisée approach would take on a little of the character of conceptual politics – applied to the language of scholarship, if not indeed the vernacular.

While we may agree with the unavoidability of Western analytical terminology, it still remains to consider carefully precisely *which* Western (German, English) terms one employs to undergo such semantic enrichment. Terms such as the German *Bürger* (≈ citizen) are already overloaded with meanings and can barely be translated adequately within Europe. It seems to me problematic, to say the least, to take such a term and try to make it amenable to the study of non-European conditions. Less culture-specific designations such as *middle class* or *civil society* may be better suited to this purpose. In the case of the normatively charged term *civil society*, however, there is a particularly great danger of writing the history of non-Western countries primarily in terms of a deficit. Incidentally, this problem of a historiography in the mode of success or failure in approaching an ideal defined by normative concepts is just as prevalent within Europe.[62] The entire historical debate about German and other *Sonderwege*, or special paths, ultimately stems from the difficulty of selecting analytical categories that recognize difference, otherness, different rhythms of change, without characterizing these as 'abnormal', 'deviant', 'backward'. The problem is particularly acute with regard to non-European societies. Here it pertains even to fundamental categories such as notions of time and space or supposed universals such as 'religion', 'individual', 'politics', whose existence and approximate meaning is uncontested in modern European history and perhaps beyond. The abstract vocabulary used in scholarship, law and many other areas, drawn largely from the common Greco-Latin tradition, had a certain standardizing effect in European history. Perhaps with the exception of the East Asian region (China, Japan), there has been no equivalent to this in the older, pre-colonial history of the non-Western countries.[63] Since the beginning of colonialization, however, the languages of colonial and semi-colonial societies have also been drawn into this inexorable tendency towards standardization. Concepts of Greco-Latin and – more recently – Anglo-American origin that have been conveyed through Western languages since the nineteenth century form a veneer, as it were, of common vocabulary, which could ameliorate the problem of translatability in the long term.

(Translation: Joy Titheridge)

Notes

1   Hans Ulrich Gumbrecht, 'Pyramiden des Geistes. Über den schnellen Aufstieg, die unsichtbaren Dimensionen und das plötzliche Abebben der begriffsgeschichtlichen Bewegung', in idem, *Dimensionen und Grenzen der Begriffsgeschichte* (Munich: Fink, 2006), 9.
2   Ibid., 7.
3   Ibid., 9.
4   Information on the group's conferences and activities can be found at <http://www.jyu.fi/yhtfil/hpscg/> (accessed 1 May 2007).
5   Cf. Melvin Richter's assessment in *The History of Political and Social Concepts. A Critical Introduction* (New York/Oxford: Oxford University Press, 1995). His criticism refers chiefly to the disproportionately greater reduction – in comparison to the *Fundamental Concepts in History* [Note: Otto Brunner, Werner Conze and Reinhart Koselleck (eds), *Geschichtliche Grundbegriffe: Historisches Lexikon zur politisch-sozialen Sprache in Deutschland* (Stuttgart: Klett-Cotta, 1972–1997)] – in the number of references to contexts and pragmatic functions of usage in

the *Historical Dictionary of Philosophy* [Note: Joachim Ritter, Karlfried Gründer and Gottfried Gabriel (eds), *Historisches Wörterbuch der Philosophie* (Basel: Schwabe, 1971–2007)]. The restrictions dictated by the format of the dictionary are increasingly regarded as an encumbrance in interdisciplinary discussion. Cf. the articles in Gunter Scholz (ed.), *Die Interdisziplinarität der Begriffsgeschichte*, Archiv für Begriffsgeschichte, special issue (Hamburg: Felix Meiner, 2000); Ernst Müller (ed.), *Begriffsgeschichte im Umbruch?*, Archiv für Begriffsgeschichte, special issue (Hamburg: Felix Meiner, 2005).

6   The yearbook was published as *Finnish Yearbook of Political Thought* from 1997 to 2002; since 2003 it has carried the current title.

7   The journal is available in printed form and online, cf. <http://contributions.iuperj.br/> (accessed 1 May 2007). [Note: the journal *Contributions to the History of Concepts* is now published by Berghahn Journals. Its editorial team consists of Sinai Rusinek, Jani Marjanen, Rieke Timçev, Ilana Brown, Yonatan Livneh and João Feres Jr. The journal's current website is <http://www.historyofconcepts.org/> (accessed 31 May 2015).]

8   Examples include Norbert Götz, *Ungleiche Geschwister. Die Konstruktion von nationalsozialistischer Volksgemeinschaft und schwedischem Volksheim* (Baden-Baden: Nomos, 2001); Jussi Kurunmäki, *Representation, Nation and Time. The Political Rhetoric of the 1866 Parliamentary Reform in Sweden* (Jyväskylä: Jyväskylän Yliopisto, 2000); Jonas Harvard, *En helig allmännelig opinion. Föreställingar om offentlighet och legitimitet i svensk riksdagsdebatt 1848–1919* (Umeå: Umeå universitet, 2006); Kari Palonen, 'Transforming a Common European Concept to Finnish: Conceptual Changes in the Understanding of Politiikka', *Finnish Yearbook of Political Thought*, 5 (2001), 113–53.

9   For France: Rolf Reichardt and Hans-Jürgen Lüsebrink (eds), *Handbuch politisch-sozialer Grundbegriffe in Frankreich 1680–1920*, 20 vols (Munich: Oldenbourg, 1985–2000); Various authors, *Dictionnaire des usages socio-politiques (1770–1815)*, 11 vols (Paris: Klincksieck, 1985–2006); as an example of a historical-semantic study on the twentieth century: Damon Mayaffre, *Le poids des mots. Le discours de gauche et de droite dans l'entre deux-guerres. Maurice Thorez, Léon Blum, Pierre-Étienne Flandin et André Tardieu (1928–1939)* (Paris: Champion, 2000); for Spain: Javier Fernández Sebastián and Juan Francisco Fuentes (eds), *Diccionario Político y Social del Siglo XIX Español* (Madrid: Alianza Editorial, 2002); on the Brazilian project: João Feres Júnior, 'For a Critical Conceptual History of Brazil: Receiving Begriffsgeschichte', *Contributions to the History of Concepts*, 1/2 (2005), 185–200; for initial information on the planned project 'Iberconceptos. Proyectoa Iberoamericano de Historia Conceptual', see

<http://foroiberoideas.cervantesvirtual.com/> (accessed 14 May 2007). [Note: for further information, see also the more recent <http://www. iberconceptos.net/> (accessed 31 May 2015).]

10   Cf. Karin Tilmans, 'Applying *Begriffsgeschichte* to Dutch History. Some Remarks on the Practice and Future of a Project', *Contributions to the History of Concepts*, 2/1 (2006), 43–58; Pim den Boer, 'The Historiography of German *Begriffsgeschichte* and the Dutch Project of Conceptual History', in Ian Hampsher-Monk, Karin Tilmans and Frank van Vree (eds), *History of Concepts: Comparative Perspectives* (Amsterdam: Amsterdam University Press, 1998), 13–22. A number of studies of Dutch concepts have already been published: Nicolaas Cornelis Ferdinand van Sas (ed.), *Vaderland. Een geschiedenis van de vijftiende eeuw tot 1940* (Amsterdam: Amsterdam University Press, 1999); Eco O. G. Haitsma Mulier and Wijger R. E. Velema (eds), *Vrijheid. Een geschiedenis van de vijftiende tot de twintigste eeuw* (Amsterdam: Amsterdam University Press, 1999); Pim den Boer (ed.), *Beschaving. Een geschiedenis va de begrippen hoofsheid, heusheid, beschaving en cultuur* (Amsterdam: Amsterdam University Press, 2001); Joost Kloek and Karin Tilmans (eds), *Burger. Een geschiedenis van het begrip 'burger' in de Nederlanden van de Middeleeuwen tot de 21ste eeuw* (Amsterdam: Amsterdam University Press, 2002).

11   Cf. Peter Thiergen (ed.), *Russische Begriffsgeschichte der Neuzeit. Beiträge zu einem Forschungsdesiderat* (Cologne: Böhlau, 2006); Nikolai E. Kopasov (ed.), *Istoričeskie ponyatiya i politiceskie idei v Rossii XVI–XX veka* (Historical concepts and political ideas in Russia, sixteenth–twentieth centuries) (Saint Petersburg: Aleteyya, 2006); see also the articles by Michail Krom, Ingrid Schierle and Walter Sperling on the Russian concept of politics from the seventeenth to the twentieth century in Willibald Steinmetz (ed.), '*Politik*'. *Situationen eines Wortgebrauchs im Europa der Neuzeit* (Frankfurt am Main/New York: Campus, 2007), 206–8. Numerous studies on the history of individual Russian concepts and on the political language of Russian in general can also be found in the journal *Ab Imperio*, published since 2000 in print and online, cf. <abimperio.net/> (accessed 3 June 2015).

12   On comparative research into the Chinese world of concepts, see the project directed by Christoph Harbsmeier (Oslo): *Thesaurus Linguae Sericae (TLS). An Historical and Comparative Encyclopaedia of Chinese Conceptual Schemes*, <http://tls.uni-hd.de/home_en.lasso> (accessed 31 May 2015). [Note: link updated.] Cf. Christoph Harbsmeier, 'Concepts that make Multiple Modernities: The Conceptual Modernisation of China in a Historical and Critical Perspective', available at <http://www.hf.uio. no/ikos/english/research/projects/tls/publications/CONCEPTS-THAT-MAKE-HISTORY%5B1%5D.pdf> (accessed 31 May 2015). [Note: link

updated. The HPSC Group organizes annual conferences on different topics.]

13 See the seminal work by Margrit Pernau, *Bürger mit Turban. Muslime in Delhi im 19. Jahrhundert*, postdoctoral thesis (Bielefeld 2006) (Göttingen: Vandenhoeck und Ruprecht, 2008) [Note: English: eadem, *Ashraf into Middle Classes: Muslims in 19th Century Dehli* (New Dehli: Oxford University Press, 2013)]; eadem, 'Gab es eine indische Zivilgesellschaft im 19. Jahrhundert? Überlegungen zum Verhältnis von Globalgeschichte und historischer Semantik', *Traverse*, 14 (2007), 51–67; Monica Juneja and Margrit Pernau, 'Lost in Translation: Transcending Boundaries in Comparative History', in Jürgen Kocka and Heinz-Gerhard Haupt (eds), *Comparative and Transnational History: Central European Approaches and New Perspectives* (New York: Berghahn, 2009), 105–29.

14 Gumbrecht (2006) 15–16 and 35–6 discusses the problem of how we can approach the pre-conceptual and non-conceptual simply by referring to the metaphorology developed by Hans Blumenberg. In addition, however, the search for colloquial paraphrases and visualizations as a means of accessing the pre- and non-conceptual must also be mentioned here. On strategies for searching for the pre-conceptual, using the concept *Fremdherrschaft* ('foreign rule') as an example: Christian Koller, *Fremdherrschaft. Ein politischer Kampfbegriff im Zeitalter des Nationalismus* (Frankfurt am Main/New York: Campus, 2005), 32–3 and 131–90. Incidentally, metaphorology has not been as neglected by the exponents of philosophical conceptual history as Gumbrecht maintains. In particular, the theoretical and empirical studies by Ralf Konersmann merit mentioning: Ralf Konersmann, 'Metaphorisches Wissen', in Ralf Konersmann, Peter Noever and Peter Zumthor (eds), *Zwischen Bild und Realität* (Zürich: GTA, 2006), 10–37; Ralf Konersmann, 'Figuratives Wissen. Zur Konzeption des Wörterbuchs der philosophischen Metaphern', *Neue Rundschau*, 116/2 (2005), 19–35; Ralf Konersmann (ed.), *Wörterbuch der philosophischen Metaphern* (Darmstadt: Wissenschaftliche Buchgesellschaft, 2007). Cf. also: Ruben Zimmermann, 'Einführung: Bildersprache verstehen oder: Die offene Sinndynamik der Sprachbilder' in idem (ed.), *Bildersprache verstehen. Zur Hermeneutik der Metapher und anderer bildlicher Sprachformen. Mit einem Geleitwort von Hans-Georg Gadamer* (Munich: Fink, 2000), 13–54. One area of intensive research is the circulation of metaphors between the natural sciences (medicine) and politics, cf. Philipp Sarasin, 'Infizierte Körper, kontaminierte Sprachen. Metaphern als Gegenstand der Wissenschaftsgeschichte', in idem, *Geschichtswissenschaft und Diskursanalyse* (Frankfurt am Main: Suhrkamp, 2003), 191–230.

15 In Gumbrecht (2006), 27, Gumbrecht quite rightly remarks that Koselleck's conceptual history has always been marked by an '*indecision*

with regard to the problem of the world-referentiality of language' (emphasis in original).

16   Cf. the recent Lucian Hölscher (ed.), *Baupläne der sichtbaren Kirche. Sprachliche Konzepte religiöser Vergemeinschaftung in Europa* (Göttingen: Wallstein, 2007).

17   However, there are a number of useful studies on the history of individual concepts for briefer time periods. Cf. for example for the concept of politics: Sabine Marquardt, *Polis contra Polemos. Politik als Kampfbegriff der Weimarer Republik* (Köln: Böhlau, 1997); Kari Palonen, *Politik als Handlungsbegriff. Horizontwandel des Politikbegriffs in Deutschland 1890–1933* (Helsinki: Societas Scientiarum Fennica, 1985); Kari Palonen, *The Struggle with Time. A Conceptual History of 'Politics' as an Activity* (Münster: Lit-Verlag, 2006); and several articles in Steinmetz (2007).

18   Examples include: Georg Stötzel and Martin Wengeler (eds), *Kontroverse Begriffe. Geschichte des öffentlichen Sprachgebrauchs in der Bundesrepublik Deutschland* (Berlin/New York: de Gruyter, 1994); Karin Böke, Frank Liedtke and Martin Wengeler, *Politische Leitvokabeln in der Adenauer-Ära* (Berlin/New York: de Gruyter, 1996); Matthias Jung, Thomas Niehr and Karin Böke, *Ausländer und Migranten im Spiegel der Presse. Ein diskurshistorisches Wörterbuch zur Einwanderung seit 1945* (Wiesbaden: Westdeutscher Verlag, 2000); Georg Stötzel and Thorsten Eitz (eds), *Zeitgeschichtliches Wörterbuch der deutschen Gegenwartssprache* (Hildesheim: Olms, 2002); Heidrun Kämper, *Der Schulddiskurs in der frühen Nachkriegszeit. Ein Beitrag zur Geschichte des sprachlichen Umbruchs nach 1945* (Berlin/New York: de Gruyter, 2005); Heidrun Kämper, *Opfer-Täter-Nichttäter. Ein Wörterbuch zum Schulddiskurs 1945–1955* (Berlin/New York: de Gruyter, 2007).

19   Expressly following on from the *Fundamental Concepts in History* but with theoretical articles on its expansion and empirical studies on key concepts of the post-war era: Carsten Dutt (ed.), *Herausforderungen der Begriffsgeschichte* (Heidelberg: Winter, 2003).

20   For an overview: Jacques Guilhaumou, 'Geschichte und Sprachwissenschaft – Wege und Stationen (in) der "analyse du discours"', in Reiner Keller et al. (eds), *Handbuch Sozialwissenschaftliche Diskursanalyse*, vol. II: 'Forschungspraxis' (Opladen: Leske und Budrich, 2003), 19–65, cf. also the examples of usage given here, chiefly for the twentieth century.

21   Cf. Stephan Lessenich, 'Einleitung: Wohlfahrtsstaatliche Grundbegriffe – Semantiken des Wohlfahrtsstaats', in idem (ed.), *Wohlfahrtsstaatliche Grundbegriffe: Historische und aktuelle Diskurse* (Frankfurt am Main/New York: Campus, 2003), 9–19; see also Stephan Lessenich, 'Schluss:

Wohlfahrtsstaatliche Semantiken – Politik im Wohlfahrtsstaat' in Ibid., 419–26; the articles in this volume range from more theoretical essays to analyses of the usage of key words.

22   In overview: Peter Burke, *Languages and Communities in Early Modern Europe* (Cambridge: Cambridge University Press, 2004).

23   Cf. as a case study of the function, prestige and usage of foreign languages, chiefly French, taking Brandenburg-Prussia as an example: Volker Wittenauer, *Im Dienste der Macht. Kultur und Sprache am Hof der Hohenzollern. Vom Großen Kurfürst bis zu Wilhelm II* (Paderborn: Ferdinand Schöningh Verlag, 2007).

24   At the moment, there exist only case studies on the interrelation between the vernacular and the language of the scholars in certain genres and contexts. On the Latin, German and Italian language of citizenship cf. e.g. Ulrich Meier, *'Burgerlich vereynung*. Herrschende, beherrschte und "mittlere" Bürger in Politiktheorie, chronikalischer Uberlieferung und städtischen Quellen des Spätmittelalters', in Klaus Schreiner and Reinhart Koselleck (eds), *Bürgerschaft. Rezeption und Innovation der Begrifflichkeit vom Hohen Mittelalter bis ins 19. Jahrhundert* (Stuttgart: Klett-Cotta, 1994), 274–306; Ulrich Meier, *Mensch und Bürger. Die Stadt im Denken spätmittelalterlicher Theologen, Philosophen und Juristen* (München: Oldenbourg, 1994). On the Latin and French language of politics: Olivier Bertrand, 'Le vocabulaire politique aux XIVe et XVe siècles: constitution d'un lexique ou émergence d'une science?', *Langage & Société*, 113 (2005), 11–32. On political and social vocabulary in Latin and Swedish in the early modern period: Bo Lindberg, *Den antika skevheten. Politiska ord och begrepp i det tidig-moderna Sverige* (Stockholm: Kungl. Vitterhets Historie och Antikvitets Akademien, 2006); for the reference to Lindberg's study I am indebted to an unpublished conference paper by Jani Marjanen (Helsinki), 'The History of Concepts beyond the Nation-State? Discourses on Methodological Nationalism and *Histoire Croisée* as New Challenges' (Bielefeld, 2007). [Note: the paper mentioned has been reworked into Jani Marjanen, 'Undermining Methodological Nationalism: *Histoire Croisée* of Concepts as Transational History', in Mathias Albert et al. (eds), *Transational Political Spaces. Agents – Structures – Encounters* (Frankfurt am Main: Campus, 2009), 239–63.]

25   This is, of course, not to say that there are not calls by mediaevalists, too, to move from an exclusively word-based Historical Semantics to a sentence or text-based Historical Semantics. Cf. Ludolf Kuchenbuch, ' "Feudalismus": Versuch über die Gebrauchsstrategien eines wissenspolitischen Reizwortes', in Natalie Fryde, Pierre Monnet and Otto Gerhard Oexle(eds), *Die Gegenwart des Feudalismus/Présence du*

féodalisme et présent de la féodalité/The Presence of Feudalism (Göttingen: Vandenhoeck und Ruprecht, 2002), 293–323, (314–15); an example of a study that covers at least an entire lexical field (and the accompanying practices): Ludolf Kuchenbuch, 'Porcus donativus. Language Use and Gifting in Seignorial Records between the Eighth and the Twelfth Centruries', in Gadi Algazi, Valentin Groebner and Bernhard Jussen (eds), *Negotiating the Gift. Pre-Modern Figurations of Exchange* (Göttingen: Vandhoeck und Ruprecht, 2003), 193–246.

26   For a summary of the state of the art in this field: Bernhard Jussen, 'Ordo zwischen Ideengeschichte und Lexikometrie. Vorarbeiten an einem Hilfsmittel mediävistischer Begriffsgeschichte', in Bernd Schneidmüller and Stefan Weinfurter (eds), *Ordnungskonfigurationen im Hohen Mittelalter* (Ostfildern: Thorbecke, 2006), 227–56.

27   Sceptical: Gunter Scholtz, 'Vom Nutzen und Nachteil des Computers für die Begriffsgeschichte', in by Ernst Müller (ed.), *Begriffsgeschichte im Umbruch?* (Hamburg: Meiner, 2005), 185–94.

28   Reinhart Koselleck, 'Hinweise auf die temporalen Strukturen begriffsgeschichtlichen Wandels', in idem, *Begriffsgeschichten. Studien zur Semantik und Pragmatik der politischen und sozialen Sprache* (Frankfurt am Main: Suhrkamp, 2006), 86 [Note: English translation: Reinhart Koselleck, *Some Reflections on the Temporal Structure of Conceptual Change* (Amsterdam: Rodopi, 1994)]; cf. also Koselleck's remarks in the final volume of the lexicon both defending the lexical approach and pointing out its limits: Reinhart Koselleck, 'Vorwort', in Brunner, Conze and Koselleck (1992), v–viii.

29   An excellent overview of various research approaches between older conceptual history and historical discourse analysis is provided by: Rolf Reichardt, 'Historische Semantik zwischen *lexicométrie* und *New Cultural History*. Einführende Bemerkungen zur Standortbestimmung', in idem (ed.), *Aufklärung und Historische Semantik. Interdisziplinäre Beiträge zur westeuropäischen Kulturgeschichte*, Zeitschrift für Historische Forschung, supplement 21 (Berlin: Duncker & Humblot, 1998), 7–28.

30   Here I draw on the differentiation between various aspects of 'meaning' in Ekkehard Felder, 'Semantische Kämpfe in Wissensdomänen. Eine Einführung in Benennungs-, Bedeutungs- und Sachverhaltsfixierungs-Konkurrenzen', in Ekkehard Felder (ed.), *Semantische Kämpfe. Macht und Sprache in den Wissenschaften* (Berlin/New York: de Gruyter, 2006), 13–46 (esp. 20–33).

31   Cf. Philipp Sarasin, 'Geschichtswissenschaft und Diskursanalyse', in idem, *Geschichtswissenschaft und Diskursanalyse* (Frankfurt am Main: Suhrkamp, 2003), 10–60. *'Dieses unschuldige, selbstverständliche Verstehen ist zweifellos genau das, womit Foucault brechen wollte, … '* ('This innocent,

unchallenged understanding is without a doubt precisely that with which Foucault wished to break … '), Ibid., 29.

32   Ibid., 51–5.

33   Reinhart Koselleck, 'Einleitung', in Brunner, Conze and Koselleck (1972), xiii–xxvii, xxiii.

34   Ibid., xviii (anticipations, *Vorgriffe*) and xxi (semantic surplus, *Bedeutungsüberhänge*).

35   Ibid., xiv.

36   To see the different emphases, compare: Reinhart Koselleck, 'Begriffsgeschichte und Sozialgeschichte', in idem, *Vergangene Zukunft. Zur Semantik geschichtlicher Zeiten* (Frankfurt am Main: Suhrkamp, 1979), 107–29; Reinhart Koselleck, 'Sozialgeschichte und Begriffsgeschichte', in idem (2006), 9–31. [Note: see Reinhart Koselleck, 'Social History and Conceptual History' (Chapter 2 in this volume).] Koselleck's analysis of Gadamer is also significant: Reinhart Koselleck, 'Historik und Hermeneutik', in idem, *Zeitschichten. Studien zur Historik* (Frankfurt am Main: Suhrkamp, 2000), 97–118.

37   Cf. Reinhart Koselleck, 'Sprachwandel und Ereignisgeschichte', in idem (2006), 32–55; Reinhart Koselleck, Ulrike Spree and Willibald Steinmetz, 'Drei bürgerliche Welten? Zur vergleichenden Semantik der bürgerlichen Gesellschaft in Deutschland, England und Frankreich', in Ibid., 402–61; Michael Jeismann, *Das Vaterland der Feinde. Studien zum nationalen Feindbegriff und Selbstverständnis in Deutschland und Frankreich 1792–1918* (Stuttgart: Klett-Cotta, 1992). Dietrich Busse's critical review of the conceptual history research agenda gave important impetus to this reorientation: Dietrich Busse, *Historische Semantik. Analyse eines Programms* (Stuttgart: Klett-Cotta, 1987).

38   Cf., however, the article on the concepts of *Volk* and *Nation* which not surprisingly attains the dimensions of a monograph: Fritz Gschnitzer et al., 'Volk, Nation, Nationalismus, Masse', in Brunner, Conze and Koselleck (1992), 141–431.

39   Andreas Suter, 'Kulturgeschichte des Politischen – Chancen und Grenzen', in Barbara Stollberg-Rilinger (ed.), *Was heißt Kulturgeschichte des Politischen?*, Zeitschrift für Historische Forschung, supplement 35 (Berlin: Duncker & Humblot, 2005), 27–55, 33: '*verfahrungen und extremitäten … die wir uns nyt hetten ynbilden können*'.

40   Ibid., 31–2.

41   Ibid., 44ff.

42   '… *Falsifizierung der semantischen Systeme und Begriffe, sei es, weil der Akt der Zuschreibung nicht mehr gelingt, sei es, weil die aus derartigen Zuschreibungsakten abgeleiteten Handlungsweisen nicht mehr die erwarteten Ergebnisse zeitigen*'. Ibid., 34.

43 Another explanation – not explored in detail here – for the decline or even disappearance from usage of certain words could be an overloading with contradictory meanings. This makes their usage in certain situations dysfunctional. One could speak of a loss of meaning through polysemy being taken too far. One example of this is the increasing unsuitability of the designation *Bürger* (citizen) in parliamentary discussions on civil rights in the state parliaments during the *Vormärz* period (from 1815 to the March 1848 revolution) and in the Paulskirche in Frankfurt, where the Frankfurt parliament met during the German revolutions of 1848; cf. Willibald Steinmetz, ' "Sprechen ist eine Tat bei euch." Die Wörter und das Handeln in der Revolution von 1848', in Dieter Dowe, Heinz-Gerhard Haupt and Dieter Langewiesche (eds), *Europa 1848. Revolution und Reform* (Bonn: Dietz, 1998), 1089–1138 (1095ff.).

44 Cf. Ernesto Laclau, 'Why do Empty Signifiers Matter to Politics?', in Jeffrey Weeks (ed.), *The Lesser Evil and the Greater Good* (London: Rivers Oram Press, 1994), 167–78.

45 Cf. on the following: Willibald Steinmetz, 'Gemeineuropäische Tradition und nationale Besonderheiten im Begriff der "Mittelklasse". Ein Vergleich zwischen Deutschland, Frankreich und England', in Klaus Schreiner and Reinhart Koselleck (eds), *Bürgerschaft. Rezeption und Innovation der Begrifflichkeit vom Hohen Mittelalter bis ins 19. Jahrhundert* (Stuttgart: Klett-Cotta, 1994), 161–236, here 211–33.

46 Demands for 'politically correct' usage fall into the latter category.

47 Treated in an excellent overview by: László Kontler, 'Translation and comparison – translation as comparison', *Contributions to the History of Concepts*, 3/1 (2007), 71–102 [Note: reference updated]; further: Doris Bachmann-Medick, 'Einleitung: Übersetzung als Repräsentation fremder Kulturen', in eadem (ed.), *Übersetzung als Repräsentation fremder Kulturen* (Berlin: Schmidt, 1997), 1–18; Douglas Howland, 'The Predicament of Ideas in Culture: Translation and Historiography', *History and Theory*, 42 (2003), 45–60.

48 Ingrid Schierle, 'Semantiken des Politischen im Russland des 18. Jahrhunderts' and Walter Sperling, 'Vom Randbegriff zum Kampfbegriff: Semantiken des Politischen im ausgehenden Zarenreich (1850–1917)', both in Steinmetz (2007), 226–47 and 248–88.

49 Cf. Reinhart Koselleck, 'Hinweise auf die temporalen Strukturen begriffsgeschichtlichen Wandels' (Engl. 1994, Ger. 2002), in idem (2006), 86–98, 95–6.

50 On the 'entangled history' (*histoire croisée*) approach in historical science in general: Michael Werner and Bénédicte Zimmermann, 'Beyond Comparison: *Histoire Croisée* and the Challenge of Reflexivity', *History and Theory*, 45 (2006), 30–50.

51   Albert Hourani, *Die Geschichte der Arabischen Völker* (Frankfurt am Main: Fischer, 1992), 123.

52   This language/power issue is discussed under the umbrella term 'language rights' from a contemporary, normative political science perspective. Cf. in overview: Alan Patten and Will Kymlicka, 'Introduction: Language Rights and Political Theory: Context, Issues, and Approaches', in idem (eds), *Language Rights and Political Theory* (Oxford: Oxford University Press, 2003), 1–51.

53   See Shingo Shimada, *Die Erfindung Japans. Kulturelle Wechselwirkung und nationale Identitätskonstruktion* (Frankfurt am Main/New York: Campus, 2000); Douglas Howland, *Translating the West: Language and Political Reason in Nineteenth-Century Japan* (Honolulu: University of Hawaii Press, 2002); Douglas Howland, *Personal Liberty and Public Good: The Introduction of John Stuart Mill to Japan and China* (Toronto: University of Toronto Press, 2005).

54   Cf. Martin Fuchs, *Kampf um Differenz. Repräsentation, Subjektivität und soziale Bewegungen. Das Beispiel Indien* (Frankfurt am Main: Surhkamp, 1999), 52–4.

55   Cf. Harald Weinrich, 'Mit gemischten Sprachgefühlen', in idem, *Wege der Sprachkultur* (München: Deutscher Taschenbuch Verlag, 1988), 290–306, here 292 and 294.

56   Cf. Fania Oz-Salzberger, *Translating the Enlightenment. Scottish Civic Discourse in Eighteenth-Century Germany* (Oxford: Oxford University Press, 1995), 46 and 138–66.

57   Cf. the study by Jörn Leonhard, *Liberalismus. Zur historischen Semantik eines europäischen Deutungsmusters* (München: Oldenbourg, 2001).

58   Cf. the comments in Reinhart Koselleck, 'Begriffsgeschichtliche Probleme der Verfassungsgeschichtsschreibung', in idem (2006), 365–401.

59   On the problem of the unavailability of a 'metalanguage' for comparative historical-sematic research: Reinhart Koselleck, Ulrike Spree and Willibald Steinmetz, 'Drei bürgerliche Welten?', in Koselleck (2006), 413.

60   [Note: by using the 'approximately equal' sign ($\approx$) in the original text (here and below), the author emphasizes that the translations he gives in parentheses are only approximations, not exact equals of the original.]

61   Cf. the publications mentioned in footnote 13 above.

62   Leonhard (2001), 71, also mentions this.

63   Cf. the remarks in Jürgen Osterhammel, 'Transferanalyse und Vergleich im Fernverhältnis', in Hartmut Kaelble and Jürgen Schriewer (eds), *Vergleich und Transfer. Komparatistik in den Sozial-, Geschichts- und Kulturwissenschaften* (Frankfurt am Main/New York: Campus, 2003), 439–66, here 450–1.

Name Index

Locators followed by *n* refer to notes.

Subject Index

Locators followed by *n* refer to notes.